We the Men

We the Men

*How Forgetting Women's Struggles
for Equality Perpetuates Inequality*

Jill Elaine Hasday

OXFORD
UNIVERSITY PRESS

OXFORD
UNIVERSITY PRESS

Oxford University Press is a department of the University of Oxford.
It furthers the University's objective of excellence in research, scholarship,
and education by publishing worldwide. Oxford is a registered trademark of
Oxford University Press in the UK and in certain other countries.

Published in the United States of America by Oxford University Press
198 Madison Avenue, New York, NY 10016, United States of America.

Library of Congress Cataloging-in-Publication Data
Names: Hasday, Jill Elaine, author.
Title: We the Men / Jill Elaine Hasday.
Description: New York, NY : Oxford University Press, 2025. |
Includes bibliographical references and index.
Identifiers: LCCN 2024041461 (print) | LCCN 2024041462 (ebook) |
ISBN 9780197800805 (hardback) | ISBN 9780197800829 (epub) |
ISBN 9780197800836
Subjects: LCSH: Women—Legal status, laws, etc. —United States—History. |
Sex discrimination against women—United States—History. |
Women's rights—United States—History.
Classification: LCC KF478 .H37 2025 (print) | LCC KF478 (ebook) |
DDC 342.7308/78—dc23/eng/20241212
LC record available at https://lccn.loc.gov/2024041461
LC ebook record available at https://lccn.loc.gov/2024041462

DOI: 10.1093/9780197800836.001.0001

Printed by Integrated Books International, United States of America

To my We the People:

My grandparents, Rose, Irving, Dora, and Isaac
My parents, Carol and Robert
My siblings, Michael and Lisa
My husband, Allan
My children, Sarah, Daniel, and David

Contents

List of Figures

Introduction
Forgotten Women

At the end of 1922, the *Washington Times* asked Alice Paul to predict how "modern feminism" would shape "the course of history in the next 100 years."[1] Paul led the National Woman's Party, which had infuriated many men in the 1910s by picketing the White House to demand woman suffrage. She was knocked from the picket line and dragged on the ground, arrested while her assailants went free, brutalized in prison, and force fed.[2]

After the Nineteenth Amendment's ratification in 1920, Paul's optimism was buoyant. She was only thirty-five when the Nineteenth Amendment made sex-based denials of the franchise unconstitutional, and she had already helped women achieve a major victory against ferocious opposition. She saw no stopping point to what women would win in the century ahead. Paul told newspaper readers in December 1922 that it would "not require one hundred years to elect a woman President of the United States" and that women would "comprise half of the membership of Congress" before 2023. She forecast that women and men would have the same economic opportunities by 2023. In sum, she was hoping and working for a world where women participate "equally in the control of government, of family, and of industry."[3] In 1923, Paul launched her campaign for the Equal Rights Amendment she had drafted.[4] Paul wanted the Constitution to declare that: "Men and women shall have equal rights throughout the United States and every place subject to its jurisdiction."[5]

America has not reached the milestones that Paul thought would already be behind us. Although women's rights and opportunities have unquestionably expanded over the past century, progress has not been nearly fast or far-reaching enough. Sometimes courts and legislatures have dragged women backward, taking away earlier victories.

Consider politics. Our line of male presidents remains unbroken, and a 2019 survey found just a third of Americans reporting that their neighbors would be comfortable with a female President.[6] As of mid-November 2024, women fill only 28.4% of the voting seats in Congress and only 32.8% of the seats in state legislatures.[7]

Consider economics. People living in families led by a woman with no spouse present are almost twice as likely to be poor as people living in families led by a man with no spouse present.[8] The median annual earnings for women working full-time and year-round in 2023 were just 82.7% of the median annual earnings for full-time, year-round male workers, with black women earning just 66.5% of white men's earnings and Latinas earning just 57.8%.[9] Only 10.4% of the chief executives at Fortune 500 companies are women.[10] Only 21% of the equity partners in the two hundred biggest law firms are women, and only about 3% are women of color.[11]

Consider constitutional law. After more than a century of feminist advocacy, our constitutional text still does not include an explicit commitment to sex equality. The Supreme Court reversed progress in 2022 by eliminating federal constitutional constraints on abortion regulation and empowering lawmakers to compel childbearing.[12]

These facts are striking. The urgent questions are about *why* women's inequality persists and *what* we can do about it. This book adds another dimension to that crucial conversation by focusing on new answers.

In a nation whose Constitution purports to speak for "We the People," too many of the stories that powerful Americans tell about law and society include only We the Men. America's dominant modes of forgetting about women help perpetuate women's inequality, rationalizing the status quo, promoting complacency, and undercutting reform. I argue that remembering women's stories more often and more accurately can help the nation advance toward sex equality.

Two ways of forgetting about women predominate in America's stories about itself. The first centers on simply ignoring women and their struggles for equality. Some examples are concrete (literally). A 2021 survey of federal courthouses found more than 165 named for a man and just four named for a woman.[13] Only three women made a 2021 list of the fifty most frequently commemorated people in America's public monuments, compared to forty-four white men, many of them slaveholders.[14] Struggles over commemorating women have drawn much less mainstream attention than commemoration conflicts framed as centrally about race, even though many struggles over commemorating women are simultaneously intertwined with race. Perhaps our male-dominated commemorative landscape is such a perennial fact of life that it sometimes fades into the background as we enter yet another government building with a man's name over the door or walk through yet another public square featuring a man immortalized on horseback. But commemorations are not just decorative flourishes or scenery. They shape the vision of America that we carry around with us, which is why generations of women have fought to reconstruct the commemorative landscape and why they have faced such persistent resistance.

Women's erasure also runs through the stories that powerful Americans tell with torrents of words rather than blocks of concrete and stone. Politicians delivering odes to America on significant anniversaries commonly celebrate the Founders for establishing government by the consent of the governed. That account depends on excluding almost everyone who was not a white male property owner. Supreme Court opinions regularly ignore women when remembering the Court's key decisions. They skip over both rulings that offered crucial support to women striving for equality and the many cases where the Court blocked or undid women's progress. Law professors making lists of the Court's most important or most terrible constitutional judgments routinely omit decisions about women's rights.[15]

Indeed, I was surprised to discover in researching this book how frequently legal authorities and popular writers marginalize women even within discussions of women's status. When judicial opinions mention women, judges on and off the Supreme Court often write as if men decided on their own to expand women's rights and opportunities. I call these tales "spontaneous enlightenment stories," and they feature in generations of popular press and political debates as well. These stories attribute progress to consensus and men's wisdom while erasing the conflict and female agency that forward momentum required, with women needing to demand change and fight for reform against determined opponents.

Women's frequent erasure coexists with a second form of forgetting in America's dominant stories about itself: forgetting the work the nation still has to do. Many of us have encountered contemporaries who announce or assume that the United States has left the sexist bad old days behind, perhaps while offering assurances that any remaining disparities are unimportant or on the verge of disappearing as a matter of course. What I did not realize is just how early in American history those premature declarations began appearing and how important a role they have played in perpetuating inequality.

Wildly exaggerated accounts of the nation's progress toward sex equality have been common in everyday settings and rarefied legal institutions since before the Nineteenth Amendment's 1920 ratification made sex-based disenfranchisement unconstitutional. These stories forget what remains undone, even to the point of proclaiming that the United States has already achieved sex equality. For over a century, waves of popular media and schoolchildren's textbooks have been telling Americans that women have been "emancipated" (asserted as early as 1892),[16] that no one "will now seriously defend the 'subjection' of woman" (1912),[17] that "[a]ll men and women are regarded as equals before the law" (1918).[18] Popular writers and textbook authors have routinely framed these declarations in terms of American women universally, although white women have tended to be top of mind. Judges have been suggesting or proclaiming that the nation has moved past sex discrimination for almost as long as American women have been mobilizing to challenge male supremacy.

Courts routinely make their rosiest pronouncements about America's commitment to sex equality while issuing judgments that maintain or exacerbate inequality. The practice extends generations back and appears as recently as the Supreme Court's 2022 decision removing federal constitutional restraints on legislative power to prohibit abortion.[19] I call these decisions "self-contradictory victory announcements" because they simultaneously trumpet the nation's triumph over inequality and facilitate inequality's persistence. The self-contradiction serves a purpose, as the loud overstatements about American progress help judges rationalize their decisions impeding that progress. What's the urgency for safeguarding or strengthening women's rights if America has already come so far?

Politicians and political activists have capitalized on the American inclination to overstate the reach of reform. Asserting that America has already established women's equality has helped a half century of anti-feminists— like anti-suffragists before them—battle feminist mobilization and champion regression while simultaneously claiming to support women's rights. Opponents of the Equal Rights Amendment, whether today or in the 1970s and 1980s, have insisted that the amendment is unnecessary because America has already vanquished sex discrimination. That contention rang through the halls of Congress as I wrote this book, deployed whenever federal lawmakers wanted to fight against removing procedural hurdles and recognizing the ERA as part of the Constitution. Anti-feminists have wielded similarly sweeping and premature pronouncements to oppose government support for childcare programs, combat abortion rights, and condemn affirmative action.

In short, ignoring women's struggles and exaggerating the nation's progress have practical consequences. These strategies obscure how women's inequality has been an organizing feature of American life, frame the issue as wholly or nearly resolved, and promise that America can achieve any additional advances smoothly through consensus without needing organized efforts to overcome impassioned resistance. They allow judges, politicians, and other powerful Americans to criticize (supposedly) abandoned practices, while diverting attention from scrutinizing unequal practices that persist. They tell women to be satisfied and to abandon further mobilization.

Revising America's dominant stories so they remember women's ongoing struggles, and recognize how far the nation still has to go, can make the histories Americans tell simultaneously more faithful to the past and more engaging today. I have been studying and writing about sex discrimination and women's legal history for more than two decades. In the thousands of documents I found as I prepared to write this book, I uncovered many remarkable stories I never knew and learned about scores of fascinating women who Americans remember rarely or not at all. Their struggles for equality can be sobering because opposition to women's rights in the United States has long been virulent—sometimes even violent—which is not a story that America likes to tell about itself. Many times women did not win, or did not win quickly, or did not win completely, or did not win unless they were privileged along other dimensions, like race and class. But women's persistent striving for equality can inspire nonetheless, and women sometimes achieved significant victories.

Expanding America's collective memory can also enhance our understanding of the present by exposing ongoing patterns that might otherwise remain difficult to discern. The long view helped me recognize how powerful Americans have deployed self-contradictory victory announcements to shield inequality and have obscured the forces needed to produce change by attributing improvements in women's status to men acting on their own instead of women mobilizing for reform.

Most of all, transforming America's dominant stories can enrich and enlarge how Americans plan for the future, strengthening our determination to push the nation further toward sex equality. America's multigenerational struggles over women's status make clear that women's concerted efforts against fierce opposition—rather than men's spontaneous bursts of enlightenment—have propelled progress. This history revealing the centrality of conflict, and the elusiveness of easy consensus, should leave us simultaneously impatient with the pace of change and prepared for a long road ahead.

In sum, the limits of our collective memory can constrict our collective imagination. *We the Men* examines that constriction and explores the possibilities that emerge when collective memory grows.

I proceed in four parts structured to highlight how courts and the world outside the courts have operated together. Although judges commonly describe themselves as operating above the fray of politics and popular opinion, judges, politicians, journalists, and other influential commemorators have long mirrored and molded each other as they construct, disseminate, and enforce America's dominant stories about itself.

Part I—*Erasure*—focuses on how the nation's dominant stories ignore women's struggles for equality. These stories frequently leave women unmentioned or erase women's work by attributing reform to men operating on their own initiative. I trace that marginalization through judicial opinions, official and scholarly pronouncements on constitutional history and constitutional law, and the stark underrepresentation of women in America's commemorative landscape.

Chapter 1—*Courts Ignore Women's Struggles for Equality*—examines how the judiciary has left women out of the stories it tells about the nation. Supreme Court opinions recounting the Court's history routinely skip over how women and gender shaped that history. They do not mention the Court's long and remarkably persistent practice of reasoning about the Constitution on the premise that women rather than men should prioritize domesticity, which I call "Mullerism" after a pivotal early decision that permitted states to impose sex-specific restraints on women's market work. Indeed, judges on and off the Supreme Court frequently center men and ignore women even when deciding cases about women's status. This chapter introduces the concept of "spontaneous enlightenment stories" and shows how judges deploying those stories have erased women's struggles for equality and misdescribed progress as emerging from consensus rather than conflict. The Supreme Court, and many other American courts, have attributed expansions in women's rights over time to the seemingly spontaneous insights of male decisionmakers without acknowledging the feminist mobilization that pushed reform forward against vehement opposition. Many judges have likewise spent decades telling a variant of the spontaneous enlightenment story in recounting how Title VII of the 1964 Civil Rights Act came to include a prohibition on sex discrimination in employment. Courts attribute that amendment to the scheming of male segregationists desperate to defeat the bill and disregard the abundant evidence documenting the vital contributions that women made to get the sex discrimination prohibition into Title VII and keep it there. This account emphasizes men's underhandedness, rather than their high-mindedness, but similarly mischaracterizes how reform occurred by treating men as the only important actors and women as passive subjects of male decisionmaking.

Chapter 2—*Remembering America Without Remembering Women*—ties the judicial tendency to ignore women's mobilization to persistent gaps in the nation's collective memory. Commemorations weave stories about the nation through memorable occasions and everyday life. But America's commemorative landscape too often leaves women out, and there has been too little improvement over time. Our cultural habit of thinking about women's treatment as a product of consensus rather than conflict can tempt us to blame inertia for the gendered lopsidedness of America's commemorations. That would miss the deliberate forces at work. From the start, women have endeavored to add their struggles for equality to America's dominant stories about itself. Women have linked their activism to foundational expressions and symbols of American democratic ideals, like the Declaration of Independence and the Statue of Liberty. Women have sought to teach Americans about women's history. Yet efforts to focus public memory on women—whether with monuments, museums, currency redesign, or otherwise—have repeatedly faced bitter and protracted opposition, for generations and to the present day. Struggles over commemorating women have often attracted less attention than they deserve. These battles rage nonetheless because they revolve around how to understand women's place in the nation's past, present, and future.

Part II—*Distortion*—examines the wildly exaggerated accounts of American progress that coexist alongside women's frequent erasure from the nation's dominant stories. For more than a century, Americans from youth to adulthood have been hearing assessments of women's status that shield inequality and encourage complacency by overstating reform and forgetting the work the nation still has to do. I use schoolchildren's textbooks, popular media, and judicial opinions to examine this long tradition across everyday settings and elite milieus.

Chapter 3—*Courts Declare Victory Early and Often*—explores generations of judicial opinions proclaiming victory over sex discrimination. This chapter introduces another new concept, "self-contradictory victory announcements," and reveals the important role these announcements have played in defending and maintaining inequality. Many of the judiciary's sunniest proclamations about American progress have appeared in decisions denying women equality, as courts rationalize their rejection of women's claims by insisting that women already have so much. I call these decisions self-contradictory because judges boast about America's embrace of sex equality while simultaneously enforcing male supremacy. Women are not the only marginalized group to have experienced the judiciary's self-contradictory declarations, but cases perpetuating women's inequality have long been prominent triggers for self-contradiction. Over the course of the twentieth century, for example, courts announced that women's legal status had been transformed while issuing judgments that empowered states to maintain sex-specific restrictions on women's working hours, prohibitions on women entering jobs reserved for men, and obstacles to women's jury service that denied women juries of their peers. Judges trumpeted the nation's commitment to sex equality while undermining women's control over their reproductive lives, refusing to give wives rights their husbands had, and making it harder for women to escape subordination in marriage.

Chapter 4—*Popular Culture Announces Women's Emancipation*—links the judiciary's self-contradictory decisions to ideas circulating outside the courts. Many of us are familiar in our own time with popular commentary overstating the nation's progress, across multiple dimensions. This chapter reveals how early in American history proclamations about the establishment of sex equality began appearing in popular culture and how commonly media accounts have deployed those declarations to support inequality. From at least the late nineteenth century onward, scores of popular writers opining about women's place in America—and frequently giving implicit pride of place to white women—have described women's inequality as part of the past rather than the present and encouraged readers to direct their concern elsewhere. Those pronouncements have often been openly self-contradictory, with popular authors expounding on the nation's commitment to sex equality while explicitly defending persistent inequality. Textbooks have imparted similar lessons to generations of schoolchildren. Even as anti-suffragists fought mightily to maintain sex-based disenfranchisement, some schoolchildren were already reading that America had emancipated women and left their inequality behind. These declarations multiplied in the decades after the Nineteenth Amendment's 1920 ratification, as textbooks highlighted white women's voting, overlooked persistent sex discrimination, and ignored the many women of color still disenfranchised. In retrospect, it is easy to see how schoolchildren's textbooks from previous eras masked inequality and nurtured complacency by exaggerating American progress and sanitizing women's struggles for equality. But many more recent textbooks continue to overstate the extent of reform and gloss over the opposition and obstacles that women's rights activists have confronted.

Part III—*Consequences*—examines how the myth that sexism is confined to history warps the present. America's distorted stories about itself continue to have practical consequences, shielding and sustaining inequality.

Chapter 5—*Courts Protect and Perpetuate Inequality*—explores those consequences within the law that courts have made in the late twentieth and early twenty-first centuries. I focus on five decisions from the United States Supreme Court along with numerous cases from state courts, drawing on archival and primary sources to uncover a clearer picture of what was at stake in these lawsuits than judges were willing to disclose. This chapter reveals how the modern Supreme Court has relied on the premise that the nation has left sexism behind as a reason to avoid examining how contemporary policies and practices perpetuate gendered inequality. I demonstrate how the Court has deployed that strategy when affirming the constitutionality of women's exclusion from military registration, sex-specific statutory rape laws, and a sex-based rule governing the citizenship of nonmarital children born abroad. State courts have proceeded similarly when enforcing hostility to alimony and leniency about marital rape. The judicial inclination to defend inequality with sweeping exaggerations about American progress shows no sign of abating. With the hoary tradition of self-contradictory victory announcements in view, it becomes readily apparent how overly rosy accounts of women's status in contemporary America ran through the Supreme Court's 2022 decision undoing federal constitutional safeguards on legislative power over abortion.

Chapter 6—*Anti-Feminists Capitalize on America's Misremembered Past*—turns to politics and political activism outside the courts. This chapter uncovers a crucial tool in the anti-feminist arsenal, wielded by women as well as men. Using internal movement documents along with external primary sources, I show how anti-feminists over the past half century, like anti-suffragists before them, have shrewdly exploited and reinforced America's penchant for overstating progress. Proclaiming that the nation has already established women's equality has made it easier for politicians and activists to oppose feminist reform and promote regression while simultaneously purporting to support women's rights. The crusade that Phyllis Schlafly and her allies waged in the 1970s and 1980s to block the Equal Rights Amendment took full advantage of this mode of attack, repeatedly deploying assertions about the achievement of women's equality that were supposedly universal but kept white middle-class heterosexual women foremost in mind. Schlafly's ideological heirs have followed her playbook in the decades since. Conservative and reactionary legislators and activists routinely insist that America has already triumphed over sex discrimination and wield that contention against feminist mobilization, including feminist efforts to increase government support for childcare, protect abortion rights, defend affirmative action, and push for the ERA.

Part IV—*Hope*—explores how we can learn from the past to change the future. Too often, America's dominant stories about itself ignore women's struggles for equality or distort them beyond recognition by exponentially exaggerating the nation's progress. Erasing women's unfinished struggles, and glossing over the fierce resistance to those struggles, shields entrenched inequalities, promotes complacency, and denies the concerted mobilization needed to propel reform and fight regression. Foregrounding the history of women's striving for equality spotlights the persistence of women's inequality in the United States and makes clear that real progress has always required women to challenge prevailing certainties, advance uncomfortable demands, and confront powerful opponents.

Chapter 7—*Building on the Past to Create a More Equal Future*—argues for more conflict over women's status rather than less. America needs reforms that span teaching, commemoration, political representation, legislation, litigation, and everyday life. Conflict can generate change. Patiently awaiting men's spontaneous enlightenment will not. Incorporating a richer and truer history of women's struggles for equality into the nation's collective memory can reorient our understanding of how women's progress takes place, focus our attention on the battles that are still unwon, and fortify our determination to push for a more equal future as we shape the next chapters in this American story.

PART I

ERASURE

Powerful Americans often forget women when they remember American history. The nation's dominant stories about itself relegated women to the peripheries early on and that tradition has proved remarkably resistant to transformation.

Multiple institutions in American life have contributed to the intransigence. Government celebrations, official holidays, public monuments, and other features of the nation's commemorative landscape have long tended to leave women out. Americans primed to assume that women's treatment emerges from consensus instead of conflict may be tempted to blame inertia for the ongoing unevenness in the nation's commemorations. But women have fought for generations to include themselves in public memory, and those efforts have faced determined and persistent opposition to the present day.

Unsurprisingly, a culture prone to excluding women from mainstream remembrances produces judges with similar habits. Courts often ignore women when reflecting on the nation's history and the judiciary's record.

Indeed, America's dominant stories about itself provide little support for the judiciary's frequent declarations that courts operate above the political and popular fray. To the contrary, these stories illustrate how courts and the world beyond the courts can reflect and reinforce each other's inclinations. Both arenas have constructed and disseminated tales in which women are missing or marginalized, and those accounts ricochet back and forth between them.

Part I examines women's too common erasure from the stories that powerful Americans tell about their country. Each chapter has a different emphasis, although some overlap is helpful because judges are not only legal elites but also members of the broader American culture they live within. Chapter 1 centers on how courts leave women out. Chapter 2 focuses on women's exclusion from America's commemorative landscape outside the courts.

Chapter 1
Courts Ignore Women's Struggles for Equality

Judges recounting stories about the nation frequently exclude women and their struggles for equality. This erasure sometimes takes the form of not discussing women at all. Supreme Court Justices have repeatedly offered selective accounts of the Court's past that ignore how women and gender fit into the story. Those omissions warp the remembrances in at least two ways simultaneously. They overlook approximately half the population, suggesting that the Court's treatment of women falls outside mainstream judicial history. Failing to consider women also makes it harder to understand how the Court has regulated men and masculinity, by diverting attention from exploring why the Court has governed men and women differently.

Excluding women from stories about the nation is nonetheless so routine for the judiciary that courts have ignored women's struggles for equality even when—or especially when—discussing improvements in women's status over time. American women have spent over a century and a half mobilizing against sex discrimination and battling powerful resistance to reform. But both the Supreme Court and courts further down the judicial hierarchy (known as lower courts) have repeatedly misdescribed progress as emanating from consensus rather than conflict, ignoring how women's concerted efforts propelled reform forward and instead attributing change to men's spontaneous enlightenment. A less common flipside of these spontaneous enlightenment stories credits reform to men's deviousness, while still misdescribing men as the only important actors needed to produce progress and women as passive beneficiaries of decisions men made on their own initiative. These tales erase women's mobilization and struggle, even from the history of women's rights.

Lochnerism but Not Mullerism

The Supreme Court is obsessed with *Lochner v. New York* (1905).[1] The Court's decision in that case struck down a state law limiting bakers to a sixty-hour work week,[2] on the theory that the bakers had a constitution-ally protected "freedom of contract" that gave them the right to work for as many hours as they wished.[3]

For decades, the Court has continually condemned *Lochner* for distorting constitutional interpretation to enforce the normative "predilections" of the Justices who decided the case.[4] Generations of Justices across the ideological spectrum have revisited *Lochner*, often because they want to accuse their colleagues of behaving like the *Lochner* Court did. The Justices take Lochnerism to be one of the worst insults they can hurl at each other's decisionmaking.[5]

While *Lochner* is notorious, its female counterpoint attracts exponentially less attention. Three years after *Lochner*, a laundry owner named Curt Muller came before the Court challenging his conviction for violating a state law limiting his female employees to a ten-hour workday.[6] The Court's unanimous decision against the laundry owner in *Muller v. Oregon* (1908) announced that the Justices' hostility to constraints on employment applied only to male employees and established a different constitutional framework to govern women's work.[7] *Muller* shared *Lochner's* penchant for constitutionalizing ideology, with the Justices using their constitutional decisionmaking to impose their personal views about how the world should work. But where *Lochner* read laissez-faireism into the Constitution, *Muller* constitutionalized the conviction that women's primary roles and responsibilities are domestic.

Muller held (ruled) that states could restrict women's working hours, even though states had to leave men unrestrained.[8] The Court treated all women as if they were mothers or future mothers and decreed that women's familial responsibilities outweighed any interest women had in working and earning more.[9] On the Justices' account, curbing a woman's "contractual powers" with sex-specific restrictions on her market participation operated "for the benefit of all."[10] Women would be better off because their "physical structure and the performance of maternal functions" left them too weak and vulnerable to protect themselves from employment conditions that conflicted with their domestic obligations.[11] Men, children, and "the race" as a whole would be better off because limiting a woman's market work would help ensure "a proper discharge of her maternal functions."[12] The term "race" often had multiple meanings in this era: the human race generally, the white race specifically, and white Anglo-Saxons more narrowly still. Many elites thought about America in demographic terms and treated women's reproductive capacity as a resource for nation building.[13] Fears that native-born white Protestant women were having too few children—while the wrong women were producing too many—helped drive waves of legal regulation, including criminal prohibitions on abortion.[14]

The Court's 1908 decision in *Muller* shaped women's employment opportunities for decades. Between 1909 and 1917, nineteen states and the District of Columbia enacted their first laws limiting women's working hours in some contexts and twenty additional states expanded limits they already had.[15] By the start of 1933, forty-two out of forty-eight states had such restrictions.[16] Most of these states restricted women's working hours across multiple occupations and industries. The consistent exceptions were for domestic service and farm labor,[17] backbreaking work particularly associated with women of color.

As a general matter, legal caps on working hours can help employees who would otherwise lack the bargaining power to secure humane working conditions. Many progressives—women as well as men—supported *Muller* at the time. They thought protecting women from exploitation was better than protecting no adult workers at all and wanted the Court to recognize that government regulation of the workplace can be appropriate, with the hope that this recognition would eventually lead the Court to question *Lochner*.[18] To be clear, I think this progressive reaction was an understandable response to the obstacles that *Lochner* created for reformers. I also recognize that some women benefited from the laws *Muller* permitted because they wanted shorter workdays than they had the leverage to negotiate for on their own.

That said, sex-specific limits on working hours could make both market work and motherhood harder for women. Restricting women but not men further entrenched sex stratification in employment, legalizing women's exclusion from desirable occupations that men dominated. These laws helped confine female workers to the low-wage dead end where exploitation was most likely and male interest in doing the work was most absent.[19] Ironically, legislation that purported to protect women could block their access to better jobs, higher pay, and promotion prospects. Legislation that purported to prioritize female domesticity could jeopardize women's domestic lives by undermining women's ability to support their families.

For example, a 1913 New York law banned women from working in factories between ten at night and six in the morning.[20] As a federal study later concluded, such prohibitions hindered or blocked women from holding some "highly skilled, well paid" jobs, like work in printing factories.[21] Many of the female printers thrown into unemployment had children or other dependents to support.[22] New York's highest court relied on *Muller* to uphold (affirm the constitutionality of) the statute in 1915.[23] The state court explained that it was constitutionally irrelevant whether the law "will inflict unnecessary hardships on a great many women who neither ask nor require its provisions by depriving them of an opportunity to earn a livelihood by perfectly healthful labor."[24]

That same year, a group of women workers formed the Women's League for Equal Opportunity to oppose sex-specific restrictions on women's employment.[25] The group's first President was Ella Sherwin, a printer who had to work longer hours for less pay after New York banned her night work.[26] Sherwin explained that laws purporting to protect working women often functioned as "protection for the men" by shielding men from female competition for sought-after jobs.[27] "Welfare legislation, if persisted in, will protect women to the vanishing point," she warned, draining "women out of all highly paid and highly organized trades."[28] Female printers in New York ultimately spent $10,000 and "incalculable energy" lobbying "each session of the legislature" for a statutory exemption to permit them to work at night,[29] which they finally won in 1921.[30]

Meanwhile, New York continued to expand its sex-specific restraints on women's work. The legislature targeted women in the transit industry in 1919, barring them from working at night and restricting their total hours.[31] Brooklyn Rapid Transit promptly informed 1,531 female employees that they were losing their jobs as "conductorettes," "ticket choppers and agents."[32] Margaret Hinchey was one of two hundred suddenly unemployed women who assembled to protest the 1919 law and join the Women's League for Equal Opportunity. She emphasized that working for the BRT had been an opportunity for women "to get employment away from the drudgery of domestic work" and declared that leaving domestic service for the BRT had made women "healthier and happier."[33] Isabel Liley similarly reported that her transit job, "a steady position with good pay," had been an improvement over her previous employment in a field where the wages were too low and the conditions too grueling to attract male applicants. "Before coming to the B.R.T.," Liley observed, "I worked twelve, fourteen, and eighteen hours a day as a trained nurse without anyone taking heed to my welfare."[34]

New York also prohibited most waitressing at night,[35] and the United States Supreme Court relied on *Muller* to uphold that prohibition in 1924.[36] Some waitresses wanted to work late shifts, when the tips were larger, the job was generally easier, and the schedule was more compatible with some women's domestic responsibilities.[37] Women opposed to the ban on night waitressing managed to get a repeal proposal before the New York Legislature in early 1929, half a year before the stock market crash that October. But the state Federation of Labor urged lawmakers to retain the prohibition, contending that allowing waitresses to work at night "would throw 5,000 men waiters out of work."[38] The prohibition stayed in place.[39]

Muller's approval of sex-specific restrictions on women's employment remained enforceable law that lower courts could wield into the 1970s,[40] long after the Court overturned *Lochner* in 1937.[41] A 1969 federal survey found thirty-eight states and the District of Columbia still imposing some sex-specific constraints on women's time at work,[42] and twenty-six states with sex-specific prohibitions on women holding certain jobs.[43] Chapter 3 will explore more of the sex-specific employment laws that *Muller* enabled for decades.

Muller's impact also extended far beyond the workplace. When the Supreme Court in 1937 upheld legislation that gave women a financial incentive not to vote, the opinion cited *Muller* as support.[44] Chapter 3 will dive into that case as well. State courts denying women equal opportunities and responsibilities deployed *Muller* similarly in the middle decades of the twentieth century, invoking that precedent when permitting a public college to keep women out,[45] or upholding women's exclusion from juries.[46]

Examining *Muller* and *Lochner* together better captures how the Supreme Court regulated state power over individuals in the twentieth century, including women in the story as well as men. Juxtaposing the two decisions also brings each into sharper focus. *Lochner* skipped the exuberantly gendered language *Muller* embraced because the Justices saw men as regular human beings and women as deviations from that baseline. But *Lochner* was not about the Justices' gender-neutral views on labor regulation and individual autonomy. *Lochner* turned on the Court's assumptions about masculinity, male labor, and male autonomy specifically and exclusively. Even when the *Lochner* Court repeatedly referenced the rights of persons and individuals to organize their working lives as they saw fit, the Justices meant the rights of men.[47]

Justice David Brewer made the gendered logic of both *Lochner* and *Muller* explicit in an essay published just months after he wrote the Court's *Muller* opinion. Brewer had been part of the *Lochner* majority, and he explained that *Lochner* recognized every man's right "to pursue happiness according to his own ideas of what will bring happiness. If he thinks that working for twelve hours is better for him and will inure to his happiness to a greater extent than labor for a less time and his work be attended with no special risks, then he has the right to work for that length of time."[48] Brewer understood such autonomy as a quintessentially masculine prerogative that he himself enjoyed. He wrote as if all men were able-bodied, powerful, and ensconced in workplaces as mentally invigorating and physically pleasant as a Justice's chambers or a cabinet secretary's office: "Here is a man; strong, vigorous, healthy. Why should he not be permitted to contract for more than eight hours' labor—for nine, ten, or a dozen, if he wishes? There is scarcely a man in charge of any department at Washington who does not work over ten hours a day. There is not a justice of our court who does not work longer, and all of us look reasonably healthy. The Declaration of Independence and the constitution give us the right to determine these questions for ourselves."[49]

In contrast, Brewer was certain that the Constitution did not endow women with the same rights. He presumed that legal authorities could expect and require women—but not men—to subordinate their individual desires to their domestic duties. Brewer recounted that he wrote *Muller* "in the firm belief that there was something in [woman's] place and work in life which justified the legislature in forbidding her to contract for factory work beyond a limited time. The race needs her; her children need her; her friends need her, in a way that they do not need the other sex."[50] While the Constitution protected men's right to live for themselves, the law could push women to live for others.

The Supreme Court has remembered and castigated *Lochner* endlessly. But when the Court recalls this pivotal episode, the accounts do not discuss how women and gender fit into the story and do not mention *Muller*.[51] Indeed, the Court rarely mentions *Muller*, even in cases about women's rights.[52]

Legal scholars compiling lists of the Supreme Court's most important or most terrible constitutional judgments have similar habits. They routinely spotlight *Lochner* as an exemplar of horrible misjudgment, declaring that *Lochner* occupies "the lowest circle of constitutional Hell"[53] and "would probably win the prize, if there were one, for the most widely reviled decision of the last hundred years."[54] *Muller*, in contrast, does not make their lists of important or terrible decisions,[55] and sometimes is not even cited in their books or articles.[56]

As we will see, *Muller*'s insistence on women's domesticity has long characterized the law's treatment of women and remains a powerful driver of legal regulation to the present day.[57] But Mullerism—reasoning about the Constitution on the premise that women rather than men should prioritize domestic roles and responsibilities—is not a word in circulation, much less a dreaded insult integral to the Court's understanding of its history. I believe I am the only one who uses the term.

Men's Spontaneous Enlightenment Instead of Women's Mobilization

One way to erase women from the nation's stories about itself is to tell those stories without mentioning how women and gender fit within them.

Another approach treats women only as subjects rather than actors. Judges have frequently left women out even when writing about women's status. This section explores how courts have repeatedly attributed expansions in women's rights over time to men's spontaneous enlightenment. The next section turns to courts crediting such expansion to men's scheming. Both accounts misdescribe the pathways to reform, treating women as if they were passive witnesses to male decisionmaking and erasing how generations of women have fought for their equality against fierce resistance.

Let's start with the beginning of the Supreme Court's modern case law on sex discrimination. As *Muller* suggests, pervasive sexism has been perfectly legal for most of American history. Even after the Fourteenth Amendment declared in 1868 that states could not deny "any person" "the equal protection of the laws,"[58] it took the Supreme Court a hundred and three years to place any constitutional limits on sex discrimination. *Reed v. Reed* (1971), which held that Idaho could not automatically prefer men over women as the administrators of their relatives' estates, was the first Supreme Court decision invalidating a statute for denying women equal protection.[59] Two years later, a four-Justice plurality in *Frontiero v. Richardson* held that the uniformed services could not give servicewomen fewer benefits and provided the Justices' first sustained explanation for why sex discrimination was a constitutional problem.[60] This explanation included the only discussion of women's history the Court would offer for decades.[61] *Frontiero's* lead opinion is called a plurality opinion because it attracted more votes than any other opinion in the case, while failing to win the five votes needed to create a majority opinion.

Women's struggles for equality did not appear in the story *Frontiero* told. Justice William Brennan's plurality opinion acknowledged with bland understatement "that our Nation has had a long and unfortunate history of sex discrimination," but never touched on the long history of women's striving for equal rights.[62] For example, the plurality's discussion of the Nineteenth Amendment's ratification in 1920 aligned with the popular accounts that misdescribe this milestone as emerging from consensus rather than conflict. The Justices never mentioned women's multigenerational campaigning to make this victory possible or the entrenched opposition suffragists had to overcome.[63] Chapter 4 will explore many popular accounts along similar lines.

The *Frontiero* plurality likewise ignored the feminist mobilization that had prodded an overwhelmingly male Congress toward recent "increasing sensitivity to sex-based classifications." *Frontiero* proceeded as if federal lawmakers had acted entirely on their own initiative in enacting the 1963 Equal Pay Act and the 1964 Civil Rights Act to combat sex discrimination in employment and in passing the Equal Rights Amendment in 1972 and sending it the states for ratification.[64] Much of this book will examine mobilization that *Frontiero* omitted.

Frontiero's plurality also treated white women as synonymous with all women, repeatedly excluding women of color. The Justices' argument for why sex discrimination raised constitutional concerns turned on a comparison between sex discrimination and race discrimination written as if every woman was white and every African American was male. *Frontiero* observed that "throughout much of the 19th century *the position of women in our society was, in many respects, comparable to that of blacks* under the pre-Civil War slave codes. *Neither slaves nor women* could hold office, serve on juries, or bring suit in their own names, and married women traditionally were denied the legal capacity to hold or convey property or to serve as legal guardians of their own children."[65] The phrasing seemed oblivious to the possibility that someone could be both black and female.

Indeed, *Frontiero's* central metaphor for sex discrimination erased women of color. On the Justices' account, sex discrimination had placed women "on a pedestal" that proved to be "a cage."[66] That story could only be about (relatively privileged) white women, as contending that America had put women of color "on a pedestal" would be far-fetched.

Frontiero likewise focused on white women's experiences with voting. The plurality's historical narrative proceeded as if all women "were guaranteed the right to vote" in 1920.[67] This is perhaps the commonest misdescription of the Nineteenth Amendment, and we will see popular writers and textbook authors repeat it routinely as well.[68] In fact, the United States Constitution has never guaranteed anyone the right to vote.[69] Instead, the Constitution prohibits certain grounds for disenfranchisement. The Nineteenth Amendment established one of those prohibitions, providing that "[t]he right of citizens of the United States to vote shall not be denied or abridged by the United States or by any State on account of sex."[70] But legal authorities—on their own or in cahoots with citizen accomplices—denied many women the vote after 1920, particularly women of color.

For example, some women could not vote after 1920 because of their marriage. The Expatriation Act of 1907—passed as women's push for the Nineteenth Amendment intensified—provided that American women automatically lost their citizenship when they married foreign men.[71] The Supreme Court upheld this law in 1915, discerning no constitutional problem with a statute that merged the "identity of husband and wife" and gave "dominance to the husband."[72]

Congress's marital expatriation scheme remained wholly intact until 1922, when lawmakers passed the Cable Act to allow some American women to keep their citizenship when marrying a foreigner.[73] Women's organizations had lobbied extensively for the Cable Act,[74] and this legislative victory was a first step toward recognizing that women's citizenship should not be contingent on which man they married.

Yet the Cable Act did not go nearly far enough. After 1922, marriage could still cost an American woman her citizenship, whereas matrimony never jeopardized an American man's citizenship. Congress confined the Cable Act's protections to women who married foreign men eligible for naturalization. An American woman still lost her citizenship if she married "an alien ineligible to citizenship," such as a man who had immigrated from Asia.[75] Moreover, if an American woman who had married an eligible foreigner lived in her husband's country for two years, or lived anywhere outside the United States for five years, the Cable Act presumed that she had surrendered her American citizenship.[76]

Women's organizations convinced Congress to amend the Cable Act several times.[77] But the United States did not abandon its policy of marital expatriation for women until 1934. Even then, women who had previously lost their citizenship by marrying did not automatically become Americans again, so the consequences of marital expatriation persisted indefinitely.[78]

Legal authorities also barred women from voting after 1920 because they lived in territories of the American empire rather than within a state. For example, literate women did not win the right to vote in Puerto Rico until 1929,[79] and the territorial legislature did not remove that literacy requirement until 1935.[80] The first federal court to hold that women in the U.S. Virgin Islands were entitled to vote did not issue that decision until the end of 1935.[81]

Most of all, laws on the books and practices on the ground blocked women from voting after 1920 because of their race. Congress imposed multiple racial prohibitions that made some immigrants, especially from Asia, ineligible for naturalization and hence suffrage.[82] Congress did not repeal the last of those statutory bans until 1952, when federal law finally declared that eligibility for naturalization "shall not be denied or abridged because of race or sex or because such person is married."[83]

African American women were theoretically eligible to vote in 1920, but whites often denied them that right in practice, especially in Southern states, through the same mechanisms deployed to disenfranchise black men. That included violence, intimidation, economic retaliation, and legal maneuvers like poll taxes, literacy tests, white primaries, understanding requirements, and 'good character' requirements.[84] Texas used similar strategies to keep Mexican Americans from voting.[85]

A 1961 federal commission surveyed voter registration in counties where more than five percent of the adult population was African American. It found "at least 129 counties in 10 States" where less than one-tenth of the African American adults were registered. In twenty-three of those counties across five states, no African Americans were registered at all.[86]

Congress did not provide that all Native Americans born in the United States were United States citizens until 1924.[87] Even then, some states continued to deny Native Americans the vote. They imposed literacy tests, refused to recognize Native Americans living on reservations as state residents, withheld voting rights because Native Americans were exempt from some state taxes, and/or contended that Native Americans were ineligible to vote because they were under the federal government's guardianship.[88]

The United States did not make significant efforts to ensure that people of color could access the polls until Congress enacted the 1965 Voting Rights Act.[89] The Supreme Court hobbled this statute in 2013 by striking down a key enforcement mechanism,[90] and battles over voting and voter suppression continue to this day.[91]

Erasing women's struggles for equality—and erasing women of color entirely—helped the *Frontiero* plurality attribute the persistence of restrictions on women's rights to the "romantic paternalism" of well-intentioned, if misguided, male lawmakers, rather than their vehement opposition to women's demands for reform.[92] At the same time, these strategic omissions allowed Brennan to write the plurality opinion as if improvements in women's status over time had emerged from the spontaneous enlightenment of male decisionmakers, unprompted by women's activism. Apparently, men just gave women the Nineteenth Amendment and congressmen decided on their own initiative to pass the Equal Rights Amendment and enact statutory prohibitions on sex discrimination in employment.[93]

Indeed, *Frontiero* linked the Justices' own decisionmaking to men's spontaneous enlightenment rather than women's striving. The Supreme Court remained all-male through the 1970s. Brennan had so little self-awareness about sexism that he was still refusing to hire female law clerks when he wrote *Frontiero*'s plurality opinion.[94] Nonetheless, he framed *Frontiero* as if the male Justices had realized on their own that sex discrimination was an "unfortunate" problem that the Supreme Court brethren needed to address.[95]

In fact, the Court began to take sex discrimination claims seriously only after feminists within and outside the legal profession propelled those claims forward. The *Frontiero* litigation itself is a prime example.

Lieutenant Sharron Frontiero's dispute with the military began when she saw her paycheck.[96] After marrying in December 1969,[97] Frontiero had expected the Air Force to give her the increased housing and health care benefits that every serviceman automatically received when he married.[98] But as she soon discovered, federal law denied those benefits to married servicewomen, unless the woman could prove that her husband depended on her for more than half his support.[99] This policy both assumed that men earned more than women and helped make that so. A male lieutenant performing the same work as Frontiero, with a wife earning the same income as Frontiero's husband, would receive more compensation from the military than Frontiero did.

Frontiero considered herself "a flaming feminist."[100] She sued the military in 1970 while still serving in the Air Force.[101] The death threat she received during the litigation did not deter her.[102]

When Frontiero brought her case to the Southern Poverty Law Center, an elated attorney there recognized that the suit presented an opportunity to translate the recent resurgence in feminist mobilization into legal reform. As Frontiero later explained: "It was like the idea of equal rights was in the air, but lawyers were looking for a real name and face and situation to put with it."[103]

By the time Frontiero's litigation reached the Supreme Court, the American Civil Liberties Union Women's Rights Project was involved as well. Future-Justice Ruth Bader Ginsburg was the project's first director.[104] She later recalled how Frontiero became one of several cases the ACLU argued before the Court in the 1970s as part of a concerted strategy to educate the Justices about sex discrimination and change how they interpreted constitutional law.[105] The ACLU's brief—which Ginsburg co-wrote—discussed the nineteenth-century woman's rights movement and its intersections and overlaps with movements for abolition and racial justice, women's long battle for suffrage, heroines like Sojourner Truth, and the feminist activism in the 1960s and 1970s that pushed lawmakers and judges to reexamine women's legalized inequality.[106] But the Frontiero Justices acknowledged none of that, opting to present an account of America's past that omitted the history of women's struggles for equality that feminists had highlighted for the Court.

Frontiero's erasure of women's struggles fit within a long judicial tradition. Since the nineteenth century, state courts had been recounting improvements in women's status over time without acknowledging that women had pushed for those changes and unsettled the status quo enough to make progress possible. Instead, courts attributed expansions in women's rights to male decisionmakers: "wise modern" lawmakers,[107] "just and enlightened" legislators and judges,[108] the "more enlightened and humane notions" of courts and legislatures,[109] the judiciary's "spirit of enlightened reason and true progress."[110] Courts either wrote about these powerful men as if they had acted entirely on their own or portrayed them as responding to an "enlightened public opinion" whose origins were never specified.[111] In either case, the accounts commonly emphasized that changes in women's status had emerged from consensus rather than conflict, with the law evolving "steadily"[112] and smoothly to produce reform "by common consent."[113]

Frontiero's erasure of women's struggles for equality also reflected and reinforced a long intellectual tradition—forged when the historical profession almost entirely excluded women.[114] From the start, America's histories and textbooks tended to push women to the margins.

Historian Henry Adams, a descendant of two Presidents,[115] noted as early as 1907 that "American history mentioned hardly the name of a woman."[116] Woman's rights advocates were keenly aware of the exclusion. The 1908 convention of the National American Woman Suffrage Association declared that "the text books used in our Schools and Colleges do not show a proper recognition of woman's work and influence in the history and development of nations." The association resolved "to investigate the matter with a view to securing the publication of unbiased, complete and up to date text books, especially in History and in Civics."[117]

Pauline Steinem (whose granddaughter, Gloria, would become a prominent feminist generations later)[118] led the association's education committee and proposed the 1908 resolution.[119] Steinem's committee proceeded to contact approximately four hundred school superintendents and twenty-six textbook publishing companies.[120] "The impression conveyed by our textbooks," Steinem reported in 1909, "is that this world has been made by men and for men, and the ideals they are putting forth are colored by masculine thought." Textbooks focused on "masculine activities," ignored women's work, and did "not show the slightest appreciation of the significance of the 'Woman's Movement.'" Indeed, Steinem found that "[t]he movement itself is not thought worth mentioning."[121]

This erasure persisted for generations. Many of the histories and textbooks the *Frontiero* Justices could have read when they were students, lawyers, or judges either did not discuss women, or did so hastily, or mentioned women's status only to attribute improvements to men's benevolence.[122]

Professor Arthur Schlesinger observed in 1922 that "[a]n examination of the standard histories of the United States and of the history textbooks in use in our schools raises the pertinent question whether women have ever made any contributions to American national progress that are worthy of record."[123] Schlesinger linked women's exclusion from America's history books to the fact "that all of our great historians have been men and were likely therefore to be influenced by a *sex* interpretation of history all the more potent because unconscious."[124] In the middle decades of the twentieth century, Schlesinger would play a key role in the founding of what became Harvard's Arthur and Elizabeth Schlesinger Library on the History of Women in America.[125] As early as 1922, in the wake of women's multigenerational battle for the Nineteenth Amendment, he argued that "the pall of silence which historians have allowed to rest over [women's] services and achievements may possibly constitute the chief reason why the women have been so slow in gaining equal rights with the men in this the greatest democracy in the world. The men of the nation have, perhaps not unnaturally, felt disinclined to endow with equality a class of persons who, so far as they knew, had never proved their fitness for public service and leadership in the past history of the country."[126]

Almost a quarter century later, Mary Beard observed that "Professor Schlesinger's appeal of 1922 for some consideration of women's contributions to the making of history effected no immediate revolution in the thinking of his gild."[127] Beard had been a suffragist with the National Woman's Party in the 1910s. She went on to write pathbreaking histories of women, albeit without a position in a university history department.[128] In 1921—when Beard was fresh from the Nineteenth Amendment victory—she coauthored a book with her husband that predicted that historians would no longer ignore "women's political power," "their labor, their education, their status in society, their influence on the course of events." The 1921 book anticipated that history would be "rewritten and the past rediscovered in the light of the new age."[129]

By 1946, Beard recognized that her prediction had yet to come true. Her *Woman as Force in History* explored how "[w]omen have done far more than exist and bear and rear children." They "have been a force in making all the history that has been made."[130] Beard observed that America's historians still routinely excluded women from their accounts or mentioned women only to describe them as subjects upon which men acted, without agency, desires, struggles, and achievements of their own. In her words: "the conventional view of women as negligible or nothing or helplessly subject to men in the long past continued largely to direct research, thinking, and writing about American history."[131]

Unsurprisingly, the professors Beard criticized did not review her work favorably. Jack Hexter, a historian "of modern freedom,"[132] called Beard's book "rather waspish" and denied that "male historians" had allowed "male prejudice" to distort their scholarship.[133]

Nonetheless, perusing mainstream histories from the middle of the twentieth century quickly confirms Beard's observations. Ralph Henry Gabriel, a professor of American history at Yale,[134] published a 452-page tome in 1940 on *The Course of American Democratic Thought*. A reviewer lauded Gabriel for presenting "an extraordinary range of American personalities."[135] When Gabriel's book appeared, women had already spent generations mobilizing for equality and only twenty years had passed since the Nineteenth Amendment's ratification. Yet Gabriel never discussed women's efforts to include themselves in American democracy.[136]

William McNeill, a celebrated historian at the University of Chicago, published *The Rise of the West: A History of the Human Community* in 1963. The book won a National Book Award and rave reviews.[137] One historian called McNeill's work "not only the most learned and the most intelligent, it is also the most stimulating and fascinating book that has ever set out to recount and explain *the whole history of mankind*."[138] McNeill's epic *History of the Human Community* consumed more than eight hundred pages, but the twenty-one page index had no entries for woman, women, female, wife, family, or marriage.[139]

Samuel Eliot Morison was an American historian with a towering reputation.[140] He taught decades of undergraduates at Harvard, but only men.[141] Harvard was still excluding women from its college when Morison retired in 1955.[142] Morison reportedly closed his classes to students from Radcliffe, Harvard's nearby sister college, because he thought the women were "frivolous."[143]

Morison published his *History of the American People* in 1965. "It's my legacy to my country," he told the *New York Times*. "It represents my cumulative knowledge over almost 50 years and my mature thinking about American history."[144] The book was 1,150 pages, but spared only a few sentences for women's rights.[145] Morison reported that "the Women's Rights movement" "included a number of sensible women reformers" and a "lunatic fringe."[146]

Since the Court decided *Frontiero* in 1973, the field of women's history has flourished. Scholars have uncovered abundant material about women's activism in the nineteenth and twentieth centuries that the Justices could draw on if they chose.[147] But the Court still frequently ignores women's struggles for equality.

The 2015 decision invalidating same-sex marriage prohibitions is illustrative.[148] Justice Anthony Kennedy's majority opinion in *Obergefell v. Hodges* reviewed the legal history of marriage, seeking to demonstrate that the law had "evolved in substantial ways over time" and could change again.[149] Women's activism has driven marriage reforms, pushing judges and legislators to remove many legal disabilities long imposed on wives. Yet *Obergefell*, like *Frontiero*, did not link women's expanded rights in marriage to women's persistent advocacy for those rights against powerful resistance. Instead, *Obergefell* observed that "women gained legal, political, and property rights" over time without acknowledging the feminist mobilization that spurred those changes. Here again, changes in women's "role and status" appeared to spring from spontaneous enlightenment. According to the Court, "society" simply "began to understand that women have their own equal dignity."[150]

Obergefell also followed *Frontiero* in suggesting that the Court's decision to extend equal protection to women was the product of enlightened Justices acting on their own initiative. *Obergefell* never mentioned the feminist litigators who had worked to transform how the Court understood women's constitutional rights. Even Ruth Bader Ginsburg, Kennedy's then-colleague who joined the *Obergefell* majority, went unmentioned.[151] Instead, *Obergefell* explained that the Justices who "invoked equal protection principles to invalidate laws imposing sex-based inequality on marriage" were "[r]esponding to a new awareness," one the Justices had seemingly developed on their own.[152]

I would never contend that feminists are the only activists excluded from the Court's opinions as the Justices foreground their own insightfulness and independence in developing the law. For example, *Brown v. Board of Education* (1954) did not discuss how the National Association for the Advancement of Colored People (NAACP) strategized for decades to undermine Jim Crow's constitutional foundations and push the Court toward rejecting racially segregated public education.[153]

But *Obergefell*'s silence about women's struggles for sex equality is striking, especially because the opinion did describe the social movement working to legalize same-sex marriage. *Obergefell* emphasized that "extensive litigation," "referenda, legislative debates, and grassroots campaigns, as well as countless studies, papers, books, and other popular and scholarly writings," had contributed to a "societal discussion of same-sex marriage and its meaning" that "led to an enhanced understanding of the issue."[154]

By necessity, this chapter cannot provide a complete account of all the work, resilience, bravery, and grit that generations of Justices have erased when they kept women's mobilization for equality out of their stories about America. I can start, however, by observing that many important advances in women's rights took generations to achieve. Winning the Nineteenth Amendment required seventy-two years of struggle after America's first woman's rights convention demanded woman suffrage.[155] Another forty-five years of struggle were required before the 1965 Voting Rights Act began to combat women of color's systematic disenfranchisement.[156] Why did these steps forward take so long? The short answer is that the opposition was ferocious.

Many anti-suffragists warned that allowing women to vote would jeopardize the pillars of civilization. When Congress debated a woman suffrage amendment in 1887,[157] Senator Joseph Brown of Georgia thundered his disapproval: "This movement is an attempt to reverse the very laws of our being, and to drag woman into an arena for which she is not suited, and to devolve upon her onerous duties which the Creator never intended that she should perform."[158] A 1915 tract denouncing "socialism, feminism, and suffragism" as "terrible triplets" worried that turning women into voters could "destroy the unity of the family."[159]

As suffragists noted, some of the commonest arguments against enfranchising women were in tension with each other. Alice Duer Miller highlighted these contradictions in a 1914 poem parodying the anti-suffrage literature that presented lists of arguments against female voting.[160] Miller was a poet, playwright, and bestselling novelist.[161] Her poem, *Our Own Twelve Anti-Suffrage Reasons*, first appeared in her *New York Tribune* column, *Are Women People?* It read:

1. Because no woman will leave her domestic duties to vote.
2. Because no woman who votes will attend to her domestic duties.
3. Because it will make dissension between husband and wife.
4. Because every wife will vote exactly as her husband does.
5. Because bad women will corrupt our politics.
6. Because bad politics will corrupt our women.
7. Because women have no power of organization.
8. Because women will form themselves into a woman's party.
9. Because men and women are so different that they must have different duties.
10. Because men and women are so much alike that men with one vote each can express themselves and us, too.
11. Because women cannot use force.
12. Because the militants can and do use force.[162]

Miller's wit was sharp, as usual. But arguments against woman suffrage consistently pointed in the same direction, even when they contradicted each other. Anti-suffragists opposed enfranchising women because they knew that women belonged at home and they feared that suffrage was incompatible with female domesticity.

The *New York Times*, for example, spent the 1910s promoting strident opposition to woman suffrage.[163] The fervor of this advocacy can appear outlandish now that the Nineteenth Amendment is no longer controversial. That shift over time perhaps explains why the *Times*'s coverage of the Nineteenth Amendment's centennial included just a single allusion to the newspaper's history of anti-suffragism, a parenthetical noting that female anti-suffragists "received admiring coverage in The New York Times."[164] But in the 1910s, *New York Times* editors—like other anti-suffragists—understood the woman suffrage question as the ultimate referendum on women's place in society and they were determined to preserve the status quo.

States were free to expand their own voting rolls before the Nineteenth Amendment forced their hands. When the New York Legislature gave the state's male voters the opportunity in 1915 to decide whether to enfranchise women, the *Times* spent almost two thousand words urging men to reject this "objectionable and unreasonable derangement of the political and social structure." The editors warned that permitting women to vote would cause "a radical reorganization of society" that would leave everyone worse off. Women, who were innately suited for "housewifery" and "the care of infants," would be condemned "to do men's tasks, to bear men's burdens." Men might have to do housework because "if the women were to take up man's duties, who is to assume the women's duties?" The *Times* editors knew that it was not "worth while to subvert the whole order of human society by putting women to do men's work."[165] They exulted when the suffrage measure lost, declaring that men had voted woman suffrage "down for the good of the State and the good of the women. The essential American conservatism, the old-fashioned notion of the position and duties of women, prevailed."[166]

Countering such vehemence took multigenerational commitment and perseverance. Carrie Chapman Catt was president of America's largest suffrage organization, the National American Woman Suffrage Association, during the final push for the Nineteenth Amendment.[167] In 1923, she published *Woman Suffrage and Politics* to recount the path to that victory.

Catt described women's "pauseless campaign" after the Fourteenth Amendment permitted states to continue excluding women from voting. Between 1868 and 1920, suffragists "were forced to conduct fifty-six campaigns of referenda to male voters; 480 campaigns to get Legislatures to submit suffrage amendments to voters; 47 campaigns to get State constitutional conventions to write woman suffrage into State constitutions; 277 campaigns to get State party conventions to include woman suffrage planks; 30 campaigns to get presidential party conventions to adopt woman suffrage planks in party platforms, and 19 campaigns with 19 successive Congresses." As Catt recalled in 1923: "Hundreds of women gave the accumulated possibilities of an entire lifetime, thousands gave years of their lives, hundreds of thousands gave constant interest and such aid as they could. It was a continuous, seemingly endless, chain of activity. Young suffragists who helped forge the last links of that chain were not born when it began. Old suffragists who forged the first links were dead when it ended."[168]

Even a few years after the Nineteenth Amendment's 1920 ratification, reminders of the effort women had to expend and the resistance women had to overcome to reach that milestone made some men uncomfortable. The *New York Times* review of Catt's book chastised "the suffragists" for not taking "their victories like ladies" and advised them to "moderate their language toward those"—meaning, men who had fought suffrage—"who have long forgotten and forgiven the battle and have turned, as is the practice of Americans, to the issues of today."[169]

In fact, the passages I just quoted from Catt understate the mobilization needed to achieve the Nineteenth Amendment. Winning that amendment required more than working long and hard within conventional political channels. Women braved multiple confrontations with violent opponents. Anti-suffragists did not confine themselves to "romantic paternalism," as the *Frontiero* Justices suggested.[170]

Suffragists held a parade in the District of Columbia on March 3, 1913, the day before Woodrow Wilson's presidential inauguration. Some white men watching the parade responded to the peaceful protest with "nothing less than riots."[171] Newspapers reported that: "Five thousand women, marching in the woman suffrage pageant today, practically fought their way foot by foot up Pennsylvania avenue through a surging mob."[172]

The mob wielded both harassment and violence. "Women, old and young, were subjected to every form of jeering obscenity as they struggled through the crowd, in scores of instances rowdies actually seized and mauled young girls."[173] The suffragists "were spit upon, slapped in the face, tripped up, pelted with burning cigar stubs, and insulted by jeers and obscene language."[174]

The police "stood by with folded arms and grinned."[175] As the *New York Evening Post* remarked, "the uniformed police seemed to have gained the impression that the suffrage parade was disapproved by their superiors and that the women had no particular right to their protection. More than one policeman remonstrated with for neglect of his duty replied: 'Wait till you see how we shall handle the crowds tomorrow. You people have no business here at all. Very well, go on and take my number.'"[176]

A few years after that parade, Alice Paul was leading the National Woman's Party, a new group that had become the more militant wing of the suffrage movement. These women were notorious for peacefully picketing in front of the White House, which was an unprecedented tactic.[177] They continued picketing after the United States entered World War I in 1917 and emphasized the contradictions between President Wilson's declarations about promoting democracy abroad and America's denial of democracy to its own female citizens.[178]

The response was explosive, as three days in August 1917 illustrate. On August 14, a mob of men attacked the party's headquarters, Cameron House, while the police let the violence unfold for hours.[179] Cameron House is only a few hundred feet from the White House, and the mob included servicemen in uniform and federal employees out of their offices at the end of the workday.[180] Men pelted the suffragists' building with eggs and tomatoes.[181] Someone shot a bullet through a second-floor window and it whizzed over a suffragist's head.[182]

Sailors assaulted the women they could reach. Lucy Burns was standing at the threshold to Cameron House. "Three sailors in uniform sprang on her, dragged her and her banner to the curb, and tore the banner to bits." Georgiana Sturgis was on the second-floor balcony. Men climbed up using a ladder they had taken from a nearby theater and a sailor hit Sturgis "with his clenched fist." She asked him, "Why did you do that?" He said he didn't know and "with a violent wrench he tore the banner from her hands and ran down the ladder."[183]

The suffragists stayed on task. Ten women snuck out to picket while the mob was still attacking their headquarters. Men intercepted eight of the women and destroyed their banners, but two women reached the White House gates without being spotted.[184]

The next day, August 15, the suffragists returned "as usual" to their posts in front of the White House. The women faced a mob of "sailors, small boys and hoodlums" while the police "obligingly left the scene."[185] "Alice Paul was knocked down three times. One sailor dragged her thirty feet along the White House sidewalk in his attempts to tear off her Suffrage sash, gashing her neck brutally."[186] Sailors also knocked down other suffragists. One woman "was struck by a soldier in uniform and her blouse torn from her body."[187]

The picketing suffragists returned the following day, August 16. This time, "fifty policemen led the mob in attacking the women. Hands were bruised and arms twisted by police officers and plainclothes men." Rather than protect the peaceful protesters, "[t]he police fell upon these young women with more brutality even than the mobs they had before encouraged."[188]

American newsmen were apparently unable or unwilling to provide detailed photographs of anti-suffrage violence, which helped shield the violence from scrutiny.[189] But a suffragist artist refused to let the violence go undepicted. Nina Allender's cartoons for the National Woman's Party attracted widespread attention.[190] Her cover art for a September 1917 edition of the *Suffragist* newspaper shows a male mob surrounding suffragists to wrest their banners from their hands and destroy them. One delighted hooligan has ripped the word "democracy" from a woman's banner and claimed it for himself. The drawing (Figure 1.1) was captioned: "Training for the Draft."[191] It illustrated how women battling for suffrage faced their own ferocious combatants, at a time when the nation was drafting young men to fight World War I.[192]

Figure 1.1 Nina Allender, *Training for the Draft*, Suffragist, September 29, 1917.
Source: National Woman's Party

Women's activism in the years preceding the 1965 Voting Rights Act spurred still more violent opposition. Consider the brutality that Fannie Lou Hamer confronted more than four decades after the Nineteenth Amendment's ratification when she mobilized to make the right to vote a practical reality for African Americans in Mississippi. The *Frontiero* Justices surely did not have women like Hamer in mind when they attributed the persistence of restrictions on women's rights to "romantic paternalism" that had placed women "on a pedestal."[193]

Hamer had spent her life as a sharecropper in Sunflower County, Mississippi, working in the cotton fields from about the age of six.[194] She attended her first civil rights meeting in August 1962, when she was forty-four.[195] She later said that she had not known that voting was a possibility for black people before the Student Nonviolent Coordinating Committee came to town.[196] At the meeting, Hamer volunteered to try to register. She recalled feeling that there was no point "being scared. The only thing they could do to me was kill me and it seemed like they'd been trying to do that a little bit at a time ever since I could remember."[197]

The Fifteenth Amendment declared race-based disenfranchisement unconstitutional in 1870, and the Nineteenth Amendment made the same proclamation about sex-based disenfranchisement in 1920.[198] But when Hamer raised her hand in 1962, few black women in Mississippi had actual access to the polls. White Mississippians blocked almost all black people from voting through the relentless deployment of violence, intimidation, economic retaliation, and legal shenanigans like literacy test requirements.[199] Mississippi did not publicize its voter registration statistics, for obvious reasons. A federal commission drew on unofficial information to report that the state's registration rate for people of color was just 6.7% in 1964, compared to 69.9% for whites.[200] The racial disparity was even more extreme in Sunflower County, which was not only where Hamer lived but also home to Senator James Eastland.[201] He was an unabashed segregationist who had announced on the Senate floor "that so far as the State of Mississippi is concerned, we have fully and finally determined that we shall master our own destiny, that we shall maintain control of our own elections, and our election machinery, and that we will protect and preserve white supremacy throughout eternity."[202] The registration rate for people of color in Sunflower was just 1.4% in 1964, compared to 80.6% for whites.[203]

On August 31, 1962, Hamer traveled with seventeen other African American volunteers to the Sunflower County courthouse in Indianola and experienced firsthand how white Mississippians kept black citizens disenfranchised.[204] Police officers met the volunteers at the courthouse.[205] When it was Hamer's turn to take the literacy test, the registrar required her to interpret a provision of the Mississippi Constitution, which her schooling had not addressed and she knew nothing about.[206]

The reprisals were swift and unending. On the drive home, the police intercepted the volunteers and took the group to jail on the pretext that their "bus was painted the wrong color."[207] The police fined the driver $100, but finally agreed to take $30. That was still a large enough sum that all the volunteers had to pool their money together to pay the fine.[208] The episode, Hamer later said, was meant "to frighten us to death."[209]

By the time Hamer got home, the owner of the plantation where she had been working as a sharecropper for eighteen years already knew where she had been.[210] W.D. Marlow III told Hamer that if she did not withdraw her registration application, she would have to leave his plantation, which meant losing both her livelihood and her housing.[211] Hamer left that night.[212] She went to stay with a friend.[213] Ten days later, night riders fired sixteen shots into the friend's house.[214]

Hamer was undaunted. She studied the Mississippi Constitution, returned to the courthouse in December 1962, and passed the literacy test. After that victory, cars and trucks filled with armed white men would slowly pass by her house at all hours of the night.[215] But Hamer remained committed to civil rights organizing and eventually became a field secretary for the Student Nonviolent Coordinating Committee.[216]

On June 9, 1963, Hamer was arrested in Winona, Mississippi. She had been traveling by bus with several other black civil rights organizers, heading home after a voter registration workshop in South Carolina.[217] Some of the organizers sat in the white part of the segregated restaurant in the Winona bus station and Hamer was arrested along with them.[218]

Officers locked Hamer in a jail cell and she could hear the police beating her colleagues.[219] Before it was Hamer's turn, a state highway patrolman called her hometown to ask about her. He was enraged when he learned about her activism, hurled racist and misogynistic slurs, and told her: "We are going to make you wish you was dead."[220]

In 1964, Hamer testified before the Credentials Committee of the 1964 Democratic National Convention about the sexualized racial violence that came next. The highway patrolman ordered two African American prisoners to beat her with a blackjack. In her words: "I began to scream and one white man got up and began to beat me in my head and tell me to hush. One white man—my dress had worked up high—he walked over and pulled my dress, I pulled my dress down and he pulled my dress back up."[221]

After the beating, Hamer "couldn't get up" and "couldn't bend [her] knees." Her hands had "turned *blue*."[222] Four days later, her body remained "just as hard as a bone."[223]

Hamer's televised testimony before the Credentials Committee sparked a wave of media attention and helped generate momentum for the 1965 Voting Rights Act.[224] When Hamer spoke to the nation about the brutality her quest for "first-class" citizenship had triggered, she turned the national anthem's confident description of the United States into a challenge, asking: "Is this America, the land of the free and the home of the brave?"[225]

When Hamer spoke to a reporter at an African American newspaper, she elaborated on the sexual assault she had endured in the Winona jail. "One of the white policemen pulled my dress up," Hamer recounted a few days after the beating, "and they were trying to feel under my clothes."[226]

In short, women have spent generations fighting for equality. They have had to upend the status quo, challenge existing power arrangements, and face ferocious opposition. Consensus and the spontaneous enlightenment of male decisionmakers have not been sufficient to transform women's lives. Women won progress through conflict.

Let's turn now to another story that courts have repeatedly told when discussing women's status. This account also overlooks how women have mobilized and treats men as the only important actors generating reform. But here, the judiciary's story about how women's rights expanded centers on men who were devious schemers rather than enlightened thinkers.

Men's Scheming Rather than Women's Striving

When the bill that became the 1964 Civil Rights Act began moving through Congress in 1963, its employment discrimination provisions reached discrimination based on race, color, religion, or national origin.[227] On February 8, 1964, however, the House amended Title VII of the multipart bill to include a prohibition on sex discrimination in employment.[228] Once added, the new prohibition stayed put and became law along with the rest of the statute on July 2, 1964.[229] Title VII proved to be an extraordinarily important advance for sex equality.

The dominant story of how Title VII came to include a prohibition on sex discrimination in employment attributes this momentous reform to men's machinations and ignores women's mobilization. In particular, the story focuses on the scheming of the congressman who introduced the sex amendment on the floor of the House, Representative Howard W. Smith of Virginia, an ardent segregationist determined to maintain white supremacy.

Courts have spent decades discussing the origins of the sex discrimination prohibition in Title VII as if Smith and his segregationist allies were the only proponents. They report that Smith "may have hoped to scuttle the whole Civil Rights Act and thought that adding language covering sex discrimination would serve as a poison pill."[230] They recount that "[t]he suave and subtle Southerners in Congress who put sex into the Civil Rights Act of 1964" had their "strategy" backfire "and a giant step towards 'women's lib' was perhaps unintentionally taken."[231] They declare that "[t]his Court—like all Title VII enthusiasts—is well aware that the sex discrimination prohibition was added to Title VII as a joke by the notorious civil rights opponent Howard W. Smith."[232] They explain that the sex amendment "came from a powerful Congressman from Virginia who may have been attempting to derail the proposed law by adding a classification that would be seen as controversial."[233] They describe the sex amendment to Title VII as "merely one congressman's gamble in an effort to thwart the adoption of the Civil Rights Act of 1964."[234]

Some judges have used this account of Title VII's origins as a rationale for interpreting the sex discrimination prohibition narrowly. When the United States Court of Appeals for the Fifth Circuit held in 1975 that Title VII permitted employers to subject male and female employees to different dress and grooming requirements, the court discussed no proponents of the sex amendment except for Smith, insisted that "nothing of import emerged from the limited floor discussion," and concluded that "Congress in all probability did not intend for its proscription of sexual discrimination to have significant and sweeping implications."[235] The Seventh Circuit relied on the same mode of reasoning in 1984 when holding that Title VII allowed employers to discriminate against transgender employees.[236] The court emphasized that the "sex amendment was the gambit of a congressman seeking to scuttle adoption of the Civil Rights Act" and declared that "[t]he total lack of legislative history supporting the sex amendment coupled with the circumstances of the amendment's adoption clearly indicates that Congress never considered nor intended that this 1964 legislation apply to anything other than the traditional concept of sex."[237]

Accounts of Title VII's origins that focus exclusively on Smith and his segregationist cronies have also been popular outside the courts for decades. The first leaders of the Equal Employment Opportunity Commission disseminated such accounts to justify their lassitude about enforcing the sex amendment. Franklin D. Roosevelt Jr., who became the EEOC's inaugural

Chair in 1965,[238] defended the Commission's conclusion that Title VII per-mitted employers to use sex-specific help wanted ads by explaining that "[t]he provision in the law covering women was inserted at the last minute because 'Howard Smith, certainly no friend of equal opportunity,' wanted to create 'ridicule and confusion.'"[239] Herman Edelsberg, the EEOC's Executive Direc-tor, told a labor conference in 1966 that the sex amendment was a "fluke," "conceived out of wedlock."[240]

Men who worked in the Justice Department while Congress was debating the Civil Rights bill wrote about the origins of the sex amendment simi-larly. Richard Berg, who became the EEOC's first Deputy General Counsel in July 1965,[241] published an article about Title VII in December 1964 when he was still an attorney in the Justice Department's Office of Legal Counsel.[242] Berg mentioned no proponents of the sex amendment beyond Smith and his colleagues "from the South" and described the provision "as an orphan" for which no one had "felt any responsibility."[243] Norbert Schlei, who led the Office of Legal Counsel when the Civil Rights bill was moving through Congress,[244] wrote in 1976 to reflect on Title VII's origins. He described Title VII as "amended *by its enemies* to add sex as a prohibited basis of discrimination."[245]

Judges presenting womanless accounts of how Title VII came to include a prohibition on sex discrimination in employment have also been able to draw on decades of books,[246] articles,[247] and news reports that attribute the sex amendment to Smith's scheming and discuss no other proponents beyond Smith's segregationist allies.[248] This work describes the sex amendment as "Representative Smith's blunder,"[249] a "joke,"[250] an "accident,"[251] "a historical fluke,"[252] "a misfired political tactic on the part of opponents of the Act."[253] On these accounts, Smith was the sole mastermind behind the sex amendment. Female proponents are never mentioned.

In fact, women within and outside Congress played crucial roles in getting the sex discrimination prohibition into Title VII and keeping it there. The womanless story about the origins of the sex amendment that many courts and commentators have told for decades erases women's struggles for their own equality, much like the judiciary's spontaneous enlightenment stories do.

The National Woman's Party sent waves of letters to federal lawmakers in December 1963 and January 1964, urging members of Congress to expand the Civil Rights bill so the legislation reached sex discrimination along with discrimination based on race, color, religion, or national origin.[254] Emma Guffey Miller (the party's Chair and President), Nina Horton Avery (the head of the party's Virginia committee), and Lynn Franklin (another party member from Virginia) sent personalized letters to Smith. These letters appealed to Smith's biases and presented an argument that Smith would eventually make on the House floor when advocating for the sex amendment to Title VII.[255] They told Smith that white women—specifically, "the female members of the native-born Caucasian citizens embracing the tenets of the Christian religion"—would be left unprotected from discriminatory treatment unless the Civil Rights bill prohibited sex discrimination as well.[256]

Why did the National Woman's Party devote so much attention to Smith? As the dominant story about Title VII emphasizes, Smith despised the 1964 Civil Rights Act and voted against it.[257] Indeed, he used his power as Chair of the House Rules Committee to delay the legislation's progress for as long as he could.[258] Smith defended white supremacy in the language of private autonomy, describing the Civil Rights bill as an unprecedented "grab for executive power over the private lives of all American citizens."[259]

But the National Woman's Party also knew that Smith had long been sympathetic to white women mobilizing for sex equality.[260] He supported the Equal Rights Amendment as early as 1945.[261] In 1956, Smith argued for including sex discrimination within the jurisdiction of a proposed civil rights commission.[262] He declared on the House floor that "there is no question of doubt that economically women are discriminated against in salaries and wages" and explained that "if this iniquitous piece of legislation is to be adopted, we certainly ought to try to do whatever good with it that we can."[263]

In 1964, the letters from the National Woman's Party about the Civil Rights bill soon had a visible impact in Congress. At a January 9 hearing of the House Rules Committee, a congressman mentioned "discriminatory laws in favor of women."[264] Representative Katharine St. George of New York, a longtime advocate for equal pay and the Equal Rights Amendment,[265] spoke up immediately. She kept the conversation from shifting to other topics by asking: "Yes, what about them?"[266] Smith then took the opportunity that St. George had helped create to report that he had just received a letter from the National Woman's Party asking why the Civil Rights bill did not reach sex discrimination. Smith emphasized that the party was "serious about" the issue and announced: "I think I will offer an amendment."[267] The next day, Smith wrote Emma Guffey Miller, the party's Chair and President, to tell her he would "certainly support" a sex amendment.[268]

On January 26, 1964, May Craig interviewed Smith on *Meet the Press*. Craig was the longtime Washington correspondent for a group of Maine newspapers,[269] as well as a former member of the National Woman's Party who had been harassed and shoved when she marched in the 1913 suffrage parade the day before Wilson's presidential inauguration.[270] By 1964, she had appeared on *Meet the Press* for over a decade and was famous enough to have been the subject of a *New Yorker* cartoon,[271] a *Vogue* profile,[272] a *Life* photo essay,[273] and multiple other magazine or newspaper features.[274] Craig described herself as "Hell-fire on equal rights for women,"[275] and boasted that she specialized in "quick, simple, and escape-proof questions."[276] When Craig interviewed Smith, she followed up on the discussion at the Rules Committee hearing, told Smith that she supported including a sex discrimination prohibition in the Civil Rights bill, and asked Smith whether he would introduce such an amendment on the House floor. Smith said that he "might do that" and declared: "I am always strong for the women, you know."[277]

A few days later, Katharine St. George made it difficult for Smith to forget about women's rights. She raised the subject of sex discrimination again at another hearing of the House Rules Committee that Smith chaired on January 29, 1964.[278]

Smith rose on the House floor to introduce the sex amendment to Title VII on February 8, 1964, with a speech that simultaneously voiced concern about workplace sex discrimination and mined the subject of female grievances for laughs.[279] The House agreed to the amendment that same day, voting 168 to 133.[280] The *Congressional Record* does not indicate which representatives voted which way, much less reveal each representative's motivations. But segregationists were clearly not the only ones who supported the sex amendment. The segregationists alone did not have enough votes.

When Smith brought the sex amendment to the House floor, there were only eleven women serving in the House and just two in the Senate.[281] Congressmen were accustomed to hearing other male voices during congressional debates, almost exclusively.

The timbre of the conversation shifted after Smith introduced his proposal. Five congresswomen had come prepared to seize the moment and speak in favor of the sex amendment. They highlighted the pervasiveness, the persistence, and the perversity of sex discrimination in employment.[282]

Representative Frances Bolton of Ohio, the first congresswoman to speak, reported that she had been planning to propose an amendment adding a sex discrimination prohibition to the Civil Rights bill.[283] Katharine St. George emphasized that women had long "fought" to expand their opportunities.[284]

Representative Catherine May of Washington acknowledged the women's organizations that had advocated for federal prohibitions on sex discrimination. She referred to the letter she had received from the National Woman's Party and noted that "[t]he League of Women Voters, some Federated Women's Clubs, the National Federation of Business and Professional

Women have joined the National Woman's Party in consistently asking that wherever laws or Executive orders exist which forbid discrimination on account of race, color, religion, or national origin that these same laws and orders should also forbid discrimination on account of sex." May declared that she was supporting the sex amendment "on behalf of the various women's organizations in this country that have for many years been asking for action from the Congress in this field, and who see this as the one possibility we may have of getting effective action."[285]

Representative Edna Kelly of New York asked: "Why restore civil rights to all and fail to give equal opportunity to all?"[286] Catherine May and Representative Martha Griffiths of Michigan worried that white women would be left without protection from employment discrimination unless Title VII included a sex discrimination prohibition.[287]

Like critics from earlier in the twentieth century, both Griffiths and St. George castigated sex-specific restrictions on women's work. Griffiths declared that "[m]ost of the so-called protective legislation has really been to protect men's rights in better paying jobs."[288] St. George highlighted examples illustrating how women-only labor laws prevented "women from going into the higher salary brackets," observing that women "cannot run an elevator late at night and that is when the pay is higher" and "cannot serve in restaurants and cabarets late at night—when the tips are higher—and the load, if you please, is lighter."[289] In contrast to this legislation reserving desirable jobs for men, St. George had "never heard of anybody worrying about" women who clean offices in the middle of the night.[290]

Representative Edith Green of Oregon was the only congresswoman to speak against the sex amendment. Green had written the 1963 Equal Pay Act,[291] and she hoped that "the day will come when discrimination will be ended against women." But Green was concerned that adding the sex amendment to Title VII might later "be used to help destroy this section of the bill."[292]

After the House agreed to the sex amendment, a woman watching from the gallery reportedly shouted, "We made it! We made it! God bless America!"[293] Two days later, on February 10, the House passed the entire Civil Rights bill by a 290 to 130 vote.[294] The legislation—including Title VII's sex amendment—was headed to the Senate.

Women inside and outside Congress immediately mobilized to protect the sex amendment. The National Woman's Party was part of this effort,[295] and it included many other women as well.

Martha Griffiths, the congresswoman who had spoken for the sex amendment at the most length on February 8, told the White House "that if that amendment came out of that bill, I would send my speech door to door in every member's district who had voted against it, and in my opinion those who voted against it would never return to Congress."[296]

May Craig used a February 16 newspaper column to celebrate the sex amendment as "a continuation of the long battle of women for first-class citizenship."[297] Three weeks later, she deployed one of her "escape-proof questions" to protect the provision. Craig prodded Senator Hubert Humphrey of Minnesota, the Senate's Democratic Whip, about the sex amendment during a March 8 interview on *Meet the Press*. After declaring "I am all for women," Humphrey stated: "I think we can accept that provision, and it is a workable one."[298]

The Civil Rights bill also needed Republican support in the Senate to overcome filibustering that could block a vote on the legislation by extending debate indefinitely. When Senator Everett Dirksen of Illinois, the Republican Minority Leader, announced at an April 7 GOP policy lunch that he would push for removing the sex amendment, women got him to back down.[299] Senator Margaret Chase Smith of Maine, who was campaigning to be the Republican presidential nominee,[300] spoke up and marshaled Republicans to oppose Dirksen's plan.[301] She was a longtime supporter of the Equal Rights Amendment and the Senate's only female Republican.[302] The National Federation of Business and Professional Women's Clubs (BPW) also flooded Senate offices with letters advocating for the sex amendment and ensured that Dirksen heard from many female constituents. Marguerite Rawalt, a past BPW President,[303] later recalled that the BPW sought help from women's groups in Illinois and she had "never seen a faster action among our women's organizations."[304] The BPW "made the telegraph wires hot, and got the letters pouring in."[305] Dirksen "got so many telegrams from Illinois and so many remonstrances from the rest of us."[306]

Rawalt was part of a network of women who had kept in contact after serving on President John Kennedy's Commission on the Status of Women.[307] These women strategized together about how to protect the sex amendment to Title VII. Pauli Murray, another alumna of the presidential commission, was in this group. After Dirksen announced his opposition to the sex amendment, Murray agreed to write a memo defending the provision.[308]

Murray was an African American feminist who would go on to write pathbreaking scholarship about utilizing Title VII to combat discrimination against women.[309] In the spring of 1964, she was pursuing doctoral work at Yale Law School.[310] Murray had the insight, the time, and the freedom from government employment to write a penetrating twenty-five page analysis of the persistence and pervasiveness of sex discrimination, its intersections, overlaps, and parallels with race discrimination, and the need for federal intervention.[311]

Where Howard Smith, the National Woman's Party, and some congresswomen had emphasized how the sex amendment to Title VII would help white women, Murray's April 14, 1964, memo argued that black and white women would "share a common fate of discrimination" without the sex amendment "since it is exceedingly difficult for a Negro woman to determine whether or not she is being discriminated against because of race or sex."[312]

Rawalt and her allies circulated Murray's memo in the Senate, the Justice Department, and the White House. They also sent a copy to Lady Bird Johnson, President Lyndon Johnson's wife.[313] Murray received a letter back from Bess Abell, the First Lady's social secretary, acknowledging Murray's "convincing and persuasive" memo and reporting "that as far as the Administration is concerned, its position is that the Bill should be enacted in its present form."[314]

In short, many women mobilized and strategized to get the sex discrimination prohibition into Title VII and to keep it there. They were active participants rather than passive bystanders to male decisionmaking.

While some of the story I just told is revealed in private letters and unpublished documents, substantial evidence of the roles that women played in Title VII's origins has been easily accessible for decades. The speeches of the five congresswomen who championed the sex amendment on the House floor are in the *Congressional Record*, one of the first places anyone should look for legislative history.[315] A published hearing report—another obvious source for legislative history—documents the House Rules Committee hearing where Howard Smith discussed a letter he had received from the National Woman's Party.[316] It seems safe to assume that at least some of the judges and commentators who focused only on Smith and his segregationist allies in recounting the origins of the sex amendment read those references to women in the legislative history and ignored them.

Women and women's historians have also spent years trying to ensure that Americans remember women's roles in Title VII's origins. The National Woman's Party began publicizing its "heroic campaign" for the sex amendment immediately after the House passed the Civil Rights bill, and party members continued to recount that history into the 1970s.[317] One of the party's former national chairs used a 1967 newspaper interview to summarize the story that the National Woman's Party wanted told: The sex amendment to Title VII "was a great achievement. Oh, I know most men call it a fluke," Ernestine Powell explained, "but it wasn't anything of the sort. It was a long hard fight and we won."[318]

Representative Martha Griffiths similarly spent time in the 1960s and 1970s reminding both the public and her fellow federal legislators about how she had "fought vigorously for the amendment" as "one of the principal supporters of the amendment."[319] Griffiths quoted the speeches that she and Katharine St. George had delivered on the House floor on February 8, 1964, and used that legislative history to argue that Title VII overrode state laws imposing sex-specific restrictions on women's work.[320] Griffiths also informed multiple audiences that she had already been planning to introduce a sex amendment before she learned about Howard Smith's intentions, but had decided after Smith's interview with May Craig to wait for Smith to introduce the amendment because she thought Smith's sponsorship would increase the amendment's chances of success.[321]

Other women shared their own stories of mobilizing to secure Title VII's prohibition on sex discrimination in employment. Marguerite Rawalt wrote an essay published in 1983 that recounted how the BPW helped protect the sex amendment as the Civil Rights bill went through the Senate.[322] Pauli Murray's 1987 memoir described the writing and circulation of her April 1964 memo.[323] Decades of women's historians, in turn, have discussed how women's advocacy shaped Title VII.[324]

But the womanless account of how Title VII came to include a prohibition on sex discrimination in employment persists within and outside the judiciary, despite all the contrary evidence. One potential explanation for this story's longevity is that describing the origins of the sex amendment as if only a wily male politician and his segregationist cronies were responsible fits comfortably within a long-established pattern of erasing women's striving for equal rights. Judges, like too much of the culture that surrounds them, are used to centering men and sidelining women, even when—or especially when—discussing how women's status improved over time. An account of Title VII's origins that presents men as the only important actors needed to propel reform and women as passive beneficiaries seems familiar, rather than overdue for more investigation.

As we have seen, courts too frequently leave women out of their stories about the nation. They omit women and gender entirely, or they treat women as subjects upon which men act and ignore how women have fought for their own progress. Either way, women and their struggles for equality are missing.

Chapter 2
Remembering America Without Remembering Women

The judicial tendency to ignore women reflects and reinforces persistent gaps in America's collective memory. Our commemorative landscape too frequently promotes a vision of the nation that pushes women away and men forward, and there has been far too little improvement over time. Official celebrations of important anniversaries have long excluded or sidelined women when telling stories about the nation. Women are too often left out when powerful Americans erect monuments, designate federal holidays, name public buildings, or otherwise construct the memorials that run through everyday life and memorable occasions.

Americans primed to assume that women's treatment reflects consensus more than conflict may be tempted to fault inertia for the continued unevenness of the nation's commemorations. That misses the intentional forces at work.

From the start, women mobilizing for equality have endeavored to enrich and expand America's dominant stories about itself. Women have linked their activism to core American narratives, arguing for women's rights by invoking the Declaration of Independence, the Constitution's Preamble, the Boston Tea Party, the Statue of Liberty, and other foundational expressions and symbols of American democratic ideals. Women have worked for more than a century and a half to make women's history common knowledge and to draw on that past in pushing for reform.

But attempts to focus public memory on women—whether with monuments, museums, currency design, or otherwise—have repeatedly faced determined and protracted opposition, for generations and to the present day. Battles over commemorating women have attracted much less attention than commemoration conflicts framed as centrally about race, even though many struggles over commemorating women are simultaneously intertwined with race. Battles over commemorating women rage nevertheless.

Women Strive to Include Themselves in America's Stories

Women mobilizing for equality have sought from their earliest days of organization to place their cause at the center of America's past, present, and future. The first woman's rights convention in the United States, held in 1848 in Seneca Falls, New York, issued a Declaration of Sentiments that rewrote the Declaration of Independence to include women on equal terms.[1] It declared "We hold these truths to be self-evident: that all men and women are created equal" and presented a list of grievances that compared the "history of repeated injuries and usurpations on the part of man toward woman" to King George's tyranny toward the colonists.[2]

The Declaration of Sentiments identified woman's rights crusaders as rightful heirs to the Founding Fathers and insisted that the American Revolution would remain unfinished so long as men subordinated women. The protest also made clear that the Declaration of Independence's focus on political liberty had been far too narrow. The Declaration of Sentiments demanded both female enfranchisement and an "equal station" for women in every other arena, calling for equality in marriage and the family, the end of sex discrimination in employment, equal educational opportunities, the abolition of the sexual double standard, the promotion of sex equality in religious worship, and more.[3]

Over the next century and beyond, woman's rights activists would continue to take strength from America's veneration of the revolutionaries and self-conception as a nation founded on a revolutionary commitment to democracy. When Elizabeth Cady Stanton, the intellectual driving force behind much early woman's rights activism, demanded in 1854 that New York legislators enact "a revision of your state constitution—a new code of laws" to free women from subjection to men, Stanton proclaimed that she spoke for "the daughters of the revolutionary heroes of '76."[4]

Women similarly seized on the Boston Tea Party's centennial in 1873 as an opportunity to remind their fellow Americans that the revolutionaries had recognized "that taxation without representation was unjust tyranny."[5] Suffragists in Chicago formed "an anti-tax league."[6] Suffragists in Boston marked the Tea Party's centennial with a rally in Faneuil Hall,[7] one of the sites where protesting colonists had gathered in the weeks before the Boston Tea Party.[8] Suffragists in New York met "to demand that the freedom for which our forefathers struggled shall be given to us also."[9]

Indeed, suffragists did not let an important national anniversary pass without attempting to make women's struggles for equality part of the story.

The New York Woman Suffrage Society sent a memorial to Congress in January 1876 after lawmakers proposed spending a million and a half dollars to celebrate the Declaration of Independence's centennial. The suffragists estimated that female taxpayers would bear a third of that expense and decried "the outrage" of imposing "upon a disfranchised and unrepresented sex the enormous burden of half a million dollars, to be given to the dominant sex to help them in their rejoicings over a liberty from which these tax-payers are excluded."[10] When July 4, 1876, arrived, women marked the occasion with protests emphasizing the contradictions between America's celebrations of independence and its refusal to extend self-government to women. "The women of Washington Territory," for example, joined "with their sisters throughout this nation in a protest against being compelled to submit to laws which they have no voice in framing; against being compelled to pay taxes to support a government in which they are not allowed representation; against being tried in courts of justice, and by juries composed entirely of men."[11]

The National Woman Suffrage Association asked to have one minute during the official centennial ceremony in Philadelphia to present a *Declaration of Rights of the Women of the United States* that Matilda Joslyn Gage and Elizabeth Cady Stanton had written and many suffragists had signed.[12] The women were undeterred when General Joseph Hawley, the politician and Union Army veteran leading the United States Centennial Commission,[13] refused their request.[14]

Susan B. Anthony, Stanton's closest ally and a tireless mobilizer, had spent more than a year determined to produce a "Centennial Screech for freedom," a "Woman's Centennial growl."[15] She arrived at the centennial ceremony with four other suffragists and waited until a male worthy had recited the Declaration of Independence. With the moment ripe, the women stood, went to the speaker's stand, and disrupted the official program. Anthony handed acting Vice President Thomas Ferry a copy of the women's Declaration, and the women distributed additional copies to the audience.[16]

The protesters then walked "to the platform in front of Independence Hall, under the very shadow of the Washington Monument," and Anthony read the women's Declaration aloud.[17] Independence Hall has extraordinary resonance as a site for protest because men debated and signed the Declaration of Independence and the Constitution inside that building. The women's Declaration proclaimed that "[t]he history of our country the past hundred years, has been a series of assumptions and usurpations of power over woman, in direct opposition to the principles of just government, acknowledged by the United States as its foundation."[18] Where the 1776 Declaration had announced "that all men" had "unalienable Rights" to "Life, Liberty and the pursuit of Happiness,"[19] the women's Declaration sought to extend those rights to women. It insisted "that woman was made first for her own happiness, with the absolute right to herself—to all the opportunities and advantages life affords, for her complete development," and denied "that dogma of the centuries, incorporated in the codes of all nations—that woman was made for man—her best interests, in all cases, to be sacrificed to his will."[20]

Some newsmen "decided to omit this part of the proceedings from their reports."[21] But the protesters wanted to capture the attention of their contemporaries and leave a "record for the daughters of 1976."[22] They wrote articles and letters to the editor that recounted "[t]he most important part of the day's proceedings in Philadelphia,"[23] called the 1776 Declaration "the old Declaration of Independence,"[24] and decried the hypocrisy of men who glorified the revolutionaries' revolt against tyranny "while they themselves are practicing the same high handed tyranny upon the other half of the people."[25]

Women similarly sought to enmesh themselves in the story of the Constitution's centennial in 1887. "No women had been invited to participate in any of the public observances," so the National Woman Suffrage Association needed to strategize to make women's voices heard.[26] After the suffragists learned that President Grover Cleveland would attend a reception during the festivities, Lillie Devereux Blake appeared at the building's gate with a journalist who convinced the guard to admit them both.[27] Blake was one of the suffragists who had joined Anthony in disrupting the celebrations for the Declaration of Independence's centennial.[28] Eleven years later, Blake approached Cleveland at the reception for the Constitution's centennial, shook the President's hand, and gave him a document.[29] The written protest drew on the Constitution's Preamble, which begins: "We the People of the United States."[30] The suffragists declared "that the words of the Preamble have been falsified for a hundred years" because women "are allowed no voice, direct or indirect, in framing this Constitution or executing its provisions." They decried this "century of injustice," demanding that the Constitution "be interpreted in accordance with the simple words in which it is framed" and insisting "that in the future all the people of the nation shall have an equal voice in choosing the rulers whose high mission it shall be to guide a true Republic on its course of glory."[31]

Women also had the foresight to engage with new national symbols as they emerged. New York suffragists recognized the 1886 unveiling ceremony for the Statue of Liberty as a chance to highlight the "monstrous absurdity" of having "Liberty embodied as a woman, in a land where no woman has political liberty."[32] The "male managers of the pageant" refused to let the New York

State Woman Suffrage Association participate in the unveiling ceremony at the base of the statue.[33] So the suffragists chartered a boat, flew their association's banner, and held a protest in New York Harbor in front of the statue as the official ceremony unfolded.[34] Lillie Devereux Blake, who led the New York suffragists,[35] explained beforehand that "while men at the base of the great statue are honoring Liberty represented as a woman, we women on board our boat will uplift our voices in demanding liberty for woman."[36] At the protest, the two hundred suffragists on board unanimously adopted a resolution Blake proposed. The wry statement redirected stereotypes about female inconsistency back at men, declaring "that in erecting a statue of Liberty embodied as a woman in a land where no woman has political liberty men have shown a delightful inconsistency which excites the wonder and admiration of the opposite sex."[37]

Suffragists seeking to embed their struggles in America's dominant stories about itself did not confine that project to formal occasions. They addressed popular expressions of democratic commitments as well, producing new versions of patriotic songs like the *Battle Hymn of the Republic*,[38] *Yankee Doodle Dandy*,[39] and *America*.[40] The rewritten lyrics sought to harness the widespread appeal of these odes to American democracy while redirecting the songs' messages. Rather than celebrate American self-government as a completed achievement, suffragist songwriters decried women's continued exclusion. For example, the original version of *America* that Samuel Francis Smith wrote in 1831 begins:

> My country! 'tis of thee,
> Sweet land of liberty—
> Of thee I sing:
> Land, where my fathers died;
> Land of the pilgrim's pride;
> From every mountain-side,
> Let freedom ring.[41]

Elizabeth Boynton Harbert called her version *The New America*. She composed the song for the National Woman Suffrage Association's January 1883 convention,[42] and women sang *The New America* at many suffrage meetings thereafter.[43] The song proclaimed that woman's rights advocates were seizing the revolutionaries' mantle to wrest liberty and justice from a withholding nation. The first verse declared:

> Our country now from thee,
> Claim we our liberty,

In freedom's name.
Guarding home's altar fires,
Daughters of patriot sires,
Their zeal our own inspires
Justice to claim.[44]

After the Nineteenth Amendment's 1920 ratification, the National Woman's Party continued to tie women's struggles to America's revolutionary legacy and to insist that the American Revolution would remain unfinished so long as women were unequal and unfree. A party official explained in 1924 that the Equal Rights Amendment would be "a declaration of the equality of women in our fundamental law, to which women can point in time of need, as men now point to the Declaration of Independence."[45] A promotion for a 1931 party conference asked members: "wouldn't you like to have been present at the Boston Tea Party?" Party leaders promised that their meeting offered "a similar opportunity" to "share in the actual shaping of the history of your country" and gather with "Americans who believe in Liberty."[46] Alice Paul— the party's driving force for decades—was still linking the fight for the ERA to the American Revolution in 1975, when the ERA needed to win ratification in four more states and the Declaration of Independence's bicentennial was approaching. Still an optimist, Paul contended that the "whole country" was "waking up to the fact that" the bicentennial was celebrating "the principle of liberty but not its application" to women. For women "to have liberty," Paul argued, they needed equality.[47]

The National Organization for Women also strove to make women's struggles for equality part of the stories surrounding key national anniversaries and symbols. Feminists founded NOW in 1966 after the Equal Employment Opportunity Commission showed little interest in enforcing Title VII's prohibition on sex discrimination in employment.[48] On the bicentennial of the Boston Tea Party, NOW held a march and rally in Boston that connected the battle for the ERA to the colonists' protest by demanding: "No taxation without equal rights."[49] NOW spent the Declaration of Independence's bicentennial highlighting how women's quest for independence remained ongoing, with a counterrally in Philadelphia on July 4, 1976, and the launch of an eight-week vigil for the ERA in front of the White House.[50]

NOW also repeatedly returned to the Statue of Liberty to spotlight the contradictions between the nation's purported commitments to democracy and its actual treatment of women. Members of NOW and other feminist groups "symbolically seized the Statue of Liberty" on August 10, 1970,[51] the day the House first voted in favor of the ERA.[52] The women reimagined the statue as a feminist icon, hanging a giant banner from a tenth-story balcony on the statue's base that read: "Women of the World Unite!"[53] As one NOW member explained, the demonstrators wanted to highlight the irony "that a woman symbolizes the abstract idea of liberty, but in reality we are not free."[54] After Congress's deadlines for states to ratify the ERA passed without the amendment winning enough ratifications,[55] NOW marked the Statue of Liberty's centennial in 1986 with a protest in New York Harbor emphasizing that "women still have not achieved full legal equality and rights in America."[56]

Women have long paired their efforts to build on the power of familiar stories about the nation with concerted work to teach Americans new stories. For over a century, women mobilizing for equality have strived to disseminate knowledge about women's history so women can invoke this past in pushing for further change.

Early woman's rights activists were writers as well as makers of history. In 1881, Elizabeth Cady Stanton, Susan B. Anthony, and Matilda Joslyn Gage published the first volume of what ultimately became a six-volume *History of Woman Suffrage*.[57] This *History* was not nearly as comprehensive as it purported to be. It centered on Stanton and Anthony, highlighted the editors' friends but not their rivals, and mentioned little about women of color.[58] Still, the thousands of pages in the *History of Woman Suffrage* provided overwhelming evidence of the editors' desire to have the early woman's rights movement—and their roles within it—remembered and built upon. The first volume began by declaring that the editors sought "to put into permanent shape the few scattered reports of the Woman Suffrage Movement still to be found, and to make it an arsenal of facts for those who are beginning to inquire into the demands and arguments of the leaders of this reform."[59] Anthony sent free copies of the first three volumes to twelve hundred public libraries in America and Europe while also giving the volumes "to hundreds of schools and to countless individuals, writers, speakers, etc., whom she thought it would enable to do better work for the franchise."[60]

Hallie Q. Brown wanted her *Homespun Heroines and Other Women of Distinction* (1926) to inspire future generations by teaching them about "the history-making" African American women who came before them.[61] Brown was a suffragist and leader in the African American women's clubs movement.[62] She compiled and edited dozens of biographical essays "to preserve for future reference an account of these women, their life and character and what they accomplished under the most trying and adverse circumstances." Brown explained that she had prepared the book "with the hope that" young people "will read it and derive fresh strength and courage from its records to stimulate and cause them to cleave more tenaciously to the truth and to battle more heroically for the right."[63]

Both mainstream and more militant suffragists wrote histories recounting their battle for the Nineteenth Amendment in the hope that Americans would remember and learn from this past. Carrie Chapman Catt drew on the archives of her National American Woman Suffrage Association to explore in *Woman Suffrage and Politics* (1923) why winning the Nineteenth Amendment took so long.[64] She wanted her assembly of "the facts and deductions drawn from them" to be a resource for "the advocates, perhaps especially the women advocates, of each recurring struggle in the evolution of democracy."[65] Doris Stevens's *Jailed for Freedom* (1920) and Inez Haynes Irwin's *The Story of the Woman's Party* (1921) provided insider accounts of how the National Woman's Party had pursued the Nineteenth Amendment in the face of brutal opposition.[66] The party's Committee on Distribution of Historical Data reported in 1929 that it had sent over four hundred copies of *Jailed for Freedom* to colleges and universities in the past year.[67]

Even when not writing their own history books, women mobilizing for equality have framed and built upon historical narratives about women's past. Alice Paul and her National Woman's Party launched the campaign for the Equal Rights Amendment with a 1923 conference in Seneca Falls. Paul's decision to bring the spotlight to Seneca Falls foregrounded the historical significance of the first woman's rights convention and claimed the mantle of those foremothers.[68] When the National Woman's Party announced its Seneca Falls event, "the women of 1923" described their conference as "linked up with" the 1848 Seneca Falls Convention "as one-half of a whole is joined with the other because it is part and parcel of it."[69] At the 1923 meeting, the leaders of the National Woman's Party unanimously committed themselves to winning the ERA and declared that their organization was "dedicated to the same equal rights program as that adopted on this spot seventy-five years ago."[70] They called the ERA "the Lucretia Mott amendment,"[71] honoring one of the women who joined with Elizabeth Cady Stanton to convene the 1848 Seneca Falls Convention.[72] Paul hoped that drawing on women's past by tying "this amendment to the 1848 movement" would accelerate change in the present, explaining at the 1923 conference that "[i]t is easier to get support for something with tradition behind it and which has grown respectable with age than for something new-born from the brain of the Woman's Party."[73] Paul also invoked future commemorations, predicting that if women limited themselves to tackling sex discrimination state-by-state, "they will be celebrating the 150th anniversary of the 1848 convention without being much further advanced in equal rights than we are."[74]

The National Woman's Party fought tirelessly for the ERA, but America did not see mass mobilization for women's rights over the next four decades. When women's mobilization for equality resurged starting in the late 1960s, many feminists identified themselves as part of a "Second Feminist Wave."[75] The term linked their activism to the wave of woman's rights activity that led to the Nineteenth Amendment, summoning that past as women organized to make history of their own.

Feminists in this second wave marked the fiftieth anniversary of the Nineteenth Amendment's ratification with a Women's Strike for Equality that simultaneously recognized how long women's struggles for equality had been underway and underscored how far those struggles still had to go. Betty Friedan, one of the founders of the National Organization for Women, first proposed the strike.[76] She later said that when she attended college in the late 1930s and early 1940s, "the first century of struggle for women's rights had been blotted out of the national memory and the national consciousness."[77] The Women's Strike was designed to make Americans remember the Nineteenth Amendment as a national milestone and was meant to harness the power of that remembrance to advance a feminist agenda that included advocating for equal educational and employment opportunities, reproductive rights, and access to childcare.[78] Women organized marches and rallies on August 26, 1970, in approximately forty cities across the nation.[79] One report estimated that New York City's march down Fifth Avenue and rally in Bryant Park attracted almost twenty-five thousand participants, including "women (and, for that matter, men) of every age, color, political persuasion, and style of dress."[80] The march and rally in the District of Columbia were similarly diverse, drawing "Weatherwomen and League of Women Voters members; black women, suburban housewives, professionals, office workers, women of the peace movement, Black Panthers and religious orders."[81] Some of the oldest marchers, in New York and elsewhere, had been part of the suffrage movement fighting for the Nineteenth Amendment.[82]

The 1977 National Women's Conference, the first such conference the federal government had ever sponsored,[83] also drew on the history of women's struggles for equality in mobilizing for a wide-ranging agenda that sought "equal rights, equal status, and equal responsibilities with men."[84] In the weeks before the meeting, more than two thousand women relayed a torch from Seneca Falls to the conference in Houston.[85] The first runner received the torch from the great-grandniece of a woman who attended the 1848 Seneca Falls Convention.[86] The last runner handed the torch to Susan B. Anthony's grandniece.[87] The crowd in the Sam Houston Coliseum cheered wildly the next day when the torch was brought to the stage after its 2,610-mile journey.[88] Bella Abzug, a former congresswoman from New York who was the conference's presiding officer, restored order with a gavel that Susan B. Anthony had wielded and declared: "The road to Houston started more than a century and a half ago when American women began organizing to win their rights of citizenship. The torch of freedom we see here today is a symbol of our past victories and our hopes for future ones."[89]

Since then, women mobilizing for equality have often chosen to wear white, as the suffragists did before them.[90] This sartorial strategy connects women's present and past campaigns, making visible the length of women's struggles for equality and women's continued engagement in those battles. Over the past decades, female demonstrators have worn white when marching and mobilizing for the ERA or for reproductive rights.[91] Female elected officials have worn white to express their commitments to women's equality and to vote for legislation that would expand women's rights and opportunities.[92] Female candidates have worn white when pursuing milestone political offices. Geraldine Ferraro wore white to accept the Democratic vice presidential nomination in 1984.[93] Hillary Clinton wore white to accept the Democratic presidential nomination in 2016,[94] and women wore white to vote for her.[95] Kamala Harris wore white to deliver her victory speech in 2020 as Vice President-elect.[96] Women's multigenerational deployment of this strategy means that wearing white can now invoke many layers of remembrance simultaneously. Harris's white suit called back to Clinton and Ferraro along with the suffragists.

Building on that tradition, women held events across the nation to honor the Nineteenth Amendment's centennial and to underscore how women's struggles for equality remain unfinished.[97] Women also erected lasting remembrances of the milestone.[98]

The Lucy Burns Museum now occupies the former site of the Occoquan Workhouse in Virginia,[99] where suffragists from the National Woman's Party arrested for picketing the White House were jailed, force fed, and brutalized.[100] Burns—Alice Paul's closest collaborator in the battle for the Nineteenth Amendment—led most picketing for the National Woman's Party and spent more days in jail than any other American fighting for woman suffrage.[101]

The Turning Point Suffragist Memorial, located on the Workhouse's grounds, features statues of Carrie Chapman Catt, Alice Paul, and Mary Church Terrell.[102] Terrell was the founding president of the National Association of Colored Women and a founding member of the NAACP.[103] Her many years of activism against discrimination and for voting rights included advocating for the Nineteenth Amendment by participating in the National Woman's Party pickets in front of the White House.[104]

Women in New York successfully mobilized for the installation of the first monument in Central Park featuring real women, rather than mythical or fictional ones like Alice in Wonderland. Supporters unveiled the Women's Rights Pioneers Monument on the day of the Nineteenth Amendment's centennial, August 26, 2020. It depicts Susan B. Anthony, Elizabeth Cady Stanton, and Sojourner Truth, an African American abolitionist and suffragist.[105]

In short, women have spent more than a century and a half working to make their struggles for equality part of America's dominant stories about itself. Women have strived to link their activism to famous expressions and symbols of American democratic ideals. They have sought to make women's long record of fighting for equal rights more widely known and to build on that knowledge in pushing for reform.

But as the next section explores, America's dominant stories have proved much more resistant to transformation than generations of women have hoped they would be. Despite women's many efforts, women are still too often left out.

Women's Exclusion from America's Commemorative Landscape

America's commemorative landscape reflects the nation's prevailing stories about itself and reinforces those stories by weaving them into everyday life and memorable occasions. This landscape has long featured accounts of America's past, present, and future in which women are missing or marginalized. I will start by exploring how American officials have celebrated pivotal dates in United States history and then turn to examine who the nation remembers when erecting monuments, naming public buildings, designating public holidays, or otherwise commemorating individuals.

Officials marking the Declaration of Independence's centennial treated women's status as irrelevant to general pronouncements about the nation. President Ulysses S. Grant launched the yearlong celebration by exalting "this centennial year of our national existence as a free and independent people."[106] Acting Vice President Thomas Ferry, speaking at the July 4, 1876, ceremony in Philadelphia that the suffragists disrupted, likewise proclaimed that the American revolutionaries had "pledged their lives, their fortunes, and their sacred honor to the abstract principle of the freedom and equality of the human race" and praised the revolutionaries for creating a nation where "the people alone hold the sole power to rule."[107] Both statements ignored how men's laws denied women freedom, equality, and the vote—while also obfuscating the nation's ongoing commitment to legalized white supremacy and long history of slavery and Native American removal. Indeed, both Grant and Ferry paired their pronouncements about the rights the American people purportedly enjoyed with masculine descriptions of the nation and its citizenry. Grant called the centennial the moment when Americans would be "commencing our manhood as a nation."[108] Ferry celebrated the Declaration of Independence for its commitment to "the sovereignty of manhood."[109]

President Grover Cleveland ignored women even when their struggles for equality were vividly before him. As the suffragists' banner protesting female disenfranchisement waved in New York Harbor, Cleveland proceeded with his speech at the Statue of Liberty's unveiling in 1886. He described the American government as "resting upon popular will" and vowed: "We will not forget that Liberty has here made her home."[110]

Cleveland's determination to ignore women's demands for equal citizenship remained steadfast when he spoke a year later at the Constitution's centennial. The President urged Americans attending Philadelphia's centennial celebration to recognize "how completely" the Constitution had "met every national peril and every national need."[111] At that point, the Supreme Court and every other male bastion of power interpreted the Constitution to permit women's disenfranchisement and women's legal subordination within marriage, at work, and everywhere else.[112] Cleveland's implication was that granting women more rights, including suffrage, was not a "national need." When Cleveland quoted Benjamin Franklin to declare that "God governs in the affairs of men," the President seemed to mean that sex specifically and presume that the Constitution established a male republic.[113]

In fact, Cleveland opposed enfranchising women. He instructed readers of the *Ladies' Home Journal* in 1905 that "the stern, rugged" political sphere was divinely allocated to men and warned that the "clamorous leaders" of the woman suffrage movement sought "a radical and unnatural change" that would subvert "sane and wholesome ideas of the work and mission of womanhood" by taking women from their "allotted sphere of home."[114] For Cleveland, "a good wife" was "a woman who loves her husband and her country with no desire to run either."[115]

Anthony was undeterred. After one of Cleveland's screeds appeared in the *Ladies' Home Journal*, Anthony told her local newspaper that the piece was "Ridiculous! Pure fol-de-rol," and asked: "Why isn't the woman herself the best judge of what woman's sphere should be?"[116]

The rebuke inspired cartoonist Charles Lewis Bartholomew. His 1905 drawing for the front page of the *Minneapolis Journal* (Figure 2.1) showed Anthony chasing after Cleveland with a rolled-up "Ladies Home Trouble" under one arm and a "Woman Suffrage" umbrella in her other hand as she tried to bop Cleveland on the head. Uncle Sam laughed behind them, perhaps poking fun at both.[117]

The dispute between Cleveland and Anthony over suffrage may seem quaint. But less had changed decades later than one might imagine.

The Declaration of Independence's bicentennial in 1976 arrived at a time of intense feminist mobilization, with the ERA out for ratification by the states.

Figure 2.1 Charles Lewis Bartholomew, *What Shall We Do with Our Ex-Presidents?—Susan B. Anthony Knows.*, Minneapolis Journal, April 26, 1905.
Source: Library of Congress

Yet the official celebrations placed women at the margins of the nation's stories about itself. President Gerald Ford began the bicentennial year by lauding the American people for dedicating themselves in 1776 "to the principles of liberty, equality, individual dignity, and representative government,"[118] which did not describe how the new nation had treated any woman or many men. When Ford spoke in Philadelphia on July 4, 1976, he praised the Founders for recognizing "that both powers and unalienable rights belong to the people,"[119] an account of the American Revolution that implicitly assumed the perspective of the privileged white men granted rights of self-government at the Founding. Thirteen more paragraphs passed before Ford mentioned women's long disenfranchisement, with a cursory and inaccurate statement framed as if the Nineteenth Amendment guaranteed voting rights and gave all women access to the polls: "Later still, voting rights were assured for women."[120] Like his predecessors a century earlier, Ford told a story about the nation that depended on marginalizing women's experiences.

Officials relegated women to the peripheries again when the Constitution's bicentennial arrived in 1987. President Ronald Reagan celebrated the bicentennial in Philadelphia by contending that the Founders built their government on the principle that all "men" were "equal," a remembrance that ignored how the Founders refused to extend equality to many men and all women.[121] Warren Burger, who retired from the Supreme Court to chair the Bicentennial Commission, repeatedly praised the Founders for establishing "government by the will of the governed" without acknowledging that the Founders denied most Americans the right to govern themselves.[122] The volume that the Bicentennial Commission published to mark the occasion made almost no reference to women's status under the Constitution and mentioned the Nineteenth Amendment in just a few sentences.[123]

This tradition in official celebrations fits into a commemorative landscape that persistently marginalizes women to the present day. Congress has created legal public holidays for commemorations that lawmakers consider important enough to merit the closing of federal offices. The federal government's annual schedule of remembrance is pervasively familiar in the United States and helps structure the year. Three legal public holidays honor men: Christopher Columbus, Martin Luther King, Jr., and George Washington. But Congress has never designated a legal public holiday to celebrate an important woman in American history or to recognize women's struggles against sex discrimination.[124]

Congress also pays posthumous tribute to the "most eminent" Americans by having their bodies lie in state (if they served in the government or the military) or in honor (if they were private citizens).[125] Aside from designating a legal public holiday, this is one of the most significant commemorations that

Congress can create. Forty-one men and four unknown soldiers have been so remembered, compared to just two women—civil rights activist Rosa Parks and Supreme Court Justice Ruth Bader Ginsburg.[126]

Smaller commemorations tend to sideline women as well. The Postal Service's commemorative stamps record and shape the nation's collective memory. They spotlight individuals whose achievements Americans do or should know about and indicate which historical figures the Postal Service thinks will appeal to the stamp-buying public. A survey of the commemorative stamps issued between the start of 2000 and the end of 2005 found that the Postal Service featured a woman on just 17.4% of the stamps depicting individuals—26 out of 149.[127]

United States passports convey stories about the nation to Americans traveling internationally and to the international community. The State Department revamped United States passports in 2007 to include thirteen inspirational quotations. A State Department official touted the "American Icon" redesign as one that "really, truly reflects the breadth of America as well as the history," and declared: "We tried to be inclusive of all Americans."[128] The redesigned passport pages told a different story. Twelve of the thirteen quotations came from men, suggesting that women were far less likely to be American icons.[129]

Women's relegation to the peripheries of America's stories about itself is similarly apparent in physical space, expressed in brick, metal, and stone as well as words. This erasure shapes the places we go in our daily lives, the buildings we enter when seeking justice, and the sites we visit to learn about America.

For example, post offices are local outposts of the United States government embedded in daily life and every community. Congress began naming post offices after individuals in 1967.[130] A 2019 count found that a woman's name was on less than twelve percent of the post offices honoring individuals—just 98 out of 823.[131]

A woman's name is almost never on the building when people enter federal courthouses to sue or be sued, to face criminal charges, to serve as jurors, or to work as judges, lawyers, or administrators. A 2021 review of named United States courthouses found more than 165 federal courthouses named for a man and just four named for a woman.[132]

The millions of people who visit America's monuments every year rarely encounter women's stories there. A 2017 survey found that only nine out of 411 national park sites (2.2%) commemorated women's history.[133] A 1996 survey of the listings in the National Register of Historic Places "associated with significant persons" found that just 3.7% of those listings were for women—approximately 360 listings out of 9,820.[134]

Public outdoor sculptures are common in the United States, but rarely feature women. By the early twentieth century, sculptor Janet Scudder was already convinced that an "obsession of male egotism" was "ruining every city in the United States with rows of hideous statues of men—men—men—each one uglier than the other—standing, sitting, riding horseback—every one of them pompously convinced that he is decorating the landscape!"[135] Decades later, a 2011 survey found that only 7.6% of America's public outdoor sculptures of individuals depicted women—just 394 sculptures out of 5,193. Excluding older monuments from the calculations did not make the results look much better. Only 11.3% of the public statues of individuals installed between 1960 and 2011 depicted women—just 184 out of 1,624.[136] A 2021 survey reviewed 48,178 public monuments in the United States and identified the fifty most frequently commemorated people.[137] Just three women made the list (Joan of Arc, Harriet Tubman, and Sacagawea), compared to forty-four white men, many of them slaveholders.[138]

I am not contending that women's efforts to include themselves in America's stories have all been futile. Those efforts have unquestionably had some success—accelerating over time—in influencing how powerful Americans speak about their nation. To take some prominent examples, President Barack Obama's second inaugural address in 2013 and President Joseph Biden's inaugural address in 2021 each included a reference to women's struggles for equality. Obama invoked the first woman's rights convention along with mobilizations for racial justice and gay rights when he declared that the truth "that all of us are created equal" had "guided our forebears through Seneca Falls and Selma and Stonewall."[139] Biden observed that Kamala Harris's swearing-in as Vice President came a hundred and eight years after the 1913 suffrage parade in the District of Columbia when "thousands of protestors tried to block brave women marching for the right to vote."[140] Harris's address accepting the Democratic vice presidential nomination in 2020 foregrounded the generations of African American women who worked for "equality, liberty, and justice for all" and named six of them: Fannie Lou Hamer and Mary Church Terrell as well as Mary McLeod Bethune, Shirley Chisholm, Constance Baker Motley, and Diane Nash. Harris observed that "We're not often taught their stories" and proclaimed that "as Americans, we all stand on their shoulders."[141]

These were important moments of recognition. Yet women are still too often missing from America's stories about itself, and the pace of change has been much slower than generations of women strived for it to be. Consider a 2017 survey of K–12 social studies standards in the fifty states and the District of Columbia. The survey found just five standards that included Hamer and none that included Terrell. Indeed, only three of the six women Harris named—Bethune, Hamer, and Nash—made any list.[142]

Opposition to Remembering Women

It can be tempting for Americans who think about women's status as emerging from consensus rather than conflict to assume that women's ongoing marginalization in the commemorative landscape simply reflects inertia. Conflicts over the prospect of commemorating women are much less well-known than commemoration battles framed as centrally about race,[143] even though many conflicts over commemorating women are simultaneously intertwined with race.

But women's efforts to focus national memory on women and their struggles for equality have repeatedly faced powerful resistance, across generations and to the present day. This section explores opposition to women's monuments, to the construction of the American Women's History Museum, and to the placement of Harriet Tubman's portrait on the twenty-dollar bill. We can start with the odyssey of the statue that the National Woman's Party donated to Congress in 1921.

The National Woman's Party wanted to create a lasting monument to women's struggles for equality that would connect the party's work to the 1848 Seneca Falls Convention. While the fight for the Nineteenth Amendment was still raging, the party commissioned Adelaide Johnson to sculpt a monument featuring three founders of the nineteenth-century woman's rights movement: Elizabeth Cady Stanton and Lucretia Mott, who organized the 1848 meeting, and Susan B. Anthony, who became Stanton's closest collaborator shortly thereafter.[144] Johnson, "the sculptor of the movement for the emancipation of women,"[145] had made separate busts of the three women decades earlier, with Anthony and Stanton posing for her in person.[146]

Johnson departed for the marble quarries of Italy in May 1920 and created a new sculpture that depicted Stanton, Anthony, and Mott emerging from a rough-hewn marble block that could symbolize the constraints women were escaping and the unfinished work ahead.[147] Johnson included an inscription celebrating the "Woman's Revolution," which read in part: "Woman, first denied a soul, then called mindless, now arisen, declared herself an entity to be reckoned."[148]

The party's plan was to place the monument in the Capitol Rotunda, the soaring space beneath the dome that connects the House and Senate.[149] Alice Paul even named a date for the unveiling—February 15, 1921, the hundred and first anniversary of Anthony's birth.[150] Johnson had the monument deposited in front of the Capitol's law library on February 5.[151] The Rotunda seemed poised to have its first statue of women.[152]

The hitch was that Congress had not agreed to accept the statue, much less place it in the Rotunda, which is the "heart of the Capitol."[153] As February 15 approached, many congressmen left little doubt about their disapproval and made excuses for why Congress could not take the statue.[154] Vice President Thomas Marshall, who had opposed enfranchising women,[155] announced that he would never support placing the monument in the Capitol.[156]

Alice Paul was determined, as usual. She publicized endorsements from Florence Harding, the President-elect's wife, and Christine Gillett, the wife of the Speaker of the House.[157] With the monument at the door and the pressure mounting, Congress's Joint Committee on the Library agreed on February 10 to accept the donation and to allow women to hold an unveiling ceremony in the Rotunda on February 15.[158] Dozens of women's groups participated in the unveiling, and the Speaker of the House formally accepted the gift to Congress.[159]

The women's moment of glory was fleeting. The Library Committee had insisted when accepting the monument that it would leave the Rotunda "immediately" after the unveiling ceremony and go to the Capitol's lower level.[160] After the unveiling, the statue moved to that dark space—known as "the crypt"—which housed no other artwork.[161]

The Library Committee also sought to downplay the monument's feminism. The committee had demanded that the inscription remain covered throughout the unveiling.[162] The inscription was hidden against a wall when the statue moved to the crypt.[163] By October 1921, the Library Committee had the inscription painted over.[164]

The statue stayed entombed in the crypt for seventy-six years, out of the light and out of the Rotunda—the prime space where Congress celebrates American history. A reporter observed in 1965 that the statue "could hardly be less prominently displayed without concealing it entirely."[165] This 1965 photograph (Figure 2.2) suggests how the monument looked when hidden away.[166]

For generations, women who wanted to congregate at a site of female commemoration went to the Capitol's crypt. The National Woman's Party rallied for the ERA there and celebrated an anniversary of the Nineteenth Amendment's ratification in the crypt.[167] Feminists carried that tradition into the last decades of the twentieth century. The National Woman's Party and the National Organization for Women held a ceremony in the crypt on February 15, 1971, the fiftieth anniversary of the unveiling ceremony in the Rotunda

Figure 2.2 Capitol Crypt, Washington, D.C., February 12, 1965.
Source: Library of Congress

and the hundred and fifty-first anniversary of Susan B. Anthony's birth. Young girls in the "Now or Never Choir" sang patriotic songs rewritten to highlight women's ongoing quest for full inclusion in American democracy, including a revised *Battle Hymn of the Republic* that began:

> Mine eyes have seen the glory
> Of the coming of LIBERTY.[168]

Feminists were in the crypt again in 1973, showering the suffrage monument with roses as part of a rally to push for the ERA and commemorate the Nineteenth Amendment's anniversary.[169] The National Organization for Women was in the crypt in 1990 to mark the seventieth anniversary of the Nineteenth Amendment,[170] and NOW held a news conference in front of the suffrage monument to advocate for the ERA in 1993.[171] Women went back into the crypt in 1995 to mark the Nineteenth Amendment's seventy-fifth anniversary.[172] As the assembled women themselves sometimes noted, the suffrage monument's relegation to the crypt vividly illustrated the burial of women's struggles for equality in the peripheries of America's stories about itself.[173] As late as 1996, the statue even lacked a placard naming Stanton, Anthony, and Mott.[174]

Women in and outside Congress spent years trying to elevate the monument.[175] Over the decades, Congress repeatedly rebuffed proposals to relocate the statue,[176] or restore its inscription.[177] "An official of the house" explained in 1928 that Congress had moved the suffrage monument to the crypt because "it was distinctly out of place in the rotunda" sharing space with statues of great men like Abraham Lincoln, George Washington, and Alexander Hamilton.[178] Almost seven decades later, the Speaker of the House, Newt Gingrich, refused to schedule a House vote on moving the statue out of the crypt. Gingrich reportedly explained that he wanted to avoid association with "a bunch of liberal women," which could serve as a reference to the memorialized women along with those pushing for the statue's relocation.[179]

Congress finally agreed in 1996 to move the monument, which went into the Rotunda in 1997.[180] But even the congressional resolution authorizing the move treated the commemoration as optional rather than essential. Congress refused to finance the transfer and specified that "the Portrait Monument" would stay in the Rotunda for just one year.[181] As Representative Carolyn Maloney of New York observed, authorizing only a temporary relocation suggested that the suffragists' Nineteenth Amendment victory "was not historically significant enough to merit the statue's full-time display in the Rotunda alongside statues of our great male leaders."[182]

The monument's long-term prospects in the Rotunda remain uncertain. While the statue has remained there to date, some legislators have attributed the inactivity to the difficulty of moving such a heavy and large piece.[183] Congress has never made the monument's place in the Rotunda permanent and never restored the feminist inscription.[184]

Getting the suffrage monument out of the crypt was a limited victory in another way as well. That statue always told an incomplete story about the fight for female enfranchisement, one focused exclusively on white women. Its composition replicated the constraints that many white suffragists placed on their vision of equality. Both Alice Paul and her more mainstream counterpart, Carrie Chapman Catt, urged Southern segregationists to support the

Nineteenth Amendment by assuring them that the amendment would not disrupt the tactics that Southern states deployed to keep people of color disenfranchised.[185] Indeed, both argued that the Nineteenth Amendment would bolster white control over Southern elections by swelling the number of white voters.[186]

That entanglement with white supremacy persisted beyond the Nineteenth Amendment's ratification. Immediately after the 1921 unveiling of the Stanton, Anthony, and Mott monument, the National Woman's Party held a convention in Washington to set the party's future course.[187] Paul refused to prioritize African American women's urgent concerns. She was unsupportive when a delegation of sixty black women met with her before the convention to ask for her party's help in pushing for a congressional investigation into "the flagrant violations of the intent and purposes of the Susan B. Anthony Amendment in the elections of 1920" that had systematically denied the vote to African American women in the South.[188] The proposal did not have Paul's backing at the convention and was defeated.[189]

Paul also refused to let Mary Talbert, a leader in the African American women's clubs movement, address the 1921 convention.[190] Talbert wanted Congress to enact anti-lynching legislation.[191] More than four thousand African American men, women, and children would be lynched in twelve Southern states between 1877 and 1950.[192] But Paul argued that anti-lynching legislation was "not a woman's measure" and worried "that the appearance of Mrs. Talbert on our program talking about lynching would inflame the Southerners, both in and out of her organization."[193]

Congress, meanwhile, was unwilling to protect black women's rights or to commemorate black women's struggles for equality. To the contrary, the Senate passed a bill in 1923 that would have permitted the United Daughters of the Confederacy to erect on public land in Washington "a monument in memory of the faithful colored mammies of the South."[194] Jane W. Blackburn Moran, chair of the committee commissioning the statue, told the press that she planned to call the monument "The Fountain of Truth."[195] In fact, the commemoration was designed to propagate the lie that black women had been content with their enslavement and pleased to care for the children of their enslavers. Representative Charles Manly Stedman of North Carolina, a Confederate veteran,[196] championed the bill by informing his fellow congressmen that these enslaved women had "desired no change in their condition of life. No class of any race of people in bondage could be found anywhere who lived more free from care and distress. The very few who are left look back to those days as the happy and golden hours of their lives."[197]

African American opposition could not stop the bill in the Senate,[198] but did succeed in keeping the bill from advancing to a vote in the House.[199] Black women were among the most determined critics.[200] Mary Church Terrell assailed the proposed monument, including in a widely reprinted letter to the editor. She predicted that if the monument was erected, thousands of black people would "fervently pray" for lightning to strike it down "so that the descendants of black mammies will not forever be reminded of the anguish of heart and the physical suffering which the mothers and grandmothers of the race endured for nearly 300 years."[201]

Decades later, the fight to get Stanton, Anthony, and Mott out of the crypt inspired the National Political Congress of Black Women to advocate for a federal monument commemorating black women's struggles for equality. By 1997, the organization had launched a campaign to memorialize Sojourner Truth in the Capitol, either by adding her image to Johnson's statue, by including Truth in a new suffrage monument for the Rotunda and placing Johnson's work elsewhere, or by installing a separate sculpture of Truth.[202] C. DeLores Tucker, the group's National Chair and Convening Founder, declared that "African-American women are no longer invisible and their contributions to this nation should not be as well."[203]

After years of lobbying and many unsuccessful bills,[204] Congress finally agreed in 2006 to accept and display a bust depicting Sojourner Truth.[205] The monument unveiled in Emancipation Hall in 2009 made Truth the first African American woman honored with a sculpture in the Capitol— 233 years after the nation's founding.[206] It represents a long overdue step toward remembering the women of color in the antislavery movement and the push for woman suffrage.[207] But Congress did not place Truth in the Rotunda.[208] The 1921 suffrage monument remains the only sculpture of women to appear there.

Let's turn now from struggles over women's monuments to opposition to the American Women's History Museum. Congresswoman Carolyn Maloney emerged from the battle over moving Stanton, Anthony, and Mott into the Rotunda convinced that America needed its first national museum dedicated to women's history.[209] Maloney's 1998 bill highlighted how the nation's existing museums had left women out, observing that between 1963 and 1997 "only 2 exhibits were authorized on women's history at the National Museum of American History."[210]

Maloney and her allies within and outside the legislative branch pushed for the construction of a women's history museum through multiple Congresses. In testimony and debates, Maloney reiterated that there was no "museum in America dedicated to the achievements of half of our population" and linked this absence to women's exclusion from America's stories about itself.[211] In her words: "Women stand on historical quicksand. With each step we take forward, the steps behind us disappear."[212]

Ultimately, women spent decades fighting for a national women's history museum. The mobilization required so much time and effort because it faced persistent countermobilization from lawmakers and anti-feminist activists who opposed devoting more commemorative attention to women's history—especially the history of women's struggles for equality.

In 2010, Senator Tom Coburn of Oklahoma and Senator Jim DeMint of South Carolina placed a hold on legislation that would have permitted a non-profit group to buy land from the federal government at fair market value and construct a national women's history museum with private funds.[213] The bill had passed the House in 2009,[214] but the hold implicitly threatened a filibuster in the Senate. Coburn and DeMint presumed that any possibility of eventual federal funding for a national women's history museum was unacceptable, explaining that they were placing their hold because "taxpayers simply cannot be guaranteed" that the museum would not ask for federal financial support "in the future." The senators also asserted that a national women's history museum would be duplicative.[215] Coburn's office elaborated on that latter objection by contending that the proposed museum would duplicate "more than 100 existing entities that have a similar mission." Coburn's hundred-item list did not name any museums exploring the full sweep of American women's history, as no such museum existed. Instead, the list included museums with far narrower missions, like Indiana's Quilters Hall of Fame and Texas's National Cowgirl Museum and Hall of Fame.[216]

Coburn and DeMint imposed their hold two days after Concerned Women for America asked DeMint for a hold.[217] That group had mobilized in the late 1970s and early 1980s to stop the ERA's ratification.[218] A few decades later, Penny Nance was leading the organization and she fought against building a women's history museum.

Nance wrote an opinion piece for the *Washington Times* in 2010 after the Coburn/DeMint hold was in place. Much like the senators, Nance saw no need to add more women's history to America's stories about itself. She called the proposed institution a "repeat-museum," asserting that "[c]ountless museums" had "already highlighted the landmark contributions of women and placed them in historical context." Nance appeared to be particularly concerned that a national women's history museum would focus public attention on women's struggles for reproductive autonomy. She emphasized that the nonprofit group advocating for the museum's construction included many board members who supported reproductive rights, and she criticized the museum website that the nonprofit had created for including "numerous online resources on the history of birth control." Nance concluded her attack on the "duplicative, politically motivated project" by appealing to Congress as a masculine institution: "Congress, how about you man up and tell the liberals 'no' for once?"[219]

Nance was still fighting to stop the women's history museum years later. In 2014, Congress was on the verge of creating a commission that would study the prospect of building a museum. Nance and seven other prominent conservatives wrote to every member of the House urging opposition to the measure. The letter criticized the museum's website for its favorable discussion of Bella Abzug,[220] the feminist congresswoman who subsequently presided over the 1977 National Women's Conference in Houston.[221]

Phyllis Schlafly, who spearheaded the battle against the ERA in the 1970s and 1980s,[222] signed this letter.[223] She told her supporters in 2014 that no more work was needed to include women in America's commemorations, ignoring all evidence of women's underrepresentation to assert "that women are honored and represented in every other national museum and monument dedicated to presenting the vast history of the American story."[224] Schlafly also appeared to be concerned that a national women's history museum would draw attention to women's struggles for equality. Without citing any evidence, she charged that the "museum would be slanted to represent the feminist ideology and would not provide an accurate portrayal of American women."[225]

Congresswoman Michele Bachmann of Minnesota lauded the anti-feminists opposing the museum and voiced similar arguments on the House floor in 2014. She contended that a national women's history museum was unnecessary because "[t]here already are 20 women's museums in the United States" and maintained that such a museum would "enshrine the radical feminist movement that stands against the pro-life movement, the pro-family movement, and the pro-traditional marriage movement."[226]

Congress ultimately authorized a women's history museum commission in 2014 when lawmakers folded the measure into a giant appropriations bill.[227] The commission's 2016 report highlighted women's underrepresentation "in the main sites of public history" and assured readers that the museum would present "controversial or difficult subjects" "with input from all sides, in well-researched ways."[228]

Opposition continued. After the House passed a bill in February 2020 to authorize building a national women's history museum,[229] Senator Mike Lee of Utah blocked the measure in the Senate.[230] Lee phrased his opposition in the language of the museum's proponents, insisting that his objection to the women's museum was "a matter of national unity and cultural inclu-sion." But his ultimate argument was familiar. Like many museum opponents before him, Lee downplayed the evidence that existing museums routinely overlooked women's history and asserted that America's national museums already wound "all the myriad strands of America's triumphant history into one imperfect but heroic story."[231]

Congress never passed stand-alone legislation authorizing construction of a women's history museum. Instead, supporters maneuvered around their persistent opponents by managing to insert the museum authorization into an omnibus appropriations bill that Congress needed to pass at the end of December 2020.[232]

As of this writing, the museum remains without a physical home. In October 2022, the Smithsonian's Board of Regents recommended two pos-sible building sites on the National Mall.[233] Either choice would amplify the museum's impact. The Mall is the preeminent commemorative venue in the United States and receives more than thirty-three million annual visitors.[234] But Congress has yet to provide the additional authorization required to build there.[235]

Like museums and monuments, currency is another important site of pub-lic commemoration. I will conclude this chapter by exploring the opposition to placing Harriet Tubman's image on the twenty-dollar bill.

Only two women have ever appeared on America's paper currency. Martha Washington, the first President's wife, graced the front of a one-dollar silver certificate the United States first issued in 1886.[236] Pocahontas, a Native Amer-ican woman who was kidnapped and imprisoned by Jamestown colonists before converting to Christianity and marrying a colonist,[237] knelt for bap-tism on the back of a twenty-dollar bill first issued in 1863.[238]

Many Americans have noticed women's absence. In 2014, President Barack Obama spoke about receiving a letter from "a young girl" who provided "a long list of possible women" to depict on America's currency.[239] The next year, a grassroots "Women on 20s" campaign ran online polls propos-ing women to depict on the front of the twenty-dollar bill.[240] The campaign inspired Senator Jeanne Shaheen of New Hampshire, who introduced an April 2015 bill spotlighting the issue and followed up with a June 2015 letter to President Obama urging him to place a woman's image on the twenty.[241]

Two weeks after Shaheen's letter, Obama's Treasury Department announced forthcoming changes to the design of the ten-dollar bill. Alexander Hamilton, the first Treasury Secretary, had long appeared alone on the front of the ten. The plan was to redesign the ten to feature both Hamilton and a woman "who was a champion for our inclusive democracy."

The department solicited the public's input into which woman Treasury Secretary Jacob Lew should select.[242]

Some Hamilton devotees found this plan unacceptable, and their numbers had swelled since the 2015 premiere of a blockbuster musical about Hamilton's life. Fans of the musical, and its creator, urged Lew to reconsider.[243] He did.

Lew announced a new plan in April 2016. Hamilton would remain alone on the front of the ten-dollar bill. The redesigned back side would depict the 1913 suffrage parade preceding Wilson's inauguration, along with five suffragists: Susan B. Anthony, Lucretia Mott, Alice Paul, Elizabeth Cady Stanton, and Sojourner Truth. However, the Treasury Department would redesign the twenty-dollar bill as well, with Harriet Tubman replacing President Andrew Jackson on the front.[244] Jackson was a slaveholder who removed Native American tribes from their lands.[245] Tubman was an abolitionist and suffragist who freed herself and hundreds of others from bondage before becoming a Union scout, spy, and nurse during the Civil War.[246]

The news that the United States government would honor Tubman on the front of the twenty-dollar bill sparked immediate opposition. Donald Trump was pursuing the Republican nomination for President in April 2016.[247] The day after Lew's announcement, Trump denounced the decision to place Tubman on the twenty as "pure political correctness." Trump wanted to keep Jackson on the front of the twenty because "Andrew Jackson had a great history" and has "been on the bill for many, many years and really, you know, represented somebody that really was very important to this country." Trump declared that "it would be more appropriate" to place Tubman's image on "another denomination," suggesting "maybe we do the two dollar bill or we do another bill."[248] The two is the least used bill. In 2016, more than seven twenty-dollar bills circulated for each two-dollar bill in circulation.[249]

Two months later, Representative Steve King of Iowa proposed a provision that would have blocked the Treasury Department from redesigning any currency. King's argument for thwarting change ignored the many people who had advocated for women's inclusion on United States currency. He contended that keeping Jackson on the front of the twenty would be "unifying" and called the plan to put Tubman on the twenty "a divisive proposal on the part of the president."[250]

After Trump became President in 2017, his Treasury Department announced that the introduction of the new twenty-dollar bill would be delayed and spent years repeatedly refusing to indicate whether the redesigned twenty would feature Tubman.[251] Meanwhile, every reference to Tubman appearing on the front of the twenty—or other suffragists appearing on the back of the ten—vanished from the Treasury Department's website after Trump took office and stayed gone throughout Trump's first term.[252] Trump hung Andrew Jackson's portrait in the Oval Office, visited Jackson's plantation, and declared himself "a fan."[253]

One of Trump's former White House staffers published a tell-all memoir in 2018. She recounted Trump's reaction when she gave him a memo in 2017 about placing Tubman on the twenty. Trump reportedly looked at a photograph of Tubman and asked: "You want to put that face on the twenty-dollar bill?"[254] The question implied that Tubman did not look like someone who belonged in that place of honor, or did not look like someone Trump found physically attractive, or both.

As of this writing, neither the redesigned twenty-dollar bill nor the redesigned ten has appeared. The Biden administration announced in January 2021 that it was committed to placing Tubman's portrait on the front of the twenty.[255] But Trump's victory in the 2024 presidential election has made that commemoration uncertain, perhaps unlikely.

In sum, generations of women have strived to include themselves and their battles for equality within America's dominant stories. Yet women are still too often forgotten when powerful Americans reflect on their country, and efforts to incorporate women into America's remembrances have faced protracted opposition for generations. When courts leave women and their mobilization out of stories about the nation, the judges are reflecting and reinforcing persistent gaps in America's collective memory. Too often, women are excluded and erased.

PART II

DISTORTION

Women's erasure from America's dominant stories about itself coexists with another form of forgetting—wildly exaggerated declarations of success that forget the work the nation still has to do. Here too, courts and the world beyond the courts have mirrored and molded each other's habits. Both judges and popular writers have long tended to overlook or understate persistent inequities when describing women's status, even to the point of asserting that America has already achieved sex equality.

Many of us are familiar with that distortion in our own time. But I was surprised to discover just how early the premature declarations of victory began appearing. Indeed, such declarations ran through judicial opinions and popular writing even before the Nineteenth Amendment's 1920 ratification made sex-based disenfranchisement unconstitutional.

These sources also reveal that powerful Americans have commonly deployed exaggeration to oppose reform and roll back progress. Overly rosy assessments of women's rights and opportunities have played an important role in shielding inequality and promoting complacency.

This part examines the hoary tradition of overstating the nation's progress toward sex equality before Part III focuses on the modern consequences for law and politics. Chapter 3 explores generations of judicial opinions declaring victory over sex discrimination. Chapter 4 links that judicial pattern to more than a century of popular media and schoolchildren's textbooks proclaiming that America has left women's inequality behind.

Chapter 3
Courts Declare Victory Early and Often

Within a few decades after the first woman's rights convention in 1848, judges were already writing as if the nation had moved beyond sex discrimination. Courts embraced that theme throughout the twentieth century, offering sweeping proclamations about American progress that ignored persistent legal restraints on women.

Courts have made many of their rosiest pronouncements about the nation's embrace of sex equality while issuing judgments denying women equal rights. Over the course of the twentieth century, for example, courts declared that women's legal position had been transformed while upholding sex-specific restrictions on women's working hours, prohibitions on women entering jobs reserved for men, and obstacles to women's jury service that denied women juries of their peers. Judges crowed about America's commitment to sex equality while undermining women's control over their reproductive lives, excluding wives from rights their husbands enjoyed, and making it harder for women to escape subordination in marriage.

I call these decisions self-contradictory victory announcements because they simultaneously perpetuate inequality and present it as part of the past rather than present. Women are not the only marginalized group that courts have subjected to such contradiction, but cases sustaining women's inequality have long been prominent triggers for self-contradictory victory announcements. The self-contradiction serves a purpose, as the insistent overstatements about American progress help judges rationalize their decisions impeding that progress. How could there be any urgency to women's claims if the nation has already embraced sex equality?

Premature Proclamations

Well before the Nineteenth Amendment, courts began suggesting or declaring that America had established women's equality. These premature proclamations sound ridiculous in retrospect, but judges issued them routinely.

To fully appreciate the prematurity, let's begin by considering how the Supreme Court obstructed women's progress in the nineteenth century. Virginia and Francis Minor went to the Court in 1875 determined to establish that the right to vote was an inherent privilege of federal citizenship, protected against state infringement by the Fourteenth Amendment's ratification in 1868.[1] She was the president of the Woman's Suffrage Association of Missouri, and he was her husband and lawyer. By 1869, they were already developing the argument that the Fourteenth Amendment guaranteed women's enfranchisement.[2] They sued after a Missouri registrar refused to let Virginia Minor register to vote in the 1872 election for President and Congress.[3] When the Missouri Supreme Court sided with the registrar, the Minors appealed to the United States Supreme Court.[4] The unanimous Justices conceded that American citizenship extended to women, but held that the Constitution "does not confer the right of suffrage upon any one."[5] *Minor v. Happersett* (1875) left states free to prohibit women from voting and left suffragists without a viable constitutional argument to make for female enfranchisement. *Minor*'s judgment that citizens have no constitutional right to vote—inseparable from the Court's refusal to enfranchise women—remains in force to this day.[6]

The Supreme Court also empowered states to exclude women from the legal profession. Myra Bradwell had launched the *Chicago Legal News* in 1868, and it quickly became one of the nation's leading legal newspapers.[7] Bradwell insisted "that woman has a right to think and act as an individual—believing if the great Father had intended it to be otherwise—he would have placed Eve in a cage and given Adam the key."[8] She appealed to the United States Supreme Court after Illinois's highest court refused to admit her to the Illinois bar in 1869, which meant that she was not authorized to practice law in the state.[9] The Illinois judges had voiced "no doubt" about Bradwell's qualifications and acknowledged that the state statute governing law licenses did not explicitly exclude women from legal practice.[10] But the judges emphasized that lawmakers had enacted the statute when the idea "[t]hat God designed the sexes to occupy different spheres of action, and that it belonged to men to make, apply and execute the laws, was regarded as an almost axiomatic truth." The Illinois court concluded that the legislature could not have expected that the privilege of having a law license "would be extended equally to men and women."[11] The United States Supreme Court affirmed the state's decision in *Bradwell v. Illinois* (1873), holding that the federal Constitution did not constrain the power of states to grant or deny law licenses as they saw fit.[12]

Two decades later, Belva Lockwood challenged state power to limit lawyering to men. She was already decades into a trailblazing legal career by the time her case reached the Supreme Court. Lockwood had been admitted to the District of Columbia bar in 1873.[13] She had successfully lobbied Congress for an 1879 statute authorizing women's admission to practice law before the

United States Supreme Court and had been the first woman admitted under the new legislation.[14] Lockwood became even more well-known when she ran for president in 1884 as the candidate of the National Equal Rights Party.[15] She applied for admission to the Virginia bar in or around 1894. The applicable Virginia statute provided that "any person duly authorized and practising as counsel or attorney at law in any State or Territory of the United States, or in the District of Columbia, may practise as such in the courts of this State." But Virginia's highest court rejected Lockwood's application nonetheless.[16] When Lockwood appealed to the United States Supreme Court, the unanimous Justices deciding *In re Lockwood* (1894) reaffirmed that states were free to prohibit women from practicing law—even if that meant reading women out of a statute that explicitly applied to everyone.[17]

The Supreme Court's eagerness to impede women's access to public life was entangled with the Justices' embrace of common law principles of coverture, which placed married women under their husbands' control without their own legal identity.[18] These principles were part of the common law because generations of judicial decisions, rather than legislation, drove their development. For example, every Justice in *Barber v. Barber* (1859) agreed that a wife ordinarily could not have a separate legal residence from her husband. No matter where she actually lived, coverture meant that her husband chose her official home.[19]

Three Justices in *Bradwell* invoked coverture principles in endorsing women's exclusion from the legal profession. They signed a concurring opinion because they agreed with the majority's result, but wanted to advance their own explanation for why Bradwell should lose her suit.[20] Their concurrence foregrounded the common law "maxim" "that a woman had no legal existence separate from her husband, who was regarded as her head and representative in the social state," and emphasized that "many of the special rules of law flowing from and dependent upon this cardinal principle still exist in full force in most States."[21] With the long and ongoing tradition of married women's legal subordination squarely in view, the concurring *Bradwell* Justices anticipated the Court's unanimous decision in *Muller v. Oregon* (1908) and reasoned about the Constitution on the assumption that women belonged at home.[22] Justices Joseph Bradley, Noah Swayne, and Stephen Field were certain that the United States Constitution permitted states to deny women access to an "independent career" because "[t]he constitution of the family organization, which is founded in the divine ordinance, as well as in the nature of things, indicates the domestic sphere as that which properly belongs to the domain and functions of womanhood." After dismissing unmarried women as "exceptions to the general rule," the concurrence announced: "The paramount destiny and mission of woman are to fulfil the noble and benign offices of wife and mother."[23]

Yet less than six years after *Bradwell*, the Court declared in *Reynolds v. United States* (1879) that America rejected "the patriarchal principle."[24] The case centered on the constitutionality of a federal criminal prohibition on polygamous marriage,[25] part of a flurry of federal legislation targeting polygamy and pressuring the Mormon Church to renounce the practice.[26] In upholding the polygamy prohibition, the Court linked "polygamous marriages" with "despotism" and "monogamous" marriages with democracy.[27]

The self-celebration was doubly ironic. First, the Utah territory, where many polygamists lived, was arguably one of the most democratic places in the United States in 1879. The territorial legislature had enfranchised women in 1870.[28] Utah women voted until 1887, when Congress chose the year of the Constitution's centennial to enact an anti-polygamy statute with a provision reinstating women's disenfranchisement in the Utah territory.[29]

Second, the Court could only describe monogamous marriage as democratic in 1879 by focusing on men's prospects and ignoring women's rights. Monogamous marriages respected male equality, translating one man/one vote in politics into one man/one wife in matrimony. But American marriages were not internally democratic, even if monogamous. As the Court had repeatedly insisted, husbands exercised legal dominion over their wives.

Nonetheless, *Reynolds* gave the Court an opportunity to place rhetorical distance between patriarchy and the (white) nation in a context where the only men losing legal prerogatives were reviled outsiders to mainstream Christianity. *Reynolds* described polygamy as foreign to the white men running the United States, "a feature of the life of Asiatic and of African people" that "has always been odious among the northern and western nations of Europe."[30] With that hierarchical cultural and racial distance asserted, *Reynolds* contended that banning polygamy kept "the patriarchal principle" out of America's "government" and "society."[31]

The Court's suggestions that the law already promoted women's equality became more emphatic as struggles over woman suffrage intensified. *Holden v. Hardy* (1898) upheld state legislation setting maximum hours for men working in underground mines or smelters, employment that the Court conceded was so extraordinarily hazardous that restricting male labor was permissible.[32] When the Justices wanted to emphasize that the nineteenth century had "originated" important "legal reforms," they used women as one of their illustrations. *Holden* announced that "[m]arried women have been emancipated from the control of their husbands and placed upon a practical equality with them with respect to the acquisition, possession and transmission of property."[33] The claim was manifestly false in 1898. Indeed, it was untrue seven decades later. As late as the 1960s, some states still limited married women's property rights, including a wife's right to sell her property without her husband's permission.[34]

Meanwhile, lower courts in the late nineteenth and early twentieth centuries often wrote as if America had already triumphed over sex discrimination, especially in the law governing marriage. While conflict over woman suffrage raged, federal and state judges routinely announced that married women had been "completely,"[35] "fully,"[36] and "wholly emancipated,"[37] that the husband's "legal supremacy" was "gone, and the sceptre has departed from him,"[38] that "legislation in this country" tended "to make husband and wife equal in all respects in the eye of the law,"[39] that there was "absolute equality of the husband and wife."[40]

The declarations of victory could be remarkably untethered from reality. Consider 1878 New Hampshire. Sex-based distinctions pervaded New Hampshire statutes, governing marriage, militia service, work, property, crime, and more.[41] In August 1878, the state legislature permitted women to vote at local school district meetings, but otherwise rebuffed woman suffragists and maintained female disenfranchisement.[42] That same month, the New Hampshire Supreme Court declared that New Hampshire was one of "many" states where "the legal distinctions between the sexes" had "been swept away."[43] The court never explained why women's disenfranchisement and all of New Hampshire's other laws treating women differently than men did not count as sex-based legal distinctions.

Women could not vote in any elections in 1914 Missouri.[44] Indeed, Missouri's male electorate went to the polls in November of that year to reject a proposed state constitutional amendment that would have enfranchised women.[45] A Missouri appellate court nonetheless proclaimed in June 1914 that the married woman's "status as a citizen has, through education and religion, been by common consent raised up to, if not higher than, that of her brother man."[46] The court's declaration of victory purportedly achieved "by common consent" likewise failed to explain how women could be equal citizens while men denied them the vote, along with other markers of full membership in the polity. For example, Missouri did not permit women to serve on state juries until 1945.[47] Even then, Missouri law considered female jurors inessential and made jury service optional for women until the United States Supreme Court struck down that sex-based exemption in 1979.[48]

Judges in the half century after the Nineteenth Amendment's 1920 ratification were yet more inclined to make sweeping pronouncements about American progress. When the Supreme Court struck down a minimum wage law for women working in the District of Columbia, the Justices framed their 1923 opinion as if the nation was already on the cusp of sex equality and legal authorities were poised to abandon all sex distinctions not grounded in physical differences of the sort that *Muller* purportedly recognized.[49] *Adkins v. Children's Hospital* declared that "the ancient inequality of the sexes, otherwise than physical, as suggested in the *Muller Case* has continued 'with diminishing intensity.' In view of the great—not to say revolutionary— changes which have taken place since that utterance, in the contractual, political and civil status of women, culminating in the Nineteenth Amendment, it is not unreasonable to say that these differences have now come almost, if not quite, to the vanishing point."[50]

Lower courts similarly suggested that America had left sex discrimination behind. A Pennsylvania court declared in 1925 that "by constitutional amendment and modern legal development, sex has ceased to be a factor in the determination of woman's legal rights and status."[51] A federal court in Tennessee called 1928 the "age of the Nineteenth Amendment, rights of women, feminism, women office holders, and general emancipation of the sex."[52] The Nebraska Supreme Court deemed 1940 "an era of feminine equality,"[53] while a New York appellate court announced in 1948 that women enjoyed "equal rights with the male sex."[54]

Judicial proclamations of coverture's demise also appeared regularly in the half century after 1920. The Supreme Court announced in 1960 that "a wife's legal submission to her husband has been wholly wiped out, not only in the English-speaking world generally but emphatically so in this country."[55] The Supreme Court in 1966 described "the peculiar institution of coverture" as "quaint" and "obsolete."[56] Lower courts echoed and amplified those pronouncements, declaring that "[t]here is every evidence of complete emancipation for the wife in America,"[57] that "the present day tendency" was "to emancipate women completely,"[58] that "[t]he emancipation of married women by modern legislation" conferred "upon them equality in personal and property rights,"[59] that "husband and wife are partners and equals."[60]

In fact, restrictions on women's rights within and outside marriage remained pervasive in the half century after the Nineteenth Amendment's ratification. Although generations of women had mobilized for equality, wives continued to experience myriad legal disabilities, including limits on a married woman's rights to contract, own and transfer property, conduct business, serve as a guarantor, and establish a legal residence apart from her husband.[61] Many employers openly denied women equal pay, used sex-specific help wanted ads, favored men in hiring and promotion, and/or otherwise disadvantaged female workers.[62] Most states had sex-based laws regulating women's working hours, access to jobs, and jury service.[63]

The Supreme Court routinely upheld women's legal subordination in the half century after 1920.[64] Even with the Nineteenth Amendment in place, the Justices kept Mullerism alive and well. They still read the Constitution convinced that women's participation in public life was unnecessary because women's true place was at home.[65]

Consider *Breedlove v. Suttles* (1937). Just fourteen years after *Adkins* suggested that the Nineteenth Amendment signified a transformation in women's legal status,[66] *Breedlove* interpreted the Nineteenth Amendment so narrowly that the Supreme Court upheld legislation giving women a financial incentive not to vote.[67]

Georgia imposed a poll tax, as did many states intent on disenfranchising African Americans and other people of color.[68] Georgia legislators cloaked their racist agenda in race-neutral statutory language, but had no compunctions about explicit sex discrimination. Georgia's annual poll tax for state inhabitants between the ages of twenty-one and sixty (who were not blind) provided that women, unlike men, could avoid tax liability by not registering to vote.[69]

Breedlove acknowledged that husbands might refuse to spend money so their wives could vote, and the Court recognized that the sex distinction in Georgia's poll tax reflected coverture principles. Indeed, the Court observed that "[t]he laws of Georgia declare the husband to be the head of the family and the wife to be subject to him."[70] However, the Court never suggested that Georgia's dedication to male dominance might undercut the constitutionality of its poll tax.

To the contrary, the Court's argument that the statute treated women "reasonably" turned on how well the law enforced coverture's premises. *Breedlove* cited *Muller* as an instructive precedent and embraced the framework of that earlier decision, reading the Constitution with the assumption that women belonged at home. As the unanimous *Breedlove* Justices explained, husbands had direct obligations to the state. They had to pay for the public schools, which the poll tax helped fund. In contrast, women's obligations were domestic. They were responsible "for the preservation of the race."[71] This was another instance where the term "race" invoked multiple meanings. Given *Breedlove*'s approval of the poll tax, I take the Court's reference to racial preservation to focus on white reproduction.

In short, the Supreme Court in the half century after the Nineteenth Amendment's 1920 ratification continued to endorse and enable a legal regime institutionalizing white male supremacy. Yet that did not stop the Justices, or lower court judges, from repeatedly suggesting that women and men were already legal equals.

In 1971—after a long history of such pronouncements—the Supreme Court finally struck down a law for denying women equal protection.[72] As this chapter and Chapter 5 will explore, the Justices' commitment to sex equality has remained uneven and Mullerism persists.[73] But judicial proclamations about the achievement of sex equality have continued apace. The Supreme Court announced in 1980 that: "Nowhere in the common-law world—indeed in any modern society—is a woman regarded as chattel or demeaned by denial of a separate legal identity and the dignity associated with recognition as a whole human being. Chip by chip, over the years those archaic notions have been cast aside so that no longer is the female destined solely for the home and the rearing of the family, and only the male for the marketplace and the world of ideas."[74] The Supreme Court declared in 2015 that "the law of coverture was abandoned" "[a]s women gained legal, political, and property rights, and as society began to understand that women have their own equal dignity."[75] Lower courts similarly told women: "You've come a long way, baby."[76]

Self-Contradictory Victory Announcements

Many of the judiciary's rosiest proclamations about American progress have appeared in decisions denying women equal rights. These decisions contradict themselves when they trumpet the nation's commitment to sex equality in the process of upholding sex discrimination. But the insistent declarations of success help judges rationalize their rejection of women's claims and deny their role in maintaining inequality.

Women's rights cases are not the only ones to feature courts' self-contradictory victory announcements. I could write another chapter exploring self-contradictory decisions that enforced white supremacy while proclaiming that America had established racial equality. Think of *Plessy v. Ferguson* (1896), where the Supreme Court announced "the legal equality" of African Americans and whites while upholding racial segregation in public transportation.[77]

Courts have also boasted about America's commitment to equality while shielding other forms of discrimination. For example, a federal district court in 2012 upheld Nevada's prohibition on same-sex marriage and simultaneously declared that discrimination based on homosexuality had "been largely erased."[78]

But while women are not the only marginalized Americans subjected to self-contradictory decisions, cases perpetuating women's inequality have been persistent triggers for judicial self-contradiction. Many of these decisions reason about women's access to public life by prioritizing women's domestic responsibilities, making disentangling public and private spheres implausible. However, for ease of discussion in the remainder of this chapter, I will first consider the long tradition of self-contradictory victory announcements in decisions about women's employment and jury service before turning to self-contradiction in decisions about women's reproductive lives and rights within marriage.

We can start by revisiting *Muller v. Oregon* (1908), which upheld sex-based limits on women's contractual rights while contending that women had equal contractual rights with men. Recall that *Muller* permitted restrictions on women's working hours, although the Court would not tolerate such constraints on men.[79] Oregon could impose special disabilities on female workers because the Justices agreed that women, unlike men, needed to subordinate their autonomy to domesticity.[80] Yet *Muller* nevertheless described women and men as legal equals in Oregon. After quoting a 1900 Oregon Supreme Court decision announcing that "[t]he current runs steadily and strongly in the direction of the emancipation of the wife," *Muller* declared "that, putting to one side the elective franchise, in the matter of personal and contractual rights [women] stand on the same plane as the other sex."[81] The statement helped the Court dismiss the plaintiff's complaints about sex discrimination, but *Muller* never explained how women could simultaneously have equal contractual rights with men and fewer contractual rights than men.[82]

The Illinois Supreme Court soon replicated *Muller*'s self-contradiction. *W.C. Ritchie & Co. v. Wayman* (1910) upheld a statute limiting women's working hours "in mechanical establishments or factories or laundries."[83] If the legislation had applied to male employees in those workplaces, it would have been "an arbitrary interference with the right of men to contract for their labor, and unconstitutional and void."[84] The Illinois judges endorsed different rules for women because they followed *Muller*'s lead and interpreted the Constitution on the presumption that women's domestic obligations outweighed their interests in working and earning more. *Ritchie* emphasized that "weakly and sickly women cannot be the mothers of vigorous children" and explained that limiting women's working hours "would tend to preserve the health of women and insure the production of vigorous offspring by them."[85] The court maintained a regime that imposed sex-specific restraints on women's contractual rights, but the judges simultaneously suggested that women and men were already contractual equals in the eyes of the law. They obscured inequality and encouraged complacency by announcing: "The legislation passed in comparatively recent years in this state, and in general by the states of the Union, has emancipated women, so that they now have the right to contract substantially as do men."[86]

Goesaert v. Cleary (1948) proclaimed that women's legal status had been transformed while refusing to alter women's legalized inequality.[87] This United States Supreme Court decision upheld a 1945 Michigan law that prohibited women from bartending in cities with fifty thousand or more people, unless the woman was "the wife or daughter of the male owner" of the bar.[88] Restrictions on female bartending had been a familiar feature of the legal landscape before Prohibition began in 1920.[89] The Michigan statute was part of a wave of legislation that the for-men-only bartenders' union helped push through statehouses after Prohibition ended in 1933.[90] By 1948, the bartenders' union was able to report to its membership that Michigan was one of seventeen states with an "anti-barmaid law."[91]

Male bartenders often presented their opposition to female bartending as a public-spirited quest to promote morality.[92] Louis W. Wulff, the president of the International Barmen Association, told the press in 1936 that he supported "a ban on" "barmaids" because: "Liquor alone can cause enough trouble, why add women." Wulff proceeded to blame women for the male transgressions they would purportedly provoke: "When you put a pretty miss behind the bar you invite trouble. You get all the gay young blades—and the old ones too—hanging about the bar until all hours."[93]

Moralizing aside, female bartending was financially frightening for the bartenders' union because bar owners could get away with paying women less. For example, a December 1945 article discussing the union's advocacy for anti-barmaid legislation in Missouri observed that female bartenders "work for $20 to $30 a week" while "the union minimum scale is $40 to $45."[94]

In more candid moments, barmen acknowledged the economic stakes. Blocking women from invading what one local agent for the bartenders' union called "the sacred professional realms of the male" kept bars from employing "women drink-mixers" to evade "the established prices fixed for male bartenders."[95] Barmen were determined to protect their market power, keeping their earnings up and their jobs secure.[96]

The Michigan law *Goesaert* upheld exemplifies how barmen benefited from these prohibitions. The statute facilitated men's economic success while denying women the same opportunities and reinforcing female domestic obligations. A male bar owner could tend his own bar. He could also profit from the bartending of his wife or daughter—whether or not he paid his relative for her labor—and Michigan did not require him to be present while his wife or daughter worked. In contrast, female bar owners could neither employ their daughters as bartenders nor bartend in their own establishments. If a woman was not the wife or daughter of a male bar owner, Michigan prohibited her from bartending in larger cities.[97] Male bartenders faced little female competition.

Perhaps unsurprisingly, Michigan did permit women to work as cocktail waitresses,[98] which was probably more dangerous—and less lucrative— than pouring drinks from behind a bar. One Michigan barmaid in this era explained why she would "not be a waitress" by reporting: "I'm safer back here. Out there you have to keep smacking down the customers."[99]

Challenging the constitutionality of Michigan's legislation was an uphill battle. In the years since *Muller*, the United States Supreme Court had rejected many other attempts to combat legislative constraints on female employment that kept work sex stratified.[100] State courts had been upholding anti-barmaid laws,[101] and the Michigan Supreme Court had swiftly dismissed a constitutional challenge to Michigan's statute.[102]

Four Michigan women sued in federal court nonetheless. Valentine Goesaert and Carolyn McMahon each owned a bar where they bartended for themselves.[103] Gertrude Nadroski was a bartender.[104] Margaret Goesaert bartended in her mother's bar.[105] Anne R. Davidow, a pioneering feminist attorney in Michigan,[106] represented them.[107] She secured affidavits (sworn statements) from twenty-three other Michigan women who recounted their successful history as bartenders and their need for the income that bartending generated.[108] After the *Goesaert* plaintiffs lost in a three-judge federal district court, they appealed to the United States Supreme Court.[109]

The Supreme Court did not record the oral argument in *Goesaert*, so I do not know exactly what the Justices said as they questioned Davidow and Michigan's lawyer in person. But Davidow recounted the proceedings in a 1978 interview. She reported that after the lunch recess "the Solicitor General of the state of Michigan came in with a couple of the judges," which made her suspect that Michigan's lawyer had "been to see somebody." Justice Felix Frankfurter then "heckled" Davidow from the bench while informing her that "the days of chivalry aren't over."[110] Presumably, Frankfurter either failed to recognize the irony or felt that Davidow's effrontery in pursuing this suit excused him from any obligation to treat her chivalrously.

Davidow left the Supreme Court thinking that the outcome of the case "was all cut and dried" against her clients. The Michigan Solicitor General had kept his remarks defending the law "short and sweet." "Frankfurter, the big liberal, had made so light of" the women's constitutional challenge, treating it as "such a frivolous thing to bring before the Court."[111]

Indeed, Frankfurter's majority opinion in *Goesaert* made clear that the Court did not take the women's case seriously. The opinion was less than three pages long and strained for erudite jocularity.[112] Frankfurter began with a gratuitous reference to "the alewife, sprightly and ribald, in Shakespeare" and assured readers: "Beguiling as the subject is, it need not detain us long." To ask whether Michigan's statute was constitutional was "one of those rare instances where to state the question is in effect to answer it."[113] *Goesaert* refused to "give ear to the suggestion that the real impulse behind this legislation was an unchivalrous desire of male bartenders to try to monopolize the calling."[114] Instead, the majority simply announced that lawmakers could reasonably believe that "bartending by women" could "give rise to moral and social problems," and the Justices did not bother to name what those problems might be.[115] After *Goesaert*, the legal regime that had controlled women's labor for generations remained intact. States were still empowered to draw "a sharp line between the sexes" that excluded women from jobs they wanted and prioritized women's domestic duties over their economic opportunities.[116] But even as the *Goesaert* Justices further entrenched legal rules denying women rights reserved for men, the Court declared that there had been "vast changes in the social and legal position of women."[117] The proclamation of progress achieved apparently made it easier to dismiss women's complaints about persistent discrimination so cavalierly.

Goesaert's consequences reverberated for decades. The decision delighted and encouraged the bartenders' union. Within a few months, union leadership was already reporting that "our people" had gone "to work to mobilize support for similar measures" in other states.[118] Anti-barmaid legislation still governed nine states as late as 1969.[119] The union's lobbying for those bans allegedly continued as late as 1970.[120] That year, a union official testified before the Senate Judiciary Committee to urge opposition to the Equal Rights Amendment.[121] The union wanted to emphasize that mothers are responsible "for the health, care, and safety of those children" in ways that fathers are not and to warn lawmakers that the ERA would jeopardize sex-specific restrictions on women's work that prioritized women's domestic obligations.[122] The Court finally overruled *Goesaert* in 1976, in a footnote.[123]

The Supreme Court's decisions upholding sex-based obstacles to women's jury service were similarly replete with self-contradiction. Consider *Fay v. New York* (1947).[124] By the time that case arose, the Supreme Court had long endorsed women's exclusion from juries. Two-thirds of a century earlier, *Strauder v. West Virginia* (1880) had found race-based discrimination in juror selection unconstitutional while proclaiming that states could make jury service open only "to males, to freeholders, to citizens, to persons within certain ages, or to persons having educational qualifications."[125] The Court's determination to protect state power to marginalize women from jury service remained unshaken after the Nineteenth Amendment. In *Fay*, two men convicted in New York challenged the constitutionality of state legislation creating an automatic exemption from jury service that women, but not men, could choose to invoke.[126] More than a quarter century after the Nineteenth Amendment's 1920 ratification, New York's law was not unusual in assuming that men were essential to civic life while women were unnecessary. As the *Fay* Court highlighted, a 1942 survey had found that twenty states absolutely barred women from jury service and fifteen additional states provided that women could "claim exemption because of their sex."[127] *Fay* upheld that regime, concluding that "[t]he contention that women should be on the jury is not based on the Constitution."[128]

The Court's opinion in *Fay* epitomized self-contradiction. The Justices saw the long history of women's exclusion from juries as a reason to uphold rather than challenge the practice, asserting: "It would, in the light of this history, take something more than a judicial interpretation to spell out of the Constitution a command to set aside verdicts rendered by juries unleavened by feminine influence."[129] With the persistence of women's exclusion in mind, the Court was certain that New York's law did not violate the Fourteenth Amendment and sure that the Nineteenth Amendment placed no constitutional checks on states beyond "the grant of the franchise."[130] The Court perpetuated an entrenched legal order that dismissed "feminine influence" on juries as superfluous. But the Justices simultaneously proclaimed that "a changing view of the rights and responsibilities of women in our public life" had "progressed in all phases of life, including jury duty."[131] Here again, the Court's declaration of progress achieved helped rationalize the Justices' disinterest in disrupting the status quo. Why rush matters along with "constitutional compulsion" if reform was already proceeding apace?[132]

The Justices returned to self-contradiction in *Hoyt v. Florida* (1961), which announced women's "enlightened emancipation" while treating women as marginal citizens and denying women juries of their peers.[133] An all-male jury had rejected Gwendolyn Hoyt's "temporary insanity" defense and convicted her of second-degree murder for killing her husband with a baseball bat.[134] Hoyt thought female jurors would have brought different perspectives to her trial and more receptivity to her arguments. She challenged the constitutionality of Florida's jury law.[135] That law produced overwhelmingly or exclusively male juries by automatically including men on jury rolls while requiring women to tell the state they wanted to be included.[136] As lawmakers surely knew, few women—or men—would choose to serve on a jury. By 1957, the year of Hoyt's trial, "some 220 women" had volunteered for jury duty in Hillsborough County, Florida.[137] The county compiled a list of ten thousand potential jurors that included just ten women.[138]

Hoyt's briefs to the courts hearing her appeals revealed her side of the story. Her husband, Clarence, was violent.[139] On "one of his rare visits home," he "became extremely angry with the defendant and beat her unmercifully."[140] He flaunted his infidelity, and "strange women" called the house.[141] Gwendolyn had "a long history of epilepsy which became progressively worse over the years, causing permanent brain damage, and which was greatly aggravated by the conduct of her husband."[142] Clarence's "complete and total rejection" of her, together with her "long suffering and her mental condition, greatly affected by her epilepsy," led her to lose "all semblance of sanity for a few moments."[143]

The men on the Supreme Court expressed little interest in considering the case from Hoyt's perspective. They presented Hoyt simply as a scorned wife, reporting that the killing "occurred in the context of a marital upheaval involving, among other things, the suspected infidelity of appellant's husband, and culminating in the husband's final rejection of his wife's efforts at reconciliation."[144] With Hoyt dismissed, the Justices focused their attention on the women who might serve as jurors.

The Court's opinion left no doubt about the Justices' continued commitment to Mullerism. *Hoyt*'s explanation for why Florida's system was "reasonable" insisted that women's primary responsibilities were domestic and their participation in public life contingent on their obligations at home.[145] As the Court proclaimed: "Despite the enlightened emancipation of women from the restrictions and protections of bygone years, and their entry into many parts of community life formerly considered to be reserved to men, woman is still regarded as the center of home and family life. We cannot say that it is constitutionally impermissible for a State, acting in pursuit of the general welfare, to conclude that a woman should be relieved from the civic duty of jury service unless she herself determines that such service is consistent with her own special responsibilities."[146]

The passage is doubly striking. First, the Court made no mention of women mobilizing for reform and battling powerful opposition, even when deciding a case where a woman was driving the litigation and challenging the unequal regime that male authorities had imposed upon her. Instead, the Justices attributed improvements in women's status to "enlightened" (male) decision-makers who had freed women from "restrictions and protections" seemingly spontaneously.

Second, the Court embraced self-contradiction. The Justices trumpeted women's "emancipation" while upholding legislation that sidelined women from civic life and jeopardized women in criminal proceedings. Declaring women emancipated suggested that the work of freeing women from unjust constraints was complete and further change unnecessary—even as the Court's version of women's emancipation left Mullerism intact, women marginalized, and all-male juries deciding the fates of criminal defendants. Hoyt's loss had implications well beyond Florida. In 1961, seventeen other states and the District of Columbia "accorded women an absolute exemption" from jury service "based solely on their sex." Three more states barred women from jury service even if they volunteered.[147]

The Supreme Court did not place constitutional limits on state power to regulate jury service by sex until 1975,[148] which gave states years to follow Hoyt's lead. In Archer v. Mayes (1973), for example, Virginia's highest court upheld a state law creating a sex-specific exemption from jury service that a woman could invoke if she had legal custody over and was "responsible for a child or children sixteen years of age or younger or a person having a mental or physical impairment requiring continuous care during normal court hours."[149] As with the Florida law Hoyt upheld, Virginia's statute presumed that women rather than men were their families' caregivers and should prioritize that domestic obligation. Archer endorsed this presumption, insisting that Virginia's statute was "reasonable" because "women are still regarded as the center of home and family life and they are charged with certain responsibilities in the care of the home and children." The Virginia court affirmed and protected a deep-rooted legal tradition treating women as peripheral citizens whose jury service was unnecessary. But the court simultaneously obscured that inequality and encouraged complacency by declaring "that women have been emancipated from restrictions and protections of the past, and, in most respects, they now enjoy the same legal status as men."[150]

Let's turn to self-contradictory victory announcements in decisions about marriage and women's bodies. The same courts that sought rationalization through self-contradiction when limiting women's participation in economic and civic life have a long history of boasting about the nation's embrace of sex equality while making it harder for married women to escape subordination, denying wives rights available to their husbands, and undercutting women's control over their reproductive lives.

Consider Thompson v. Thompson (1910), where the Supreme Court announced that the legal system was emancipating married women while issuing a judgment that blocked battered wives from suing their violent husbands for damages.[151] Under the common law that generations of courts developed and deployed, married women had no right to initiate litigation on their own because they had no separate legal identity.[152] *Thompson* centered on the meaning of a 1901 federal statute providing that married women in the District of Columbia could now "sue separately" "for torts committed against them, as fully and freely as if they were unmarried."[153] Jessie Thompson reported that her husband, Charles, had beaten her on seven occasions, and she invoked this statute in suing him for assault and battery.[154] The Court declared that the law governing the District fit within a wave of state legislation "passed in pursuance of the general policy of emancipation of the wife from the husband's control."[155] Yet after proclaiming that lawmakers were freeing married women from their husbands' domination, the Court proceeded to interpret the statute at issue in *Thompson* on the presumption that Congress did not want "to revolutionize the law governing the relation of husband and wife as between themselves."[156] The Justices argued that permitting a wife to sue her husband "for injuries to person or property" would be such a "radical and far-reaching" change that the Court could allow Thompson's suit to proceed only if the statute's language was "so clear and plain as to be unmistakable evidence of the legislative intention."[157] In fact, the statute's language was straightforward. The law specified that wives could sue "for torts committed against them, as fully and freely as if they were unmarried," in a context where unmarried women could pursue assault and battery claims against men who attacked them.[158] Nonetheless, the Justices insisted that Congress had not spoken with "irresistible clearness."[159] The Court had proclaimed that the law was emancipating married women, but that only obscured the Justices' determination to resist reform.

Twentieth-century state courts likewise turned to self-contradiction in developing doctrines of interspousal tort immunity, which prohibited litigation where one spouse was suing the other seeking damages for injuries inflicted. Courts protected husbands' prerogatives to abuse their wives while excusing the judiciary's complicity and promoting complacency by declaring that the law had already emancipated married women. The Washington Supreme Court announced in 1911 that state lawmakers had enacted legislation whose "object" was "abolishing the tyranny of sex," and then the judges interpreted that legislation to preserve the common law disability that blocked women from suing their husbands for willfully infecting them with incapacitating venereal disease during marriage.[160] The Tennessee Supreme Court in 1915 trumpeted the state's progress while holding that women could not seek damages from men who assaulted them during marriage.[161] The governing Tennessee statute from 1913 provided that a married woman was "fully emancipated" and could "sue and be sued with all the rights and incidents thereof, as if she were not married."[162] But the judges simultaneously declared that married women had been freed from subjection and insisted that lawmakers did not want "to empower a wife to bring an action against her husband for injuries to her person."[163]

Courts were similarly inclined to self-contradiction when denying married women compensation for their domestic labor. Despite the prevalence of declarations about the "complete emancipation of married women" "and their exaltation to an equality with, if not to a superiority over, their husbands," judges were certain that a wife was not entitled to compensation for doing her husband's housework.[164] Glossing over the chasm between the unrestrained proclamations about progress achieved and the unchanged reality made logical consistency elusive. For example, a federal court in Alabama announced in 1916 that the state had "liberated the wife" from the "indefensible thralldom" of the common law, which "treated the wife as though she were the chattel of the husband."[165] But at the same time, the court insisted that a married woman was still obligated to serve as her husband's "housekeeper" and prohibited from making an enforceable agreement with her husband to be paid for that labor.[166] As the judge declared, a wife was not "entitled to any compensation for services ordinarily and naturally incumbent upon her in that beautiful relation which she assumed by her marriage vows."[167] The rosy progress reports helped mask how little had changed.

Judges also deployed self-contradiction when refusing to give married women rights their husbands enjoyed. If a third party harmed a man's wife, courts had long empowered the husband to pursue his own litigation against the wrongdoer and collect damages for the loss of consortium he suffered when his wife was injured.[168] In contrast, courts routinely held for much of the twentieth century that a married woman could not pursue a consortium claim against a third party who injured her husband.[169] Midcentury judges denied married women remedies because of their sex while referring to the era as "these days of the total emancipation of married women,"[170] "these enlightened times of legal equality between the sexes."[171] The self-congratulatory declarations of victory helped rationalize the judiciary's refusal to treat wives as favorably as husbands. How important could the right to sue for consortium damages be if married women were already emancipated and equal?

Decades later, the United States Supreme Court in *Planned Parenthood of Southeastern Pennsylvania v. Casey* (1992) announced the end of women's legal subordination while upholding lawmaking that doubted women's decisionmaking capacity and undermined women's control over their reproductive lives. *Casey* reviewed a Pennsylvania law that impeded women's access to abortion. Among other provisions, Pennsylvania banned abortion unless the woman visited a doctor to receive information the state wanted her to hear and then waited at least twenty-four hours before returning for the abortion.[172] As *Casey's* plurality acknowledged, requiring two separate medical appointments made accessing abortion more difficult for many women—especially women who were poor, lived far from abortion providers, and/or struggled to get time away from husbands, employers, or others. Practical realities meant the two-visit requirement would delay some women's abortions by much longer than a day.[173]

Casey upheld this provision, with a plurality opinion suggesting that distrust of women's decisionmaking capacity was appropriate.[174] The plurality argued that Pennsylvania could constitutionally require the transmission of state-approved information and impose a twenty-four-hour waiting period to ensure that women's decisionmaking was "wise,"[175] "mature,"[176] and "thoughtful and informed."[177] The clear implication was that women might be unwise, immature, thoughtless, or uninformed without the state's intervention. Indeed, the plurality wrote as if women might not understand what they were doing if they accessed abortion without first submitting to the state information/waiting period requirement, describing Pennsylvania's law as "reducing the risk that a woman may elect an abortion, only to discover later, with devastating psychological consequences, that her decision was not fully informed."[178] The plurality emphasized that women do not have "a constitutional right to abortion on demand,"[179] using language that invoked disrespect for women's judgment to dismiss the idea that legal authorities should permit women to make decisions about abortion without interference.

This mode of reasoning belittled women and empowered states to undercut women's autonomy. Some women subject to the state information/waiting period requirement that *Casey* upheld would be forced into childbearing because they were unable to evade a domineering husband twice in order to secure an abortion.

But the *Casey* Court nonetheless asserted that its reading of the Constitution no longer denied women equality, in or out of marriage. *Casey* declared that "[t]he ability of women to participate equally in the economic and social life of the Nation has been facilitated by their ability to control their reproductive lives," without acknowledging that the *Casey* decision reduced women's reproductive autonomy.[180] *Casey* contended that the Court's "present understanding of marriage and of the nature of the rights secured by the Constitution" rejected "the common-law understanding of a woman's role within the family," which had placed wives under their husbands' control.[181] *Casey* proclaimed that "[t]he Constitution protects all individuals, male or female, married or unmarried, from the abuse of governmental power."[182]

Casey was self-contradictory, yet not unusual. Courts have been suggesting or declaring that America has left women's inequality behind since before the Nineteenth Amendment. Writing rosy proclamations about the nation's progress often particularly appeals to judges when they issue decisions impeding that progress. The self-contradictory victory announcements loudly insisting that women already have so much help judges rationalize their choices and deny their part in perpetuating inequality.

Chapter 4
Popular Culture Announces Women's Emancipation

The decades of judicial victory announcements fit into a well-established cultural tradition outside the courts. Generations of insistent voices in popular media have described women's inequality as part of the past rather than the present. These proclamations shielding ongoing discrimination and discouraging mobilization began before the Nineteenth Amendment and have been a steady drumbeat through the century of popular writing since ratification. Although the absurdity of the media's earliest declarations has become ever more apparent with the passage of time, more recent work overstates the nation's progress with equivalent brio. Popular authors have routinely framed their accounts as universal descriptions of women's place in America, while usually giving white women implicit pride of place.

As with judicial proclamations, the media's victory announcements have frequently been self-contradictory. Popular writers have described the vanquishing of sex discrimination as a national triumph even as they warn that equal rights and opportunities have been disastrous for women. Some authors have embraced more explicit self-contradiction when undercutting reform, boasting about America's commitment to sex equality while openly defending persistent inequality, opposing progress, and even pushing regression.

These media messages have built on lessons that generations of schoolchildren have heard. Some textbooks were already declaring women emancipated while suffragists and anti-suffragists furiously battled over female disenfranchisement. Assertions that America had left women's inequality behind multiplied in the decades after the Nineteenth Amendment's 1920 ratification, as textbooks highlighted white women's voting, overlooked persistent restraints on women's rights, and ignored the many women of color still blocked from the polls. Here too, it can be easy to recognize, especially in retrospect, how textbooks from earlier eras masked inequality and promoted complacency by exaggerating progress and sanitizing women's struggles. But more recent textbooks continue to overstate the nation's advances and underemphasize the entrenched opposition and obstacles that women's rights activists have confronted.

Popular Stories for Adults

Many twenty-first-century Americans are personally familiar with media accounts exaggerating the nation's progress, across many dimensions. Think of the incessant talk about "post-racial" America that surrounded Barack Obama's 2008 election as America's first black president.[1] A Cleveland *Plain Dealer* columnist announced that "America has completed its evolution into a racial meritocracy."[2] The *Wall Street Journal* presented Obama's victory as an opportunity to "put to rest the myth of racism as a barrier to achievement in this splendid country."[3]

Still, it was surprising to discover how early in American history pronouncements about the establishment of sex equality began appearing in popular media and how often pontificators have deployed those pronouncements to support inequality. The press began describing women's emancipation as an accomplished fact while suffragists fought powerful opposition and sex-based denials of the franchise remained constitutional, widespread, and part of a comprehensive legal regime denying women rights and opportunities.[4] No woman could vote in Texas in 1892 and restrictions on women's employment were legal and ubiquitous,[5] but the *Austin Daily Statesman* nonetheless announced that women had been "emancipated from the thraldom of home duties and invited into the gladiatorial arena of business, literature and politics."[6] The *St. Louis Globe-Democrat* published words of wisdom from a writer opining in 1897 that "American women were emancipated without a siege, and so long ago that nobody can remember the date."[7] A widely reprinted 1912 article in the *Chicago Record-Herald* similarly emphasized consensus rather than conflict when describing the transformation in women's status, suggesting that no one "will now seriously defend the 'subjection' of woman."[8] A year later, police in the nation's capital stood by as a mob of white men harassed and attacked suffragists peacefully marching on the eve of Woodrow Wilson's inauguration.[9]

Popular writers frequently used these sunny pronouncements to present America's purported egalitarianism as a distinction that set the United States apart from the rest of the world. No woman could vote in Arkansas in 1904,[10] but an article in the *Arkansas Gazette* nonetheless contended that "[o]ur women are the freest in the world, enjoying every privilege of citizenship."[11] That same year, a writer in the *Minneapolis Tribune* overlooked Minnesota's sex-based restrictions on the franchise to assert "that in our country women are emancipated in all that the term implies."[12] A 1906 essay in the *Chicago Tribune* described "[t]he American" as a man who was "acknowledging his wife as his equal, and declaring before the world that she is the most emancipated woman on the face of the earth."[13] The *Spokane Spokesman-Review* boasted in 1910 about "[t]he emancipation of woman from the traditional tyranny to which her European sister has been subjected."[14] In reality, the United States was not an egalitarian trailblazer for women. American suffragists observed, for example, that New Zealand abolished sex-based restrictions on the franchise in 1893.[15] Within Europe, Finland eliminated sex-based voting requirements in 1906, when many American women remained disenfranchised.[16]

Popular proclamations of American women's emancipation often focused particular attention on the law of marriage. Newspapers in the late nineteenth and early twentieth centuries echoed and amplified judicial assertions about the demise of common law principles of coverture, promoting complacency and disregarding women's protests by ignoring persistent legal disabilities that limited married women's rights to operate independently of their husbands.[17] The *Brooklyn Daily Eagle* was ready to report in 1888 "that every old law which made the husband master of the wife has been erased."[18] The *Chicago Tribune* contended in 1895 that "[t]he laws" of Illinois had "emancipated married women."[19] The *Raleigh News & Observer* placed coverture in the past in 1911, announcing: "Married women are emancipated. A twenty year fight is ended."[20]

Influential law journals disseminated that story as well. Harvard Law School Professor Joseph H. Beale, Jr., advised readers of the *Harvard Law Review* in 1905 that "married women were emancipated from the control of their husbands" during the nineteenth century.[21] Epaphroditus Peck, a Yale Law School valedictorian who became a Connecticut judge and then a state legislator, taught domestic relations law at his alma mater for a decade.[22] He announced coverture's eradication in 1916 and gave men the credit, proclaiming in the *Yale Law Journal* that Connecticut was one of "many" states where "the ancient law concerning married women has been swept away, and an equality of personal and property rights has been established" through "the action of male voters, male legislators and male judges."[23] That assertion was meant to support Peck's endorsement of a common anti-suffrage argument. In his words: "Connecticut women can hardly argue that they need the suffrage because of the unwillingness of men to give them fair and equal treatment as to their personal and property rights."[24]

Declarations of America's triumph over sex discrimination multiplied in the half century after the Nineteenth Amendment's 1920 ratification, with writers undercutting women's ongoing struggles for reform by framing women's inequality as a solved problem. The *Buffalo Morning Express* proclaimed in 1921 that "the battle for sex equality has been won."[25] A 1928 article in the *New York Times* presumed "that things have gone just about as far as possible in making the American woman equal to the American man."[26] The introduction to a 1931 book on *Woman's Coming of Age* openly discouraged feminist mobilization. The authors declared that "Feminism has attained its ends," "has practically fulfilled its mission," and "has nothing more to offer," reporting that "[e]conomic emancipation" had been "fortified by political and educational independence, and these in turn by moral independence."[27] The next year, a psychologist similarly announced in the 1932 *Oakland Tribune* that "[t]he fight for feminism is over. Woman has everything that she has ever wanted."[28] The *Dayton Daily News* proclaimed in 1949 that "[t]he feminist revolution is complete," explaining that "[f]ifty years ago the emancipation of women was a thing to argue about" but now "emancipation is a fait accompli."[29] The *Birmingham News* assured subscribers in 1958 that: "Women became emancipated long ago in law."[30]

The victory announcements frequently relied on overstated accounts of what the Nineteenth Amendment had accomplished that erased the many women of color who remained disenfranchised and ignored the persistent restrictions on women's rights and opportunities that continued to deny women access to the best jobs, exclude women from the most elite colleges, and subordinate wives to their husbands.[31] The *Kansas City Star* declared in 1921 "that today women are emancipated from all the traditional shackles except fashion. They have an amendment of their own and their votes command the same market price as those of the long privileged men."[32] Frederick Lewis Allen, a self-described "retrospective journalist," announced in his bestselling *Informal History of the Nineteen-Twenties* (1931) that "the winning of the suffrage had its effect. It consolidated woman's position as man's equal."[33] A historian told readers of the *Woman's Home Companion* in 1955 that women had "been emancipated politically as well as educationally and economically."[34] As struggles to enfranchise women and men of color intensified in the years preceding the 1965 Voting Rights Act, a 1960 article in the *Iowa City Press-Citizen* contended that "[t]he emancipated woman" had already "gained freedom, equality and the ballot."[35] The 1962 *Chicago Tribune* likewise centered white women when fostering complacency, reporting that the nation had adopted "universal suffrage" in 1920 and proclaiming that "the New Woman is working out a comfortable equality."[36]

Some of the victory declarations attributed the nation's triumph to women's past efforts. A columnist advised readers of the *Atlanta Constitution* in 1932

that "[a] few brave and intelligent women, desiring nothing more than justice, demanded and eventually obtained recognition of the fact that women
are people. Women were 'emancipated.' They were given the right to vote; the
law recognized them as man's equal."[37] A Maryland newspaper announced in
1940 that "[w]omen sought and achieved equality with men" and observed
that "[t]he great social movements of the Nineteenth Century were nearly
all originated and fought for by women."[38] An Indiana newspaper in 1959
interviewed Landrum Bolling, the president of Earlham College, for an article discussing how Earlham's curriculum prepared female students for lives as
homemakers. Bolling declared it "clear that the 'battle of feminism' has been
won long ago."[39] Radcliffe College President Mary Bunting likewise described
sex equality as a victory fought for and achieved, announcing in 1961 that "the
bitter battles for women's rights are history. The cause has been won."[40] Paul
Woodring, education editor for the *Saturday Review*, proclaimed in 1963 that
women had "achieved emancipation and equality of opportunity." He credited the "complete" "victory" to women's mobilization but almost mocked
the women who had mobilized, which hardly encouraged readers to follow
in their footsteps. As Woodring explained: "With emancipation the feminist
movement came to an end, and the suffragettes of a bygone day now seem
more than a little ridiculous to a generation of coeds who have forgotten how
recently their present status was achieved and how great was the struggle of
those responsible for it."[41]

At least as often, however, popular writers in the decades after the Nineteenth Amendment emphasized that women were not primarily responsible
for America's purported success in leaving women's inequality behind. Some
authors gave industrialization all the credit. Will Durant, a popular historian
who would later win a Pulitzer Prize,[42] spoke to a Manhattan audience of
more than fifteen hundred in 1926 and reached many more when the *New
York Times* reported the event. After predicting that "[t]he first quarter of the
twentieth century will in the future be known, not for the World War, but
for the emancipation of woman," Durant insisted that "[t]he industrial revolution was the cause of her liberation."[43] *Glamour* made that argument still
more emphatically in 1942. What gave woman "her financial independence"
and "economic and legal equality with men"?[44] *Glamour* did not mention
the generations of mobilized women who had fought to expand their rights
and opportunities against fierce resistance. Instead, the magazine declared:
"This is going to hurt, but the fact—the cold, scientific low-down—is that the
'emancipated,' independent career woman as we know her today is nothing
more nor less than a by-product of the machine age. Thanks to the machine,
women's domestic life became less burdensome."[45]

Other popular writers erased how feminist mobilization had propelled change forward through conflict by attributing the transformation in women's status to men's enlightenment rather than women's efforts to overcome formidable opposition to reform. John Macy was a public intellectual celebrated in his time as "one of the most important American literary critics."[46] His reflections on the nation's progress centered men and relegated women to the peripheries as mostly passive beneficiaries. Macy reported in 1926 that "certain economic and social disabilities which women suffered for centuries have been rectified, largely through the efforts of enlightened men."[47] He contended "that the greatest expressions of Feminism, the most eloquent and effective pleas for emancipation of women, have come not from women but from men."[48] John Erskine was a Columbia professor and popular novelist.[49] He described men as the key actors responsible for purportedly making America "a woman's world," explaining in 1936 that "the finer spirits among my sex tried to improve the feminine lot."[50] Russell Lynes wrote about women's status when he was the managing editor of *Harper's* and an influential tastemaker.[51] His 1957 book breezily assumed that equality between husbands and wives was well-established, quipping: "Whereas it was once a question of 'Who wears the pants in this family?' it is now a matter of pants all around, and the children are as likely to cling to Father's apron strings as Mother's."[52] On Lynes's account, men had engineered this metamorphosis. He remembered the Nineteenth Amendment as a gift rather than a battle, ignored the women of color who remained disenfranchised, and opined: "It is doubtful that when men let women have the vote, back in 1920, they foresaw the sort of social revolution that they were letting loose on themselves."[53]

The theme persisted when feminist mobilization resurged in the late twentieth century. Women striving for equality confronted not only direct opposition in the political arena, but also decades of popular media suggesting or declaring that women should demobilize because the inequities they were protesting were either already rectified or on the precipice of vanishing without concerted effort. As determined anti-feminists campaigned to stop ratification of the Equal Rights Amendment,[54] the *New York Times* chose to publish a lengthy excerpt from a then-forthcoming book that described defenders of the status quo as passive rather than active and contended that "powerful inertial forces opposing change in the United States have a way of abruptly caving in." The writer insisted at the end of 1981 that there was a national consensus against sex discrimination "in questions of jobs, salary, access to education, or property rights," announcing: "That battle, however painful, has been uncomplicated and, except for what amounts to a mopping-up operation, seems to have been won."[55] By April 1982, when

Congress's extended deadline for states to ratify the ERA was just two months away, it was clear that ERA opponents had succeeded in blocking timely ratification.[56] But an essay in the *Spokane Spokesman-Review* nonetheless asserted that "the battle, and the war," for women's equality "is mostly won" and proclaimed that "[t]he activist breed of woman is no longer needed."[57] The declaration of progress achieved was simultaneously a call for feminist quiescence.

Time repeatedly framed the work of the women's movement as complete. A 1989 cover story announced that feminism's "triumphs" had "rendered it obsolete, at least in its original form and rhetoric," and then quoted a Harvard professor who was ready to tell *Time*'s readers: "Saying the women's movement is dead is like saying the cold war is dead. No. No. It's over. It's won."[58] The magazine was back a year later with another story on "the success of the women's movement" contending that "[y]oung Americans inherit a revolution that has largely been won."[59] When this pronouncement appeared in 1990, the median woman working full-time and year-round earned just 71.6 cents for every dollar a full-time, year-round male worker made.[60] A 1990 survey of America's 799 largest publicly traded industrial and service companies found that only 0.47% of the best-compensated officers and directors were women—19 out of 4,012.[61] The House of Representatives was less than seven percent female in 1990, and only two women served in the Senate.[62] Indeed, *Time*'s own editors during the previous decade had repeatedly recognized that men continued to monopolize the pinnacles of power. They named just one "Woman of the Year" in the 1980s while six different men won "Man of the Year," and two of those men won twice.[63]

While some popular writers in the late twentieth century gave feminists credit for sparking the transformation that now purportedly rendered further struggle unnecessary, others implicitly or openly discouraged continued mobilization by downplaying the contributions of organized women's rights activity. A popular book on the anthropology of *America Now* emphasized that economic forces had been more important than activism, asserting in 1981 that: "Women's liberation did not *create* the working woman; rather the working woman—especially the working housewife—created women's liberation."[64] A 1983 opinion piece in the *Baltimore Sun* "almost a year" after the expiration of Congress's extended deadline for states to ratify the ERA suggested that Americans should not find this feminist defeat worrisome because the nation was already on the cusp of sex equality and deliberate efforts to expand women's rights and opportunities were unnecessary: "Most of the socio-demographic goals sought by most women in America have pretty well happened, or are happening, with a speed that is quite remarkable," and "most of" this transformation "was happening on its own" rather than through "conscious political design."[65]

As the twentieth century ended and the twenty-first began, popular media continued to promote complacency by describing women's struggles for equality—and resistance to those efforts—as parts of the past rather than the present. On these accounts, feminism's work was over and done because sex equality was an uncontroversial commitment that America had readily embraced. A wave of magazines and newspapers popularized the term *duh feminism* in the 1990s.[66] The point of the catchphrase was to treat feminism as a "dead" part of the past rather than a live concern requiring ongoing mobilization for legal and social change.[67] The term disregarded women's multigenerational striving and strategizing for equality in the face of persistent opposition to suggest (in the words of a *Chicago Tribune* journalist) that feminism "won because it is so obvious."[68] Along similar lines, a journalist writing in the *Atlanta Journal-Constitution* in 1999 described "radical feminism" as "passé" "because all of us—or nearly all of us—are members of the faith" and announced: "The war's over, and the right side won."[69] An *Orlando Sentinel* column declared in 2000 that "most of feminism's goals have been met," rendering feminism "nearly" "artificial."[70] Years later, the same journalist opined in the *Washington Post*. The piece discussed resistance to Hillary Clinton's 2016 campaign to be the first female president while describing feminism as "obsolete through acceptance" and proclaiming that young women "really can have it all."[71]

Popular Self-Contradiction

Popular victory announcements have often been as self-contradictory as the judicial declarations of victory that Chapter 3 examined. Popular writers have a long history of congratulating the nation for its triumph over sexism while simultaneously insisting that equal rights and opportunities have been terrible for women. The self-contradiction and push against feminist mobilization have sometimes been even more blatant, with some popular authors declaring that America has embraced sex equality while explicitly defending persistent inequality and advising complacency or regression.

I will start with the dire warnings to women. In the decades after the Nineteenth Amendment's 1920 ratification, newspapers, magazines, and books were full of praise for egalitarian ideals and American progress paired with advice that implicitly urged women to run from feminism by detailing the supposed downsides of equality for women. A New Jersey newspaper published a lengthy interview in 1931 with Ernest Boyd, a prominent literary critic.[72] Boyd celebrated "the great philosophies and ideals which have influenced the world since the beginning of time" and attributed them to men, asserting that "[j]ustice, freedom, liberty were all male ideas." While lauding those lofty principles in the abstract, Boyd contended in the same interview that "[t]he primary result of emancipation has been to complicate the problems of life and to drag women down to the level of men." "Emotionally, emancipation has had a bad effect on woman."[73]

A 1948 *Esquire* article bragged that the American woman was "the most independent and free of women anywhere" while insisting that American women were also "[t]he most unhappy and dissatisfied."[74] That dual assertion—nominally about all American women, but with white women clearly top of mind—was ubiquitous, as popular postwar writers treated sex equality as both a national accomplishment and a catastrophe for women. A 1951 review in the *Chicago Tribune* reasoned from the premise "that women are in a sorry plight with all their enlightenment. For with all their education, pay envelopes, kitchen gadgets, and this and that, American women are frustrated, dissatisfied, sometimes inefficient and inadequate, and unhappy."[75] The introduction to *Life*'s 1956 special issue on *The American Woman: Her Achievements and Troubles* emphasized the purported downsides of equality while also erasing the women who fought for equal rights before the twentieth century.[76] It began by declaring: "To be an American woman today is to be cast in an exciting, challenging and difficult role—exciting because the sky seems to be the limit in education, work and freedom; challenging because the whole concept of 'woman's rights' is still relatively new—scarcely more than 50 years old; and difficult because the new freedom has produced a backwash of unforeseen emotional and psychological problems for the emancipated woman."[77]

Some authors published book-length warnings. Ferdinand Lundberg and Marynia Farnham's 1947 bestseller on the *Modern Woman* gave the United States and other Western nations credit for easily recognizing "the correctness—moral and historical—of the feminist program" while the authors belittled the contributions of feminists themselves.[78] Their account glossed over generations of conflict to contend that "[v]arious rights and privileges that a minority among [women] laid boisterous claim to for the first time in history were quickly conceded, as to a bothersome child."[79] With that asserted, Lundberg and Farnham devoted the bulk of their book to arguing that feminism "spelled only vast individual suffering for men as well as women, and much public disorder."[80] Hendrik de Leeuw's *Woman: The Dominant Sex* (1957) called American women "not only the most privileged, but, paradoxically, the most dissatisfied persons in the world." He ignored generations of opposition to feminist mobilization to contend that the nation's women "had liberty and uncounted privileges dished up on a gold platter" and reported that "many have gone berserk with their newly acquired power."[81] Eric John Dingwall's 1957 book on *The American Woman* declared that her apparent success in "attaining all for which she had so long striven" had "seemed to bring her no nearer to serenity, tranquility and the enjoyment of her gains."[82]

Assertions about the injuries that equality had supposedly inflicted on women were so prevalent that they created marketing opportunities for midcentury entrepreneurs. Marie Murphy, vice president of a "relaxation equipment" manufacturer, told the press in 1959 that "women have become so aggressive, are engaged in so many activities, that the strain builds to a point at which it has to erupt." She predicted that "if women between the ages of 40 and 60 don't slow down they won't be around to boast of their longevity."[83]

Warning women remained a favorite media pastime as feminism resurged in the late twentieth century, with popular authors emphasizing that feminist mobilization and American progress could leave women feeling worse. The *Washington Post* advised of the hazards in 1968, as the modern women's movement was launching. That year, the median woman working full-time and year-round earned just 58.2 cents for every dollar a male full-time, year-round worker made.[84] Explicit constraints on women's rights and opportunities remained commonplace, and the Supreme Court's first decision striking down legislation for denying women equal protection was still three years in the future.[85] The Court had never placed any constitutional limits on the many state laws restricting access to abortion.[86] Feminists were vigorously pushing for reform, but the *Post* nevertheless proceeded as if America had already triumphed over sex discrimination. An article announced that "the legal emancipation of the female" had been "followed by The Pill, which has emancipated her in still another way." The *Post* writer claimed these national accomplishments while simultaneously suggesting that the developments threatened women's happiness: "the thought that they may be shortchanging their families by pursuing personal interests, troubles many women." "The times are changing, and that's the problem."[87] The *Miami Herald* featured a doctor's warning in 1982 that "[w]omen have liberated themselves into dope" and the miseries of drug addiction.[88] A *Boston Globe* columnist proclaimed in 1986 that feminism had been "triumphant" while describing the purported consequences of that victory as "grim news for the women and children and decent men who need stable families and homes to give their lives comfortable, tangible meaning and hope for the future."[89] That same year, a *Newsweek* cover story informed the nation that an unmarried college-educated woman in her thirties or forties had little chance of finding a husband.[90] The story described men as "postfeminist" while advising that "many men don't want to put up with the hassles of a two-career family."[91]

The warnings were on bookshelves as well. William Novak's widely discussed 1983 book on *Roadblocks to Romance* praised "the women's movement" for achieving "many impressive gains" and addressing "some glaring social injustices" while reporting that the movement was "a major source of conflict between the sexes."[92] Novak suggested that increased scrutiny of heterosexual relationships had diminished women's chances of romantic fulfillment, declaring: "Whereas men and women used to be together, by 1975 much of society was polarized: women were on one side, men on the other, and between the two lay a valley of hostility and distrust."[93] Connell Cowan and Melvyn Kinder's bestselling *Smart Women, Foolish Choices* (1985) sounded a similar alarm.[94] The book characterized "the core tenets of feminism" as "well-taken and just" while cautioning readers that "[a]ngry women frighten men."[95] Cowan and Kinder repeatedly described feminism as a potential impediment to women forming fulfilling intimate relationships with men.[96] They reported a "tendency on the part of women today, especially smart ones, to make even greater 'errors' with the opposite sex than they might have done in previous years" and offered advice for the "career-oriented" woman who "is likely to feel that her love relationships with men are disappointing, frustrating, and very confusing."[97]

Books continued to emphasize how progress threatened women's fulfillment as one millennium closed and another unspooled. Karen Lehrman's 1997 book on *Women, Sex & Power in the Real World* generated considerable media attention for simultaneously boasting about the nation's "tremendous political and social" progress and detailing the supposed downsides of that progress for women. The book reasoned from the premise that "[w]omen are not 'oppressed' in the United States, and they're no longer (politically at least) even subjugated. What they very well might be, though, is overwhelmed and confused."[98] Michael Segell reflected on "thirty years of feminism and gender equality" in his 1999 book on *Manhood After Feminism*.[99] He observed "an epidemic of romantic malaise and confusion" and a dearth of romantic heterosexual relationships "of any consequence."[100] Samantha Parent Walravens compiled *Torn*, a 2011 collection of women's essays. She reported that "the Women's Movement" had "freed us from domestic bondage and opened the doors to economic opportunity" but emphasized that: "In trying to have it all, women today have pushed themselves to the limit."[101] Lori

Gottlieb offered perhaps the bluntest warning in *Marry Him*, her 2010 book for unmarried women like herself who wanted husbands.[102] Gottlieb declared that she would not "give back the gains of feminism for anything," but advised her marriage-minded readers: "feminism has completely fucked up my love life."[103]

Other popular authors have trumpeted America's embrace of sex equality while openly defending persistent inequality and promoting complacency or regression. These self-contradictory victory announcements flourished in the decades after the Nineteenth Amendment's 1920 ratification. Willard Waller, a sociology professor at Barnard College who wrote frequently in the popular press, delivered the mixed message to newspaper readers across the country in 1945.[104] He credited the United States with "generations of feministic progress," culminating in "the conditions of freedom and equality that have existed in the United States since" the first World War. Relegating women's struggles to the past set up Waller's dismissal of the "old-fashioned feminist" who "will say that a woman is the mistress of her own body; the nation has no right to force her to bear children." With the return of peacetime life imminent as World War II entered its final months, Waller was eager to demand that women sacrifice autonomy and self-ownership because they owed America reproduction: "A woman's ownership of her body should be subordinate to her obligation as the trustee of the race." Here again, the term "race" appeared to have multiple meanings. Like many opponents of reproductive autonomy before him, Waller was particularly concerned that "people with superior capacities" were having too few children.[105]

Midcentury authors also crowed about the nation's commitment to sex equality while defending women's absence from top jobs and advising against change. A 1950 article in the *Atlantic* contended—implausibly—that women had "equal rights in every field of endeavor" and "equal pay for equal work" while criticizing "the worried, restless, immature females who complain bitterly that there are not enough women in high executive positions in the business world and in government."[106] The article asserted that "modern women" had placed "too much emphasis on success and too little upon service" and urged complacency rather than mobilization: "The balanced, mature woman who knows her inner worth does not run around the world complaining of the injustice of men."[107] Helen Sherman and Marjorie Coe's 1955 book on *The Challenge of Being a Woman* declared that American women were "no longer considered second-class citizens" while offering rationalizations for why only a "relatively small number of women" hold "top positions in this country."[108] Sherman and Coe took for granted that this sex stratification was "best explained not by men's desire to keep [women] out but by an insufficient drive on the part of the women themselves to get in."[109] So should women strive harder to promote themselves if their purported lack of ambition was the crucial obstacle to reaching the peaks of power in a nation where women had "the most freedom, the greatest amount of formal education, and the widest opportunities to enrich our lives"?[110] Sherman and Coe went in a different direction. They counseled women to prioritize male career advancement, instructing readers it is "up to you to gear the routine of the household to your husband's needs, to be his attractive official hostess, and to live (and *like* living!) where he thinks it wise in the light of his best job opportunities."[111]

Indeed, popular advice-givers often paired their boasts about the nation's triumphs in establishing sex equality with pointers directing women to privilege their husband's interests. A marriage counselor proclaimed in the 1956 *Woman's Home Companion* that "[w]e are proud, and rightly so, of the democratic form that marriage in America has assumed." But when the counselor announced "the new equality of marriage," he simultaneously told "the modern wife" to "see to it that her husband's sense of authority and leadership remains intact and that he is not robbed of his masculine role of protector and provider."[112]

The resurgence of feminist mobilization in the late 1960s and early 1970s spurred more self-contradictory victory announcements. The *Shreveport Times* declared in 1967 that "women are emancipated" while defending a status quo where "scientific, technical and governmental careers" were "usually reserved to men." The newspaper opposed "the prospect of more working women and more farmed-out children," approvingly quoting a psychiatrist who warned that "[p]utting more women to work may mean we are turning out more for the Gross National Product, but it also may mean we are turning out more ill people."[113]

Three years later, Eric Sevareid's televised commentary for *CBS Evening News* on the day of the Women's Strike for Equality, August 26, 1970, simultaneously suggested that organized efforts to promote sex equality were unwarranted and conceded that the goals of the women's movement were unmet. Sevareid began by announcing to his nationwide audience "the plain truth" "that most American men are startled by the idea that American women generally are oppressed," and he shared the "article of faith among men that no husband ever won an argument with a wife." At the same time, Sevareid acknowledged that the United States had yet to achieve the "three practical aims" the leaders of the Women's Strike emphasized: "equal opportunities in employment and education, abortion on demand, and child care centers." Rather than explore that tension, Sevareid told Americans that "the militant women" wanted to be thought of "as persons, not as women" and advised his audience that this could not be done, contending: "It is hard enough to separate nationality from personality and impossible to separate one's personality from one's sex."[114]

Less than four years after that—with none of the Strike's goals satisfied—a syndicated columnist announced that it was "time for the postfeminist phase to begin." The columnist framed further feminist mobilization as unnecessary, declaring in 1974 that "[t]he American woman" was already "on her way" to "complete economic, political and educational equality" with more "open choices" than ever before. But he simultaneously insisted that women with children actually had no options. For mothers, but not fathers, children had to "take priority over everything else."[115]

Popular authors continued to deploy self-contradictory victory announcements to promote complacency or regression as one millennium ended and another began. USA Today published an opinion piece in 1994 that declared "that most of the political work" of feminism was "done" while simultaneously urging universities and employers to structure their policies around the understanding that a woman's "'no' doesn't always mean 'no.'"[116] Of course, discouraging feminist mobilization would facilitate that policy goal. A syndicated newspaper columnist reinforced gendered expectations about women's domestic obligations while announcing in 2002 that America had moved to "the post-feminism era" where women "take for granted that they can do whatever they want." The premise that women no longer needed to worry about constraints on their choices seemed designed to preempt objections to his prodding women toward prioritizing domesticity. The columnist worried that "children were losing out on something as mothers aggressively pursued careers" while expressing no interest in exploring whether a man's employment negatively impacted his children.[117]

Popular Stories for Children

Popular writers crowing about America's commitment to sex equality—while erasing women's ongoing struggles and the work the nation still needs to do—have been addressing audiences familiar with those messages since childhood. Schoolchildren's textbooks disseminate visions of the nation to impressionable readers, feature stories designed to resonate widely, and constitute the only history books that some Americans ever peruse. Generations of schoolchildren have read textbooks that nurture complacency and discourage mobilization by glossing over persistent inequality and its many fierce defenders to suggest or declare that the nation has left sexism behind.

As with the popular press, some textbooks began bragging about America's embrace of sex equality while anti-suffragists feverishly battled against female voting and sex-based disenfranchisement remained constitutional and widespread. Roscoe Lewis Ashley's *American History* (1907) recounted the "emancipation of women" and contended that women had become "independent." Ashley was writing more than a decade before the Nineteenth Amendment. He acknowledged that only four states gave women the same voting rights as men and took for granted that employers paid women less, but did not let those facts disturb his conclusion that women were already emancipated and independent.[118] Wilbur Gordy's *History of the United States for Schools* (1913) was published more than a half century before many elite colleges admitted women. Gordy nonetheless contended that "[w]omen now have educational advantages equal to those of men."[119] Albert Bushnell Hart's *New American History* (1917) agreed that American women had "equal educational opportunities" and seized the opportunity to boast about American superiority, proclaiming that: "The United States has gone further than any other large country in acknowledging that women are a part of the make-up of the nation and are entitled to a share in the public national life."[120] A year later, when Grace Turkington's *My Country* (1918) appeared, thirty-three out of forty-eight states maintained sex-based restrictions on the franchise.[121] Although women had spent decades mobilizing for equality, discrimination against women at work, in marriage, and in every other arena was still legal and customary throughout the nation.[122] Yet Turkington nevertheless assured young readers that "[a]ll men and women are regarded as equals before the law," as if this was a principle legal authorities already upheld rather than one they routinely rebuffed despite women's persistent activism for reform.[123] Waddy Thompson's *History of the People of the United States* (1919) likewise ignored pervasive and legalized sex discrimination to assert that women had "secured, in nearly every state, equal rights with men in matters of property, education, and employment."[124]

Textbook proclamations that America had achieved sex equality became more common in the decades after the Nineteenth Amendment's 1920 ratification, even as some of the obstacles that women faced actually expanded. Rolla Tryon's *The American Nation Yesterday and Today* (1930) declared that "the ideal of equal rights for women" had been "realized."[125] William Hamm's *The American People* (1938) reported women's "economic emancipation," insisting in an era when employers openly paid female workers less and excluded them from the best jobs that women had "ceased to be dependent upon some man—father or husband—for the necessities of life."[126] These rosy accounts discouraging criticism of the status quo were all the more disconnected from reality because they appeared as powerful Americans were rolling back progress. Public officials and private companies responded to the Great Depression by intensifying their longstanding hostility to employing married women, a form of discrimination that simultaneously assumed and exacerbated wives' economic dependence on their husbands. Before the 1929 stock market crash that launched the Depression, the National Education Association's 1927–28 survey of cities with at least 2,500 people found just 39.0% of the cities reporting that they hired married women as new teachers and just 49.2% reporting that they retained female teachers who wed. Those figures dropped to 23.4% hiring and 37.1% retaining in the 1930–31 survey.[127] The New England Telephone and Telegraph Company and the Northern Pacific Railway fired married female employees in 1931.[128] For five years beginning in 1932, federal law provided that layoffs of federal employees would target married people whose spouses also worked for the federal government.[129] Predictably, over three-fourths of the people who had lost their jobs by the end of 1934 because of this legislation were wives rather than husbands.[130] Public opinion polls uncovered few Americans willing to defend married women's right to work.[131] Eighty-two percent of the participants in a 1936 poll—including seventy-nine percent of the surveyed women—answered "no" when asked whether they approved "of a married woman earning money in industry or business if she has a husband capable of supporting her." George Gallup, director of the American Institute of Public Opinion, remarked that it was "an issue on which voters are about as solidly united in opposition as on any subject imaginable including sin and hay fever."[132]

After World War II, Fremont Wirth's *United States History* (1949) announced that "[e]qual political rights for women" had been "attained."[133] John Hicks's *Short History of American Democracy* (1949) contended that "[l]egal discriminations against women" had been "brought near the vanishing point."[134] The declarations presented sex discrimination as an issue already resolved or on the precipice of disappearing. They depended on omitting all contrary evidence, including the Supreme Court's recent decisions reinforcing women's second-class citizenship. *Goesaert v. Cleary* (1948) permitted states to ban women from jobs that men wanted. *Fay v. New York* (1947) allowed states to exclude or marginalize women from jury service and deny women juries of their peers. *Breedlove v. Suttles* (1937) upheld state legislation creating a financial incentive for women not to vote.[135]

Many textbooks from the middle years of the twentieth century identified 1920 or the 1920s as the moment when America established sex equality. These texts purported to speak about all women. But they highlighted white women's voting while erasing the women of color who remained disenfranchised. Melville Freeman's *The Story of Our Republic* (1938) reported that the 1920s "saw women win their goal of equality," including "not only the full privilege of voting, but freedom from old social customs and traditions—the right to work, play, dress, and live as they pleased."[136] Leon Canfield's *The United States in the Making* (1948) announced the "emancipation of women" and explained that "[b]y 1920 [women] had not only attained legal equality, but had won as well the right to vote and hold office throughout the United States."[137] Leland Baldwin and Mary Warring's *History of Our Republic* (1965) maintained that America had achieved sex equality in 1920, contending that "[d]uring the Gilded Age the old legal barriers were swept away and women came to have the same rights as men, except that they did not all get the right to vote until 1920."[138]

Textbooks often insisted that the nation had established sex equality through consensus rather than conflict, as enlightened men allied with reform-minded women. William Long's *America* (1923) asserted that men had responded to women's campaigning for suffrage with "the masculine conviction that whatever the women of America want they will surely have." Long then described the Nineteenth Amendment in those expansive terms, reporting that the amendment "gave to American women everywhere equal political rights with men."[139] Eugene Barker's *The Building of Our Nation* (1948) explained that "men and women alike" had "recognized" in the nineteenth century "[t]he injustice of" denying women equal rights and opportunities. On Barker's account, this shared understanding had made eradicating sex discrimination simple. Barker asserted "that almost everything which women demanded" at the 1848 Seneca Falls Convention "has long since been granted them as matter of right."[140] Recall that the Seneca Falls advocates sought an "equal station" for women in every realm, including employment, education, marriage, and the family.[141] Paul Boller and Jean Tilford's *This Is Our Nation* (1961) similarly emphasized in discussing the success of the nineteenth-century woman's rights movement that "many prominent men" had "supported the movement."[142]

Unsurprisingly, these consensual accounts of women's history overlooked or underemphasized the powerful opposition that generations of suffragists fought against and strategized around. Barker described enfranchising women as a logical inevitability: "Since the United States wanted to be democratic—since the United States wanted to govern according to the wishes of its inhabitants—it was clear that, sooner or later, political rights would have to be extended to women."[143] Assumptions about the inevitability of woman suffrage became easy to make after the Nineteenth Amendment was no longer controversial. Barker glossed over the uncomfortable reality that many Americans at the time thought democracy did not require female voting.

James Frost's *History of the United States* (1968) reported that "[t]he patriotic services rendered by women during World War I quickly broke down resistance to the idea of women voting."[144] Women's contributions during World War I may have increased support for suffrage. Carrie Chapman Catt certainly celebrated those contributions as she led the National American Woman Suffrage Association (NAWSA).[145] President Wilson followed suit.[146] But anti-suffragism remained common after World War I, including among pivotal male politicians.

The Nineteenth Amendment passed the Senate on June 4, 1919, with just two votes to spare.[147] Maud Wood Park, NAWSA's lead congressional lobbyist,[148] thought the war had not swayed "a single vote" in Congress.[149] She concluded that the amendment managed to squeak through the Senate because of the state victories suffragists had already won.[150] Phrased bluntly, senators from states that enfranchised women feared alienating their female constituents and losing their seats.

Ratifying the Nineteenth Amendment required agreement from thirty-six state legislatures, so suffragists could afford no more than twelve holdouts. Eight states had already rejected the amendment by the time Tennessee became the thirty-sixth state to ratify.[151] Winning Tennessee took tireless campaigning that almost failed.[152] The Tennessee House approved the Nineteenth Amendment on August 18, 1920, with no votes to spare.[153]

In retrospect, it is easy to see that schoolchildren's textbooks from earlier eras sanitized women's struggles for equality and denied how sex discrimination remained legal, ubiquitous, and ardently defended. But many textbooks from more recent decades continue to obscure inequality and promote complacency, glossing over the persistent opposition and obstacles that women's rights activists have encountered while emphasizing or overstating America's progress.

Sometimes modern textbooks discount how central women's inequality has been to American history or downplay the vehement resistance to reform. John Garraty's *The Story of America* (1991) suggested that a sophisticated understanding of the past required suspending critical judgments about the Founders' commitments to white supremacy and male dominance, instructing young readers that "[t]o condemn George Washington for owning slaves and taking control of his rich wife's property would only show that we did not understand Washington and the Revolution."[154] James Banks's *United States: Adventures in Time and Place* (2001) did not discuss violent anti-suffragism or mention the furious men who harassed and assaulted suffragists as they marched in Washington the day before Wilson's 1913 presidential inauguration. Instead, the book advised teachers to use a newspaper report describing a more obscure suffrage demonstration in 1912 New York where "[t]he sight of the impressive column of women striding five abreast up the middle of the street stifled all thought of ridicule."[155] Daniel Boorstin's *History of the United States* (1981) similarly understated how difficult winning the Nineteenth Amendment had been, ignoring the amendment's razor-thin margin of victory in the Senate to assert that "President Wilson's support, in 1919, helped the suffrage amendment pass Congress with little opposition."[156]

Sometimes modern textbooks provide unrealistic estimates suggesting that barriers to women's equality should cause little concern because they are already on the verge of vanishing. Robert Divine's *America Past and Present* (2011) observed that "by 2004 women's wages still averaged only 76.5 percent of men's earnings," but told readers that "experts predicted" women would "reach pay equity with men" in "2018."[157] That year has passed and the gender pay gap has not disappeared as a matter of course. A recent report estimates based on past trends that America's gender pay gap will not close for full-time, year-round workers until 2066 and will not close for all workers until 2088.[158]

Sometimes modern textbooks obscure persistent inequality by overstating past reform. Exaggerating the Nineteenth Amendment's impact is routine. Textbooks report that the amendment "guarantee[d] all women the right to vote,"[159] "guaranteed every adult woman the right to a voice in the government of the country,"[160] extended "the right to vote" "to all women,"[161] gave "all women" the vote.[162] Daniel Boorstin contended that the Nineteenth Amendment made women "first-class citizens."[163] This amendment did end sex-based voting prohibitions. But it guaranteed neither the right to vote nor women's first-class citizenship. Struggles for sex equality, and battles over voting and voter suppression, rage to this day.[164]

Modern textbooks also commonly highlight more recent constitutional and statutory prohibitions on sex discrimination without discussing constraints on the reach of those prohibitions. Textbooks report that the 1964 Civil Rights Act banned sex discrimination in employment without mentioning how the Supreme Court has narrowed the scope of that legislation.[165] They observe that "[i]n 1971 the Court ruled that unequal treatment based only on sex violated the Fourteenth Amendment" without explaining how the Court has limited the boundaries of equal protection.[166] I will cite just two out of many examples here, and Chapter 5 will explore several more. *Geduldig v. Aiello* (1974) held that pregnancy discrimination is not a form of sex discrimination for purposes of the Fourteenth Amendment's Equal Protection Clause.

This decision exempts a pervasive form of gendered bias from the more demanding review, known as heightened scrutiny, that the Court applies in equal protection challenges to sex-based laws.[167] *Personnel Administrator v. Feeney* (1979) effectively confined the constitutional law of sex discrimination to focus only on government action that explicitly differentiates by sex. This decision makes legislation and regulation written in sex-neutral language essentially immune from challenge as unconstitutional sex discrimination— no matter how disproportionately the law harms women.[168] Both *Geduldig* and *Feeney* preserved important barriers to women's equality, and ignoring them leaves those setbacks out of the story.

In sum, decades of judicial opinions declaring victory over sex discrimination reflect and reinforce a longstanding cultural tradition outside the courts that similarly undercuts reform and promotes complacency through distorted tales about the nation. Like judges, popular authors for adults and children have spent more than a century exaggerating American progress toward sex equality, glossing over the opposition and obstacles that generations of women's rights activists have fought, and conveniently ignoring or actively defending persistent inequality.

PART III

CONSEQUENCES

How we think and talk about the world shapes what we do within it. America's distorted stories about itself have practical consequences to the present day.

The long tradition of wildly overstating the nation's progress toward sex equality has continued to skew American law and politics in the late twentieth and early twenty-first centuries, with each arena echoing and enforcing the other. Modern judges have relied on the premise that the United States has left sexism behind as a reason to avoid examining how contemporary policies and practices perpetuate women's inequality. Politicians and political activists have deployed declarations about America's achievement of sex equality to oppose feminist reform and promote regression while simultaneously purporting to support women's rights.

This part explores how the contention that sexism is confined to history warps the present. Chapter 5 focuses on the courts. Chapter 6 examines politics and political activism outside the courts.

Chapter 5
Courts Protect and Perpetuate Inequality

Generations of judges have been eager to tie women's inequality to times long past and places far away. Even as coverture's enforcement of male dominance continued to constrain women's lives in and out of marriage, nineteenth-century courts were already calling coverture principles "feudal,"[1] badges "of infirmity or serfdom,"[2] "the offspring of a rude and barbarous age."[3] Judges writing in the half century after the Nineteenth Amendment's 1920 ratification similarly described coverture as "feudal,"[4] "medieval,"[5] "ancient and medieval,"[6] "archaic,"[7] "outmoded,"[8] and from "a barbarous age."[9] These labels sounded like insults and functioned that way in some respects. Americans do not associate the Middle Ages with good government or stellar quality of life. But calling coverture medieval or feudal linked that regime to the Old World centuries before the founding of the United States, framing women's legal subordination as foreign to America's practices instead of integral to them.

The Supreme Court in the last decades of the twentieth century and the first decades of the twenty-first has accelerated and expanded these efforts to associate women's inequality with distant history rather than the here and now. The Court described coverture as "medieval" as early as 1960.[10] In January 1975, less than four years had passed since the Justices first struck down legislation for denying women equal protection.[11] But the Court was already calling sex stereotypes "archaic," as if sexism was a relic from a bygone age rather than an organizing feature of modern life.[12] At least fourteen of the Court's subsequent decisions similarly describe sexism as "archaic."[13] The Court also commonly chooses related adjectives, calling sexism "outdated,"[14] "outworn,"[15] "outmoded,"[16] or an "old" notion.[17] As with "medieval," these terms express disapproval while simultaneously suggesting that the Court and the nation have jettisoned such old-fashioned ways of thinking and governing.

This chapter explores how the urge to tie sexism to the past rather than the present has shaped judicial arguments and decisionmaking over the past half century and as recently as *Dobbs v. Jackson Women's Health Organization*, the

2022 Supreme Court decision removing federal constitutional constraints on legislative power to prohibit abortion.[18] Judges have used the premise that America has embraced sex equality as a springboard for upholding policies and practices without exploring how they maintain or exacerbate inequality. I focus on four United States Supreme Court cases preceding *Dobbs*, turn to state court decisions to place the Supreme Court's work in a wider judicial context, and then consider *Dobbs* itself. Examining archival and primary sources helps reveal a clearer picture of the stakes of this litigation than judges were willing to disclose.

The United States Supreme Court in the Decades Before *Dobbs*

Let's start with the late twentieth century and *Rostker v. Goldberg* (1981), which upheld women's exclusion from military registration.[19] The Supreme Court's decision perpetuated women's unequal citizenship with unequal responsibilities, while relying on the contention that America had repudiated sexism.

The United States has never included women in military registration or conscription. The congressmen who established the modern registration system after World War II, like lawmakers before them, governed with the certainty that women's ultimate responsibilities were domestic.[20] With that assumed, the Eightieth Congress—in office for 1947 and 1948—proceeded as if women's exclusion from registration required virtually no discussion.[21] The congressmen constructing America's postwar military apparatus were willing to let women volunteer for military service. But even then, lawmakers expected servicewomen to resign upon marriage and structure their lives around wifely duties. Federal legislators repeatedly invoked General Dwight D. Eisenhower's assurance that "few" servicewomen would stay long enough to earn retirement benefits because (in Eisenhower's oft-cited words) enlisted women "will come in and I believe after an enlistment or two enlistments they will ordinarily—and thank God—they will get married."[22] Congressmen also made a point of confirming that the military would continue to discharge servicewomen who became pregnant.[23] Military leaders offered multiple assurances, with Rear Admiral T.L. Sprague explaining "that under those circumstances, a woman's loyalty and duty are to her family and no longer to the service."[24]

Judges endorsed and enforced these ways of thinking. In the 1960s and 1970s, federal district and appellate courts (the lower federal courts that hear trials and appeals from those trials) routinely upheld the constitutionality of women's exclusion from military registration and conscription. They either treated the exclusion as so commonsensical that explanation was superfluous, or they took the opportunity to reaffirm their commitment to Mullerism and reason about the Constitution on the assumption that domesticity was women's core obligation.[25] *United States v. St. Clair*, a 1968 federal district court decision from New York, was a prime example of the latter approach and other courts quoted it extensively.[26] *St. Clair* recognized that Congress's decision to exclude women from registration and the draft rested on the same precept that the Supreme Court had recently affirmed in *Hoyt v. Florida* (1961)—that women were "still regarded as the center of home and family life."[27] District Judge Dudley Bonsal's opinion declared that Congress had "followed the teachings of history that if a nation is to survive, men must provide the first line of defense while women keep the home fires burning."[28] During oral argument, Bonsal had elaborated on how Congress's decision to prioritize women's domesticity promoted national security, suggesting that "[t]he theory was that women would stay home and have children so there'd be some soldiers for the next war."[29]

Federal legislators and judges had to revisit the issue of women's exclusion from military registration in the early 1980s. The United States had stopped drafting men in 1973 and stopped registering them in 1975.[30] But after the Soviet Union invaded Afghanistan, President Jimmy Carter wanted to reinstate registration to increase military readiness and demonstrate resolve.[31] Carter was both a Navy veteran and an Equal Rights Amendment advocate.[32] In February 1980, he asked Congress to authorize the registration of women along with men.[33] Carter highlighted the contributions that volunteer servicewomen were making to the military and emphasized that "[e]qual obligations" and "equal rights" were intertwined.[34]

Carter's proposal arrived while ERA ratification battles were keeping national attention on the law's treatment of women.[35] Congress chose continuity over reform, enacting legislation in June 1980 that funded registration for men but not women.[36] *Rostker* was a constitutional challenge to women's exclusion.[37]

The suit had begun in 1971, when four young men opposed to the Vietnam War brought a sweeping challenge to the constitutionality of registration and the draft.[38] The litigation proceeded slowly through the federal courts in Pennsylvania, although judges found it easy to dismiss all but one of the plaintiffs' arguments.[39] Judges would not hold that registration or conscription constituted involuntary servitude, or took property without due process, or violated the First Amendment.[40] The plaintiffs' constitutional objection to the sex-specificity of the law governing involuntary military service was harder to push aside.[41] In 1976, the Supreme Court had instructed the judiciary to subject explicitly sex-based legislation to heightened scrutiny, which is supposed to be a more skeptical and rigorous mode of judicial review than what courts apply to ordinary laws.[42] Using the heightened scrutiny framework, a three-judge federal district court concluded in July 1980 that male-only registration was unconstitutional.[43] If that judgment had stood, Congress would have had to choose between ending registration or expanding it to include women. But the Supreme Court reversed.[44]

The Supreme Court's argument in *Rostker* was grounded on the contention that the nation's lawmakers had left sexism behind. After introducing the case and reviewing the history of judicial deference to Congress about military affairs,[45] Justice William Rehnquist's majority opinion cited the hearings, floor debates, and committee reports where federal legislators had "extensively considered" Carter's 1980 proposal.[46] The Court wanted to emphasize at the outset that Congress had "thoroughly reconsider[ed] the question of exempting women from" military registration "and its basis for doing so."[47] Why did the Justices think this was such an important point to foreground? *Rostker* insisted that the extensiveness of Congress's 1980 discussion "*clearly establishes* that the decision to exempt women from registration was not the accidental by-product of a traditional way of thinking about females."[48]

The operative assumption appeared to be that sexism might explain the actions of long-ago Congresses, but would not infect contemporary lawmaking. Some discriminatory statutes might survive because legislators kept old laws on the books "unthinkingly or reflexively and not for any considered reason."[49] But if a modern-day Congress considered an issue "at great length, and Congress clearly expressed its purpose and intent," that was reason enough to conclude that Congress's decision did not reflect "a traditional way of thinking about" women because contemporary lawmakers have discarded such biases.[50]

Invoking the premise that modern legislators had moved beyond sexism helped take attention away from the Court's failure to examine the actual record thoroughly. *Rostker* highlighted how often Congress had discussed Carter's proposal while ignoring much of the content of that discussion.

The legislative history that the *Rostker* Court left out makes clear that the lawmakers who rejected Carter's proposal to register women—like the lawmakers who instituted the post-World War II registration system—presumed that men were obligated to serve their nation on the battlefield while women were responsible for staying home with their children. A 1980 report from the all-male Senate Armed Services Committee on military appropriations for

the upcoming year included a section that explained the committee's opposition to female registration, in less than five full pages.[51] *Rostker* quoted or
cited that report twenty-three times for insight into Congress's reasoning, but
never mentioned key passages that are impossible to miss in the short section
on registering women.[52] The undiscussed part of the Senate report made
the "specific" finding that the Carter administration had "given insufficient
attention to necessary changes in Selective Service rules, such as those governing the induction of young mothers, and to the strains on family life that
would result from the registration and possible induction of women."[53] The
committee recounted that "witnesses representing a variety of groups" had
testified "that drafting women would place unprecedented strains on family
life, whether in peacetime or in time of emergency."[54] The committee declared
that: "A decision which would result in a young mother being drafted and a
young father remaining home with the family in a time of national emergency
cannot be taken lightly, nor its broader implications ignored. The committee is strongly of the view that such a result, which would occur if women
were registered and inducted under the administration plan, is unwise and
unacceptable to a large majority of our people."[55]

Rostker similarly chose to ignore how individual lawmakers opposed to
registering women in 1980 used congressional hearings and floor debates
to present domesticity as a central responsibility for women rather than
men. Senator Sam Nunn of Georgia warned that registering and conscripting
women would interfere with women's domestic obligations because in "hundreds, perhaps even thousands of cases" there would be "fathers staying home
while mothers are shipped off for military service under a draft."[56] He was
certain that "society" was unprepared for the "shock" of seeing conscripted
women "leaving their husbands at home to take care of the children."[57] Senator John Warner of Virginia grounded his opposition to registering and
drafting women in his conviction that "a young mother" should not be "surrendering child care and going off to boot camp leaving the baby with the
husband."[58] Representative Marjorie Holt of Maryland critiqued Carter's proposal to register women by emphasizing that the "vast majority of" women
"want to stay home and be wives and mothers."[59] Senator Jake Garn of Utah
called the prospect of registering and drafting women "another part of the
degradation of the family, taking women out of the home."[60] He could not
"even conceive of that in the tradition of the American family and what it has
meant to society."[61]

I find it implausible to suppose that this legislative history simply escaped
Rehnquist's attention as he wrote for the Court in *Rostker*, especially given
his track record of keen interest in preserving traditional family life. Before

Rehnquist's confirmation to the Supreme Court in late 1971,[62] he wrote a memo on the ERA as an assistant attorney general in the Nixon administration. Rehnquist's 1970 memo observed that the ERA could jeopardize women's exclusion from the draft and concluded that "[t]he overall implication of the equal rights amendment is nothing less than the sharp reduction in importance of the family unit, with the eventual elimination of that unit by no means improbable."[63]

Rehnquist's majority opinion in *Rostker* relied on the premise that federal lawmakers had abandoned gendered ways of thinking as a reason to uphold Congress's recent decisionmaking without scrutinizing it. But the legislators rejecting female registration in 1980 still embraced commitments that the *Muller* Court would have applauded and shaped federal policy around the conviction that women belonged at home. Ignoring this continuity empowered lawmakers who insisted that men and women were on divergent life paths to help make that so.

As *Rostker* observed, that case was hardly the first time the Justices had upheld sex-based legislation after linking sexism to the past rather than the present.[64] Just three months before the *Rostker* decision, a plurality of the Court in *Michael M. v. Superior Court* (1981) had relied on similar reasoning to uphold a California law providing that only men and boys could be convicted of statutory rape and only girls could count as victims.[65]

California's statutory rape law had been sex-specific since the first session of the California Legislature enacted criminal legislation in 1850.[66] The legal framework established amidst the state's founding remained in place for generations, even as California lawmakers gradually raised the age of consent from ten (in 1850), to fourteen (in 1889), to sixteen (in 1897), to eighteen (in 1913), where it stayed.[67] When California incorporated its 1850 statute into a penal code in the 1870s, the code commissioners' note explained that the "provision embodies the well settled rule of the existing law; that a girl under ten years of age is incapable of giving any consent to an act of intercourse which can reduce it below the grade of rape." What the note discussed was unobjectionable. Of course, a girl younger than ten cannot consent to sex. What the note did not mention also spoke volumes. California's commissioners expressed no concerns about the decisionmaking capacity of equally young boys.[68]

The California Supreme Court echoed and amplified this line of reasoning when enforcing the state's sex-specific statutory rape law, explaining that the criminal prohibition reflected legislative concerns about female decisionmaking intertwined with legislative determination to safeguard female chastity. *People v. Verdegreen* (1895) reported that "[t]he obvious purpose of" the criminal prohibition was "the protection of society by protecting from violation the virtue of young and unsophisticated girls."[69] Society could not depend on girls to make prudent choices when faced with "the insidious approach and vile tampering" of male seducers, so the state needed to intervene because preserving "the virtue of young girls" was imperative.[70]

Almost seven decades later, the California Supreme Court offered the same basic account of the statutory rape law. If anything, *People v. Hernandez* (1964) emphasized the state's doubts about female decisionmaking even more emphatically. The court observed that California's sex-specific provision "conclusively presumed" that "the male" was "responsible for" sexual activity he participated in and simultaneously "presumed" that a girl younger than eighteen was "too innocent and naive to understand the implications and nature of her act."[71] *Hernandez* also elaborated on how California's sex-specific law reflected the legislature's judgment that female virtue—unlike its male counterpart—was essential for social order, reporting: "The law's concern with her capacity or lack thereof to so understand is explained in part by a popular conception of the social, moral and personal values which are preserved by the abstinence from sexual indulgence on the part of a young woman. An unwise disposition of her sexual favor is deemed to do harm both to herself and the social mores by which the community's conduct patterns are established. Hence the law of statutory rape intervenes in an effort to avoid such a disposition."[72]

California courts continued to acknowledge that the state's sex-specific prohibition on statutory rape was designed to safeguard female chastity from male lust even as the constitutional law governing sex discrimination started to shift. As late as 1975, a California appellate court took for granted that this criminal prohibition protected girls from "the desires and designs of older people of the opposite sex who are on the prowl."[73]

Michael M. brought a brighter spotlight to California's choice to define statutory rape as a sex-specific crime. The case began when a young man charged with statutory rape in 1978 challenged his prosecution on the ground that California's statute unconstitutionally discriminated based on sex.[74] A successful suit would have meant that California could keep its statutory rape prohibition only by rewriting the legislation in sex-neutral terms.

Michael Douglas McMillan—his lawyers used his full name when litigating in California and it was all over the California press—was an unlikely champion for sex equality.[75] He had reportedly turned to violence after the sixteen-year-old he was kissing, Sharon, refused to take off her pants.[76] Sharon testified at the preliminary hearing that McMillan had "slugged [her] in the face" "about two or three times," leaving bruises.[77] In her words: "I said,

'No,' and I was trying to get up and he hit me back down on the bench and then I just said to myself, 'Forget it,' and I let him do what he wanted to do."[78]

The District Attorney's office had pursued the statutory rape charge after deciding that there was insufficient evidence to win a forcible rape conviction.[79] I suspect that the prosecutors who reached this conclusion were worried that judges and jurors would be unsympathetic to Sharon if they considered her unchaste. Charging McMillan with statutory rape made questions about Sharon's consent legally irrelevant. Even then, judges did not write about Sharon kindly. The California Supreme Court introduced her by reporting that "Sharon, 16, engaged in sexual intercourse after an amorous interlude on a park bench."[80] When the case reached the United States Supreme Court, Justice Rehnquist's plurality opinion wasted little time before observing that Sharon "had already been drinking" when she met Michael.[81]

Justice Harry Blackmun went further when writing about Sharon in his concurring opinion explaining his own reasons for upholding California's law. Americans often remember Blackmun as a liberal icon for writing the majority opinion in *Roe v. Wade* (1973), the now-overruled decision where the Supreme Court first placed constitutional limits on legislative power to restrict abortion.[82] But Blackmun revealed a different side of himself eight years later in his *Michael M.* concurrence. He insisted that it was "only fair" to Michael "to point out that his partner, Sharon, appears not to have been an unwilling participant in at least the initial stages of the intimacies that took place the night of June 3, 1978."[83] The sentence ended with a footnote quoting Sharon's preliminary hearing testimony, including her account of Michael's violence.[84] Blackmun did not express sympathy for Sharon. Immediately after that footnote, he described "Petitioner's and Sharon's nonacquaintance with each other before the incident; their drinking; their withdrawal from the others of the group; their foreplay, in which she willingly participated and seems to have encouraged; and the closeness of their ages" as "factors that should make this case an unattractive one to prosecute at all."[85] Note Blackmun's deployment of the term "foreplay," which suggested that the "initial" "intimacies" Sharon had consented to would naturally lead to intercourse.

A half year after McMillan's statutory rape arrest, he reportedly attacked another woman while robbing the store where she was working as a clerk. Police reported that McMillan knocked the woman to the ground by striking her head with a tire wrench, choked her with an apron he wrapped around her neck, and threatened to murder her if she disclosed the robbery to anyone.[86] She had attended school with McMillan,[87] and reportedly identified him to the police shortly after the attack.[88] He pled guilty.[89]

Meanwhile, McMillan's challenge to California's statutory rape law proceeded. The judges hearing *Michael M.* in the California Supreme Court and the United States Supreme Court were not adjudicating the wisdom of punishing McMillan in particular. They were assessing the constitutionality of the sex-specific criminal prohibition in all contexts, including where both parties had consented to sex without coercion.[90]

California's Supreme Court upheld the law in early November 1979.[91] At the time, there was some possibility that the California Legislature might make statutory rape a sex-neutral offense before McMillan's litigation went any further. John Knox, a Democratic Assemblyman, had introduced a bill in April 1979 that would have rewritten the state's statutory rape prohibition to criminalize nonmarital sex with anyone under eighteen when the perpetrator was "more than 5 years older than the victim."[92]

But Knox's bill did not become law. In October 1979, a retired California Municipal Court Judge, Coleman Stewart, wrote an opinion piece in his local newspaper contending that Knox's bill would "[l]egalize sexual attacks on a minor as long as there is less than five years of age difference between the attacker and the victim."[93] The accusation misdescribed how Knox's statutory rape provision would have functioned. If someone sexually attacked a child, other criminal prohibitions beyond the statutory rape law would penalize that conduct. Nonetheless, the charge became the centerpiece of a Republican direct mail campaign launched as computer technology was facilitating that strategy. In or around November 1979, the California Republican Assembly—a conservative group that claimed to have ten thousand members in California—sent a fundraising letter over the signature of Patrick Nolan, a Republican Assemblyman who would later become the Assembly's Republican leader.[94] The letter repeated retired Judge Stewart's mischaracterization of Knox's proposal and warned that the bill would render "the decent citizens of California defenseless against attack from perverted sex-crime offenders." It asked for contributions to fight Knox's bill and campaign against "the liberal Democrats who continually vote yes on this type of legislation," urged readers to deluge Knox with correspondence, and solicited signatures on petitions to the Assembly's Criminal Justice Committee.[95] For the time-pressed, the mailer included postcards preprinted with criticism to send to Knox. He reported receiving thirty-two hundred of them.[96] Knox told the media in early December 1979 that he would not be pushing for the legislation in the coming year.[97] The California Assembly never had a committee hearing or floor debate on the bill, which was officially dead by January 1980.[98]

Diane Watson, a Democrat who was the second woman and the first African American woman elected to the California Senate,[99] then introduced a bill in March 1980 that would have criminalized any nonmarital sex with someone under eighteen.[100] The available legislative history makes reconstructing what happened to Watson's bill difficult. The California Senate's records just indicate that the bill was scheduled for a committee hearing in April 1980 and that the hearing was canceled at Watson's request. The legislative session adjourned in November 1980 without further action on Watson's bill.[101]

At least one more reform effort emerged that year, but was no more successful. In May 1980, Leo McCarthy, a Democrat who was the Speaker of the California Assembly,[102] proposed a preprint bill that would have made statutory rape a sex-neutral crime. For example, McCarthy's draft legislation would have criminalized sex with anyone younger than fourteen and would have criminalized sex with a fourteen- or fifteen-year-old when the perpetrator was at least four years older than the child.[103] By July, California newspapers were reporting that McCarthy was circulating his preprint and inviting public discussion.[104] But McCarthy never transformed the preprint into an officially introduced bill in 1980, and the state's sex-specific statutory rape law remained unchanged when McMillan's appeal reached the United States Supreme Court.[105] The Justices upheld the law's constitutionality in March 1981.[106]

Like the *Rostker* Court, the *Michael M.* plurality used the premise that modern lawmakers had left gendered thinking behind as a reason not to inquire further. Without providing any citations or quotations, the plurality reported that: "Subsequent to the decision below, the California Legislature considered and rejected proposals to render [the statutory rape prohibition] gender neutral, thereby ratifying the judgment of the California Supreme Court."[107] The statement ignored how the legislative maneuvering had produced no committee hearings, floor debates, or votes. The plurality saw no need to dive into what California legislators had actually said and done in 1979 and 1980 or to examine how generations of California authorities had previously explained this criminal provision. Instead, the plurality took the simple fact that some lawmakers had recently thought about the statutory rape provision as "enough to answer petitioner's contention that the statute was the accidental by-product of a traditional way of thinking about females."[108] The Justices assumed and insisted that contemporary legislators had jettisoned "outmoded" ideas about women and relied on that assumption when avoiding further investigation.[109]

Michael M.'s framing of gendered reasoning as part of the past rather than the present was particularly ironic because the plurality's own opinion illustrated how legal authorities continued to presume that women rather than men would organize their lives around domestic responsibilities. The California prosecutors seeking to convict McMillan under the sex-specific statutory rape law apparently recognized that the state's long-standing explanations for this criminal provision—the inadequacy of female decisionmaking and the preciousness of female virtue—no longer seemed as convincing as they once had. By 1978, California's lawyers had developed a new justification for the law. They contended that the statute was meant to prevent nonmarital teenage pregnancies, which sounded like a still-viable policy goal—even if there was no evidence that California had enacted or maintained the statutory rape prohibition for that reason.[110] Rather than explore the available evidence on California's actual legislative motivations, the *Michael M.* plurality seized on this new justification.[111] The plurality explained that subjecting only males to conviction for statutory rape was fair because "the risk of pregnancy itself constitutes a substantial deterrence to young females" contemplating sexual relations. In short, the plurality argued that the possibility of conceiving an unwanted pregnancy was threat and punishment enough for women or girls having sex with teenage boys. In contrast, the plurality maintained that a man or boy "*by nature*, suffers few of the consequences of his conduct" if he impregnates a teenage girl: "No similar natural sanctions deter males. A criminal sanction imposed solely on males thus serves to roughly 'equalize' the deterrents on the sexes."[112]

This claim purported to rest on biological sex differences rather than "the baggage of sexual stereotypes."[113] Yet the assertion that males avoid "virtually all of the significant harmful and inescapably identifiable consequences of teenage pregnancy" depended on the implicit presumption that fathers will neglect their nonmarital children while mothers raise them—another version of Mullerism's insistence that women must prioritize domesticity while men may prioritize themselves.[114] Biology neither requires mothers to participate in their children's lives nor dictates that fathers escape procreation's consequences. A man evades those consequences when he does not raise his child.

Michael M. both assumed women's disproportionate responsibility for nonmarital children and helped maintain that disparity. Nurturing and supporting a child are infinitely harder from prison. But the Justices upheld a statute that subjected only males to incarceration, even when both participants were the same age and shared decisionmaking equally. The Justices relied on the premise that America had moved past sexism as a reason to uphold a sex-based statute without exploring how the legislation perpetuated inequality.

There was one last irony. The years courts spent rationalizing and affirming California's sex-specific law ultimately helped McMillan escape punishment. He was on parole from the robbery and assault case by the time the United States Supreme Court decided *Michael M.* on March 23, 1981.[115] California moved quickly to proceed with McMillan's statutory rape trial only to discover that he had already disappeared.[116] After McMillan was finally found and arrested in August 1984, California scheduled his statutory rape trial for that October. But Sharon was twenty-three by then and perhaps unwilling to revisit what happened years earlier. The District Attorney's investigators were unable to locate her and subpoena her to testify.[117] The District Attorney reported in mid-October 1984 that law enforcement authorities believed that Sharon had left the region voluntarily. Without the state's key witness, the District Attorney asked the trial court to dismiss the statutory rape charge against McMillan.[118] California did not make statutory rape a sex-neutral offense until 1993.[119]

We will return shortly to how framing sexism as part of the past rather than the present has shaped the Supreme Court's constitutional decisionmaking, following that story into the new millennium. But before leaving the late twentieth century, I wanted to explore how this framing has also shaped the judicial response to Title VII's statutory prohibition on sex discrimination in employment—the prohibition whose inclusion in the 1964 Civil Rights Act Chapter 1 discussed.

Consider *Hishon v. King & Spalding* (1984).[120] When the Court decided that case three years after *Michael M.* and *Rostker*, Justice Lewis Powell, Jr., drew on the premise that sex discrimination was no longer a problem to urge skepticism about a woman's allegations of workplace bias. Elizabeth Anderson Hishon had been an associate in a large Atlanta law firm from 1972 until 1979, when the partners terminated her employment because they decided not to elevate her to partnership.[121] She sued in federal court in Atlanta, contending that the firm, King & Spalding, had violated Title VII by discriminating against her because of her sex.[122] Hishon, a real estate attorney, later explained that she was "not typically one to march in a parade. But there comes a point—and I reached that point—where you have to take a stand."[123]

Indeed, even a cursory review of the situation provided ample reason to suspect that sexism might have warped King & Spalding's decisionmaking. The firm was founded in 1885, but had hired only one female attorney before Hishon.[124] Hishon's predecessor spent 1944 to 1977 as King & Spalding's sole "permanent associate,"[125] watching as more than fifty men who joined the firm after her became partners while she was never promoted.[126]

King & Spalding's annual gala reflected and reinforced the centrality of white Christian men to the firm and the marginalization of everyone else. The firm held these celebrations at the Piedmont Driving Club. Many King & Spalding partners were members of this exclusive club—including the leader of the firm's real estate department, where Hishon worked.[127] But Piedmont barred Jews and African Americans from joining and admitted white Christian women only "by inheritance."[128] King & Spalding did not hire its first Jewish associate until 1967 and did not hire its first African American associate until 1971.[129]

Hishon lost in the federal district and appellate courts. The judges who dismissed her case did not consider the merits of her allegations or give her the opportunity to conduct discovery investigating whether King & Spalding had evidence that would support her claim that the firm had discriminated against her. Instead, the lower courts accepted King & Spalding's argument that the firm's decision to deny Hishon partnership did not count as an employment decision within the meaning of Title VII's prohibition on sex discrimination in employment.[130] It was a bold assertion. The firm had hired Hishon, set the terms and conditions of her work, and fired her pursuant to King & Spalding's "up-or-out policy" when the partners chose not to promote her.[131]

District Judge Newell Edenfield's explanation for his narrow reading of Title VII was explicitly gendered and solicitous about other societal hierarchies as well. He analogized a law firm's decisions about which associates to promote to a man's decision about which woman he wanted to marry, perhaps the most intimate choice of his life. Hishon—who was white, Christian, and in her thirties when King & Spalding denied her partnership—had not reported experiencing race, religious, or age discrimination.[132] But Judge Edenfield, who was a partner at a Georgia law firm before his appointment to the bench, seemed well aware that those biases also pervaded law firms.[133] His 1980 opinion insisted that Title VII left law firms selecting new partners as unconstrained as a man deciding whether to propose, even when firms (like romantic suitors) preferred partners of a particular sex, race, religion, and age. On Edenfield's account, "worthy and desirable qualities" for a business partner—or a wife—"are not necessarily divided evenly among the applicants according to race, age, sex or religion, and in some they just are not present at all. To use or apply Title VII to coerce a mismatched or unwanted partnership too closely resembles a statute for the enforcement of shotgun weddings."[134] The United States Court of Appeals in Atlanta affirmed in 1982.[135] The Supreme Court agreed to hear the case and resolve whether a law firm's decisions about who to select as partners are subject to Title VII.[136]

By that point, Hishon's lawsuit had been focusing years of public attention on King & Spalding's treatment of women. The firm made at least two adjustments after Hishon filed suit. By the time the district court issued its judgment in 1980, King & Spalding had hired its first female partner, an achievement Judge Edenfield duly noted.[137] By the time the Supreme Court heard oral argument in the fall of 1983, the firm had a second female partner.[138]

But the fundamentals of King & Spalding's culture and power dynamics appeared unchanged despite the national spotlight. In the summer of 1983—when Supreme Court oral argument was imminent—King & Spalding reportedly held a "bathing-suit competition" featuring "stunned" and "humiliated" female summer associates. First prize reportedly went to a woman about to begin her third year at Harvard Law School. The King & Spalding partner who bestowed the award reportedly announced: "She has the body we'd like to see more of."[139]

That October, Justice Powell used the Supreme Court oral argument as an opportunity to publicize his doubts about Hishon's contention that King & Spalding had discriminated against her. Powell's skepticism did not rest on a review of Hishon's evidence, as the lower courts had denied Hishon the opportunity to gather and present her evidence on the merits. Instead, Powell's predisposition to discount Hishon's allegations came from his foundational assumption that sex discrimination—like race discrimination—was a historical problem now overcome. Powell reportedly had "a look of incredulity on his face" during oral argument.[140] He asserted from the bench that a law firm partner "selecting new partners" wants "the strongest possible person regardless of sex, color, or race." Powell conceded that this "may not have been true 20 or 30 years ago when people had lots of prejudices they don't have now." But he insisted that America had left such biases behind, proclaiming that he could not "imagine a law firm deliberately discriminating against somebody if the firm made a judgment that the individual would increase the profits of the law firm."[141]

Powell made these pronouncements at a time when almost every partner in a large law firm in the United States was a white man. A 1984 survey covering ninety-two of the hundred biggest law firms found that just five percent of the partners were female, only 0.65% were black, and only 0.22% were Hispanic.[142]

Powell's own experience with law firm practice mirrored the demographics at King & Spalding. Powell was a named partner in Virginia's biggest law firm before he joined the Supreme Court.[143] All his partners in Hunton, Williams, Gay, Powell and Gibson were white men.[144] On October 22, 1971, the day President Richard Nixon sent Powell's nomination to the Senate,[145] an

African American lawyer reported that one of the senior partners in Powell's firm had told him in December 1969 that it would "be a very long time before this firm considers hiring a black associate, because the older partners would object."[146] Powell denied that his firm discriminated, but admitted belonging to two clubs that barred African Americans and Jews from membership.[147]

Decades after Powell expressed doubts about Hishon's case at oral argument, white men continue to dominate large law firm partnerships. A 2020 survey of the two hundred biggest law firms in the United States found that twenty-one percent of the equity partners were female, around four percent were Asian/Pacific Islander, almost three percent were Hispanic/Latinx, just under two percent were black, and 0.14% were Native American.[148]

The Supreme Court ultimately held in *Hishon* that Title VII reaches a law firm's decisions about who to choose as partners, so firms can face liability if they discriminate based on race, color, religion, sex, or national origin.[149] But this hard-fought victory was just a first step. Title VII plaintiffs have low success rates.[150] The crucial next question for people like Hishon was whether and when courts would be willing to conclude that a firm actually had discriminated.

Powell's concurrence addressed this pivotal issue. He suggested that courts should be skeptical about plaintiffs alleging bias, contending that: "In admission decisions made by law firms, it is now widely recognized—as it should be—that in fact neither race nor sex is relevant."[151] Powell was used to writing about race this way,[152] and he did not cite any evidence establishing that law firms had moved beyond race and sex discrimination. He simply insisted that it was true. Here again, a Justice had begun with the premise that Americans had left discrimination in the past and relied on that foundational assumption as a reason to direct scrutiny away from how ongoing practices maintain inequality.

King & Spalding was perhaps less confident that the partners' decision-making had been unbiased. The Supreme Court's ruling meant that Hishon was "entitled to her day in court to prove her allegations."[153] King & Spalding apparently found that prospect unappealing. Less than a month after the Supreme Court announced its decision, the firm settled with Hishon. The terms were undisclosed, but the firm reportedly paid Hishon a "substantial" sum.[154]

I will turn now from the late twentieth century to the early decades of the new millennium. *Sessions v. Morales-Santana* (2017) intertwined incremental progress with further entrenchment of a gendered status quo.[155]

This case considered legislation governing when nonmarital children born abroad can obtain United States citizenship.[156] Federal law on the subject has been sex-specific since Congress first explicitly addressed the citizenship status of this category of children in a 1940 statute.[157] Luis Ramón Morales-Santana's suit focused on the constitutionality of sex-specific parental residency requirements.[158] Morales-Santana was born in the Dominican Republic in 1962 to unmarried parents, one of whom was a United States citizen.[159] If his mother had been the citizen parent, Morales-Santana would have been a United States citizen at birth so long as his mother had lived in the United States for at least one continuous year before Morales-Santana was born.[160] But Morales-Santana's father was the parent with United States citizenship.[161] Federal law blocked a citizen father in that situation from conveying his citizenship to his foreign-born nonmarital child unless the father had lived in the United States before his child was born for periods totaling at least ten years, including at least five years after the father turned fourteen.[162] Morales-Santana's father was twenty days short of satisfying this requirement when Morales-Santana was born, having left the United States just before turning nineteen.[163]

Morales-Santana held that the Constitution prohibits Congress from imposing parental residency requirements that distinguish between the children of citizen fathers and the children of citizen mothers.[164] Justice Ruth Bader Ginsburg's majority opinion emphasized how sex-differentiated parental residency requirements embodied legislative assumptions that mothers will be committed to their nonmarital children while fathers will "care little about, and have scant contact with, their nonmarital children."[165] The Court explained that the lengthy parental residency requirement for the foreign-born nonmarital children of American fathers reflected Congress's concerns about whether those fathers "would counteract the influence" that foreign mothers would have on their children. "For unwed citizen mothers, however, there was no need for a prolonged residency prophylactic: The alien father, who might transmit foreign ways, was presumptively out of the picture."[166]

Morales-Santana repeatedly associated this mode of gendered reasoning with the past rather than the present. The Court called the sex-differentiated parental residency requirements "stunningly anachronistic" and described the assumption "that unwed fathers are invariably less qualified and entitled than mothers to take responsibility for nonmarital children" as an "obsolescing view."[167] The opinion emphasized that the sex-specific requirements dated "from an era when the lawbooks of our Nation were rife with overbroad generalizations about the way men and women are," a time before the Court subjected sex-based legislation to heightened scrutiny.[168] The statement linked the legal regime to bygone lawmakers and glossed over the many more recent legislators who had maintained and even expanded sex-based citizenship rules long after the advent of heightened scrutiny. Most notably, a 1986 federal statute kept in place the one-continuous-year parental residency requirement for the foreign-born nonmarital children of American mothers while providing that an American father could transmit his United States citizenship to a nonmarital child born abroad on or after November 14, 1986, only if the father had lived in the United States before his child was born for periods totaling at least five years, including at least two years after the father turned fourteen.[169] The 1986 statute also added a new obstacle to United States citizenship that the nonmarital children of American fathers face and the nonmarital children of American mothers avoid. Going forward, a nonmarital child born abroad to an American father and a foreign mother must establish that his "father unless deceased has agreed in writing to provide financial support for the child until such child reaches the age of eighteen years."[170] Subsequent Congresses have permitted this sex-specific regime to survive into the twenty-first century.

Morales-Santana's efforts to tie gendered reasoning to long-gone history rather than more current events helped direct attention away from exploring how legal authorities continue to embrace and accommodate presumptions about men spurning their domestic responsibilities. In fact, aspects of the Court's own decisionmaking in *Morales-Santana* protect congressional commitments to sex stereotypes and perpetuate gendered access to citizenship.

First, consider the remedy the Court devised in *Morales-Santana*, which did not help a single additional person acquire United States citizenship. After the Court decided that the Constitution prohibits sex-differentiated parental residency requirements, the Justices had at least two options in restructuring parental residency regulation for foreign-born nonmarital children. One was to extend Congress's openness to the children of American mothers so this welcome also greeted the children of American fathers. The other was to extend Congress's skepticism about the children of American fathers so this wariness also applied (prospectively) to the children of American mothers.[171] The Court took the latter path, arguing that Congress would have made that choice.[172] I have no doubt that retaining lengthy parental residency requirements for the nonmarital children of American fathers does reflect Congress's policy preferences, in both the mid-twentieth century as well as today. But *Morales-Santana* did not explore whether Congress's commitment to preserving those restrictions is entangled with lawmakers' persistent expectations about paternal disengagement. After *Morales-Santana*, Congress can still govern on the premise that acquiring United States citizenship through a nonmarital American father should be difficult because most men in that situation will have scant contact with their children—so long as lawmakers subject the nonmarital children of American mothers to the same parental residency regulation.

Second, *Morales-Santana* discussed sex stereotypes about committed mothers and irresponsible fathers as if they were historical relics while simultaneously endorsing the continued constitutionality of another sex-based citizenship rule that evinces and enforces the same gendered assumptions. *Morales-Santana* made clear that the Court remains committed to its 2001 decision in *Nguyen v. Immigration and Naturalization Service*.[173]

Nguyen upheld Congress's paternal acknowledgment requirement, which provides that an American father seeking to transmit United States citizenship to a foreign-born nonmarital child with a foreign mother must formally acknowledge paternity before the child turns eighteen—by either legitimating the child, declaring paternity in writing and under oath, or obtaining a court order establishing paternity.[174] The requirement and its deadline do not apply to foreign-born nonmarital children with American mothers and foreign fathers.[175]

Like sex-based parental residency rules, the paternal acknowledgment requirement rests on gendered expectations that women's domestic responsibilities are mandatory and men's optional. Congress first enacted the paternal acknowledgment requirement in 1940, after President Franklin D. Roosevelt's administration proposed it.[176] Roosevelt had instructed his Secretary of State, Attorney General, and Secretary of Labor "to review the nationality laws of the United States," "recommend revisions," and "codify those laws into one comprehensive nationality law for submission to the Congress."[177] The executive branch's report to Congress explaining the administration's proposed paternal acknowledgment requirement emphasized that the mother of a nonmarital child was "bound to maintain it as its natural guardian" while mentioning no similar natural ties or obligations between fathers and their nonmarital children.[178]

Indeed, the paternal acknowledgment requirement not only reflects gendered assumptions about paternal disengagement, it also makes distant relationships more likely. The requirement can separate fathers and children who would otherwise be closer by denying children United States citizenship because their fathers failed to formalize paternal acknowledgment in time. Tuan Anh Nguyen's American father, Joseph Boulais, had raised him in Texas from the age of five. Their emotional and biological ties were indisputable. But the United States denied Nguyen citizenship and considered him deportable because his father did not complete the proper paperwork before Nguyen turned eighteen.[179] Boulais later reported that he had assumed Nguyen was a United States citizen and not known about the paternal acknowledgment requirement until too late.[180]

The paternal acknowledgment requirement also helps shirking fathers evade responsibility. Suppose an American father does not want to devote any time or money to his foreign-born nonmarital child. Suppose he hopes to keep his American family from learning about the child.[181] The paternal acknowledgment requirement means that the child is unlikely to become a United States citizen with the right to live in her father's country unless she has her father's timely cooperation. The rule facilitates paternal escape by subjecting children to what one federal district judge called "the personal vagaries and consciences of their fathers."[182] In contrast, federal law does not offer a ready-made escape route to American mothers hoping to shed their maternal obligations. A mother's cooperation is unnecessary to make her foreign-born nonmarital child a United States citizen.

Nguyen's judgment upholding the paternal acknowledgment requirement protected and perpetuated the same gendered assumptions about maternal duty and paternal disengagement that *Morales-Santana* suggested were "anachronistic" and "obsolescing."[183] The *Nguyen* opinion also appeared to reason within those assumptions, enshrining a version of Mullerism in the twenty-first century. *Nguyen* emphasized that: "One concern in this context has always been with young people, men for the most part, who are on duty with the Armed Forces in foreign countries." *Nguyen* then presented statistics suggesting that many American men were in the military when their foreign-born nonmarital children were conceived. The Court observed that the United States stationed 1,041,094 members of the military abroad in 1969—Nguyen's birth year—and stationed 252,763 abroad in 1999.[184] Why highlight that information in defending the law? The paternal acknowledgment requirement applies whether or not the father was enlisted at the time of conception. However, Americans are especially primed to expect paternal neglect from servicemen who father nonmarital children with foreign women while stationed abroad. Foregrounding the prevalence of servicemen helped the *Nguyen* Court imply that Congress was right to assume that nonmarital fathers will absent themselves from their children's lives.

Yet *Morales-Santana* endorsed the *Nguyen* decision and the continued constitutionality of the paternal acknowledgment requirement. Indeed, *Morales-Santana* seemed to discount the harm the paternal acknowledgment requirement inflicts. *Nguyen* had called that requirement a "minimal" hurdle "to the acquisition of citizenship."[185] *Morales-Santana* agreed, contending that the paternal acknowledgment requirement could "fairly be described as minimal."[186] This was a remarkable way to characterize an immovable deadline that denies United States citizenship to people who would be citizens if their American parent was female.

These aspects of *Morales-Santana* are particularly striking because Ruth Bader Ginsburg wrote the Court's opinion.[187] Ginsburg devoted much of the 1970s to feminist litigation, including in the *Frontiero v. Richardson* case that Chapter 1 discussed.[188] Justice Ginsburg dissented in *Nguyen*, joining an opinion that criticized the paternal acknowledgment requirement and the *Nguyen* majority for enforcing sex stereotypes.[189]

But the five other Justices who joined Ginsburg's majority opinion in *Morales-Santana* included two conservatives with perhaps unshakable commitments to *Nguyen*.[190] Justice Anthony Kennedy wrote for the *Nguyen* majority and so was particularly invested in that precedent.[191] Chief Justice John Roberts, Jr., clerked for William Rehnquist, who sided with Kennedy in *Nguyen*.[192] When Ginsburg wrote *Morales-Santana* for a majority that needed at least one conservative vote to eliminate sex-differentiated parental residency requirements, she definitely wanted to keep her majority coalition and perhaps feared that a majority opinion written by another Justice would be worse. She chose to draw on a common story that America tells about itself and associate sex stereotypes with the past rather than the present.

State Courts

Strategically exaggerating progress also appeals to state courts, within and beyond constitutional cases. This section places the United States Supreme Court's decisionmaking in a wider judicial frame by highlighting two important contexts where state judges have leaned on overstated proclamations about American advances when choosing not to examine whether their decisions contribute to women's inequality. The first example focuses on legal hostility to alimony and the second explores legal leniency for marital rape.

Courts adjudicating alimony disputes began exaggerating women's market opportunities as early as the 1950s. In 1955, for example, the median woman working full-time and year-round earned just 63.9 cents for every dollar a full-time, year-round male worker made.[193] Legislators and judges were content to let sex discrimination pervade work life and expected women to prioritize household labor over market employment.[194] But the Florida Supreme Court nevertheless insisted in a 1955 decision affirming a denial of alimony that "the opportunities for self-support by the wife are so abundant," proclaiming: "Times have now changed. The broad, practically unlimited opportunities for women in the business world of today are a matter of common knowledge."[195]

A New York appellate court adjudicating an alimony dispute in 1956 quoted the Florida Supreme Court's declaration about women's "practically unlimited opportunities" and agreed that "[t]he position of the wife has changed."[196]

The resurgence of feminist mobilization in the late 1960s and early 1970s inspired more divorcing or divorced men to make assertions along these lines when seeking to avoid or terminate alimony obligations. Sometimes they presented arguments in court that emphasized the rise of the "Women's Liberation movement" and "the recent emancipation of women socially and economically and particularly in the area of employment opportunity."[197]

Sometimes divorcing men had additional public forums available to them. James Hayes chaired the California Assembly's Judiciary Committee in 1969 and coauthored California's Family Law Act, which restructured the state's divorce law and instituted no-fault divorce (divorce without having to prove spousal wrongdoing).[198] The new legislation provided that judges considering whether and to what extent to award alimony should take into account "the ability of the supported spouse to engage in gainful employment without interfering with the interests of the children of the parties in the custody of such spouse."[199] By the end of July 1969, the bill had passed the California Legislature and was awaiting Governor Ronald Reagan's signature, which would come on September 4.[200] Hayes took advantage of this interim. On August 8, 1969, he presented the California Assembly with a report he had written for the Assembly's Judiciary Committee and declared that the report "represents the Committee's intent."[201]

Hayes's committee report insisted that the nation was leaving women's inequality behind and argued that this premise should guide courts deciding whether to award alimony or to modify an existing award. In his words: "When our divorce law was originally drawn, woman's role in society was almost totally that of mother and homemaker. She could not even vote. Today, increasing numbers of married women are employed, even in the professions. In addition, they have long been accorded full civil rights. Their approaching equality with the male should be reflected in the law governing marriage dissolution and in the decisions of courts with respect to matters incident to dissolution."[202]

James Hayes produced this report while in the midst of divorcing his wife, Janne. She had four children with James and had not worked in the market since 1941, the year she married him.[203] James and Janne agreed to a property settlement in 1966 that required him to pay her $650 a month until she remarried or either of them died.[204] The alimony order that the California Superior Court ultimately issued in the summer of 1969 tracked this agreement.[205] The

Hayes divorce became final in November 1969, shortly before the Family Law Act went into effect at the start of 1970.[206]

Soon after his divorce, James took the time to publish an article about the Family Law Act in the *American Bar Association Journal*. The 1970 article contended that "[t]he California Legislature" had "concluded that [married women's] approaching equality with the male should be reflected in the law governing marriage dissolution, support and custody." This pronouncement appeared under a heading that told the legal profession: "Women's Rights Observed by California Legislature."[207]

In August 1972, Governor Reagan appointed James to be a Los Angeles County Supervisor.[208] James won a full term in the November 1972 election.[209] Just three years had passed since his divorce, and his new job paid $36,393 a year.[210] But James had remarried and was eager to shed his obligations to his first wife.[211] Five weeks after the election, he went back to California Superior Court seeking to terminate his alimony payments to Janne.[212]

James's brief insisting that he should owe Janne nothing quoted the passage he had written into the Judiciary Committee report about married women's "approaching equality"—without identifying James as the author of that language.[213] James's emphasis on American progress toward sex equality seemed designed to gloss over persistent gendered disparities that left men like him economically secure and women like his former wife economically vulnerable. Janne's full-time assumption of domestic duties freed James to pursue career success and political power, and he departed their marriage with those assets. At the same time, Janne's homemaking meant that she did not develop her market skills or earning capacity, and she departed their marriage with those liabilities. The alimony that James had promised to pay was Janne's only source of income.[214] Her March 1973 brief responding to James explained that she was not qualified for any job "except for the most menial" and was physically incapable of performing that kind of labor because of multiple disabling conditions, including arthritis, asthma, rheumatism, and scoliosis.[215] The brief described Janne as "a housewife for some 30 years" and argued: "To tell her that she has now attained equality which means that she must now go out and support herself is a cruel and inhuman joke and a perversion of the equality movement."[216]

Three weeks after receiving Janne's brief, the California Superior Court agreed to reduce James's alimony obligation. The judge lowered the required monthly payments in phases so they dropped from $650 to $300 by October 1974.[217]

James was still unsatisfied and went back to court in June 1974. By that point, his annual income had risen to $39,288.[218] Nonetheless, he tried again for a judicial order terminating his alimony obligation.[219] This time, another California Superior Court judge agreed to reduce the alimony to $200 a month starting in July 1975.[220] With her alimony slashed to the bone, Janne applied for food stamps from the federal government and welfare benefits from her county.[221] James was unabashed about Janne's resort to public assistance for the impoverished, telling the press: "It frankly doesn't embarrass me at all."[222]

James's run of legal victories ultimately hit an obstacle he helped construct. In October 1975, the California Court of Appeal held that the property settlement James had reached with Janne created a monthly obligation for him to pay her $650 that was not subject to judicial modification.[223] Yet even that judgment did not dissuade James from continuing to litigate in an effort to evade his responsibilities.[224] Janne was still depending on food stamps as of 1977.[225] Meanwhile, the mode of reasoning that James Hayes pursued as a legislator and a litigant persisted.

Many courts denying, reducing, or terminating alimony in the years after the resurgence of feminist mobilization relied on overstated accounts of the nation's progress in achieving sex equality. Even by the end of the 1970s, the median woman working full-time and year-round still earned just 59.7 cents for every dollar a male full-time, year-round worker made.[226] A 1979 federal government survey tracking the civilian noninstitutional population found that just 49.4% of married women whose husbands were present had any participation in the civilian labor force.[227] But courts were already declaring in the 1970s that "women now enjoy equal access to the economy's employment opportunities,"[228] that "the woman is as fully equipped as the man to earn a living."[229] The loud pronouncements about women's supposedly equal opportunities helped take attention away from ongoing inequities and the actual obstacles that the specific women before the court were facing.

Consider *Tan v. Tan* (1972), where the Illinois Appellate Court unanimously upheld the termination of Margaret Tan's alimony payments from her ex-husband, Harry.[230] Margaret's employment prospects were grim. As she testified, she had not worked in the market since the mid-1950s.[231] Margaret explained that she had disabling conditions that made standing painful and reported that her foot problems had worsened because Harry had used violence and threats to keep her in high heels.[232]

In her words: "Harry Tan insisted that I wear high heels and he beat me up when I refused to wear them, and he insisted that I wear them, and he said he was going to kill me if I didn't, and he knocked me to the floor and tried to kill me and so I wore the heels."[233] Margaret also testified that Harry "just laughed at" her when she told him that wearing high heels was painful.[234] And: "He struck me and said he would leave me if I didn't wear them."[235]

The Illinois Appellate Court devoted a single sentence to Margaret's testimony about Harry's abuse before declaring a few paragraphs later that it would "take judicial notice of the recent emancipation of women socially and economically, and particularly in the area of employment opportunity. Women are no longer restricted to certain types of jobs, and they are entitled under the law to equal pay for equal work."[236]

That blanket pronouncement about the "change in the status of women" hardly applied to the *Tan* case.[237] The litigation revealed no reason to believe that Margaret's relationship with Harry had been "socially" emancipated, and Margaret was not about to take the working world by storm, especially given her testimony that Harry's abuse had impaired her ability to stand. But the sweeping proclamation helped the court avoid addressing whether judicial hostility to alimony—along with judicial willingness to gloss over domestic abuse—might contribute to women suffering disproportionately at divorce.

Judges have also relied on overly cheery accounts of American progress toward sex equality when enforcing lopsided prenuptial agreements that deny or limit alimony. Implicitly or explicitly, they echo "the Madison Avenue pronouncement that 'you've come a long way, baby.'"[238]

The Pennsylvania Supreme Court's 1990 decision in *Simeone v. Simeone* provides an illuminating example.[239] When Frederick Simeone married Catherine Walsh in 1975, he was a thirty-nine-year-old neurosurgeon with about $90,000 in annual income and around $300,000 in assets. She was a twenty-three-year-old unemployed nurse.[240] Her assets of around $3,000 were one-hundredth the size of his.[241]

Frederick had a lawyer, who prepared a prenuptial agreement for Catherine and Frederick to sign.[242] It provided that Catherine would receive no more than $25,000 in total support payments at divorce, payable in weekly installments of $200.[243] Frederick's lawyer presented Catherine with the document late on the Friday afternoon the day before the wedding, when she could not delay signing if she wanted the nuptials to proceed on schedule.[244] Catherine did not have a lawyer, and Frederick's lawyer did not advise her about the legal rights the agreement would take from her. She signed and married Frederick the next day.[245] She had a baby with Frederick in 1977.[246] Catherine and Frederick separated in 1982 and began divorce proceedings in 1984.[247] By 1984, Frederick's annual income exceeded $820,000.[248] In 2008, he would open a museum to display his multimillion-dollar race car collection.[249]

The Pennsylvania Supreme Court enforced the prenuptial agreement, "discarding" precedent that allowed judges to assess a prenup's reasonableness and inquire "into whether parties had attained informed understandings of the rights they were surrendering."[250] The court's decision rested on the premise that women and men now had "equal status" under "the law" and "in our society." *Simeone* explained that society had advanced "to the point where women are no longer regarded as the 'weaker' party in marriage, or in society generally" and declared that there was no "viability in the presumption that women are uninformed, uneducated, and readily subjected to unfair advantage in marital agreements. Indeed, women nowadays quite often have substantial education, financial awareness, income, and assets."[251]

Those generalized pronouncements wholly misdescribed the specific dynamics of Catherine's engagement to Frederick. Catherine did not "have substantial education, financial awareness, income, and assets." Frederick was the one with those advantages and he wielded them to his benefit. The court relied on its declarations about the nation's progress as a reason to disregard the actual power imbalances in the relationship at issue and not explore whether enforcing prenuptial agreements like the one Frederick had Catherine sign would contribute to women's economic precariousness at divorce.[252]

Let's turn now from the law governing divorce to the law governing ongoing marriages. Judges have also relied on inflated accounts of American progress to divert attention from exploring whether the more lenient treatment of marital rape perpetuates women's inequality.

The common law that generations of American courts enforced made husbands absolutely exempt from prosecution for raping their wives.[253] The nineteenth-century woman's rights movement was determined to change that. Indeed, the movement's leaders described establishing a wife's right to refuse her husband's sexual demands as even more important than suffrage, reasoning that women would never be equal and free unless they controlled how many children they had and when.[254] Elizabeth Cady Stanton wrote an 1855 public letter declaring that "[t]he rights, to vote, to hold property, to speak in public, are all-important; but there are great social rights, before which all others sink into utter insignificance. The cause of woman is," Stanton explained, a question "of human rights—the sacred right of a woman to her own person." As she asked: "Did it ever enter into the mind of man that woman too had an inalienable right to life, liberty, and the pursuit of her individual happiness? Did he ever take in the idea that to the mother of the race, and to her alone, belonged the right to say when a new being should be brought into the world? Has he, in the gratification of his blind passions, ever paused to think whether it was with joy and gladness that she gave up ten or twenty years of the heyday of her existence to all the cares and sufferings of excessive maternity?"[255] Lucy Stone, another driving force in the woman's rights movement, agreed in 1855 that the marriage "question underlies, this whole movement and all our little skirmishing for better laws, and the right to vote, will yet be swallowed up, in the real question, viz, has woman, as wife, a right to herself? It is very little to me to have the right to vote, to own property &c. if I may not keep my body, and its uses, in my absolute right. Not one wife in a thousand can do that now, & so long as she suffers this bondage, all other rights will not help her to her true position."[256]

Consensual accounts of American history remember the first woman's rights movement as a success, but the movement did not win the right of sexual self-possession for married women that leading advocates had identified as more crucial than the vote. Throughout the nineteenth century and for most of the twentieth, no state would prosecute a husband for raping his wife.[257] Judges ignored this inconvenient reality when making sweeping pronouncements about America's embrace of sex equality. For example, a New York court did not mention men's immunity from prosecution for raping their wives when boasting in 1935 about "the present day tendency to emancipate women completely." Instead, the court simply asserted that the law had "recognized that [a married woman's] body is not her husband's but her own."[258]

At least twelve states still treat sex crimes more leniently if they occur within marriage—prohibiting a narrower range of conduct, establishing lesser penalties, or creating special obstacles to prosecution.[259] States have rewritten their laws in sex-neutral language, so they now expound on a spouse's prerogatives rather than a husband's.[260] But the available evidence suggests that the underlying behavior remains highly gendered, with the law's continued leniency overwhelmingly benefiting men and jeopardizing women.[261]

The Virginia Supreme Court in *Weishaupt v. Commonwealth* (1984) relied on overstated declarations about the nation's progress to direct attention away from exploring whether shielding marital rape reflects and reinforces women's inequality.[262] The case centered on Ronald Weishaupt's alleged rape of his wife, Janet.[263] She had moved out in November 1981 and consulted an attorney about obtaining a divorce, but the lawyer had advised her not to file for divorce until she and Ronald had been separated for a year. One night three weeks short of a year's separation, Janet was at a friend's sixth-floor apartment.[264] Ronald scaled the exterior of the building, climbed onto the balcony, dragged and shoved Janet into the bedroom, pinned her down, and forced intercourse on her while she resisted and screamed.[265]

Virginia indicted Ronald for rape.[266] The jury—perhaps straining for a way to hold Ronald less than fully accountable for his brutality—found Ronald guilty of attempted rape and sentenced him to two years in prison.[267]

Ronald appealed.[268] The state had convicted him pursuant to a rape statute that did not differentiate based on marriage. But he contended nonetheless that the common law's marital rape exemption remained in force in Virginia.[269] In Ronald's view, "he had an absolute right to do what he did."[270] The Virginia Supreme Court upheld his conviction, concluding "that a wife can unilaterally revoke her implied consent to marital sex where, as here, she has made manifest her intent to terminate the marital relationship by living separate and apart from her husband; refraining from voluntary sexual intercourse with her husband; and, in light of all the circumstances, conducting herself in a manner that establishes a *de facto* end to the marriage."[271]

While issuing this judgment, the Virginia Supreme Court acknowledged that "[t]he question whether a woman should be allowed to make a unilateral decision to withdraw consent to marital sex is bound up in the larger question of whether women are to be in independent control of their personal fates or whether they are to be under the control of others."[272] The *Weishaupt* majority declared that "[n]o citation to authority is required to establish that [common law] views of the dependence of women have long been cast aside."[273] The court announced that the judiciary in Virginia, as in other states, was "increasingly" recognizing the "role of the autonomy and independence of women" and breaking "with the ancient rules that cast women in a subservient posture."[274]

Those rosy proclamations about leaving women's legal subordination behind helped divert attention from an equally important part of the *Weishaupt* decision. The Virginia Attorney General had argued "that any concept of implied consent to intercourse growing out of the marital relationship" violated the Virginia Constitution by infringing "upon individual liberty." But the Virginia Supreme Court refused to require husbands to obtain "actual consent" from their wives "before each act of intercourse," choosing instead to preserve a man's entitlement to rape his wife when they are in an ongoing relationship.[275] *Weishaupt* never explained how denying married women legal control over their own bodies was consistent with "the ever increasing separateness and independence accorded women in this Commonwealth."[276]

The *Weishaupt* majority's proclamations about the law's embrace of sex equality also ignored the concurring opinion in *Weishaupt*, where three out of seven Virginia Justices agreed with the majority about upholding Ronald's conviction but presented their own reasoning for that result.[277] This concurrence did not dwell on the full humanity of married women. Its references to wives were more disrespectful, describing women who reported marital rape to law enforcement as wives who had made "a cry of 'Rape!'" The concurrence's concern focused on men and their sexual prerogatives in marriage. Indeed, the concurrence suggested that treating marital rape the same as rape outside of marriage would be unjust to husbands, observing: "While we have recognized in our cases the independence of women in this State, this recognition should not operate to discriminate against men." Virginia could prosecute Ronald because Janet had "demonstrated over a prolonged period of time a clear intention permanently to separate from the husband and such complete separation has, in fact, occurred." But the concurring Justices wanted to underscore that a husband retained the legal right to rape his wife when she had temporarily moved "to a separate room in the same house" or moved "to a residence separate from the husband" while maintaining "regular social contact" with him.[278]

Later that year, the Virginia Supreme Court overturned another husband's rape conviction.[279] Edward Alan Kizer had allegedly raped his wife after the two had separated and after she had decided that their marriage was "fractured beyond repair." Nonetheless, the court reversed Kizer's conviction on the ground that the prosecution had failed to prove "beyond a reasonable doubt that the husband knew, or reasonably should have known, that the marriage was terminated *de facto*." If a man reasonably thought his marriage was not over, he was legally free to force his wife to have sex with him.[280]

The Virginia General Assembly has since expanded the state's criminalization of marital rape. But the state still treats marital rape more leniently. While a rape conviction in Virginia ordinarily means a minimum of five years in prison, someone convicted of raping his spouse can get away with counseling.[281]

Dobbs

As we have seen, judges have repeatedly relied on the premise that the nation has moved beyond gendered ways of thinking and governing as a reason not to explore how current policies and practices perpetuate inequality. A version of this strategy recently featured in one of the most consequential Supreme Court decisions in American history. *Dobbs v. Jackson Women's Health Organization* (2022) removed federal constitutional limits on the prohibition of abortion, empowering lawmakers to compel childbearing.[282]

The *Dobbs* litigation centered on the Gestational Age Act, a 2018 Mississippi law prohibiting abortion after fifteen weeks of pregnancy "[e]xcept in a medical emergency or in the case of a severe fetal abnormality."[283] This statute was irreconcilable with the Court's precedents in *Roe v. Wade* (1973) and *Planned Parenthood of Southeastern Pennsylvania v. Casey* (1992).[284] In the almost half century since *Roe* first recognized constitutional constraints on abortion regulation, the Court had never permitted legislators to ban abortion before viability.[285]

Justice Samuel Alito, Jr., wrote for the Court in *Dobbs*.[286] He had opposed *Roe* for decades,[287] and he now had the votes to overrule it.

Alito's majority opinion upholding Mississippi's law and lifting constitutional barriers to abortion prohibition made a point of refusing to consider how denying women access to legal abortion would undermine women's status in society. The word "equality" appears only twice in the *Dobbs* majority opinion.[288] The Court dismissed in a single paragraph the possibility of subjecting abortion laws to heightened scrutiny under the Fourteenth Amendment's Equal Protection Clause.[289] *Dobbs* insisted that the Court had "neither the authority nor the expertise to" assess "the effects of the abortion right on the lives of women."[290]

But those moves did not keep the Court from wielding claims about women's status in the United States. To the contrary, with the long tradition of self-contradictory victory announcements in view, it becomes readily apparent how the *Dobbs* majority repeatedly invoked overstated accounts of women's advances to defend the Justices' decision to leap backward and eliminate a constitutional right that women had held for generations.

Even as the Court claimed not to be thinking about the practical consequences of *Dobbs*, the majority opinion drew on exaggerated reports of the nation's progress that were designed to deny the injuries that abortion prohibitions inflict on women. Mississippi, and anti-abortion groups urging the Court to side with Mississippi, had sought to mask the horrors of forced childbearing by citing improvements over time in America's treatment of women.[291] The *Dobbs* majority repeated their "arguments about modern developments," which emphasized "that attitudes about the pregnancy of unmarried women have changed drastically; that federal and state laws ban discrimination on the basis of pregnancy; that leave for pregnancy and childbirth are now guaranteed by law in many cases; that the costs of medical care associated with pregnancy are covered by insurance or government assistance."[292]

This line of advocacy depended on obscuring everything that remained unchanged. In repeating it, the *Dobbs* majority did not expound on the pains, burdens, and dangers of pregnancy and childbirth, which remain life-altering and sometimes life-threatening. A woman's risk of death from carrying her pregnancy to term is exponentially greater than her risk of dying from a legal abortion.²⁹³ *Dobbs* also did not examine the persistence of employment discrimination against pregnant women and mothers, which still sidelines many women at work or costs them jobs.²⁹⁴ And *Dobbs* did not explore the nation's continued failure to establish universal health care and guarantee paid family leave, which still jeopardizes millions of Americans. Twelve percent of reproductive-age women were uninsured in 2019 and seventy-six percent of private sector workers were without access to employer-provided paid family leave in 2022.²⁹⁵

Consider the ongoing realities in Mississippi itself. State law evinces no shift in attitude toward nonmarital pregnancy, still treating that condition as shameful while making its occurrence more likely. Mississippi permits public schools to exclude all discussion of contraceptives from their sex education classes and prohibits public schools from providing "any demonstration of how condoms or other contraceptives are applied." At the same time, the curriculum that Mississippi's "abstinence-plus" public schools must follow and that Mississippi's "abstinence-only" public schools must not contradict denigrates nonmarital pregnancy at every turn. The state wants public schools to teach students about "the inappropriateness of the social and economic burden" that nonmarital childbearing places "on others." Mississippi also wants public schools to teach "that a mutually faithful, monogamous relationship in the context of marriage is the only appropriate setting for sexual intercourse" and to provide instruction about "the current state law related to sexual conduct."²⁹⁶ That last point reinforces the others, as Mississippi still criminalizes fornication and adultery.²⁹⁷ Mississippi's childbirth rate for girls between the ages of 15 and 17 was the nation's highest in 2022,²⁹⁸ suggesting the ineffectiveness of shame as a protection against pregnancy.

Pregnancy and childbirth remain perilous in Mississippi. The state's pregnancy-related mortality rate between 2016 and 2020 was a horrifying 35.2 deaths for every 100,000 live births, and that figure encompassed a stark racial disparity. Black, non-Hispanic women in Mississippi had a pregnancy-related mortality rate of 63.3 deaths for every 100,000 live births, compared to 15.1 deaths per 100,000 live births for white, non-Hispanic women in the state.²⁹⁹

What about life as a pregnant woman or mother in Mississippi? Mississippi has no state law prohibiting private employers from engaging in pregnancy discrimination or sex discrimination more generally.³⁰⁰ If a pregnant woman or mother is unable to earn enough in the market or is pushed out of it, the state's social safety net is vanishingly thin. As Mississippi Representative Sonya Williams-Barnes and other legislative opponents of the Gestational

Age Act observed, Mississippi was "telling a woman what to do with her body and when to do it" while refusing to provide adequate assistance to needy mothers and children.[301]

When the Court decided *Dobbs* in 2022, Mississippi's Temporary Assistance for Needy Families (TANF) program offered indigent two-person families—such as a mother and child—no more than $236 a month to live on. Ordinarily, Mississippi would increase TANF benefits by up to $24 a month for each additional person in the family, so an indigent three-person family— such as a mother and two children—would receive up to $260 a month. But if a woman conceives and bears an additional child while already in the TANF program, Mississippi generally will not adjust her TANF benefits to take into account that additional need.[302] Even the pittance that Mississippi provides to TANF recipients can be exceedingly difficult to access. In 2022, Mississippi received an average of 1,542 TANF applications a month, approved an average of 131 (8.5%), and denied an average of 1,410 (91.4%).[303]

Mississippi has also refused to expand its Medicaid program under the Affordable Care Act, taking advantage of a 2012 Supreme Court decision that blocked Congress from penalizing such optouts.[304] The federal government reports that 116,917 women of reproductive age were uninsured in Mississippi in 2019 and that 42% of those women were African American.[305]

After ignoring the harms of forced childbearing, the *Dobbs* majority returned to proclamations about American progress when dismissing the dangerousness of unfettered legislative power over abortion. Drawing again on briefing from the anti-abortion movement,[306] the *Dobbs* majority sought to defend the Justices' decision to give legislatures so much control over women's lives by announcing that: "Women are not without electoral or political power. It is noteworthy that the percentage of women who register to vote and cast ballots is consistently higher than the percentage of men who do so."[307] Earlier on, the majority opinion had proclaimed that "women gained the constitutional right to vote in 1920."[308]

This line of argument similarly turned on obscuring how far America still has to go. The Court erased the women who lack access to the polls more than a century after the Nineteenth Amendment's 1920 ratification. Recall that the United States Constitution guarantees no one the right to vote.[309] In fact, *Dobbs* upheld legislation that emerged from a state notorious for distorting elections with multiple mechanisms for voter suppression, including state constitutional provisions establishing life-long felon disenfranchisement and requiring voters to present government-issued photographic identification.[310] A 2020 study estimated that Mississippi's felon disenfranchisement rule alone had disenfranchised 10.55% of Mississippi's voting-age population, including 15.96% of Mississippi's voting-age African Americans.[311] No one is elected to the Mississippi state government without surmounting—or benefiting from—the state's gauntlet of systemic disenfranchisement. A federal appellate court held in 2024 that Mississippi's felon disenfranchisement provision does not violate federal constitutional requirements.[312]

So who runs Mississippi? The Court's declaration about women's electoral and political power also diverted attention from the overwhelmingly male group of officeholders directly responsible for the Gestational Age Act. The Court never mentioned that men held 85.1% of the seats in the Mississippi legislature that passed this bill in 2018,[313] nor did the Court report that the governor who championed the bill and signed it into law was the latest in Mississippi's uninterrupted line of white male governors.[314] Boasting about women's electoral and political power while ignoring these persistent inequalities made it easier to deny how politicians can endanger women when constitutional safeguards disappear.

In sum, the American inclination to link sexism to the past instead of the present has skewed the law that judges have made in the late twentieth century and the early twenty-first. Courts rely on exaggerating the nation's progress toward sex equality when refusing to explore how ongoing policies and practices—including the judiciary's own decisions—protect and perpetuate inequality.

In the years to come, there is ample reason to predict that judicial decisions will continue to feature overstated accounts of American progress toward sex equality. As many judges have apparently realized, sweeping proclamations about the nation's advances can help rationalize judgments upholding an unequal status quo—or even pushing women backward. How could denying women the rights they seek or want to preserve be that important if women already have so much?

Chapter 6
Anti-Feminists Capitalize on America's Misremembered Past

Wild exaggerations about the nation's progress also warp political battles outside the courts. A long line of politicians and political activists have been determined to associate women's inequality with distant history rather than the here and now.

Indeed, exploiting and reinforcing America's penchant for overstating progress toward sex equality has been a key strategy for conservative and reactionary forces since as early as the anti-suffrage movement in the nineteenth and early twentieth centuries. Anti-suffragists commonly insisted that female enfranchisement was unnecessary because "all legal disabilities of women" had already "been removed by men,"[1] or were "fast passing away."[2] On their accounts, there was not "one scintilla of truth in the assertion that woman is oppressed."[3]

This chapter focuses on modern manifestations of that hoary political tradition, using internal movement documents along with external primary sources to examine a half century of activism against feminist initiatives. Anti-feminists in the late twentieth and early twenty-first centuries have wielded the contention that America has already established women's equality, leaning on that assertion as they combat feminist reform and promote regression while simultaneously claiming to support women's rights. I begin with the crusade that Phyllis Schlafly and her allies waged in the 1970s and 1980s to stop ratification of the Equal Rights Amendment, which repeatedly relied on assertions about the achievement of women's equality that purported to be universal but had white middle-class heterosexual women foremost in mind. I then turn to Schlafly's ideological heirs battling feminist mobilization in the decades since. Anti-feminists have followed Schlafly's playbook, deploying declarations of victory over sex discrimination to condemn affirmative action, lobby against government support for childcare, oppose abortion rights, fight revitalized efforts to add the ERA to the Constitution, and more.

Phyllis Schlafly and Her Allies

When feminist activism resurged in the last decades of the twentieth century, countermobilizing anti-feminists promptly tapped into the American inclination to exaggerate progress and forget what remains undone.[4] Claims that women's equality was an accomplished fact in the United States soon swirled around efforts to block the Equal Rights Amendment.

Alice Paul's allies first introduced the ERA in Congress in 1923, after Paul and her National Woman's Party launched the ERA campaign that Chapter 2 discussed.[5] Over the next decades, feminists prodded lawmakers to reintroduce the amendment in Congress after Congress, hold more than a dozen committee hearings,[6] and issue a tower of reports.[7]

The amendment's chances of success seemed to be blossoming as World War II came to a close. Between July 1945 and July 1946, the House and Senate Judiciary Committees each favorably reported the ERA out of committee, the full Senate debated the amendment over three days, and the Senate voted thirty-eight to thirty-five in favor of the ERA—a milestone even if it fell short of the two-thirds support in each chamber of Congress required for constitutional amendments.[8]

But that momentum waned amidst postwar conservativism and hit an unyielding obstacle.[9] Representative Emanuel Celler of New York, who began chairing the House Judiciary Committee in 1949 and returned to the post whenever Democrats controlled the House,[10] kept the amendment trapped in his committee for years without a hearing.[11] He had opposed the amendment since as early as 1943.[12] Celler told the press in 1957 that the ERA was "old hat" (an old-fashioned, out-of-date idea).[13]

Feminist mobilization in the late 1960s and early 1970s amplified interest in the ERA. Representative Shirley Chisholm of New York was a committed advocate. Her election as the first African American congresswoman had been front-page news in November 1968.[14] When Chisholm reintroduced the ERA in the House in May 1969, she assailed one of "the commonest arguments" against the amendment, "that women are already protected under the law and do not need legislation." Chisholm argued that "the concentration of women in lower paying, menial, unrewarding jobs and their incredible scarcity in the upper level jobs" was "[s]ufficient proof" that "[e]xisting laws are not adequate to secure equal rights for women." As Chisholm asked: "If women are already equal, why is it such an event whenever one happens to be elected to Congress?"[15]

Gloria Steinem, a feminist writer and editor who would go on to co-found *Ms.* magazine,[16] also drew attention to how sweeping exaggerations about

American progress were deployed against the ERA. Her May 1970 testimony urging a Senate subcommittee to support the amendment decried the "myth" "that women are already treated equally in this society" and emphasized "that equal pay for equal work, equal chance for advancement, and equal training or encouragement is obscenely scarce in every field."[17]

Later that year, Representative Martha Griffiths of Michigan—one of the congresswomen who had fought to add a sex discrimination prohibition to Title VII of the 1964 Civil Rights Act—mobilized support for a discharge vote that freed the ERA from the House Judiciary Committee and brought the amendment to the House floor on August 10, 1970.[18] The ERA passed the House the same day, but then died in the Senate.[19] The amendment finally got through the next Congress on March 22, 1972, when the Senate passed the ERA five months after the House had again voted favorably.[20] The amendment Congress sent to the states provided that: "Equality of rights under the law shall not be denied or abridged by the United States or by any State on account of sex."[21]

At that point, feminists needed to convince three-quarters of the state legislatures—thirty-eight—to ratify the amendment.[22] Efforts to stop the ERA intensified exponentially as ratification campaigns began.

Phyllis Schlafly was a conservative Republican activist known for the widely circulated book she wrote and privately published to promote Senator Barry Goldwater's 1964 presidential run.[23] She launched her own newsletter and fundraising operation after a more moderate rival (who supported the ERA) bested her in a bitterly fought May 1967 election for the presidency of the National Federation of Republican Women.[24] The inaugural issue of *The Phyllis Schlafly Report* appeared in August 1967, complete with appeals for donations to the "Eagle Trust Fund" and allegations of "irregularities and illegalities" in the election Schlafly had just lost.[25] Schlafly also spent the summer of 1967 urging Republican women's clubs to divert to the Eagle Trust Fund some of the dues they would have otherwise sent to the National Federation of Republican Women.[26]

The Phyllis Schlafly Report first discussed the ERA a month before the amendment passed Congress, when Schlafly devoted her February 1972 newsletter to explaining "What's Wrong with 'Equal Rights' for Women."[27] It was not immediately apparent that ERA opposition would become Schlafly's signature issue, and the next edition of her newsletter moved on to a diatribe against busing.[28] But by May 1972, Schlafly was announcing that her February attack on the ERA had drawn "the biggest response in the five-year history of this newsletter."[29] After that encouragement, she launched a multiyear crusade against the ERA, waged in newsletters, endless public appearances, and an anti-feminist manifesto, *The Power of the Positive Woman* (1977).[30] Schlafly and the organizations she founded and ran—Stop ERA and Eagle Forum—became the driving forces fighting ratification.[31]

Schlafly emphasized two central arguments. She insisted that the ERA was unnecessary because America had already achieved women's equality, and she warned that the ERA was dangerous because it threatened women's domesticity. Schlafly drew on these two themes to oppose a constitutional prohibition on sex discrimination while claiming to support sex equality.

Schlafly maintained that America had eradicated discrimination against women, as a matter of law and fact. In February 1972, only three months had passed since the Supreme Court first struck down legislation for denying women equal protection.[32] The median woman working full-time and year-round in 1972 earned just 57.9 cents for every dollar a full-time, year-round male worker made.[33] Nonetheless, Schlafly characterized "[t]he claim that American women are downtrodden and unfairly treated" as "the fraud of the century."[34] Schlafly's proclamation purported to encompass American women as a whole, but she was clearly focused on straight white middle-class women in particular. When Schlafly asserted that "[of] all the classes of people who ever lived, the American woman is the most privileged,"[35] or criticized Russia for having "women do the heavy, dirty work American women do not do,"[36] she hardly seemed to be thinking about the impoverished women of color toiling in America's agricultural fields. Schlafly's insistence that "American women do *not* want to be liberated from husbands and children" likewise dismissed women who desired female partners, nonmarital relationships, or solitude.[37]

By 1977, Schlafly was announcing "that the Positive Woman in America today faces a future in which her educational and employment options are unlimited."[38] She reported that "[t]here is no law that discriminates against women."[39] She promised that "the Positive Woman in America today has a near-infinite opportunity to control her own destiny, to reach new heights of achievement, and to motivate and influence others. Her potential is limited only by the artificial barriers erected by a negative view of herself or by the stultifying myths of the women's liberation movement."[40]

On Schlafly's account, powerful men, rather than feminist women, were responsible for the nation's progress. She endlessly emphasized that Congress had prohibited sex discrimination in employment, education, and credit, with statutes like the 1963 Equal Pay Act, the 1964 Civil Rights Act, the 1972 Equal Employment Opportunity Act, the 1972 Education Amendments, and the 1974 Equal Credit Opportunity Act.[41] Schlafly reported that this legislation meant that "[e]qual pay for equal work is guaranteed," that women have "[c]omplete protection against discrimination" in employment,[42] that women enjoy "equal employment opportunity."[43] Indeed, she proclaimed that "[f]ederal legislation is already more than adequate to assure women of everything they could reasonably want. Women are fully guaranteed equality in educational opportunities, admissions, and employment."[44] Schlafly's touting of federal civil rights laws proceeded as if male legislators had enacted prohibitions on sex discrimination easily and on their own initiative. She never discussed how feminists within and outside Congress had fought for this legislation against powerful resistance, presumably because she was loath to acknowledge the contributions of feminist mobilization.[45] Schlafly also chose not to mention that Goldwater—the politician with whom she had most closely identified herself—opposed federal prohibitions on employment discrimination and voted against the 1964 Civil Rights Act and the 1972 Equal Employment Opportunity Act.[46]

This 1976 photograph from a Stop ERA rally in the Illinois capitol rotunda (Figure 6.1) illustrates how Schlafly's campaign sought to present the amendment as unnecessary in a nation that had purportedly established women's equality.[47] Schlafly, then in her fifth year fighting ratification in Illinois,[48] sang into a bullhorn backed by singing supporters holding signs. One sign read:

Figure 6.1 *Magnifying Her Voice Against ERA,* CHICAGO TRIBUNE, April 28, 1976.
Source: Getty

"We HAVE EQUAL Job Opportunities." Another asked: "NEW ILLINOIS CONSTITUTION provides . . . . equal work, equal pay, why then, ERA?"[49]

Schlafly paired her praise for male politicians with the insistence that male inventors and capitalists had been even more crucial to women's liberation. By the 1970s, Americans had heard from a long line of cultural arbiters inclined to identify advances in household technology and consumer products—rather than changes in law and society—as the key engines driving improvements in women's lives.[50] The theme was common enough that hints could seep into America's waging of the Cold War. In 1959, then-Vice President Richard Nixon and Soviet Premier Nikita Khrushchev toured a model house that was part of the American National Exhibition in Moscow.[51] Nixon pointed to a late-model American washing machine as evidence of capitalism's superiority over communism. He told Khrushchev and the world press: "In America, these are designed to make things easier for our women."[52]

Schlafly drew on this tradition from her very first newsletter on the ERA, maintaining that legal reforms were less important for women than technological advances that facilitated housework:

The real liberation of women from the backbreaking drudgery of centuries is the American free enterprise system which stimulated inventive geniuses to pursue their talents -- and we all reap the profits. The great heroes of women's liberation are not the straggly-haired women on television talk shows and picket lines, but Thomas Edison who brought the miracle of electricity to our homes to give light and to run all those labor-saving devices -- the equivalent, perhaps, of a half-dozen household servants for every middle-class American woman. Or Elias Howe who gave us the sewing machine which resulted in such an abundance of readymade clothing. Or Clarence Birdseye who invented the process for freezing foods. Or Henry Ford, who mass-produced the automobile so that it is within the price-range of every American, man or woman.[53]

Schlafly's argument presumed that women were responsible for keeping neat homes (and hairstyles) while contending that housework was no longer burdensome for American women unable to afford servants because of the men who invented, manufactured, and sold home appliances and consumer goods. In fact, considerable research—and lived experience—made clear that housework's demands on women's time had remained remarkably consistent before and after technological advances, as new inventions led to more exacting standards rather than greater freedom.[54] Schlafly's decision to include Henry Ford, a notorious antisemite, in her pantheon of male heroes was also jarring and perhaps revelatory.[55]

But Schlafly ignored all that in her simultaneous determination to insist that modern American women had nothing to complain about and deny that feminist activism had helped improve women's lives. She told the middle class: "Militant women's liberationists did not produce automatic washers and dryers. It was the American competitive system that manufactured appliances cheap enough for the average American family to afford."[56]

Schlafly's second major line of attack fit with her odes to home appliances. If the ERA was unnecessary because women already had legal, economic, and practical equality, the amendment was dangerous because it would take women from domesticity and "deprive the American woman of her most cherished right of all -- the right to stay home, keep her baby, and be supported by her husband."[57] Schlafly charged that "[t]he women's libbers are radicals who are waging a total assault on the family, on marriage, and on children."[58] She contended that the ERA would force women to work outside the home, taking "away a woman's present *freedom of choice* to take a job — *or* to be a full-time wife and mother. In short, it will take away the right to be a woman."[59]

Schlafly's case against the ERA glossed over the deep internal tensions permeating her constitutional advocacy, her legislative assessment, and her reporting on the facts of women's lives. The constitutional tension was perhaps most glaring: Schlafly used the contention that America had already embraced sex equality as a reason *not* to include a commitment to sex equality in the Constitution. But why wouldn't the nation express its deepest values in its foundational governing document?

Schlafly's overview of the legislative landscape could also induce vertigo. She declared that "[t]here is no law that discriminates against women" while simultaneously applauding state legislation that continued to discriminate against women.[60] Some of this contradiction centered on lesbians, women Schlafly openly denigrated and lumped together with prostitutes and swingers.[61] Schlafly recognized that prohibitions on same-sex marriage were a form of sex discrimination against lesbians, but never acknowledged that the persistence of those prohibitions in every state despite growing mobilization for reform undercut her assertion that the law had already eradicated discrimination against women. Instead, she endorsed same-sex marriage bans and warned that the ERA would undo them.[62]

Schlafly similarly contradicted herself when discussing the legislative treatment of heterosexual marriage, never exploring the inconsistencies between her declarations about the end of legal discrimination against women and her praise for state statutes that continued to privilege husbands over wives. Schlafly celebrated "the laws that give the husband the right to establish the domicile of the marriage and to give his surname to his children" as "good laws designed to keep the family together."[63] She argued that this legislation was wise to uphold patriarchal control. In her words: "Every successful country and company has one 'chief executive officer.' None successfully functions with responsibility equally divided between cochairmen or copresidents. . . . If marriage is to be a successful institution, it must likewise have an ultimate decision maker, and that is the husband."[64] Schlafly did not explain how women could be legal equals while legislation still enforced male supremacy.

Schlafly's discussion of workplace law was likewise riddled with contradiction. She praised federal civil rights statutes for purportedly eradicating employment discrimination against women, but simultaneously sought to revise this legislation to augment men's legal advantages. Schlafly opposed "job preference for employed women in order to achieve arbitrary race and sex quotas," and contended that "[r]everse discrimination unjustly discriminates against the person who is trying to support a family." As those statements suggest, Schlafly paired her opposition to affirmative action for women and people of color with advocacy seeking a boost for male breadwinners in the job market. She urged Congress to amend federal antidiscrimination law "to authorize employers to give job preference in hiring and promotions and retentions during layoffs to the spouse designated as the 'principal wage earner' in each family."[65] While facially sex-neutral, this proposal would have predictably benefited married men and set back married women hoping to obtain or retain a job a man might want.

Schlafly twisted herself into more knots when dismissing inconvenient facts, such as women's underrepresentation in political leadership. Although Schlafly proclaimed that women had unlimited opportunities, she knew "that women hold only a small minority of seats in Congress, state legislatures, and national, state, and local boards and commissions."[66] Like some of the popular writers discussed in Chapter 4, Schlafly sought to explain away that stark reality by attributing female marginalization to women's supposedly insufficient drive and ambition for political success. She declared in 1977 that "[t]he fact that there may be only 18 women out of 535 members of Congress does not prove discrimination at all."[67] Instead, "[t]he small number of women in Congress proves only that most women do not want to do the things that must be done to win election—drive all those thousands of miles, shake all those strangers' hands, eat all those third-rate chicken suppers, attend political meetings every night and weekend, subject themselves to press and political attacks that impugn their integrity and their motives, and face probes into personal life and finances."[68] The meandering sentence was a nonresponsive distraction. While most women do not want to run for elected office, neither do most men. Where was Schlafly's evidence for the assertion that discrimination did not factor into women's underrepresentation in Congress? Her own career suggested that sexism still impeded opportunity—even for extraordinarily hardworking and ambitious women.

Schlafly ran for Congress in 1952 and 1970, campaigning tirelessly to become the first woman to represent her Illinois district only to lose to men twice.[69] While multiple issues potentially contributed to her defeats,[70] gender was an inescapable part of both elections. News coverage in 1952 described Schlafly as "an attractive Alton housewife,"[71] a "tall, honey-haired political fledgling,"[72] an "attractive brunet."[73] A September 1970 news article on Schlafly's second campaign reported that she was running in "a district where many persons, women among them, distrust the idea of women politicians," and observed that anyone who saw Schlafly's billboard photograph "may join the ranks of those who refer to the subject of the highway advertising as 'that woman with her mouth open.'"[74]

By the next month of her campaign, Schlafly was willing to allude to sexism as an obstacle to her political ambitions. "My opponent says a woman's place is in the home," she acknowledged when addressing an October 1970 lunchtime audience in a Shelbyville church basement. "But my husband replies that a woman's place is in the House—the United States House of Representatives."[75]

Schlafly projected optimism about her electoral chances the second time around, telling the press shortly before the election: "I think I'm ahead because no one can outwork me."[76] Yet Schlafly's unmatched work ethic did not pay off at the polls. She lost in November 1970,[77] which left her with the free time to launch her anti-ERA campaign denying the persistence of discrimination against women.

By 1980, Schlafly's energetic and effective crusade against the ERA had made her a pivotal figure in what she called "the pro-family coalition" propelling the New Right.[78] Schlafly signaled in the media that she wanted an important post in Ronald Reagan's incoming presidential administration,[79] and that ambition sparked popular commentary.[80]

She was passed over. Women held only ten of the first hundred and ten key appointments to Reagan's transition team, and each of the first ten people Reagan chose for a cabinet-level position was a white man.[81]

Despite—or because of—these tensions in her arguments, Schlafly attracted many allies who echoed her attacks on the ERA. Some of the like-minded joined Schlafly's organizations. Rosemary Thomson, the Illinois director of Schlafly's Eagle Forum from the group's founding in 1975,[82] published *The Price of Liberty* (1978), her own book castigating "Women's Lib" and "the Women's Lib Amendment."[83] Like Schlafly, Thomson simultaneously endorsed patriarchal control over the family—with the husband as "president"—and insisted that the ERA was unnecessary because "'equal rights' already are a fact for women."[84]

Other allies repeated Schlafly's arguments when mobilizing against the ERA within their own organizations. Women Who Want to Be Women, an anti-feminist group founded in Fort Worth, Texas, in or around 1974,[85] produced an anti-ERA leaflet that circulated across the nation in the mid-1970s and became ubiquitous enough to have a nickname—the "pink sheet," a reference to its frequent printing on pink paper.[86] The pink sheet paraphrased and summarized Schlafly's newsletters when explaining why "ladies" needed to fight ERA ratification by "writing a hand written letter to your local Senator and your local Representative" and "calling these men on the phone."[87]

The W's knew it was safe to assume that state lawmakers would be male, but still framed the ERA as both unnecessary and threatening for the heterosexual middle-class traditionalists who were the pink sheet's implicit audience. The sheet began by assuring the "ladies" that "no women in history have ever enjoyed such privileges, luxuries, and freedom as American women."[88] The sheet then declared that federal antidiscrimination legislation "already guaranteed" women "equal pay for equal work." It described "the 'equal pay for equal work' argument" in favor of the amendment as "deceptive," "merely a smokescreen to hide the real intent of the ERA."[89] That intent purportedly included undermining traditional family life. The leaflet warned that the ERA would "permit *homosexuals* to '*marry*' and *adopt* children" and undo legal requirements that wives and children "wear the name of husband and father."[90]

Beverly LaHaye, who founded Concerned Women for America in 1979 "to combat the goals of the feminist movement,"[91] similarly contended that there was "no need for" the Equal Rights Amendment.[92] LaHaye was a conservative Christian author and speaker whose publications included a bestselling sex manual coauthored with her husband that promised "Spirit-filled Christians" that they enjoyed sex "more on a permanent lifetime basis than any other group of people."[93] Her 1980 book, *I Am a Woman by God's Design*, attacked the ERA. Like Schlafly, LaHaye maintained that the amendment was unnecessary while warning that the "ERA *will* force upon us the rigid, unisex, gender-free mandate demanded by the women's-liberation movement, and *will* transfer the power to apply this mandate to the federal government and the federal courts."[94] LaHaye emphasized that there was "already legislation in operation that deals with" "equal pay for equal work, equal job-promotion opportunities, or equal treatment in hiring."[95]

Jerry Falwell also echoed and amplified Schlafly's case against the ERA. Falwell was a fundamentalist pastor who hosted the "Old Time Gospel Hour" on television and radio, led a Virginia megachurch, and founded what became Liberty University.[96] He had a long history of right-wing advocacy, including a sermon published in 1958 that condemned the Supreme Court's desegregation decision in *Brown v. Board of Education* (1954).[97] Falwell described segregating schools and churches as "simply respecting God's law."[98] He warned that "integration of the races" "will destroy our race eventually" because "if we mix the races in schools, in churches, etc., we must realize that the ultimate end will be the social mixing, which can only lead to marital relationships."[99] Several years later, on March 21, 1965, Martin Luther King Jr. and other religious leaders were in the midst of leading a civil rights march from Selma to Montgomery, Alabama.[100] Falwell preached at his Virginia church that evening and subsequently published his sermon.[101] He questioned "the sincerity and non-violent intentions of some civil rights leaders such as Dr. Martin Luther King Jr., Mr. James Farmer, and others, who are known to have left-wing associations" and contended that civil rights "demonstrations and marches have done more to damage race relations and to gender hate than to help."[102] Falwell advised Christians "to get off the streets and back into the pulpits and into the prayer rooms."[103] But he did not take that advice himself.

Falwell co-founded the Moral Majority in 1979 with (among others) LaHaye's husband.[104] By 1980, Falwell and Schlafly were headlining an "I Love America—Stop ERA Rally" in front of the Illinois capitol.[105] He reportedly introduced her as the "greatest citizen to come out of Illinois since Abraham Lincoln."[106] Falwell's 1980 book, *Listen, America!*, urged his enormous audience to "stand against the Equal Rights Amendment, the feminist revolution, and the homosexual revolution."[107] Falwell denounced the ERA as a "definite violation of holy Scripture" that "defies the mandate that 'the husband is the head of the wife, even as Christ is the head of the church.'"[108] Like Schlafly, he paired his commitment to patriarchal marriage with the insistence that the ERA was unnecessary. Falwell told his readers that Schlafly was "one of the most knowledgeable people I know" and summarized her anti-ERA arguments in his book: "The Equal Rights Amendment offers women nothing in the way of rights or benefits that they do not already have. In the areas of employment and education, laws have already been enacted to protect women. The only thing the Equal Rights Amendment would do would be to take away rights and privileges that American women now have in the best country in the world."[109]

Ultimately, the anti-ERA campaign that Schlafly spearheaded had the wind at its back. Schlafly's arguments drew strength from the long American tradition of overstating the nation's progress toward sex equality, often while rationalizing and enforcing limits on women's rights. Her appeals reflected and reinforced entrenched norms prioritizing women's roles as wives and mothers, presuming male headship in marriage, and denigrating homosexuality. Her side benefited from the constitutional requirement that at least three-fourths of the states must approve any amendment, which means that just thirteen dissenting states can block ratification.[110] Congress further tilted the playing field against ratification when it inserted a seven-year ratification deadline into the 1972 joint resolution sending the ERA to the states,[111] and then later enacted just a modest extension until June 30, 1982.[112]

Schlafly's own shrewdness, determination, and energy also propelled her anti-ERA crusade forward. Schlafly gave her movement the credit when only thirty-five of the required thirty-eight states had ratified the ERA by Congress's first and second deadlines.[113] Many ERA supporters, scholars, and popular commentators agreed on Schlafly's pivotal importance,[114] with some contending that ERA advocates would have won the amendment's prompt ratification if Schlafly had not mobilized.[115] Schlafly continued to revel in her triumph and champion anti-feminism for the rest of her life.[116]

Schlafly's Heirs

Schlafly's ideological heirs have recognized the potency of her strategy and followed her approach in the years since Schlafly's campaign against the ERA. Anti-feminist activists and lawmakers continue to lean on the assertion that America has already established women's equality, which helps them claim to support women's rights while they oppose feminist reform and promote regression. This section traces the persistent deployment of that assertion through the end of the twentieth century and the start of the twenty-first, before turning to how anti-feminists within and outside Congress have exaggerated American progress when fighting resurgent efforts to add the ERA to the Constitution.

Robert Bork's *Slouching Towards Gomorrah* (1996) exemplifies how declarations that America has left sex discrimination behind have remained central to anti-feminist advocacy.[117] Bork was a conservative legal scholar who served as solicitor general in the Nixon and Ford administrations and as acting attorney general for Nixon.[118] Unlike Schlafly, he managed to secure an important appointment from the Reagan administration. Reagan nominated

Bork for a seat on the United States Court of Appeals for the District of Columbia Circuit, and the Senate confirmed him in 1982.[119] Bork was back before the Senate five years later because Reagan nominated him for the United States Supreme Court.[120] Beverly LaHaye from Concerned Women for America was one of many conservatives to testify before the all-male Senate Judiciary Committee in support of Bork's confirmation.[121] But the Senate refused to confirm Bork this time,[122] and Bork resigned from the Court of Appeals in 1988 because he wanted "to speak, write, and teach about law and other issues of public policy more extensively and more freely."[123] Bork's 1996 bestseller castigated the liberal forces purportedly driving "American decline."[124] His targets included "the angry activists of feminism."[125]

Bork's argument that women should abandon feminist mobilization rested on the contention that America had already triumphed over sex discrimination. On his account, women should "drop the word 'feminism' altogether since the movement no longer has a constructive role to play; its work is done. There are no artificial barriers left to women's achievement."[126]

Bork was careful not to give modern feminists credit for the nation's purported accomplishment, assuring readers that "feminists, radical or otherwise, actually had little to do with the progress of women in the latter half of this century. The trends that would *of themselves* produce today's results were in place at least by the early 1960s."[127] Like Schlafly, Bork presumed that housework was women's responsibility. He downplayed the importance of legal and social change, instead attributing the expanded "opportunities open to women" in the second half of the twentieth century "largely" to technological advances that made "shopping, food preparation, laundering and much else . . . dramatically easier."[128] In his words: "For women the new choices are available largely because of technology, for blacks because of the success of the civil rights movement."[129] Bork presented that sharp distinction as if race and sex did not interact and as if no one could be simultaneously black and female.

Bork's book appeared amidst a spate of anti-feminist activism in the 1990s that fought feminist priorities and promoted regression by insisting that America had already left sex discrimination in the past. Laura Ingraham, a former member of the Reagan administration,[130] embraced this strategy when pursuing the eradication of affirmative action—a longtime focus of conservative activism that ultimately won a 2023 Supreme Court decision prohibiting race-based affirmative action in university admissions.[131]

Ingraham testified before a House Judiciary subcommittee in April 1995, speaking on behalf of the anti-feminist Independent Women's Forum.[132] That group had emerged out of an ad hoc predecessor called "Women for

Clarence Thomas" that had championed Thomas's 1991 confirmation to the Supreme Court notwithstanding Anita Hill's allegation that Thomas had sexually harassed her while he was her supervisor at the Department of Education and the Equal Employment Opportunity Commission.[133] Executive Director Barbara Ledeen described the IWF as an organization for women who believe that feminists should have "declared victory and gone home."[134]

By 1995, Ingraham had clerked for Justice Thomas on the Supreme Court, joined the IWF's advisory board, and drawn significant media attention.[135] Meanwhile, the IWF had set its sights on attacking affirmative action, recognizing the popular and political impact that female opponents could have. As Ledeen told the *Washington Post* in 1995, "You can't have white guys saying you don't need affirmative action."[136] The implication was that white women like Ingraham could promote that argument.

Ingraham's 1995 testimony contended that it was "time to leave" affirmative action "behind us."[137] She urged Congress to amend Title VII of the 1964 Civil Rights Act "to provide that nothing in title VII should be construed to permit gender, racial or other group preferences, quotas or set-asides."[138] After testifying, Ingraham amplified her opposition to affirmative action in the popular press. The assertion that women no longer faced discrimination at work was central to her critique. Ingraham castigated feminists for "whining about" what she called "an imaginary glass ceiling" and maintained "that women in the work force are at long last pushing against a wide open door."[139]

Ingraham was just one of many voices in the Independent Women's Forum attacking feminism on the premise that America had already eradicated sex discrimination.[140] Anita Blair was the Forum's executive vice president and general counsel in 1995.[141] She deployed exaggerations about the nation's progress in the Supreme Court brief she filed on behalf of the IWF in *United States v. Virginia*, a suit about the constitutionality of Virginia's exclusion of women from the Virginia Military Institute.[142] Blair's brief urged the Justices to uphold the state school's male-only admissions policy,[143] while simultaneously insisting that "[w]omen are not excluded from educational and professional opportunities."[144] Indeed, the brief suggested that the Court "take this opportunity to declare women emancipated."[145] Virginia ultimately lost this case in 1996,[146] and Blair's efforts as a VMI board member to take the school private rather than admit women were unsuccessful.[147] But overstating improvements in women's status continued to be a core component of Blair's anti-feminist advocacy.

Blair used media interviews to deride feminists as baselessly gloomy—along with old and unattractive—declaring that "a telltale way to find a liberal feminist" was to look for "the nasty wrinkles around her mouth that she gets from frowning."[148] She announced in a November 1997 interview "that feminism should have declared victory and gone home" "in 1977 or 1978" because: "All that was needing to be done had been done." Here again, the point of the premature declaration of victory was to characterize ongoing feminist efforts as unnecessary and even "pretty destructive."[149] Blair was comfortable asserting that "[i]n this world, the biggest enemy to truth and common sense and logic is probably feminism."[150] She criticized feminists for supporting treatment programs for men who committed domestic violence, mocking such programs as "reeducation camp."[151] She also opposed opening military fighter pilot positions to women as "not economical."[152] A few years later, in the George W. Bush administration, Blair became the Deputy Assistant Secretary of the Navy for Personnel Programs.[153]

Overstated accounts of American progress ran through the *Brief Against Feminism* that F. Carolyn Graglia published in 1998 and adapted for the IWF's magazine.[154] Graglia castigated feminists for disseminating "the myth of societal, especially male, oppression of women" and argued from that baseline in condemning affirmative action and the Equal Rights Amendment.[155] She presented her own experiences as evidence that feminists had misdescribed the nation, insisting that when she was a student and then a practicing lawyer in the 1940s and 1950s "assistance—not discrimination—and encouragement—not obstruction—had always been" her "happy lot."[156]

Graglia had ultimately left market work to stay home with her children.[157] She applauded women who did the same,[158] and criticized "government-funded child care programs."[159] Yet Graglia's portrait of life as a homemaker was grimmer than she acknowledged. She described "a housewife's life" as having "few musts (breakfast, dinner, and *sex as her husband desires*); for the rest, she can choose to do what she wishes, when she wishes."[160] Her account suggested that housewives were not entitled to refuse their husband's sexual demands. A member of the Independent Women's Forum board reviewed Graglia's book for the *Wall Street Journal* and praised Graglia for presenting "a thinking woman's argument for putting family first."[161] Phyllis Schlafly chose Graglia, who had written her *Brief* and joined the lecture circuit after her children were grown, as the Eagle Forum's 1998 "Full-time Homemaker of the Year."[162]

Christina Hoff Sommers, a philosophy professor in the Independent Women's Forum,[163] attacked feminist educational reform by asserting that America had already triumphed over sex discrimination. Sommers spoke at a December 1996 conference organized by the American Enterprise Institute, a conservative think tank that had become Robert Bork's institutional base.[164] Her central message was that it was "simply irresponsible to argue that

American women, as a gender, are worse off than American men." Sommers used that rosy assessment of the nation's progress as a springboard for condemning "the contemporary women's movement" and its ongoing agenda. Her immediate target was "[p]rograms to help girls who have allegedly been silenced and demoralized in the nation's sexist classrooms." She castigated "[t]he myth of the short-changed schoolgirl" as "a perfect example of everything that's gone wrong with contemporary feminism," including "the irresponsible victimology" and "the outcry against being 'oppressed,' coupled with massive lobbying for government action." Sommers assured her audience: "The truth is, American women are the freest in the world. Anyone who doesn't see this simply lacks common sense."[165]

The Independent Women's Forum also financed an anti-feminist handbook for female undergraduates at Georgetown University, *The Guide: A Little Beige Book for Today's Miss G* (1997).[166] A recently formed Georgetown student group, the Women's Guild,[167] spent a night in early October 1997 slipping copies of the handbook under the dormitory doors of Georgetown women embarking on their first year of college.[168] The *Guide* began with the premise that women should direct their critical scrutiny inward—to "our minds, our morals, and our conduct"—because "the fight for equality is largely a thing of the past."[169] The book proceeded to dismiss concerns that female workers confront "Wage gaps" and "Glass ceilings" as "only a Feminist hallucination."[170] It concluded by counseling women to "[s]et aside" "*Ms. Magazine*" and avoid confrontation: "If you want to conquer the world (and men), try a dash of grace, a flash of charm, a modest flirtation. Remember, the tigress who knows when to roar also knows when to purr."[171] After the *Guide*'s distribution at Georgetown, a syndicated columnist at the conservative *Washington Times* quoted this counsel and repeated the headline the *Guide* had used: *I Am Woman, Hear Me Purr.* The columnist assailed the National Organization for Women as a group "whose major issues are gay, lesbian and feminist studies which target man as oppressor" and praised the *Guide* for offering "refreshing advice to counteract the NOW message."[172]

By the fall of 1998, the Independent Women's Forum was providing "advice, assistance and support" to *Portia*,[173] a "women's issues magazine" at Yale.[174] The journal assured Yale women "that we now enter the workforce on a level playing field" and directed readers to IWF literature.[175]

As one millennium ended and another unfolded, the contention that America had already triumphed over sex discrimination continued to suffuse conservative politics. Nancy Pfotenhauer was the president of the Independent Women's Forum when she wrote an opinion piece praising President George W. Bush's 2003 State of the Union address. She called Bush's speech "the beginnings of a thoughtful agenda for the women's movement," singling out Bush's advocacy for tax cuts, interest in altering the Social Security program, and the fact "that he never suggested that women as a group need special help." Pfotenhauer did not explore whether Bush's proposals—which included eliminating the federal estate tax and reducing or eliminating federal taxation of capital gains—would exacerbate economic inequality and further strain America's social safety net. Instead, her argument that "we should *all* applaud" Bush's "refusal to treat women as 'victims' needing special government assistance" turned on the assertion that "[t]raditional feminists" were wrong to "tell us that discrimination must remain atop every woman's list of concerns." Pfotenhauer declared: "Women now have that equal opportunity. The rest is up to us."[176]

That theme also ran through the 2008 Republican campaign for president. Sarah Palin, the Alaska governor who became John McCain's running mate in the 2008 election,[177] presented women's equality as a completed accomplishment while she opposed feminist efforts to combat persistent sex discrimination. Palin's speech at the 2008 Republican National Convention proclaimed "that this is America and every woman can walk through every door of opportunity."[178] A few weeks later, Palin gave a television interview in which she simultaneously declared "that women certainly today have every opportunity that a man has to succeed and to try to do it all anyway" and criticized a federal bill to extend the statute of limitations for pay discrimination suits. Palin dismissed the bill as "a boon for trial lawyers" and announced that there were already "laws on the books" providing "that no woman could be discriminated against in the workplace in terms of anything, but especially in terms of pay."[179]

Palin's assurances that existing legislation had already addressed the problem of sex discrimination at work diverted attention from the gap in antidiscrimination law that Palin and McCain wanted to preserve. A 2007 Supreme Court decision had interpreted Title VII narrowly, barring pay discrimination claims under the statute unless the employee had filed a charge with the Equal Employment Opportunity Commission within one hundred and eighty days after her employer made an allegedly discriminatory pay decision and notified the employee of her pay.[180] An employee who did not quickly realize that her pay was unequal was left without a Title VII remedy, even if the employer's early decision to discriminate meant that the employee was paid less for her entire career. The bill Palin opposed—which Congress enacted after the McCain/Palin defeat as the Lilly Ledbetter Fair Pay Act of 2009—frees employees from the Supreme Court's restrictive reading of Title VII. The legislation restarts Title VII's statute of limitations clock whenever an employee receives a paycheck made smaller by her employer's previous decision to discriminate.[181]

Framing sex discrimination as a past problem has remained a prominent anti-feminist strategy in the years since Palin's campaign for vice president. For example, Cleta Mitchell, a conservative activist and longtime lawyer for Republican politicians and right-wing groups,[182] asserted in 2017 that all the feminist movement "could responsibly achieve, has been achieved." As with many anti-feminists before her, Mitchell's eagerness "to declare victory" was entangled with her contention that Americans should reject contemporary feminism and its ongoing agenda. She criticized "the purposeless 'women's marches'" that protested the start of Donald Trump's first presidential term in January 2017 and condemned feminist support for abortion rights, which she derided as "[t]he ugly truth" "that the women's movement has morphed into a giant abortion-rights lobby."[183] A few years later, Mitchell became notorious for her alleged efforts to promote Republican political power by undermining American elections. She reportedly aided Trump's attempt to overturn his defeat in the 2020 presidential election and mobilized election conspiracists around the 2022 midterms and the 2024 presidential election.[184]

Of course, all these declarations of victory over sex discrimination have come up against the inconvenient reality that women remain starkly underrepresented at the highest reaches of political and corporate power. Here too, anti-feminists in the last years of the twentieth century and the first years of the twenty-first have followed Schlafly's playbook, striving to explain away women's marginalization and insist that Americans should not attribute persistent disparities between women and men to ongoing discrimination.

Anti-feminists writing at the end of the twentieth century sometimes dismissed such disparities as rapidly dissipating holdovers from an earlier era whose practices the nation had supposedly left behind. When Elizabeth Larson co-chaired the Independent Women's Forum in 1995,[185] she contended that the "relatively few women sitting in the top ranks of major corporations" was "a situation that would *resolve itself* even in the absence of affirmative action."[186] Indeed, Larson primed Americans to expect a quick resolution even without systematic efforts to increase women's representation at the top. She reported that "[i]t takes 25 years to reach the position of president and 30 to reach chairman, and women have only been in managerial positions in significant numbers since the mid-seventies." "Between 1995 and 2000," then, "the first wave of women to have had unbroken, full-time business careers will have 25 to 30 years of experience behind them."[187]

Diana Furchtgott-Roth, a fellow at the American Enterprise Institute who had published a book with the Independent Women's Forum,[188] mined the same vein when attacking affirmative action in 1997. Furchtgott-Roth insisted "that women now have equality of opportunity,"[189] and mocked the idea that working women confront a "glass ceiling" as "a figment of feminist imaginations."[190] Her argument denying that persistent discrimination helped explain the paucity of women in top management posts emphasized that "[w]omen received less than 5 percent of graduate degrees in the sixties and seventies, and these are the graduates who now are at the pinnacle of their professions." As Furchtgott-Roth assured readers: "That supports the 'pipeline' theory, which holds that women have not reached the top in greater numbers because they have not been 'in the pipeline' long enough."[191]

The pipeline argument always had a built-in expiration date, though, as women's mass entry into first-rung corporate jobs receded further into history. With the passage of time, evidence mounted that women's scarcity at the top would not be rectifying itself as a matter of course once America moved a few decades beyond the 1970s. To cite just one of many examples, only 10.4% of Fortune 500 companies had female chief executives in 2024.[192]

So anti-feminists in the late twentieth and early twenty-first centuries have been more inclined to advance another explanation for why men continue to dominate the highest reaches of workplace hierarchies even after America has purportedly left sex discrimination behind. This argument contends that few top jobs go to women because few women want such success.

Melinda Ledden Sidak used that argument when testifying on behalf of the Independent Women's Forum in 1995. Sidak was a former member of the Reagan administration with a track record of unrestrained opposition to government regulation.[193] As an attorney for the Tobacco Institute, an industry lobbying group, she had fought a proposed ban on cigarette vending machines in New York City with testimony that sought to erase decades of evidence documenting smoking's dangers.[194] Sidak declared at a City Council hearing in May 1990 that "smoking has not been shown to cause cancer or any other disease."[195] The blatant falsehood reportedly backfired with the Council and prompted some audience members to jeer or hiss.[196] New York City banned cigarette vending machines from most public places later that year.[197]

In her 1995 congressional testimony for the IWF, Sidak opposed affirmative action and insisted that women's underrepresentation "in some jobs" was "not evidence of pervasive discrimination or prejudice." She seemed to attribute sex stratification in employment entirely to "the fact that many women voluntarily choose family as their work."[198]

Linda Chavez, another alumna of the Reagan administration,[199] responded similarly to a 1995 federal government report finding "that only 5% of senior managers of Fortune 2000 industrial and service companies are women."

Chavez dismissed as "almost entirely wrong" the idea "that women are being denied promotions for which they are as eager to compete and as qualified as their male counterparts." Rather than explore how discrimination might help explain women's stark underrepresentation at the top, Chavez emphasized that "most women—including professionals and midlevel executives—put their families first" and recounted women's purported unwillingness to engage in "cutthroat competition."[200]

Carrie Lukas, the vice president for policy and economics at the Independent Women's Forum in 2006,[201] dismissed the possibility that discrimination was suppressing women's pay. Her *Politically Incorrect Guide to Women, Sex, and Feminism* declared that the "battle" to make the "social, political, and all other rights of women equal to those of men" "has been won."[202] That account depended on explaining away persistent pay gaps. Lukas's effort was uncompromising, insisting: "Discrimination isn't why women make less money than men. Women make different choices and have different priorities which results in them earning less."[203]

Sabrina Schaeffer, the executive director of the Independent Women's Forum in 2015, wrote about how "women still lag behind men in the political arena" without considering sexism as a potential contributor to why "women only hold 18 percent of congressional seats, comprise 24 percent of state legislatures and hold five gubernatorial seats." Instead, Schaeffer declared that she was "a firm believer in gender differences." Schaeffer emphasized women's distaste for "the noisiness of the campaign environment" and suggested that women might naturally prefer supporting roles to elected office. After reporting that "men and women are different—we share different talents, aptitudes and interests," she asked: "if women are more inclined toward organizing bodies on the ground or writing about the implications of policy, why not embrace these strengths?"[204]

Indeed, anti-feminists have often attributed women's purportedly different preferences to nature rather than societal constraints or cultural expectations. Kate O'Beirne, a Reagan administration alumna who became a conservative columnist, editor, and commentator,[205] published a 2006 book denouncing feminists as *Women Who Make the World Worse.*[206] O'Beirne declared that "American women have more freedom in their personal and professional lives than any man or woman has ever enjoyed in recorded history."[207] But she proceeded to assail feminist support for day care,[208] even though many mothers would have no professional lives or ability to support their families without access to affordable day care. O'Beirne proclaimed that "[t]he feminist movement has long been on a collision course with what we know to be true about the natural bond between mother and child." On her account, feminists demanded that women "be every bit as committed to careers as men are, but biology won't let them have their win. Women fall madly in love with their babies in a way that devoted fathers don't."[209]

Danielle Crittenden, the founding editor of the IWF's quarterly magazine,[210] likewise framed women's disproportionate subordinating of their market participation to their family responsibilities as rooted in biological drives that preceded legal and social arrangements and were independent from them. She told a Senate subcommittee in 1998: "The fact is that when children come along, someone has to accommodate them. A woman who has carried the baby around for 9 months inside of her usually finds it natural to do so and often impossible not to."[211] The next year, Crittenden published a book announcing that "[w]hat my generation may have discovered is that we have reached the biological limits of our freedom." The idea was that women had "had every legal, economic, and social impediment removed," and any remaining disparities between men and women could not shrink without rewriting nature, which was unrealistic. In Crittenden's words: "To achieve any more, to be truly able to live the same lives as men, we'd actually have to *be* men."[212] Crittenden's claim about the disappearance of "every legal, economic, and social impediment" fit uneasily with her 1998 testimony, which advocated for preserving legal, economic, and social arrangements that impede women's ability to combine motherhood and market success. She opposed "subsidizing day care to free mom to go to work,"[213] arguing that it does not "make sense for society to attempt to reinvent itself so that" a mother "can more conveniently and inexpensively delegate the care of those babies to strangers."[214]

In short, Schlafly's ideological heirs opposing feminist efforts and promoting regression have continued to embrace her strategy, leaning on declarations about America's triumph over sex discrimination and scrambling to explain away inconvenient facts. Schlafly's battle plan even continues to guide opposition to the Equal Rights Amendment itself. The remainder of this chapter explores how anti-feminists have wielded exaggerated accounts of the nation's progress to fight the ERA in the decades since Schlafly's crusade.

The ERA's absence from the national stage was brief. By the early 1990s, some feminists within and outside Congress were already arguing that the process of ratifying the amendment could resume without starting from scratch, despite the expiration of Congress's ratification deadlines.[215] Energized by that prospect, ERA supporters began remobilizing to secure ratification in three additional states and bring the total up to the required thirty-eight.[216]

Advocates of this "three-state strategy" soon confronted ERA opponents insisting again that the amendment was unnecessary because America had already left sex discrimination behind. Elaine Donnelly had spent the 1970s and early 1980s chairing Stop ERA's national media efforts while also founding and leading Michigan's Stop ERA group.[217] She turned to the old anti-ERA arguments to fight the three-state strategy, advising the press in 1994 that "[w]omen are already full citizens under the Constitution." Like Schlafly, Donnelly paired that victory announcement with the warning that "[t]hose promoting ERA" had "an underlying agenda" that was "tied to abortion and homosexual rights." Meanwhile, Donnelly championed women's continued unequal treatment. By 1994, she was president of the Center for Military Readiness, which was fighting to maintain policies banning servicewomen from combat positions and prohibiting lesbians and gay men from serving openly in the military.[218]

More ERA opponents echoed Schlafly's arguments as renewed ratification efforts intensified. Missouri Representative Vicky Hartzler explained her opposition to ratification by declaring in 2000 "that women have all the opportunities in the world" and "we should be telling them that the past is behind us."[219] George Will, a conservative columnist, disseminated that contention in 2007, asserting that "[t]he full inclusion of women in America's regime of rights was accomplished in the 20th century without an ERA, a constitutional redundancy."[220] Phyllis Schlafly herself spoke out in 2014, when she was eighty-nine, insisting that feminists pursuing ratification were "doing it to raise money, to give people something to do, to pretend that women are being mistreated by society."[221] Nevada Senator Michael Roberson proclaimed before voting against ratification in 2017: "Women have achieved equality and are equal to men in the eyes of the law. This is a great victory, and the battle has been won."[222]

Sometimes women opposing the ERA seemed oblivious to the atypicality of their personal experiences and cited their own elite careers as evidence that the nation had moved past sex discrimination. When Florida Senator Ronda Storms called the ERA "anachronistic" in 2007, she emphasized: "You're talking to a Florida female senator who's here, who's equal, who's achieved parity with men."[223] Margaret Ransone, a Virginia state legislator, helped squash a 2014 ratification proposal and declared: "I've never felt like I was discriminated against."[224] Victoria Cobb, president of the Family Foundation of Virginia and "a third-generation opponent of the ERA," cited herself as evidence "that women didn't need a vague amendment promising vague rights." Yet Cobb's own account of her privileged perch revealed her distance from many women's lives. Cobb reported in 2018 that she led "an organization, earning the same pay as my male colleagues, while having four children with associated maternity leave and a permanent family-friendly schedule."[225]

Ultimately, ERA supporters managed to win three additional ratifications. Nevada ratified in 2017,[226] Illinois followed in 2018,[227] and Virginia ratified on January 27, 2020.[228]

To date, however, the archivist of the United States, who has the statutory responsibility to publish ratified amendments, has not recognized the ERA as part of the Constitution.[229] On the first day of Virginia's 2020 legislative session, January 8, the Trump administration's Office of Legal Counsel in the Department of Justice publicly released an opinion contending that the seven-year ratification deadline Congress had inserted into the joint resolution sending the ERA to the states was binding and unalterable, so any ratifications after 1979 were invalid.[230] The Trump administration's opinion also raised the possibility that several of the states that ratified the ERA before 1979 should not count toward the ratification total because their legislatures subsequently sought to rescind the ratifications.[231] On the same day the Trump Justice Department publicly released this opinion, the National Archives and Records Administration announced that it would "abide by the OLC opinion, unless otherwise directed by a final court order."[232]

The ERA has remained in limbo since then. Although President Biden expressed personal support for the ERA,[233] he did not direct the archivist to publish the amendment.[234] Instead, the Biden administration's Office of Legal Counsel announced in January 2022 that "[w]hether the ERA is part of the Constitution will be resolved not by an OLC opinion but by the courts and Congress."[235] ERA advocates within and outside state government have sued seeking official recognition of the amendment's ratification, but without success to date.[236] Federal lawmakers have also proposed multiple bills that would either remove the ratification deadline or directly recognize the ERA as part of the Constitution.[237]

The amendment's opponents in Congress have responded to those legislative efforts by returning to Schlafly's playbook once again. They warn that the ERA would upend the law's treatment of women while simultaneously insisting that the ERA is "unnecessary" because women "already have equal rights under the law."[238]

Some of the purported threats that Schlafly invoked to instill panic, like same-sex marriage, have receded from anti-ERA arguments because they have already materialized without the ERA. In the early 2020s, the ERA's enemies have tended to emphasize that the amendment would provide a new constitutional foundation for abortion rights, a possibility that assumed even greater significance as the Supreme Court's commitment to protecting abortion rights under the Fourteenth Amendment seemed increasingly wobbly before it collapsed completely in 2022.[239] Representative Doug Collins of Georgia asserted in 2020 that the "ERA would be used to prevent state voters from enacting any limits on abortion, up to the moment of birth."[240] That same year, Representative Jackie Walorski of Indiana agreed that the ERA would be "enshrining unrestricted abortion in the Constitution and allowing full taxpayer funding for abortion."[241] Representative Virginia Foxx of North Carolina equated support for the ERA with "attempting to write into the Constitution the right to an abortion at all three trimesters, force taxpayers to pay for them, and eliminate all conscience protections for medical providers who wish to abstain from abortion."[242] Representative Kay Granger of Texas openly expressed contempt for women who terminate a pregnancy. She maintained that the ERA would "create an unlimited constitutional right to abortion," "[a]llowing women to discard their unborn children at taxpayer expense."[243] Representative Debbie Lesko of Arizona declared in 2021 that "the ERA would be used to codify the right to abortion, undoing pro-life protections, and forcing taxpayers to fund abortions."[244] That same day, Representative Vicky Hartzler of Missouri, now a federal rather than state legislator, contended that the ERA would "eradicate State and Federal pro-life laws and policies."[245] Representative Marjorie Taylor Greene of Georgia proclaimed that the ERA would "empower the woke feminist mob" and "enshrine abortion," creating "a new constitutional right guaranteeing abortion on demand."[246]

After the Supreme Court overruled *Roe*, Senator Cindy Hyde-Smith of Mississippi declared in 2023 that "advocates of the ERA" were "no longer shy about their goal to use ERA to impose unrestricted abortion-on-demand up to the moment of birth across the nation and to enforce taxpayers to pay for this. Their apparent goal," she maintained, "is to use ERA to overturn the Dobbs decision that returned the issue of abortion to the legislative process and instead re-empower unelected judges to impose a radical abortion policy that is in line with China and North Korea."[247] Senator Lindsey Graham of South Carolina echoed the contention in the same committee hearing, arguing that the ERA "would require judges to strike down anti-abortion laws" and "mandate abortion on demand up to the moment of birth."[248]

A critical audience might take these attacks on abortion rights as evidence that American women still lack full and secure control over their own lives. Like Schlafly before them, the ERA's most recent opponents in Congress have sought to counter arguments that the nation still has work to do by pairing their warnings about the changes the ERA would purportedly unleash with declarations that America has already established women's equality. In

2021, for example, Representative Michelle Fischbach of Minnesota contended "that men and women in the United States are already equal under law" and announced that "the ERA is unnecessary, redundant, and divisive."[249] Representative James Comer of Kentucky agreed that the ERA "is simply unnecessary" as "equality under the law for men and women is already guaranteed by the Constitution and by statute."[250] Representative Fred Keller of Pennsylvania maintained that "Americans know the ERA is as unnecessary today as it was 40 years ago" and reported that "[o]ur citizens are protected under the umbrella of existing laws that shield them from sex discrimination or any kind of discrimination."[251] Representative Andrew Clyde of Georgia asserted "that men and women are already considered equals under the Constitution" and derided "the so-called Equal Rights Amendment" as "both a ridiculous fashion statement and a battle cry for many who fail to recognize the progress the United States has made since the 1970's."[252] Representative Hartzler spoke on the House floor against the ERA while proclaiming: "I rise today to celebrate the achievements women have made and reaffirm that we are already equal under current law."[253]

In sum, the nation's dominant stories about itself have practical consequences, both inside and beyond the courts. Anti-feminists in the late twentieth and early twenty-first centuries have tapped into the powerful American inclination to exaggerate progress and forget what remains undone. Schlafly, her allies, and her heirs have fought feminist reform and promoted regression by insisting that women's equality is already established and sexism already left behind.

PART IV

HOPE

Too often, Americans are primed to think about women's treatment as emerging from consensus rather than conflict. Judges, politicians, and other influential voices telling tales about the nation regularly ignore women entirely or attribute improvements in women's status to men's spontaneous enlightenment rather than women's mobilization against fervent resistance. Their stories commonly exaggerate the nation's progress beyond recognition, even to the extreme of insisting that America has easily embraced sex equality and any remaining disparities are unimportant or on the verge of disappearing on their own without organized efforts.

Forgetting women's struggles for equality—and forgetting the work the nation still has to do—shields inequality, promotes complacency, and denies how generations of women have had to come together to fight for reform and against regression. Foregrounding women's struggles highlights the persistence of women's inequality as an organizing feature of American life and makes clear that real progress has always required women to disrupt the status quo, dispute prevailing certainties, demand change, and duel with powerful opponents.

The long record of fierce conflicts over women's rights and opportunities should leave Americans committed to sex equality both impatient with the pace of progress and prepared for a lengthy road ahead. This final part of the book seeks to build on the past in strategizing for a better future.

PART IV

HOPE

Chapter 7
Building on the Past to Create a More Equal Future

Incorporating the history of women's unfinished struggles for equality into America's dominant stories about itself can prime us to think differently about the nation, reorienting our understanding of how women's progress takes place, focusing our attention on the battles that are still unwon, and fortifying our determination to fight for a more equal future. This history teaches that the United States needs more conflict over women's status rather than less. Conflict can propel progress. Patiently awaiting men's spontaneous enlightenment will not.

Chapter 7 highlights some of the unwon battles that need fighting, or continued fighting, to push progress forward—now and over the long haul. They span teaching, commemoration, political representation, legislation, litigation, and everyday life.

Teaching

I will begin with teaching because it is so formative and so concentrated in the first decades of life. Offering students more inclusive and engaging access to the past can expand their perspectives in thinking about the present and their vision in imagining the future. Teaching's centrality in shaping young minds helps explain the intensity of conflict over curriculums. Recent years have seen waves of state legislation restricting how public schools may address contentious issues, including sex discrimination as well as race, sexual orientation, and gender identity.[1] Countering that onslaught will take tremendous work. But it is well worth fighting for students' right to learn about the unvarnished past, with both its triumphs and its tragedies. Giving students more and more nuanced access to women's history can begin immediately in places where that is possible.

K-12 education is especially important because it reaches the most people, some of whom will never read a history book again. Textbooks and teachers can draw on the vibrant and ever-growing body of scholarship on women's struggles for equality in United States. While K-12 classes will be unable to cover all this material in detail, at least three overarching and interlinked points can be made clear.

The first is about inclusion. Women are not a sideshow to the main event, with stories that teachers can skip or relegate to specialized elective courses. Women's experiences are just as important as men's experiences. A generalization about American history does not work as a generalization if it excludes women. Along the same lines, generalizations about women's experiences do not work as generalizations if they treat some groups of women as irrelevant. For example, lessons should not present white women's experiences as the experiences of all women, with women of color erased.

The second point to highlight is about conflict. Americans have spent generations battling over women's status under the law and in society. Consensus and men's spontaneous enlightenment did not drive progress forward and neither did a few late, great women acting alone. Progress has required concerted mobilization to overcome determined opponents. The unequal status quo has always had ardent—sometimes even violent—defenders.

The third point to emphasize is about incompleteness. Women's rights and opportunities have expanded in myriad ways over time. But legal authorities have also sometimes reversed women's hard-fought gains, and the persistence of women's inequality remains a fault line running through American history. Relentless resistance has meant that many of the goals reform-minded women have been pursuing for generations have yet to be achieved. Progress remains in progress, rather than complete.

Of course, simply proclaiming these points is unlikely to be an effective classroom technique. I will provide some examples of how teachers can integrate the themes into their curriculum.

More accurate teaching about the Nineteenth Amendment can reveal facets of women's history that influential Americans frequently overlook or underemphasize. Too often, textbook authors, popular writers, and legal authorities characterize the Nineteenth Amendment as a gift from men that gave women the vote and a commonsensical advance for the nation.[2] This presentation misleads on multiple scores.

The Nineteenth Amendment was not a gift and many Americans— including many of the men who ran the country—did not accept it as commonsensical at the time. The Nineteenth Amendment was a multigenerational battle, with suffragists facing powerful opposition to the end. Recall that the Nineteenth Amendment passed the Senate with only two votes to spare. After that, no more than twelve state legislatures could holdout if the amendment was to become part of the Constitution. Eight states had already rejected the amendment by the time suffragists convinced the Tennessee Legislature to provide the last ratification needed for victory. The Tennessee House approved the amendment with no votes to spare.[3]

Indeed, resistance to the Nineteenth Amendment persisted even after ratification. Georgia and Mississippi refused to let any women vote in the November 1920 election, on the excuse that the Nineteenth Amendment's ratification that August had given women insufficient time to comply with the lengthy advance registration requirements in those states.[4] Georgia would not ratify the Nineteenth Amendment until 1970.[5] Mississippi would not ratify until 1984.[6]

Presenting suffrage history as if the path to the Nineteenth Amendment was smooth and harmonious can implicitly train students to anticipate that Americans will readily accept needed reforms and to assume that heated opposition to reform proposals undermines the case for their necessity. The amendment's actual history illustrates how even essential reforms can face ferocious opposition, including violence against peaceful protestors. The Nineteenth Amendment became commonsensical rather than controversial only in retrospect.

Teaching students about the Nineteenth Amendment also provides an opportunity to illustrate how women's struggles for equality remain ongoing. Every American should understand both that the United States Constitution guarantees no one the right to vote and that chasms often exist between voting rights on paper and in practice.[7] The Nineteenth Amendment prohibits sex-based denials of the franchise. But framing that amendment as conclusively establishing women's access to the polls misdescribes reality and implicitly centers white women. Laws on the books or tactics on the ground have denied many women the vote since 1920, especially women of color. Battles over voting and voter suppression rage to this day.[8]

The history of women's work provides more rich teaching opportunities. For example, this history presents an opportunity to examine how influential Americans have rationalized and defended restrictions on women's rights. Courts and commentators have often used the term "protective labor legislation" to describe the sex-specific regulation of working women that the Supreme Court upheld in *Muller v. Oregon* (1908) and that states continued to enforce for most of the twentieth century.[9] The term invokes consensus and aligned interests, suggesting that these statutes made women and society as a whole better off.[10] Rather than simply adopting the loaded phrase, teachers and students can explore whether it accurately characterizes restrictions on women's working hours, prohibitions on women holding certain jobs, and the like. While some supporters of those restraints had protective aspirations

and dreams of extending the regulations beyond female workers, this legislation legalized women's exclusion from jobs that men wanted and helped
confine working women to the underpaid dead end where exploitation was
most rampant.[11]

Classes interrogating rather than just repeating the protective moniker can
delve into specific examples. Think of the 1945 Michigan anti-barmaid statute
that the all-male bartenders' union lobbied for and the all-male Supreme
Court upheld in *Goesaert v. Cleary* (1948). That legislation safeguarded the
employment and earnings of male bartenders, but did not protect women
from anything except better jobs and higher pay. Instead of fostering female
security, the law pushed women toward economic and physical vulnerability
by closing bartending to them while keeping cocktail waitressing open. Even
the wives or daughters of male bar owners—the only women Michigan permitted to bartend in larger cities—were not protected, as the statute included
no requirement that the male owner pay his female relative or be present while
she tended bar.[12]

Teachers and students can also explore how power brokers selectively
deployed the language of protection by considering the contrast with the
Fair Labor Standards Act of 1938. Congress enacted this legislation after the
Supreme Court overturned the *Lochner v. New York* (1905) decision that
Chapter 1 discussed, and the statute has always applied to male as well as
female workers.[13] In fact, the 1938 legislation evinced a particular concern
for white male workers by excluding many occupations—such as domestic
service, laundry work, and farm labor—that were dominated by women, people of color, or both.[14] The FLSA does not use protective language when
establishing a right to time-and-a-half overtime pay for covered employees
working more than forty hours a week.[15] Congress chose the language of fairness instead. Moreover, the FLSA is explicitly concerned about preserving
employment and earning power, issues male lawmakers did not ordinarily
mention when imposing sex-specific restrictions on working women.[16]

I will turn now to higher education, specifically law school teaching. I am
not dwelling on the need to include women's past, present, and future in
liberal arts education because women's stories are likely more accessible in
liberal arts programs than anywhere else in the educational system—even
if colleges and universities still too often confine those stories to courses on
women's history or women's studies and fail to adequately integrate them into
mainline surveys in history, political science, and other core subjects.

Law schools teach far fewer students than colleges or K-12 schools, but
have outsized influence because law students are future lawyers, law professors, judges, and legislators. The same points about inclusion, conflict, and

incompleteness that I highlighted for K-12 education are vital in law schools as well. Too often, law teaching implicitly relegates women to the peripheries while foregrounding men. Women's lives under the law are equally worthy of study, and law school courses should not present those experiences as footnotes or exceptions while treating men's experiences as the ordinary baseline. When examining women's legal treatment, law school courses can highlight how judges have relied on spontaneous enlightenment stories that deny women's role in propelling legal change and obscure the battles required to win improvements in women's status. Law school courses can also explore how judges enforcing limits on women's rights and opportunities have sought to rationalize their decisions with self-contradictory victory announcements insisting that America has already achieved sex equality.

Opportunities to center women along with men abound. In constitutional law courses, professors could foster discussions about expanding the lists of the Supreme Court's most important or most terrible constitutional decisions that regularly appear in legal scholarship and shape law teaching. Law professors devising and disseminating these lists routinely omit cases about women's rights.[17] If deployed differently, these lists could become opportunities to broaden conversations rather than keeping them narrowed on the same few cases. Students could consider why no cases about women's rights have made these lists and explore which cases might be worthy additions. For example, many of the decisions this book examines would be prime candidates for inclusion on lists of the Supreme Court's worst, including *Muller* (interpreting the Constitution on the premise that women rather than men should prioritize domesticity),[18] *Breedlove v. Suttles* (1937) (upholding a poll tax and allowing states to give women a financial incentive not to vote),[19] *Goesaert* (permitting states to ban women from jobs men want),[20] *Hoyt v. Florida* (1961) (treating women as unnecessary participants in public life and denying women juries of their peers),[21] and *Dobbs v. Jackson Women's Health Organization* (2022) (empowering lawmakers to compel childbearing).[22]

The teaching of constitutional decisions already on worst-ever lists can also be more inclusive. Professors should pair class time spent on *Lochner* with roughly equal time spent on *Muller*. Each of these seminal decisions in the first decade of the twentieth century read the Justices' ideological views into the Constitution. Both were about the constitutionality of statutory restrictions on working hours, with *Lochner* rejecting them for men and *Muller* embracing them for women. Teaching *Lochner* without *Muller* alongside it runs the risk of erasing women and presenting a legal regime that applied exclusively to men as if it established a general rule.

Pairing *Lochner* and *Muller* brings both decisions into sharper focus and directs attention to key questions: Why did the Court treat men and women so differently, promoting (purportedly) unrestrained autonomy for men while pushing women to live for others? Why did *Lochner* become a Supreme Court obsession, a cornerstone of constitutional law's anti-canon, and the wellspring of persistent insults about Lochnerism, when the Court cites *Muller* much less often, *Muller* does not make lists of the Court's most significant or terrible decisions, and Mullerism is a term no one (but me) uses? Is it because the men who have dominated the Court and the legal academy have simply been more interested in how the law treats men? Is it because the Justices believe they repudiated Lochnerism long ago, but Mullerism remains a powerful driver of legal decisionmaking to the present day?[23]

Plessy v. Ferguson (1896) is another anti-canonical case, taught ubiquitously. Yet there are still opportunities to highlight different elements of the decision and draw connections across categories. Women are not the only marginalized group subjected to the judiciary's self-contradictory victory announcements. *Plessy's* endorsement of racially segregated transportation deployed that strategy as well, with the Court announcing "the legal equality" of African Americans and whites in the process of upholding legalized white supremacy.[24] Examining *Plessy's* self-contradiction can enhance discussion of that decision while simultaneously weaving women's legal history more tightly into the fabric of constitutional law teaching.

Courses beyond constitutional law should also center women along with men. For example, courses examining statutory prohibitions on employment discrimination should counter the womanless account of how Title VII of the 1964 Civil Rights Act came to include a prohibition on sex discrimination in employment. Professors and students can explore why courts and commentators have repeated this inaccurate story for decades, despite all the evidence documenting how women mobilized to get the sex amendment into Title VII and keep it there.[25] Why have so many influential Americans swallowed a tale about women's progress in which the only important actors are men? Is it because such stories remain commonplace? Is it because judges, journalists, and mainstream scholars too often ignore existing scholarship on women's legal history? Is it because schools too frequently train students to expect and accept that?

In short, teaching offers unparalleled opportunities to enrich how students understand the past, expand how they think about the present, and enliven how they plan for the future. Teachers, textbooks, and students should seize these chances as often as they can.

Commemoration

Commemorations teach outside the classroom. When they thread stories about America through memorable occasions and ordinary days, we can absorb the lessons without ever opening a book and long after leaving student life behind. Too often, America's commemorations push women into the shadows and place men alone in the spotlight. Transforming the commemorative landscape will be challenging. As we have seen, efforts to focus public memory on women have faced fierce opposition for generations.[26] This is another battle worth fighting for generations to come.

America needs both more commemoration of women and different kinds of commemoration. I will start by highlighting promising projects that Americans can build on and then propose additional ideas.

The American Women's History Museum offers an unprecedented opportunity to reshape the nation's commemorative landscape. Chapter 2 discussed the decades-long mobilization that finally managed to maneuver around conservative opposition and win congressional approval for the museum at the end of 2020. As of this writing, Congress has not authorized a building site and the museum remains years away from opening.[27]

The national women's history museum could make extraordinary contributions to public memory. It can fulfill that potential only by exploring the full, sometimes uncomfortable reality of American women's past. Foregrounding conflict, inclusion, and incompleteness is essential here as well. For example, a museum cannot faithfully examine the history of women's experiences in the United States without devoting sustained attention to the many people who fought feminist reform and promoted regression. Anti-feminism—including from women—is an important part of women's history.[28] As conservative critics have emphasized, the museum needs to remember right-wing figures like Phyllis Schlafly, one of the most influential Americans of the twentieth century.[29] Telling the full story likewise means acknowledging the boundaries that some feminists placed on their pursuit of equality. A museum cannot faithfully recount the battle for the Nineteenth Amendment without describing how white suffragists like Alice Paul and Carrie Chapman Catt entangled themselves with white supremacy.[30] Telling the full story also means recognizing that struggles and conflicts over women's rights and roles remain ongoing. The Equal Rights Amendment is a prime example, as are ongoing battles over access to the polls, as are ongoing battles over women's reproductive autonomy.[31]

The Lucy Burns Museum outside the nation's capital is less well-known than the national museum-in-progress and unlikely to ever attract the same volume of visitors. It is worth highlighting nonetheless as an illustration of how commemorations constructed on battle sites can focus public memory on the tremendous conflict that progress can require. This museum occupies the former site of the Occoquan Workhouse in Virginia,[32] where National Woman's Party suffragists arrested for picketing the White House were jailed, brutalized, and force fed.[33] Its naming honors the suffragist leader who spent more days in jail than any other American fighting for woman suffrage.[34]

The museum's location and name foreground the battle-scarred path to the Nineteenth Amendment and museum exhibits elaborate on that theme, examining the violence that men inflicted on suffragists and the determination of mobilized women who persisted nonetheless.[35] For example, a panel about the jailed suffragists' "Night of Terror" in November 1917 reports that: "Thirty new prisoners arrived at Occoquan on November 14—they were greeted by dozens of armed guards wielding clubs. Some were dragged to the Men's Workhouse, others were beaten and kicked. Lucy Burns spent the night handcuffed to her cell door. Guards threw 73-year-old Mary Nolan into her cell and bashed Dora Lewis's head against the wall, knocking her unconscious. Alice Cosu suffered a heart attack thinking Lewis had died. The suffragists began hunger strikes in protest, leading to repeated and painful force-feedings."[36] The same panel quotes Burns herself. She took notes in Occoquan that she managed to get smuggled out, and the National Woman's Party published them within days.[37] Burns's report of her forced feeding described how she "was held down by five people at the legs, arms and head." When she refused to open her mouth, a prison doctor shoved a feeding tube up her nostril. As Burns recounted: "I turned and twisted my head all I could, but he managed to push it up. It hurts nose and throat very much and makes nose bleed freely. Tube drawn out covered with blood. Operation leaves one very sick."[38] Reading these words on location at Occoquan can only magnify their impact.

Even temporary commemorations can enhance the landscape. Sharon Hayes exhibited *If They Should Ask* in Philadelphia's Rittenhouse Square for two months in the fall of 2017.[39] The sculpture featured nine half-size pedestals that Hayes modeled after pedestals uplifting statues of notable men in Philadelphia.[40] Rather than pick a few women to honor with statues on her pedestals, Hayes left the pedestals empty but inscribed.[41] The inscription began: "On this site there could be a statue to . . . ."[42] Hayes then listed more than eighty remarkable women from a roster generated collectively.[43] She had convened a diverse group of female Philadelphians to begin collecting names of women from the Philadelphia area who contributed to the city's history. Hayes also established a website so members of the general public could submit suggestions.[44]

Since 2004, Ruth Sergel has organized Chalk as an annual remembrance for the victims of the Triangle Shirtwaist Factory fire in lower Manhattan on March 25, 1911.[45] That fire killed 146 people, including 129 women.[46] They worked and died at a garment factory without sprinklers, fire doors, fire drills, fire stairs, firewalls, or other precautions against cotton's extreme flammability.[47] Their bosses had violently resisted unionization.[48] Indeed, the owners were so obsessed with control that they kept some of the factory doors locked to restrict employees' movements.[49] The fire's horrific death toll became a rallying cry as reformers pushed for workplace safety requirements and workers' rights.[50] Each March 25, volunteers participating in Chalk fan out through New York City so that someone visits every place where one of the 146 fire victims lived.[51] On the pavement in front of each victim's former home, a volunteer chalks the victim's name, age, address, and the fact that she died on March 25, 1911, in the Triangle Shirtwaist Factory fire.[52] The volunteers post a flyer about the fire near each chalking.[53]

These temporary commemorations share three features that could inspire many other projects. First, both benefit from collective wisdom and strength. *If They Should Ask* drew on many women's ideas about which female historical figures deserve commemoration. Chalk requires many people to come together to make the commemoration happen.

Second, both extend beyond their specific subjects of remembrance to simultaneously focus public attention on the overarching issue of women's scarcity in the commemorative landscape. An empty pedestal or a name chalked on the sidewalk spotlight absence, prodding observers to think about all the statues of women that would grace public spaces if memorialization was as open to women as it has been for men.

Third, both suggest immediate strategies for chipping away at a monumental task (pun intended). Consider Philadelphia as an example. When Hayes exhibited *If They Should Ask* in 2017, Philadelphia's commemorations included more than fifteen hundred sculptures of men, but only two sculptures of women.[54] Unless cities like Philadelphia suddenly become willing and able to unveil a new female statue every week (Monument Mondays?), America will not be counterbalancing generations of male-dominated memorialization within the next decades. Temporary commemorations are not adequate substitutes for more permanent additions. But *If They Should Ask* and Chalk have been vehicles for commemorating some women right away, while the work of reshaping the commemorative landscape in more lasting ways proceeds.

Going forward, reimagining America's commemorative landscape will nec-essarily be a collective and multigenerational endeavor. Many ideas for com-memoration will likely emerge at the local level and focus on remembering women and events tied to that place. I will offer my own ideas for important projects to pursue and hope they can prompt more proposals, conversation, and mobilization.

The two hundred and fiftieth anniversary of the United States in 2026 presents an immediate opportunity. As we have seen, reform-minded women have been eager from their first years of mobilization to tie women's struggles for equality to milestone anniversaries in American history. Women pursued these efforts from the outside because the official commemorations treated women as an irrelevance or an afterthought. When Susan B. Anthony and other suffragists disrupted the official centennial ceremony in 1876 or when the National Organization for Women held a counterrally on the bicentennial in 1976, the men leading the official commemorations were busy proclaim-ing that the Founders had established government by the consent of the governed.[55]

That story depends on excluding the experiences of most people in the early United States. The nation's first census, in 1790, reported that free white males aged sixteen and older constituted just 20.7% of the population in the thirteen original states plus the districts of Kentucky, Maine, and Vermont.[56] Almost every potential voter came from this narrow sliver, and even some white men could not vote at the nation's start because of state restrictions on voting, including property ownership requirements.[57] In comparison, the first census recorded that 17.8% of the people in the same area were enslaved, 39.6% were free white females, 20.3% were free white males younger than sixteen, and 1.5% were "All other free persons."[58]

When the nation's semi-quincentennial arrives in 2026, women should not be an afterthought and should not have to claw their way into the commemo-rations. When Americans remember the Founding, we should remember all of it. Freedom and self-government were part of the Founding, and so were slavery and subjection. The experiences of women, enslaved and not, were as much a part of the Founding as the experiences of men.

America's federal holidays should also be more inclusive. These celebra-tions structure the year while providing annual occasions for remembrance and reflection. But as Chapter 2 observed, Congress has never created a legal public holiday to honor a woman or to recognize women's struggles for sex equality.

Women's mobilization could generate excitement about the prospect of a new federal holiday and solicit input about which woman or women

Congress should honor. *If They Should Ask* suggests one model for gathering ideas about potential honorees. The grassroots "Women on 20s" campaign suggests another. That campaign proposed fifteen possible women to depict on the front of the twenty-dollar bill and ran online polls in 2015 to gauge popular reactions. Over a quarter million people (256,659) voted in the first poll to select finalists. More people (352,431) voted in a second poll choosing between four finalists, which Harriet Tubman won.[59] As Chapter 2 discussed, Treasury Secretary Jacob Lew ultimately announced in April 2016 a plan to place Tubman's image on the front of the twenty. That redesign will hopefully be forthcoming.

Alternatively or in addition, a grassroots campaign could explore pursuing a federal holiday that would commemorate women's struggles for equality without singling out an individual woman for remembrance. August 26, the anniversary of the Nineteenth Amendment and the Women's Strike for Equality, is one possible date.

An argument for this approach is that it recognizes another way the commemorative landscape needs to grow. Celebrating more remarkable women, one at a time, is not enough. No one woman moved the nation forward on her own, no matter how effective she was. When commemorations tell America's stories, they should include the collective mobilization required to propel progress in the face of powerful resistance.

With that in mind, America also needs more commemorations like the Lucy Burns Museum that mark battle sites in women's struggles for equality. I will offer two proposals here, but more possibilities abound.

There should be a museum in Winona, Mississippi, on the site where police jailed and attacked Fannie Lou Hamer and her civil rights colleagues on June 9, 1963.[60] Museum exhibits could contextualize that day in Winona, situating the police violence within the long history of institutionalized white supremacy and documenting the collective courage and commitment required to combat this power structure. It took until 2022 for Winona to establish an annual "Fannie Lou Hamer Day" on the anniversary of the violence and to erect a historical marker on the site where the city's jail stood in 1963.[61] The marker acknowledges that Hamer challenged "Mississippi's and the nation's White supremacists by demanding equal rights."[62] A museum could build on these important first steps and do much more, including by highlighting primary sources. For example, the federal government pursued criminal charges against five lawmen allegedly involved in the Winona atrocities.[63] The prosecution ended unsuccessfully on December 6, 1963, when an all-white male jury acquitted the defendants after only seventy-six minutes of deliberation.[64] But the trial transcript includes testimony from

Rosemary Freeman, Lawrence Guyot, Fannie Lou Hamer, June Elizabeth Johnson, Annell Ponder, Euvester Simpson, and James Harold West about the police brutality they suffered in the Winona jail.[65] Hamer recounted her experiences within and beyond Winona for the rest of her life.[66]

There should also be a battle marker at Cameron House, the former National Woman's Party headquarters where a mob of men attacked suffragists on August 14, 1917.[67] The current historical marker does not mention women or suffrage, confining itself to reporting on prominent men who visited or lived in the house.[68] A marker describing how this site steps from the White House featured in the struggle over the Nineteenth Amendment could explain the furious and far-reaching opposition to woman suffrage, remembering the servicemen in uniform and civilian federal employees who participated in the anti-suffrage mob and the policemen who allowed the violence to continue for hours. The marker could recount how suffragists persisted in picketing the White House despite assaults and arrests, and even snuck out to picket while the mob was in the midst of storming party headquarters.[69] The marker could further explain why the National Woman's Party spent only a brief time at Cameron House. A month before the mob descended, the suffragists' landlord had informed the notorious women that they would have to leave.[70] A marker at Cameron House about woman suffrage and its foes would complement the exhibits at the Sewall-Belmont House, which was National Woman's Party headquarters starting in 1929— well after the Nineteenth Amendment's ratification.[71] The Sewall-Belmont House became a national historic site in 1974 and a national monument in 2016, after the National Woman's Party fought off multiple congressional proposals over the years to demolish the building and make way for more federal office space.[72]

Commemorations of the past are so contested because historical memory shapes present thought and future action. But commemorating the past is simultaneously important and insufficient. America's commemorative landscape also needs more monuments that foreground women's ongoing struggles by focusing explicitly on today and tomorrow.

In that vein, I will close this section by proposing an Equal Pay Clock. This digital clock would present gender pay gaps along with the projected dates for their elimination, scrolling between the figures for women as a whole and for various groups of women. Recall that a recent report estimates based on past trends that America's gender pay gap will not close for full-time, year-round workers until 2066 and will not close for all workers until 2088.[73] Feminists could post an Equal Pay Clock in multiple physical locations as well as online. Ideally, at least one location would be in a well-trafficked public place that draws media attention, like Manhattan's Times Square. I modeled the idea after the National Debt Clock in Manhattan, and there is also a Climate Clock in Manhattan and a Doomsday Clock in Chicago.[74] The National Debt Clock builds visual force by spiraling ever upward, even in the time a pedestrian takes to pass on the sidewalk. The Equal Pay Clock would attract the eye by rotating between different statistics, but would build its visual force from the glacial pace of change in the projected dates.

An Equal Pay Clock would complement the annual Equal Pay Days that feminists have been marking for more than a quarter century. These commemorations highlight how many extra days women need to work in order to catch up with what men made in the previous calendar year.[75] For example, March 12 was 2024's Equal Pay Day because the average woman working full-time and year-round had to work almost fourteen and a half months—2023, plus nearly two and a half months into 2024—to catch up with what the average male full-time, year-round worker made in 2023 alone.[76] Equal Pay Days have the advantage of creating annual occasions to mobilize around, whether with a rally, legislative hearing, presidential proclamation, or otherwise.[77] An Equal Pay Clock would have the advantage of constant visibility.

None of these commemorative projects will be easy to accomplish, and they represent just a few of innumerable possibilities. Women have been battling their marginalization in America's commemorative landscape for generations, and the work of reconstructing that landscape will need to continue for generations to come. We have to keep fighting to enrich and expand the stories our commemorations tell about our nation and ourselves.

Political Representation

Let's move from commemorations entangled in politics to consider political representation more directly. I began this book with Alice Paul's predictions at the end of 1922. She forecast that it would "not require one hundred years to elect a woman President of the United States" and that women would "comprise half of the membership of Congress" before 2023.[78] Paul's predictions are now over a century old. Not one woman has ever been President. As of mid-November 2024, women fill just 28.4% of the voting seats in Congress—along with just 32.8% of the seats in state legislatures.[79] It is far too late for Paul's predictions to have yet to come true.

At this point, American women have been striving for generations to increase their representation in political office. Shortly after the Nineteenth Amendment's ratification, the National Woman's Party launched campaigns to push for women's election to Congress in 1924 and 1926.[80] Those campaigns made little headway. The November 1924 and 1926 elections each produced just one new congresswoman, a new member of the House of Representatives.[81] Two more women won special elections in 1925 to succeed their late husbands in the House.[82]

The pace of change remained agonizingly slow thereafter. Jeannette Rankin, who in November 1916 had become the first woman ever elected to Congress,[83] assessed the situation bluntly in a 1966 interview she gave at age eighty-five: "We're half the people; we should be half the Congress."[84] Note that Rankin did not predict when women would achieve equal representation in Congress. Perhaps that future seemed more distant in 1966 than it had in the heady days immediately after the Nineteenth Amendment victory. A half century after Rankin's first election to the House, women held only fourteen (2.6%) of the 535 seats in Congress.[85]

Paul's predictions and Rankin's declaration remind us not to set expectations too low. Many media stories over the past half century have described a particular election cycle as the "Year of the Woman,"[86] or announced the "Feminization of Politics,"[87] or reported a "Pink Wave" in Congress.[88] Recognizing progress is important, but premature proclamations of victory can obscure how much further America still needs to go before women are equally represented in government.

Consider 1992, perhaps the most famous Year of the Woman. The November election that year occurred in the aftermath of Clarence Thomas's ascension to the Supreme Court in 1991.[89] There were just twenty-nine women in the House when Thomas joined the Court, and only two women in the Senate that confirmed Thomas.[90] An all-male Senate Judiciary Committee— which Joe Biden chaired—questioned Thomas and Anita Hill, who reported that Thomas had sexually harassed her at work.[91] Outrage over how the Senate's men mishandled the situation and mistreated Hill added fuel to the campaigns of women running for Congress in 1992.[92] After endless media speculation about an imminent Year of the Woman,[93] the November 1992 election did boost the number of congresswomen. Yet female representation remained absurdly low. When the new Congress convened in January 1993, women held just forty-eight (11.0%) of 435 seats in the House and just six of one hundred seats in the Senate.[94] Journalistic declarations that 1992 had proved to be the Year of the Woman were wildly unrealistic.[95] Politics was still stuck in the Year/Millennia of the Man.

Anti-feminists are well aware of the tension between their premature announcements that America has already achieved sex equality and the demographics of the Presidency, Congress, and state legislatures. That is why they strive so mightily to rationalize women's political marginalization and insist that persistent sex discrimination does not help explain women's continued scarcity at the top.[96] Those arguments are meant to counter intuitions that the government should look more like the people it is supposed to serve. Feminists can build on those intuitions, even while recognizing that they coexist with persistent expectations that the typical politician will be male.

Women running for federal or state Houses of Representatives could recycle Bella Abzug's slogan from when she first ran for Congress in 1970:

> This woman's place
> is in the House
> the House of Representatives![97]

Abzug trumpeted that slogan in her successful summer primary battle against a male incumbent,[98] and many female candidates for Congress or state legislatures have since repeated it.[99]

Indeed, recall from Chapter 6 that Phyllis Schlafly used a version of the same slogan during her second campaign for Congress. "My opponent says a woman's place is in the home," Schlafly told voters in October 1970. "But my husband replies that a woman's place is in the House—the United States House of Representatives."[100] Schlafly's delivery of that line a few months after Abzug's well-publicized primary victory raises the possibility that Schlafly got the idea for the zinger from Abzug. That possibility is particularly intriguing because Schlafly and Abzug would soon become fierce antagonists. When Schlafly devoted the January 1976 issue of her newsletter to attacking the Commission on International Women's Year, she called the commission "Bella Abzug's Boondoggle."[101] Abzug and Schlafly even debated each other in person at least once, sparring over the Equal Rights Amendment at a 1979 Kentucky college symposium.[102]

If Schlafly did take inspiration from a trailblazing feminist, she took care to twist Abzug's slogan rightward. Rather than proclaiming in her own voice that women belong in Congress, Schlafly presented herself as her husband's messenger. The adjustment emphasized that Schlafly was campaigning with his approval and respecting his authority.

I prefer Abzug's version, which asserted women's right to wield political power without asking whether a man approved of that prospect. Abzug's heirs can also adapt her slogan for myriad political ambitions. Many women pursuing Senate seats have told voters that "a woman's place is in the House and the Senate."[103] Hillary Clinton's 2016 presidential campaign declared that "a woman's place is in the White House,"[104] and that slogan also appeared during

Shirley Chisholm's 1972 run for the presidency and Geraldine Ferraro's 1984 run for the vice presidency.[105]

Abzug, meanwhile, had a new slogan ready when she set her sights on the Senate. There were no female Senators in the ninety-third and ninety-fourth Congresses, in office from 1973 to 1976.[106] When Abzug ran for a Senate seat in the 1976 election and when she campaigned for other female Senate candidates, she declared: "As the saying goes, 'A stag Senate is a stagnation.'" "That's how the saying goes," Abzug explained, "because I keep on saying it."[107]

Battles to secure women's equal representation in politics have been ongoing for over a century, and victory is not yet in sight. To be sure, women do not all think and vote the same way. Abzug and Schlafly were fierce antagonists because they fiercely disagreed with each other. But Americans have never experienced what politics could look like—and what it might do—if women were just as likely as men to be in state legislatures, Congress, and the Oval Office. We need to keep pushing until every year in politics is the year of the people, rather than yet another year of the men.

Legislation

Well before women achieve equal political representation, there is much legislation to mobilize for now at both the federal and state levels. A comprehensive list would be longer than one chapter could contain, but I can highlight some of the unfinished legislative business that examining the multigenerational record of women's struggles for equality brings to the fore. I group this ongoing legislative agenda into five categories: the ballot box, the body, the bottom line, the balance, and the baseline.

The Ballot Box. I will discuss voting rights first because they are foundational to the ability to achieve all other legislative goals. As Fannie Lou Hamer, Mary Church Terrell, Alice Paul, Carrie Chapman Catt, Susan B. Anthony, Elizabeth Cady Stanton, and the countless women who fought alongside them knew, lawmakers often disregard the disenfranchised.

Too often, America's dominant stories mask injustice and encourage complacency by framing women's struggles for voting rights as parts of the past rather than the present, as if they ended with congressional enactment of the 1965 Voting Rights Act or even with the 1920 ratification of the Nineteenth Amendment's prohibition on sex-based disenfranchisement. The Supreme Court's opinion in *Dobbs v. Jackson Women's Health Organization* (2022) presents yet another example of this distorted account of American history. *Dobbs* ignored the Court's refusal to recognize an affirmative constitutional right to vote, and the many women disenfranchised since 1920, to declare that "women gained the constitutional right to vote in 1920."[108]

Struggles over voting and voter suppression are ongoing, providing the backdrop to every other legislative battle.[109] Consider the ban on abortion after fifteen weeks of pregnancy that the Mississippi Legislature enacted in 2018 and the Supreme Court upheld in *Dobbs*.[110] Polling in Mississippi found that a majority disagreed "with the Supreme Court's decision to overturn the right to an abortion."[111] So why was the Mississippi Legislature so eager to roll back female autonomy? I suspect it was relevant that men filled 85.1% of the seats in the legislature that passed the anti-abortion law *Dobbs* upheld.[112] It was also probably important that multiple methods of voter suppression distorted the elections that produced this state government.[113] Why worry about what a majority of the state population thinks if that majority does not determine who runs Mississippi?

Federal lawmakers have proposed an array of reforms to protect and expand voting rights. For example, Congress could enhance voter access by making election day a legal public holiday,[114] requiring states to offer same-day voter registration,[115] and setting national minimum standards for early voting and voting by mail.[116] Congress could combat partisan gerrymandering and promote electoral competition by establishing uniform criteria for congressional redistricting.[117] Congress could pass a revised version of the Voting Rights Act enforcement mechanism that the Supreme Court struck down in 2013, so jurisdictions with a history of voting rights violations need federal preclearance before changing election rules.[118] None of these proposals will be easy to enact, precisely because they would be politically consequential. But all are worth fighting for because voting—as a right under the law and a reality on the ground—facilitates the pursuit of every other right and opportunity.

The Body. Let's now consider one of the most important rights that voting can secure, the right to control your own body. In many arenas this book has examined, women have moved forward over time, even if progress has often been too slow and too small. Change has run in the opposite direction for reproductive rights, with the Supreme Court dragging women backward. The *Dobbs* decision removing federal constitutional constraints on legislative control over abortion is one of the biggest feminist setbacks in American history.[119] Unsurprisingly, the available evidence indicates that women were more likely than men to register to vote after a draft of the *Dobbs* majority opinion leaked in May 2022.[120]

Dobbs exemplifies and exacerbates women's legal vulnerability in the United States. Powerful Americans have boasted from the nation's earliest days about America's commitment to liberty and self-government, even as they denied women those prerogatives. Women have many more rights and opportunities now than they had at the Founding, but that fundamental contradiction persists. America continues to present itself as freedom-loving while withholding freedom from women.

A young protestor named Soraya Bata highlighted that contradiction when standing outside the Supreme Court building on June 24, 2022, the day the Justices announced their decision in *Dobbs*.[121] The sign she held read: "WE WERE NEVER THE LAND OF THE FREE."[122] Bata's sign (Figure 7.1) immediately reminded me of Fannie Lou Hamer's electrifying testimony before the Credentials Committee of the 1964 Democratic National Convention. Hamer recounted the police brutality she endured in Winona as payback for her civil rights activism and asked: "Is this America, the land of the free and the home of the brave?"[123] Like Hamer, Bata transformed the national anthem from a celebration of freedom achieved to a launching pad for protest about the many Americans still denied self-government.

As I write this chapter, much of American politics centers on conflict over whether women will control their reproductive capacities and their own lives. Congress is one battlefield, marked by competing proposals to restrict

Figure 7.1 Outside the Supreme Court, Washington, D.C., June 24, 2022.
Source: Getty

abortion nationally or to legalize abortion nationwide.[124] The battles run even more furiously through statehouses, with some legislatures protecting women's rights to make their own decisions and others forcing women into childbearing.[125] Battles also rage over ballot measures, which have energized voters and produced multiple victories for abortion rights since *Dobbs*.[126] All these battles will continue for the foreseeable future, requiring untold mobilization, commitment, and persistence from feminists within and outside government.

The *Dobbs* decision highlighted how anti-abortion forces have been leaning on exaggerated accounts of American progress to deny the injuries that abortion bans inflict on women. Chapter 5 illustrated how to counter those arguments with empirical evidence about how difficult pregnancy, childbirth, and motherhood remain in a nation with horrifying maternal mortality rates, persistent sex discrimination, and a flimsy social safety net. Anti-abortion legislatures like Mississippi's purport to be pro-life, but that asserted commitment is difficult to detect in the state's treatment of mothers and children. We can do much more to expose contradictions within the anti-abortion movement, including by demonstrating how the words and actions of anti-abortion figures contradict the movement's overly rosy depictions of American progress.

For example, anti-abortion groups have been wielding the premise "that attitudes about the pregnancy of unmarried women have changed drastically" as a rationale for denying women control over whether to carry such pregnancies to term.[127] But anti-abortion advocacy frequently undercuts the movement's assertions about an attitudinal transformation, with members of the anti-abortion movement continuing to stigmatize women who become pregnant outside of marriage. Michael J. McMonagle published a 2022 opinion piece in the *Philadelphia Inquirer* outlining his agenda as the president of the Pro-Life Coalition of Pennsylvania. Rather than demonstrating new attitudes, McMonagle described unmarried pregnancy as "this challenge of sexual promiscuity."[128] That same year, an anti-abortion advocate testified before a committee of the Indiana General Assembly, urging legislators to not "just ban abortion as a medical procedure" but also "criminalize the act of abortion." He told lawmakers: "Don't listen to clergypersons who think that teenagers in their youth group shouldn't have consequences for being promiscuous."[129] Recent letters to the editor strike similar notes, contending that "all single women should be encouraged to take responsibility for their promiscuous actions by abstinence or other available methods rather than by abortion,"[130] or castigating "abortion for convenience and the promotion of promiscuity."[131]

Indeed, women who become pregnant outside of marriage continue to be fired from institutions that oppose abortion. Victoria Crisitello was an unmarried "art teacher and toddler room caregiver" at the St. Theresa School, a part of the Archdiocese of Newark, New Jersey.[132] In 2014, the school fired her after learning that she was pregnant.[133] The school's successful defense of its requirement that employees abstain from premarital sex suggested no flight from traditional attitudes, instead emphasizing the religious view that "to engage in sex outside of marriage is a sin."[134]

Sarah Syring was an unmarried middle school English teacher at the Saint Andrew Academy, a part of the Archdiocese of Louisville, Kentucky.[135] She similarly reported being fired in 2020 after disclosing her pregnancy.[136] Her employer acknowledged terminating Syring because she violated the "Christian Witness policy."[137]

Naiad Reich was an English teacher at the Our Lady of Lourdes Regional High School, a part of the Diocese of Harrisburg, Pennsylvania.[138] She was fired in 2018 after disclosing that she had become pregnant outside of marriage, with the termination letter explaining that Reich's nonmarital pregnancy violated "the morality clause" in her employment contract.[139] In subsequent litigation, Reich's employer repeatedly emphasized that her "conduct, in intentionally conceiving a child out of wedlock and intentionally refusing to marry, constitutes not only serious and public immorality, but also constitutes public scandal."[140]

Conflicts over reproductive rights are the most visible examples of women's ongoing battles to establish and exercise control over their own bodies. But they are not the only ones. As Chapter 5 observed, at least twelve states still treat sex crimes more leniently if the perpetrator acted while married to his victim. They prohibit a narrower range of conduct, impose weaker penalties, or enforce special obstacles to prosecution. While states have rewritten their sex crime legislation in sex-neutral language,[141] the available evidence suggests that the law's persistent leniency toward sex crimes within marriage overwhelmingly benefits men and jeopardizes women.[142] These statutes protect and perpetuate prerogatives that the law has empowered husbands to wield over their wives since the nation's earliest days, denying women sexual autonomy and bodily integrity.

Yet the Supreme Court's precedents shield this legislation. The Court has made statutes phrased in sex-neutral terms constitutionally secure—no matter how disproportionately the legislation harms women. These statutes are exempt from the heightened scrutiny that judges apply to explicitly sex-based laws challenged under the Fourteenth Amendment's Equal Protection Clause, unless the plaintiff can establish that lawmakers "selected or reaffirmed" the facially neutral provision "at least in part because of, not merely in spite of, its adverse effects upon" women.[143] Proving such legislative malice is all but impossible.

The path to transforming the law on husbands' sexual prerogatives accordingly runs through legislatures rather than courts. Feminists need to keep fighting until sex crimes no longer distinguish between perpetrators based on whether they are married to their victims. It is long past time for the law to recognize that marriage should not diminish a woman's rights over her own body.

The Bottom Line. Let's turn to economics. No matter what rights exist as a formal matter, the ability to steer one's own life, access opportunities, and make decisions without the pressure of desperation often turns on finances.

The pay gap between men and women has remained remarkably unyielding over time. More than two decades ago, in 2003, the median woman working full-time and year-round earned just 75.5 cents for every dollar a full-time, year-round male worker made.[144] That figure has budged little since, rising to just 82.7 cents in 2023.[145] A robust empirical literature documents the pervasiveness of the gender pay gap, even when researchers control for other variables like education, industry, occupation, race, region, unionization, work experience, and work hours.[146]

Anti-feminists recognize that this gap is galling. That is why they are so anxious to explain it away and insist that sex discrimination does not factor into its persistence.[147] But studies confirm what many women know from personal experience—that women encounter both overt discrimination and unconscious biases at work, including when employers make pay decisions. For example, one study gave science professors application materials purportedly from an undergraduate seeking work as a laboratory manager. The applications were identical, except that approximately half the professors reviewed materials with a male name for the applicant and approximately half reviewed materials with a female name.[148] The science professors judged the male applicant to be more competent and more worthy of hiring than the identical female applicant.[149] They offered the man an average starting salary of $30,238.10, while offering the woman an average of $26,507.94—just 87.66% of the man's pay.[150]

A study of academic psychologists similarly tested the impact of varying the name on a job applicant's otherwise unchanged curriculum vitae.[151] It found that the psychologists were significantly less likely to hire a female applicant than a male applicant with the same resume. The woman was also less likely to receive positive evaluations on her research, teaching, and service.[152]

There are many more studies.[153] Researchers found that changing audition procedures at symphony orchestras so that applicants were not visible to evaluators increased the likelihood that a female musician would be hired "by severalfold."[154] Another study found that white male employees received larger pay raises than women and people of color who scored equally well on performance evaluations.[155]

Mothers can be especially vulnerable to employment discrimination. One study used two sets of equally strong job application materials and varied which set of materials identified the applicant as a parent.[156] The researchers applied for 320 jobs by sending one application as a mother and a second as a childless woman; they responded to another 318 job postings by sending one application as a father and a second as a childless man. Mothers were approximately half as likely as childless women to receive callbacks (10 versus 21). In contrast, fathers received more callbacks than childless men (16 versus 9).[157]

In short, sex discrimination at work remains widespread, limiting pay and denying opportunities. While quick solutions are elusive, there are promising and proven reform strategies available that feminists should keep pushing more legislatures to pursue.

Congress should bar employers from questioning job applicants about their prior salaries. The too-common practice of asking about pay history before deciding what pay to offer can lock workers into a cycle of unequal compensation that they cannot escape by switching jobs.[158]

Federal legislation on the subject is currently inadequate. The federal Equal Pay Act of 1963 does not explicitly address pay history.[159] Some federal courts have interpreted this statute narrowly, allowing employers to use prior salary as a rationale for denying equal pay for equal work.[160]

In the absence of a nationwide ban on pay history questions from employers, a growing number of states have seized the initiative. An October 2023 survey found that legislation in sixteen states and Puerto Rico bars employers from asking about pay history or relying on pay history to set salaries.[161] I testified in support of passing such legislation in Minnesota five times between 2020 and 2023, when the state finally enacted a ban.[162]

Multiple studies have found that state salary history bans reduce gender pay gaps.[163] These bans can also help anyone else with a history of being underpaid. A 2020 study compared counties covered under a salary history ban with uncovered counties in the same labor markets.[164] It found that the enactment of salary history bans led to more salary postings in online help wanted ads and higher wages. The pay of job changers protected under a salary history ban rose by an average of five to six percent compared to unprotected job changers. That differential was even larger for female job changers (approximately eight percent) and African American job changers (approximately thirteen percent).[165] In other words, pay history bans made workers as a whole better off while simultaneously reducing both gender and racial pay gaps.

In every Congress since 1997, lawmakers have tried without success to enact bills addressing the problem of employers relying on pay history.[166] Faced with that legislative wheel-spinning, the Biden administration promulgated regulations in 2024 that bar federal agencies from using a new hire's salary history to set her pay.[167] The Biden administration also proposed regulations in 2024 that would bar federal contractors and subcontractors from asking about or considering the pay history of job applicants whose work would fall within or be connected to a federal government contract.[168]

Legislating in this arena should be a priority. Congress should explicitly bar employers from asking about pay history. In the meantime, more states should ban the practice. Employer questions about pay history perpetuate pay discrimination.

Some of the bosses arming themselves with information about pay history simultaneously strive to limit what their workers know about pay. Survey evidence indicates that employers often have formal or informal policies that prohibit or discourage employees from discussing pay.[169] Combatting these pay secrecy policies should be another legislative priority. They perpetuate pay discrimination by making it difficult or impossible for an employee to discover that she is paid less than her peers.

Lilly Ledbetter's experience is illustrative. She spent 1979 to 1998 as a supervisor at a Goodyear Tire & Rubber plant in Alabama.[170] Approximately eighty people worked as area managers in the plant at some point during those years, but just a handful were women.[171] At the end of 1997, Ledbetter was the only female area manager and her monthly salary was $3,727. The male area managers made more, even when they had less seniority than Ledbetter. Their monthly salaries ranged from $4,286 to $5,236.[172]

Ledbetter could not make these comparisons at the time, however, because Goodyear kept its pay decisions secret.[173] She later testified that she had "the feeling" as the end of her career approached "that maybe I wasn't getting paid as much as I should, or as much as the men. But there was no way to know for sure, because pay levels were kept strictly confidential." Ledbetter did not have access to "hard evidence of discrimination" until she received an anonymous note in March 1998 comparing her salary to the salaries of three male managers.[174] Once she got that tip, Ledbetter pursued legal redress for pay discrimination.[175] As Chapter 6 discussed, she lost in the Supreme Court in 2007 when the majority disregarded the obstacles that Ledbetter had faced in discovering that she was underpaid and insisted that Ledbetter had brought her suit too late.[176] Congress responded to the Court's decision with 2009 legislation relaxing Title VII's statute of limitations.[177] That addressed the timing issue but not the pay secrecy problem.

Legislative progress against pay secrecy remains insufficient. As of October 2023, only twenty-one states and the District of Columbia had legislation protecting employees against being punished for discussing pay.[178] At least two studies have found that gender pay gaps shrink in states that provide such protection.[179] At the federal level, an executive order generally prohibits federal contractors from discriminating against employees or applicants for discussing pay.[180] Employers also violate the National Labor Relations Act when they bar covered employees from discussing pay.[181] But that act leaves out many categories of workers, including agricultural laborers, domestic servants, independent contractors, and supervisors.[182] Even when a worker falls within the NLRA's coverage, the National Labor Relations Board cannot impose punitive remedies.[183] Decades of congressional proposals to provide workers with more far-reaching and robust protection against pay secrecy have been unsuccessful to date.[184] Protecting the right to discuss pay should be a legislative priority, for both Congress and the remaining states.

In addition, federal and state legislators can pursue other strategies to combat pay secrecy. For example, lawmakers could require employers to disclose a job's wage or wage range to applicants and existing employees. Efforts to pass federal legislation along these lines have been unsuccessful so far.[185] However, eleven states had enacted wage range transparency laws as of October 2023.[186] I testified twice in 2024 in support of proposed legislation in Minnesota, which the state enacted that year.[187] The Biden administration also proposed regulations in 2024 that would require federal contractors and subcontractors to disclose in job postings what compensation they offer for positions involving work under or connected to a federal government contract.[188] A Canadian study found that laws making university faculty salaries publicly available information shrank the gender pay gap in those salaries.[189]

Unequal pay undermines women's ability to support themselves and their loved ones. It is not the only obstacle, however, particularly for women raising children in a nation that makes combining market work and motherhood extraordinarily difficult. I will turn now to those barriers and the legislative agenda to tackle them.

Mothers and fathers need access to paid leave. Despite endless proposals, Congress has kept the United States as a global outlier and never established a federal right to paid parental or family leave.[190] In the absence of a federal requirement, most employers do not offer paid leave. As Chapter 5 discussed, seventy-six percent of private sector workers did not have access to employer-provided paid family leave in 2022.[191] The federal Family and Medical Leave Act of 1993 requires covered employers to provide up to twelve weeks of unpaid leave so an eligible employee can care for a child, spouse, parent, or herself.[192] But many people cannot afford to take unpaid leave. Even if they could, a 2018 survey found that only fifty-six percent of employees in the United States fell within the FMLA's reach.[193]

The absence of federal legislation on paid leave and the eligibility hurdles for unpaid leave are facially neutral policies with disproportionate impacts on women that are entirely predictable consequences of Congress's refusals to do better. Creating a federal right to paid leave for all employees would help both women and men combine parenthood and market work.

America also needs legislation to expand access to early childhood education and childcare. The nation's public spending on these goods as a proportion of gross domestic product lags behind, with the United States thirty-fifth out of the thirty-seven market democracies in the Organisation for Economic Co-operation and Development.[194] A survey of the 2019–20 school year—the last that began before the COVID-19 pandemic—found that only 43.8% of 4-year-olds and 16.9% of three-year-olds were attending a publicly funded preschool, preschool special education, or Head Start program.[195] Existing public subsidies for childcare likewise fall short. In 2020, just eighteen percent of the 10.9 million children who met federal eligibility requirements actually received a childcare subsidy.[196]

Without access to public support, the cost of childcare can be prohibitive. The United States Department of Labor estimated childcare costs county-by-county, focusing on full-time childcare for a single child not receiving public subsidies.[197] In 2018, the latest year with data available, median childcare costs ranged from 8.0% of median family income for home-based childcare for a school-age child in a small county to 19.3% of median family income for center-based childcare for an infant in a very large county.[198]

A study from Child Care Aware of America examined the average cost of placing two children—an infant and a four-year-old—in center-based childcare in 2023. It was more expensive than median annualized rent in every state and the District of Columbia.[199] The same study compared the cost of placing an infant in center-based childcare in 2023 with median income for single parents. Childcare costs ranged from 22.8% of income in South Dakota to 63.2% of income in the District of Columbia.[200]

Unsurprisingly, multiple studies find that higher childcare costs reduce maternal employment.[201] Mothers pushed out of market work lose their paychecks and any associated benefits and opportunities, which can include health insurance, retirement plans, and promotion possibilities. On the flip side, researchers find that reductions in childcare costs and increases in the availability of public schooling for young children are associated with increases in maternal employment and reductions in poverty.[202]

Securing more government support for early childcare and education is another longstanding battle that will be difficult to win. As Chapter 6 explored, anti-feminists have fought such efforts for decades. Combating those forces is vital because public support for early childcare and education can be a lynchpin enabling women to combine motherhood and market success.

The Balance. So far, this section has focused on legislation to expand women's rights and opportunities. But equal rights and equal responsibilities are inextricably connected. The absence of one makes the other less likely. Together, they create and confirm full citizenship. I will turn now to those obligations.

Let's first consider women's exclusion from military registration. If registration is to continue, Congress needs to include women along with men. Ending male-only registration has long been unfinished business, and that has become even more obvious since the military opened all combat positions to women as of 2016.[203]

Chapter 5 examined how women's exclusion from registration has always been rooted in the assumption that women rather than men should organize their lives around domestic responsibilities. As we have seen, legislators and judges have endlessly deployed that same assumption to deny women equal rights and opportunities. Feminists have to fight against legal decisionmaking grounded on the premise that women, but not men, belong at home—even recognizing that many women enjoy their exemption from registration. Many men would also prefer not to register. That is why Congress has made registration involuntary.

The Supreme Court is not eager to revisit women's exclusion from registration. In June 2021, the Justices had the opportunity to hear an appeal challenging the Court's 1981 *Rostker* precedent upholding male-only registration. The Court declined to hear the case, with three Justices signing a separate statement that contended that "the Court's longstanding deference to Congress on matters of national defense and military affairs cautions against granting review while Congress actively weighs the issue."[204]

Congress has not been all that active. In 2016—after the military opened every combat position to women—Congress established the National Commission on Military, National, and Public Service and instructed the commission to consider whether registration should include "all citizens and residents, regardless of sex."[205] I testified before this commission in 2019 to explain the constitutional problems with male-only registration.[206] The commission's final report in March 2020 recommended including women in registration.[207] The House and Senate Armed Services Committees each held a hearing on this report in 2021,[208] but Congress has kept male-only registration in place.

It is well past time for reform. Congress should either require military registration without regard to sex or end registration altogether.

Federal law governing the citizenship of foreign-born nonmarital children offers another opportunity to equalize both rights and responsibilities. Congress should not impose a financial support requirement on citizen fathers seeking to convey United States citizenship to their nonmarital children born abroad to foreign mothers when no such requirement applies to citizen mothers in the parallel situation.[209] Congress should not impose a deadline for paternal acknowledgment when no such deadline governs recognition of a maternal relationship.[210] As Chapter 5 detailed, these sex-based rules are rooted in persistent presumptions that parental obligations are mandatory for mothers and optional for fathers, so the United States can take maternal commitment for granted while requiring fathers to prove their interest.

Feminists should push for citizenship laws recognizing that parenthood is as much a responsibility for fathers as it is for mothers. If Congress wants to ensure that viable ties exist between citizen parents and their foreign-born nonmarital children, legislation should require that directly rather than using sex as a proxy.

The Baseline. I will end this section by shifting from specifics to a baseline question: Will the Constitution include the Equal Rights Amendment's explicit prohibition on sex discrimination? The crucial next step is to push Congress to embrace the ERA's declaration that: "Equality of rights under the law shall not be denied or abridged by the United States or by any State on account of sex."[211] Federal lawmakers should either directly recognize the ERA as part of the Constitution, remove the seven-year ratification deadline that Congress inserted into the 1972 joint resolution sending the ERA to the states, or—ideally—both.[212] Such congressional endorsement would make it more difficult for the Supreme Court to resist the conclusion that the ERA's ratification is complete. The Court has never denied recognition to a constitutional amendment that Congress accepts. *Coleman v. Miller*, a 1939 Supreme Court decision sparked by a dispute over whether Kansas had ratified the Child Labor Amendment,[213] emphasized that Congress controls "the promulgation of the adoption of a constitutional amendment."[214]

Even so close to the finish line, fighting for the ERA remains arduous. Continued opposition to the amendment in Congress fits within a long history of vehement resistance to expanding women's rights and roles. The stakes are high.

Most broadly, the ERA could help transform how powerful and ordinary Americans understand the relationship between women and the Constitution. As we have seen, generations of legal authorities have excluded women from the center of constitutional law. Indeed, Justice Antonin Scalia argued in 2011 that the Constitution does not prohibit sex discrimination at all because: "Nobody ever thought that that's what it meant. Nobody ever voted for that. If the current society wants to outlaw discrimination by sex, hey we have things called legislatures, and they enact things called laws." He added: "That's what democracy is all about."[215]

This was never a compelling argument. Men barred women from voting on both the original Constitution and the Fourteenth Amendment prohibiting states from denying "any person" "the equal protection of the laws."[216] From that perspective, it is hard to see how abiding by what the men behind these constitutional provisions purportedly thought about sex discrimination would be a triumph of democratic legitimacy, rather than an importation of past injustice into the present. But in any event, women are unquestionably not an afterthought to the ERA. Adding that amendment to the Constitution would affirm women's equal citizenship and women's centrality to constitutional law.

Most practically, the ERA could help expand women's rights and opportunities. As Chapter 6 highlighted, the amendment's opponents have spent over a half century describing the ERA as simultaneously unnecessary and menacing. The first claim has always depended on denying persistent sex discrimination and dismissing ongoing disparities. The second line of attack has recently focused on arguing that the ERA would provide constitutional protection for abortion rights. That latter argument has an ironic dimension, as anti-abortion politicians and activists ordinarily refuse to acknowledge any connections between abortion rights and sex equality. But anti-abortion attacks on the ERA suggest the impact the amendment could have—eventually, if not necessarily with the current Supreme Court. Embedding the ERA's explicit prohibition on sex discrimination into the constitutional firmament would provide a new, sturdier foundation supporting feminist advocacy about constitutional rights. Indeed, feminists arguing that the ERA prohibits lawmakers from imposing abortion bans that compel childbearing could draw on how the ERA's enemies have described the amendment's consequences.

I am well aware that I have outlined an enormous legislative agenda, and I could continue for pages more. Generations of American women have pushed for laws that take their interests into account and treat them as equals. There is much more to do.

Litigation

Litigation is another arena where women need to keep fighting. Foregrounding the long history of women's unfinished struggles for equality could help. As we have seen, the decisions courts make in the present often build on assertions about the past. Judges rely on spontaneous enlightenment stories to attribute improvements in women's status over time to consensus rather than conflict. They wield the contention that America has already triumphed over inequality to rationalize decisions facilitating inequality's persistence.

Litigation is not teaching. But success in court can turn on shifting how judges view the world. The history of women's activism offers abundant material for contesting the judiciary's tendencies to deploy self-contradictory victory announcements and erase women's ongoing mobilization against powerful resistance.

Even moving judges away from describing sexism as medieval, feudal, archaic, and the like would be an improvement.[217] Those terms can seem appealing because they present sexism as a passé relic antithetical to contemporary values. But deploying those descriptors associates women's inequality with times long past and places far away, when judicial attention should focus on how inequality remains entrenched in modern America.

Of course, any discussion of litigation strategies has to consider how receptive judges will be. The United States Supreme Court has been an obstacle rather than an aid to women's pursuit of equality for most of American history. I feel comfortable stating that the current six-Justice conservative/regressive supermajority fits within that obstructive tradition. In the near term, the Court is unlikely to prioritize women's equality or to wean itself from leaning on exaggerations about the nation's progress, recently evident in the *Dobbs* decision.[218]

But advancing women's equality claims at the Supreme Court is a multigenerational project. Sometimes feminist advocates can direct their work toward securing immediate victories, and sometimes feminists have to focus on setting the stage for potential victories in the years to come. Over time, Justices will retire, Presidents will appoint replacements, and the Court may become more receptive to feminist advocacy.

Meanwhile, the United States Supreme Court is not the only important litigation venue, notwithstanding its power to bind the rest of the judiciary to its interpretation of the federal Constitution. State courts, and lower federal courts, decide exponentially more cases and offer innumerable opportunities. There can still be maneuvering room for judges interested in protecting women's rights.

That room can exist within constitutional law. After the *Dobbs* bombshell, for example, some state courts interpreted their state constitutions to protect at least some reproductive rights.[219]

That room can also exist outside constitutional law. Most litigation does not directly turn on constitutional interpretation, even when the outcome in court reflects how judges understand women's place in the world. Think of the divorce cases Chapter 5 examined, where judges framed women's inequality as part of the past rather than the present and disregarded the evidence of persistent inequality that was right before them. Disrupting that pattern could transform judicial decisionmaking without ever involving constitutional interpretation.

In short, pursuing litigation victories and striving to thwart litigation disasters remain important aspects of women's struggles for equality, whether or not the United States Supreme Court is an ally. Those battles need to continue as well.

Everyday Life

I have saved a crucial arena for the end. In our everyday lives, we can all participate in fighting for reform and against regression. The opportunities extend from public domains, like voting and demonstrating, to more private ones, like speaking with relatives, friends, and neighbors.

I hope this book illuminates how America's dominant stories about itself shield inequality and encourage complacency by forgetting women's struggles for equality and forgetting the work the nation still has to do. Recognizing those ongoing patterns can keep us alert to spontaneous enlightenment stories and self-contradictory victory announcements as they appear, prepared to place them in context, and ready to respond. We can look for opportunities to change minds and promote engagement.

We can also share an overriding lesson from the past. The long history of women's struggles for equality makes clear that progress is unlikely to be quick, easy, or achieved by anyone acting alone. Generations of women have learned that lesson and persisted nonetheless.

Jill Ruckelshaus is one of them. Starting in the 1970s, she became a key figure advocating within and outside Republican politics for feminist priorities like the ERA and abortion rights.[220] Phyllis Schlafly, who was not a fan, called her "the Gloria Steinem of the Republican Party."[221]

In 1977, Ruckelshaus spoke at a convention of the National Women's Political Caucus, a group she co-founded.[222] She offered this clear-eyed assessment and rallying cry, which I have had hanging on my wall since before I went to law school:

> We are in for a very, very long haul . . .
> I am asking for EVERYTHING YOU HAVE TO GIVE
>
> We will never give up . . .
> You will lose your YOUTH, your SLEEP,
> your PATIENCE, your Sense of HUMOR
> and occasionally . . . the understanding and support
> of people that you LOVE very much.
>
> IN RETURN, I have nothing to offer you but . . .
> your PRIDE in being a woman, and
> all your DREAMS you've ever had for your daughters,
> and nieces, and granddaughters . . .
> your FUTURE
> and the certain KNOWLEDGE that
> at the end of your days
> you will be able to look back and say that
>
> ONCE in your life
> you gave EVERYTHING you had
> FOR JUSTICE.[223]

Pursuing justice for women has always required sustained mobilization against entrenched resistance. When we come together to challenge the unequal status quo and confront powerful opponents, we need to combine urgent impatience with resilience, grit, and determination over the very long term. Feminists still have many battles to win as we work to transform a nation whose promises of empowering We the People have too often been limited to We the Men.

Acknowledgments

I am delighted to thank the many people who helped me as I wrote this book. Brian Bix, Naomi Cahn, June Carbone, Maxine Eichner, Allan Erbsen, Carol Hasday, Robert Hasday, Elizabeth Katz, Serena Mayeri, Karen Tani, and Mary Ziegler did me the enormous favor of reading the entire manuscript. I am grateful for their generosity and engagement with my work.

Many more people read individual chapters or early versions of this project. I appreciate the thoughtful comments I received from Susan Appleton, Deborah Dinner, Elizabeth Emens, Katie Eyer, Richard Thompson Ford, Joanna Grossman, Jennifer Hendricks, Melissa Murray, Douglas NeJaime, Rachel Rebouché, Reva Siegel, Barbara Welke, Rebecca Zietlow, and workshop or conference participants at the American Society for Legal History, Boston University School of Law, Brooklyn Law School, DePaul University College of Law, the Family Law Scholars and Teachers Conference, the Law and Society Association, Loyola University Chicago School of Law, Stanford Law School, the Summer Feminist Legal Theory Series, the University of Akron School of Law, the University of Florida Levin College of Law, the University of Minnesota Law School, the University of Wisconsin Law School, and Washington University School of Law.

This book would not exist without the work of many librarians and archivists. The librarians at the University of Minnesota Law Library, including Katie Baratto, Scott Dewey, Vicente Garces, Ryan Greenwood, Sandra Jacobson, Andrew Martineau, Loren Turner, and David Zopfi-Jordan, responded to my endless requests with aplomb and mastery of the interlibrary loan system. The support of these superb and dedicated librarians has made it possible for me to write three books at the University of Minnesota without research assistants. I am also thankful for the help I received from archivists at the California State Archives; the Circuit Court of Cook County, Illinois; Columbia University; Cornell University; the Detroit Public Library; Emory University; Florida State University; Georgetown University; Harvard University; the Jenkins Law Library; the Library of Congress; the Library of Virginia; the National Archives and Records Administration; the Superior Court of California, County of Los Angeles; the United States Capitol; the University of California, Berkeley; the University of Michigan; the University of North Carolina; the University of Virginia; and Yale University.

My experience at Oxford University Press has been outstanding. I would like to thank my editor, David McBride, for his enthusiasm about this project and his skillful guidance of the manuscript through the publication process. I also appreciate the care and insight that two scholars devoted to their anonymous peer reviews for the press.

Most of all, I want to thank my family. My parents, Carol and Robert Hasday, and my husband, Allan Erbsen, have spent decades reading my work and supporting all my personal and professional endeavors. My three children, Sarah, Daniel, and David, light up my life. My grandmother, Rose Rosenfelt, encouraged me to pursue opportunities she never had. I dedicate this book to my family. You are my We the People.

Notes

Introduction

1. Alice Paul, *Women Will Be Real Equals in 2023*, WASH. TIMES, Dec. 28, 1922, at 24 (emphasis omitted).

2. *See* INEZ HAYNES IRWIN, THE STORY OF THE WOMAN'S PARTY 232, 244–50, 254–55, 283–87 (1921); DORIS STEVENS, JAILED FOR FREEDOM 128, 184–91 (1920).

3. Paul, *supra* note 1, at 24.

4. *See* Alice Paul, *An Approaching Anniversary*, CHRISTIAN SCI. MONITOR (Boston), June 2, 1923, at 20; *Women Adopt Form for Equal Rights*, N.Y. TIMES, July 22, 1923 (§ 1), at 1.

5. S.J. Res. 21, 68th Cong. (1923) (internal quotation marks omitted); *see also* H.R.J. Res. 75, 68th Cong. (1923).

6. *See* Lisa Lerer, *Six Female Candidates, One Unrelenting Refrain*, N.Y. TIMES, July 4, 2019, at A1.

7. *See* CTR. FOR AM. WOMEN & POL., RUTGERS UNIV., WOMEN IN THE U.S. CONGRESS 2024 (2024); CTR. FOR AM. WOMEN & POL., RUTGERS UNIV., WOMEN IN STATE LEGISLATURES 2024 (2024).

8. *See* EMILY A. SHRIDER, U.S. DEP'T OF COM., POVERTY IN THE UNITED STATES: 2023, at 21 tbl.A-2 (2024).

9. *See* ARIANE HEGEWISCH ET AL., INST. FOR WOMEN'S POL'Y RSCH., PUB. NO. C527, GENDER AND RACIAL WAGE GAPS WORSENED IN 2023 AND PAY EQUITY STILL DECADES AWAY 4 tbl.1 (2024).

10. *See* Emma Hinchliffe, *The Share of Fortune 500 Companies Run by Women CEOs Stays Flat at 10.4% as Pace of Change Stalls*, FORTUNE, June 4, 2024.

11. *See* DESTINY PEERY, NAT'L ASS'N OF WOMEN LAWS., 2020 SURVEY REPORT ON THE PROMOTION AND RETENTION OF WOMEN IN LAW FIRMS 8, 40 (2020).

12. *See* Dobbs v. Jackson Women's Health Org., 597 U.S. 215, 231 (2022). I note at the outset that I do not mean "women" to be an exclusionary term and include transwomen within my definition of women. I also recognize that abortion regulation can directly impact anyone with the capacity to become pregnant.

13. *See* E-mail from Christi Chidester Votisek, Commc'ns Specialist, U.S. Gen. Servs. Admin., to author (July 28, 2021) (copy on file with author).

14. *See* MONUMENT LAB, NATIONAL MONUMENT AUDIT 12, 17, 19 (2021).

15. *See* AKHIL REED AMAR, AMERICA'S UNWRITTEN CONSTITUTION: THE PRECEDENTS AND PRINCIPLES WE LIVE BY 245–75 (2012); KERMIT ROOSEVELT III, THE NATION THAT NEVER WAS: RECONSTRUCTING AMERICA'S STORY 123 (2022); J.M. Balkin & Sanford Levinson, *The Canons of Constitutional Law*, 111 HARV. L. REV. 963, 1018–19 (1998); Jamal Greene, *The Anticanon*, 125 HARV. L. REV. 379, 380–87 (2011); Anita S. Krishnakumar, *On the Evolution of the Canonical Dissent*, 52 RUTGERS L. REV. 781, 781–82, 790–91, 800–03 (2000); Richard A. Primus, *Canon, Anti-Canon, and Judicial Dissent*, 48 DUKE L.J.

243, 250–57 (1998); Ilya Somin, *The Case for Expanding the Anticanon of Constitutional Law*, 2023 Wis. L. Rev. 575, 576–77.

16. *The Emancipation of Women*, Austin Daily Statesman, Sept. 9, 1892, at 2.
17. For examples of reprintings, see *World Grows Better*, Sunday Star (D.C.), Feb. 4, 1912 (pt. II), at 7; *World's Progress Morally*, L.A. Times, Mar. 17, 1912 (pt. III), at 17; *see also* Marcel Prevost, *Women Afraid of Liberty*, Wash. Post, May 28, 1905 (pt. 4), at 7.
18. Grace A. Turkington, My Country: A Textbook in Civics and Patriotism for Young Americans 336 (1918); *see also id.* at 85, 150.
19. For the decision, see Dobbs v. Jackson Women's Health Org., 597 U.S. 215, 231 (2022).

Chapter 1

1. 198 U.S. 45 (1905).
2. *See id.* at 52–65.
3. *Id.* at 60–61.
4. Moore v. City of East Cleveland, 431 U.S. 494, 502 (1977) (plurality opinion); *see also* Nat'l Pork Producers Council v. Ross, 598 U.S. 356, 382 (2023); Dobbs v. Jackson Women's Health Org., 597 U.S. 215, 240, 265, 292 (2022); Sorrell v. IMS Health Inc., 564 U.S. 552, 567 (2011); Stop the Beach Renourishment, Inc. v. Fla. Dep't of Env't Prot., 560 U.S. 702, 721 (2010) (plurality opinion); Coll. Sav. Bank v. Fla. Prepaid Postsecondary Educ. Expense Bd., 527 U.S. 666, 690–91 (1999); Planned Parenthood of Se. Pa. v. Casey, 505 U.S. 833, 861–64 (1992); Whalen v. Roe, 429 U.S. 589, 596–97 (1977); Dean v. Gadsden Times Publ'g Corp., 412 U.S. 543, 545 (1973) (per curiam); Roe v. Wade, 410 U.S. 113, 117 (1973); Harper v. Va. Bd. of Elections, 383 U.S. 663, 669 (1966); Griswold v. Connecticut, 381 U.S. 479, 481–82 (1965); Ferguson v. Skrupa, 372 U.S. 726, 729–30 (1963); Day-Brite Lighting, Inc. v. Missouri, 342 U.S. 421, 423, 425 (1952).
5. *See, e.g.*, Whole Woman's Health v. Hellerstedt, 579 U.S. 582, 641 (2016) (Thomas, J., dissenting); Obergefell v. Hodges, 576 U.S. 644, 687, 694, 696–99, 703–06 (2015) (Roberts, C.J., dissenting); *Sorrell*, 564 U.S. at 585, 591–92, 602–03 (Breyer, J., dissenting); McDonald v. City of Chicago, 561 U.S. 742, 878, 905 (2010) (Stevens, J., dissenting); *Coll. Sav. Bank*, 527 U.S. at 701–02 (Breyer, J., dissenting); Seminole Tribe v. Florida, 517 U.S. 44, 166 (1996) (Souter, J., dissenting); United States v. Lopez, 514 U.S. 549, 605–07 (1995) (Souter, J., dissenting); *Casey*, 505 U.S. at 957, 959–62 (Rehnquist, C.J., concurring in the judgment in part and dissenting in part); *id.* at 998 (Scalia, J., concurring in the judgment in part and dissenting in part); 324 Liquor Corp. v. Duffy, 479 U.S. 335, 359–60 (1987) (O'Connor, J., dissenting); Thornburgh v. Am. Coll. of Obstetricians & Gynecologists, 476 U.S. 747, 788, 797 n.5 (1986) (White, J., dissenting); Indus. Union Dep't, AFL-CIO v. Am. Petroleum Inst., 448 U.S. 607, 723–24 (1980) (Marshall, J., dissenting); Cent. Hudson Gas & Elec. Corp. v. Pub. Serv. Comm'n, 447 U.S. 557, 589, 591 (1980) (Rehnquist, J., dissenting); *Roe*, 410 U.S. at 174 (Rehnquist, J., dissenting); *Harper*, 383 U.S. at 686 (Harlan, J., dissenting); *Griswold*, 381 U.S. at 512 n.4, 514–15, 522–24 (Black, J., dissenting); *id.* at 528 (Stewart, J., dissenting).
6. *See* Muller v. Oregon, 208 U.S. 412, 416–17 (1908).
7. *See id.* at 416–23.
8. *See id.* at 423.
9. *See id.* at 422.

10. *Id.*

11. *Id.* at 421.

12. *Id.* at 421–22.

13. *See* Theodore Roosevelt, *The Law of Civilization and Decay*, 22 FORUM 575, 579, 586–87 (1897) (book review); Edward A. Ross, *The Causes of Race Superiority*, 18 ANNALS AM. ACAD. POL. & SOC. SCI. 67, 86–89 (1901).

14. *See* BREVARD D. SINCLAIR, THE CROWNING SIN OF THE AGE: THE PERVERSION OF MAR-RIAGE 69–70 (Boston, Scriptural Tract Repository 1892); HORATIO ROBINSON STORER, WHY NOT? A BOOK FOR EVERY WOMAN 62–65, 85–86 (Boston, Lee & Shepard 1866); L.D. Griswold et al., *Additional Report from the Select Committee to Whom Was Referred S.B. No. 285*, 63 J. SENATE STATE OHIO, app. at 233, 233, 235 (1867); William McCollom, *Criminal Abortion*, *in* TRANSACTIONS OF THE VERMONT MEDICAL SOCIETY, FOR THE YEAR 1865, at 40, 42–43 (Burlington, R.S. Styles 1865); J.J. Mulheron, *Fœticide*, 10 PENINSULAR J. MED. 385, 391 (1874).

15. *See* Elizabeth Brandeis, *Labor Legislation*, *in* 3 HISTORY OF LABOR IN THE UNITED STATES, 1896–1932, at 399, 459 (1935).

16. *See id.* at 458.

17. *See id.* at 459.

18. *See* NANCY WOLOCH, A CLASS BY HERSELF: PROTECTIVE LAWS FOR WOMEN WORKERS, 1890s–1990s, at 19–25 (2015); Joan G. Zimmerman, *The Jurisprudence of Equality: The Women's Minimum Wage, the First Equal Rights Amendment, and Adkins v. Children's Hospital, 1905–1923*, 78 J. AM. HIST. 188, 198–200 (1991).

19. *See* ELIZABETH FAULKNER BAKER, PROTECTIVE LABOR LEGISLATION 425–28 (1925); ALICE KESSLER-HARRIS, OUT TO WORK: A HISTORY OF WAGE-EARNING WOMEN IN THE UNITED STATES 212–14 (1982).

20. *See* Act of Mar. 15, 1913, ch. 83, § 1, 1913 N.Y. Laws 150, 150–51.

21. WOMEN'S BUREAU, U.S. DEP'T OF LAB., BULLETIN NO. 65, THE EFFECTS OF LABOR LEGISLATION ON THE EMPLOYMENT OPPORTUNITIES OF WOMEN 52 (1928).

22. *See Equal Rights: Hearing on S.J. Res. 52 Before a Subcomm. of the S. Comm. on the Judiciary*, 71st Cong. 3–4 (1931) (statement of Maud Williams); *Actual Protection vs. Theoretical Protection*, INDUS. EQUAL., July 15, 1923, at 1, 1.

23. *See* People v. Charles Schweinler Press, 108 N.E. 639, 639–44 (N.Y. 1915).

24. *Id.* at 643.

25. *See* BAKER, *supra* note 19, at 189–90.

26. *See id.* at 190; *Sees Many Jobless Women as Result of New Labor Laws*, BROOKLYN DAILY EAGLE, May 11, 1919, at 24.

27. *Sees Many Jobless Women as Result of New Labor Laws*, *supra* note 26, at 24 (quoting Ella Sherwin) (internal quotation marks omitted).

28. Anne O'Hagan, *"Protecting" Women out of Their Jobs*, 5 TOUCHSTONE 400, 402 (1919) (quoting Ella Sherwin in the *New York World*) (internal quotation marks omitted).

29. *Actual Protection vs. Theoretical Protection*, *supra* note 22, at 1; Nelle Swartz, *Employment of Women in Newspaper Offices as Proofreaders, Linotypists and Monotypists*, 6 INDUS. BULL. 37, 37 (1926).

30. *See* Act of May 3, 1921, ch. 489, § 1, 1921 N.Y. Laws 1508, 1509.

31. *See* Act of May 12, 1919, ch. 583, § 1, 1919 N.Y. Laws 1572, 1573.

32. O'Hagan, *supra* note 28, at 401 (internal quotation marks omitted).

33. *200 Conductorettes Denounce Law that Caused Discharge*, Brooklyn Daily Eagle, May 20, 1919, at 9 (quoting Margaret Hinchey) (internal quotation marks omitted).

34. O'Hagan, *supra* note 28, at 403 (quoting Isabel Liley) (internal quotation marks omitted).

35. *See* Act of May 17, 1917, ch. 535, § 1, 1917 N.Y. Laws 1564, 1564–65.

36. *See* Radice v. New York, 264 U.S. 292, 293–98 (1924).

37. *See The Farce of "Protection,"* Indus. Equal., July 15, 1923, at 4, 4; W.A. Warn, *Republicans Open Fire on 5-Cent Fare*, N.Y. Times, Feb. 27, 1930, at 5; *Women in Clashes on Night Work Bill*, N.Y. Times, Mar. 6, 1929, at 18.

38. *Women in Clashes on Night Work Bill*, *supra* note 37, at 18.

39. Warn, *supra* note 37, at 5.

40. *See* Craig v. Boren, 429 U.S. 190, 210 n.23 (1976).

41. *See* West Coast Hotel Co. v. Parrish, 300 U.S. 379 (1937).

42. *See* Women's Bureau, U.S. Dep't of Lab., Bulletin No. 294, 1969 Handbook on Women Workers 271 (1969).

43. *See id.* at 277–28.

44. *See* Breedlove v. Suttles, 302 U.S. 277, 282 (1937).

45. *See* Heaton v. Bristol, 317 S.W.2d 86, 98–99 (Tex. Civ. App. 1958).

46. *See* Commonwealth v. Welosky, 177 N.E. 656, 661–64 (Mass. 1931).

47. *See* Lochner v. New York, 198 U.S. 45, 53–54, 56–63 (1905).

48. David J. Brewer, *The Legitimate Exercise of the Police Power in the Protection of Health*, 21 Charities & Commons 238, 240 (1908).

49. *Id.* at 241.

50. *Id.*

51. *See* cases cited *supra* notes 4–5.

52. *See, e.g.*, Dobbs v. Jackson Women's Health Org., 597 U.S. 215 (2022) (*Muller* not mentioned); Sessions v. Morales-Santana, 582 U.S. 47 (2017) (*Muller* not mentioned); Whole Woman's Health v. Hellerstedt, 579 U.S. 582 (2016) (*Muller* not mentioned); Planned Parenthood of Se. Pa. v. Casey, 505 U.S. 833, 961 (1992) (Rehnquist, C.J., concurring in the judgment in part and dissenting in part) (only *Muller* citation in all the *Casey* opinions and does not discuss *Muller* as a case about women); Thornburgh v. Am. Coll. of Obstetricians & Gynecologists, 476 U.S. 747 (1986) (*Muller* not mentioned); Rostker v. Goldberg, 453 U.S. 57 (1981) (*Muller* not mentioned); Michael M. v. Superior Ct., 450 U.S. 464 (1981) (*Muller* not mentioned); Craig v. Boren, 429 U.S. 190 (1976) (*Muller* not mentioned); Frontiero v. Richardson, 411 U.S. 677 (1973) (*Muller* not mentioned); Roe v. Wade, 410 U.S. 113 (1973) (*Muller* not mentioned); Reed v. Reed, 404 U.S. 71 (1971) (*Muller* not mentioned); Griswold v. Connecticut, 381 U.S. 479 (1965) (*Muller* not mentioned).

53. Akhil Reed Amar, America's Unwritten Constitution: The Precedents and Principles We Live By 270 (2012).

54. David A. Strauss, *Why Was Lochner Wrong?*, 70 U. Chi. L. Rev. 373, 373 (2003).

55. *See, e.g.*, Amar, *supra* note 53, at 270–74; J.M. Balkin & Sanford Levinson, *The Canons of Constitutional Law*, 111 Harv. L. Rev. 963, 1018 (1998); Jamal Greene, *The Anticanon*, 125 Harv. L. Rev. 379, 380 (2011); Anita S. Krishnakumar, *On the Evolution of the Canonical Dissent*, 52 Rutgers L. Rev. 781, 788–90 (2000); Richard A. Primus, *Canon, Anti-Canon, and Judicial Dissent*, 48 Duke L.J. 243, 244–45 (1998).

56. *See* Amar, *supra* note 53; Balkin & Levinson, *supra* note 55; Primus, *supra* note 55.

57. *See infra* Chapters 3, 5–6.

58. U.S. CONST. amend. XIV, § 1.

59. *See* 404 U.S. 71, 71–77 (1971).

60. *See* 411 U.S. 677, 678–91 (1973) (plurality opinion).

61. The Court did not revisit the subject until 1996. *See* United States v. Virginia, 518 U.S. 515, 531–34 (1996) (suggesting the judiciary has a constitutional responsibility to remediate the law's history of promoting women's subordination).

62. *Frontiero*, 411 U.S. at 684 (plurality opinion).

63. *See id.* at 685.

64. *Id.* at 687.

65. *Id.* at 685 (emphasis added).

66. *Id.* at 684.

67. *Id.* at 685.

68. *See infra* Chapter 4.

69. *See* Minor v. Happersett, 88 U.S. (21 Wall.) 162, 165–78 (1875).

70. U.S. CONST. amend. XIX.

71. *See* Act of Mar. 2, 1907, Pub. L. No. 59-193, § 3, 34 Stat. 1228, 1228–29.

72. Mackenzie v. Hare, 239 U.S. 299, 311–12 (1915).

73. *See* Cable Act, Pub. L. No. 67-346, 42 Stat. 1021 (1922).

74. *See Naturalization and Citizenship of Women: Hearings Before the H. Comm. on Immigr. & Naturalization*, 67th Cong. 570–71 (1922) (statement of Maud Wood Park, National League of Women Voters); 62 CONG. REC. 12,060 (1922) (statement of Rep. Albert Johnson); *The New Law*, WOMAN CITIZEN, Oct. 7, 1922, at 18.

75. Cable Act § 3.

76. *See id.*

77. On women's advocacy, see *Amendment to the Women's Citizenship Act of 1922: Hearings on H.R. 10208 Before the H. Comm. on Immigr. & Naturalization*, 71st Cong. 4–15, 23–38 (1930); 72 CONG. REC. 11,884 (1930) (statement of Sen. Royal Copeland); *Cleaning up the Cable Act*, BULL. NAT'L LEAGUE WOMEN VOTERS, Feb. 1930, at 1; *The New Cable Bill*, 16 EQUAL RTS. 74 (1930). For Cable Act amendments, see Act of July 3, 1930, Pub. L. No. 71-508, 46 Stat. 854; Act of Mar. 3, 1931, Pub. L. No. 71-829, 46 Stat. 1511; Act of July 2, 1932, Pub. L. No. 72-248, 47 Stat. 571; Act of June 25, 1936, Pub. L. No. 74-793, 49 Stat. 1917; Act of July 2, 1940, Pub. L. No. 76-704, 54 Stat. 715.

78. *See* 78 CONG. REC. 9489–91 (1934) (Senate ratifying Convention on the Nationality of Women); CANDICE LEWIS BREDBENNER, A NATIONALITY OF HER OWN: WOMEN, MARRIAGE, AND THE LAW OF CITIZENSHIP 243 (1998).

79. *See* Act of Apr. 18, 1929, No. 27, § 1, 1929 P.R. Laws 180, 180.

80. *See* Act of Mar. 23, 1935, No. 4, § 1, 1935 P.R. Laws 146, 146.

81. *See In re* Application of Williams, No. 14-1935, slip op. at 16 (D.V.I. Dec. 27, 1935) (copy on file with author; Harvard Law School Library, Albert Lévitt Papers).

82. *See* Nationality Act of 1940, Pub. L. No. 76-853, § 303, 54 Stat. 1137, 1140; Act of Dec. 17, 1943, Pub. L. No. 78-199, § 3, 57 Stat. 600, 601; Act of July 2, 1946, Pub. L. No. 79-483, § 1, 60 Stat. 416, 416.

83. Immigration and Nationality Act, Pub. L. No. 82-414, § 311, 66 Stat. 163, 239 (1952).

84. *See* CAROL ANDERSON, ONE PERSON, NO VOTE: HOW VOTER SUPPRESSION IS DESTROY-ING OUR DEMOCRACY 4–17 (2018); MANFRED BERG, "THE TICKET TO FREEDOM":

THE NAACP AND THE STRUGGLE FOR BLACK POLITICAL INTEGRATION 149–51 (2005); ALEXANDER KEYSSAR, THE RIGHT TO VOTE: THE CONTESTED HISTORY OF DEMOCRACY IN THE UNITED STATES 227–29, 235–37, 247–50, 258–59, 262–63 (2000); 1 VOTING: 1961 COMMISSION ON CIVIL RIGHTS REPORT 5, 27, 30, 163–64 (1961); MICHAEL WALDMAN, THE FIGHT TO VOTE 142–45, 161–63 (2016); Ralph J. Bunche, *The Negro in the Political Life of the United States*, 10 J. NEGRO EDUC. 567, 569–76 (1941); Liette Gidlow, *The Sequel: The Fifteenth Amendment, the Nineteenth Amendment, and Southern Black Women's Struggle to Vote*, 17 J. GILDED AGE & PROGRESSIVE ERA 433, 443 (2018); *infra* text accompanying notes 193–226.

85. *See* DAVID MONTEJANO, ANGLOS AND MEXICANS IN THE MAKING OF TEXAS, 1836–1986, at 251–52, 292 (1987).

86. VOTING, *supra* note 84, at 111.

87. *See* Act of June 2, 1924, Pub L. No. 68-175, 43 Stat. 253.

88. *See* TO SECURE THESE RIGHTS: THE REPORT OF THE PRESIDENT'S COMMITTEE ON CIVIL RIGHTS 40, 161 (1947); Daniel McCool, *Indian Voting, in* AMERICAN INDIAN POLICY IN THE TWENTIETH CENTURY 105, 107–13, 116 (Vine Deloria, Jr. ed., 1985); Jeanette Wolfley, *Jim Crow, Indian Style: The Disenfranchisement of Native Americans*, 16 AM. INDIAN L. REV. 167, 181–90 (1991).

89. Voting Rights Act of 1965, Pub. L. No. 89-110, 79 Stat. 437.

90. *See* Shelby County v. Holder, 570 U.S. 529, 556–57 (2013).

91. *See, e.g.*, ANDERSON, *supra* note 84, at 44–158; Alexandra Berzon & Nick Corasaniti, *Trump Allies Quietly Push to Reduce Key Voter Rolls*, N.Y. TIMES, Mar. 4, 2024, at A15.

92. Frontiero v. Richardson, 411 U.S. 677, 684 (1973) (plurality opinion) (internal quotation marks omitted).

93. *See id.* at 685, 687.

94. *See* SETH STERN & STEPHEN WERMIEL, JUSTICE BRENNAN: LIBERAL CHAMPION 399–401 (2010).

95. *Frontiero*, 411 U.S. at 684 (plurality opinion).

96. For Frontiero's rank, see *id.* at 680.

97. *See* Brief of American Civil Liberties Union *Amicus Curiae* at 3, Frontiero v. Richardson, 411 U.S. 677 (1973) (No. 71-1694) [hereinafter ACLU Brief].

98. *See* Cris Carmody, *Judge Ginsburg's Ex-Clients Reflect Upon Their Cases*, NAT'L L.J., June 28, 1993, at 34; Kay Lazar, *Fight for Equality Recalled*, BOS. SUNDAY HERALD, Mar. 16, 2003, at 7.

99. *See Frontiero*, 411 U.S. at 678–79 (plurality opinion).

100. *A 'Flaming Feminist' Lauds Court*, N.Y. TIMES, May 22, 1973, at 36 (quoting Sharron Frontiero) (internal quotation marks omitted).

101. *See* ACLU Brief, *supra* note 97, at 3–5.

102. *See* Lazar, *supra* note 98, at 7.

103. Carmody, *supra* note 98, at 34 (quoting Sharron Frontiero) (internal quotation marks omitted).

104. *See* Ruth B. Cowan, *Women's Rights Through Litigation: An Examination of the American Civil Liberties Union Women's Rights Project, 1971–1976*, 8 COLUM. HUM. RTS. L. REV. 373, 375 (1976).

105. *See* Ruth Bader Ginsburg & Barbara Flagg, *Some Reflections on the Feminist Legal Thought of the 1970s*, 1989 U. CHI. LEGAL F. 9, 11, 14–18.

106. *See* ACLU Brief, *supra* note 97, at 15–18.

107. Lane v. Bryant, 37 S.W. 584, 585 (Ky. 1896).

108. Nelson v. Metro. St. Ry. Co., 88 S.W. 781, 783 (Mo. Ct. App. 1905).

109. Fulton v. Fulton, 39 N.E. 729, 731 (Ohio 1895).

110. Haynes v. Nowlin, 29 N.E. 389, 389 (Ind. 1891).

111. Rivard v. Mo. Pac. Ry. Co., 165 S.W. 763, 767 (Mo. 1914); Dondero v. Turrillas, 94 P.2d 276, 280 (Nev. 1939).

112. Szymanski v. Blumenthal, 52 A. 347, 348 (Del. Super. Ct. 1902).

113. Claxton v. Pool, 167 S.W. 623, 629 (Mo. Ct. App. 1914); *see also* Cosper v. Valley Bank, 237 P. 175, 176 (Ariz. 1925); Appeal of Robinson, 33 A. 652, 653–54 (Me. 1895); Peter v. Byrne, 75 S.W. 433, 435–36 (Mo. 1903); Millington v. Se. Elevator Co., 239 N.E.2d 897, 898 (N.Y. 1968); Crowell v. Crowell, 105 S.E. 206, 210 (N.C. 1920); Strouse v. Cohen, 18 S.E. 323, 324 (N.C. 1893); Sturgineger v. Hannah, 11 S.C.L. (2 Nott & McC.) 147, 148–49 (1819); Schultz v. Christopher, 118 P. 629, 629 (Wash. 1911).

114. On this exclusion, see GERDA LERNER, LIVING WITH HISTORY/MAKING SOCIAL CHANGE 38–51 (2009).

115. *See* GARRY WILLS, HENRY ADAMS AND THE MAKING OF AMERICA 11–15 (2005).

116. THE EDUCATION OF HENRY ADAMS 387 (1907).

117. FORTIETH ANNUAL REPORT OF THE NATIONAL-AMERICAN WOMAN SUFFRAGE ASSOCIATION HELD AT BUFFALO OCTOBER 15TH TO 21ST, INCLUSIVE, 1908, at 88 (Harriet Taylor Upton ed., 1908) [hereinafter FORTIETH ANNUAL REPORT].

118. *See* Sandra Gurvis, *Toledo Trendsetter: Pauline Perlmutter Steinem*, PATHWAYS, Winter 2019, at 10, 10. For more on Gloria Steinem, see *infra* Chapter 6.

119. *See* FORTIETH ANNUAL REPORT, *supra* note 117, at 85–88.

120. *See* FORTY-FIRST ANNUAL REPORT OF THE NATIONAL-AMERICAN WOMAN SUFFRAGE ASSOCIATION HELD AT SEATTLE, WASHINGTON JULY 1ST TO 6TH, 1909, at 58–59 (Harriet Taylor Upton ed., 1909).

121. *Id.* at 62.

122. *See, e.g.*, REUBEN POST HALLECK, HISTORY OF OUR COUNTRY FOR HIGHER GRADES 521 (1923); WILSON PORTER SHORTRIDGE, THE DEVELOPMENT OF THE UNITED STATES 704 (1929).

123. ARTHUR MEIER SCHLESINGER, NEW VIEWPOINTS IN AMERICAN HISTORY 126 (1922).

124. *Id.*

125. *See* RADCLIFFE COLLEGE, THE ARTHUR AND ELIZABETH SCHLESINGER LIBRARY ON THE HISTORY OF WOMEN IN AMERICA: 1964–1966 TWO YEAR REPORT 1 (1966).

126. SCHLESINGER, *supra* note 123, at 126–27.

127. MARY R. BEARD, WOMAN AS FORCE IN HISTORY: A STUDY IN TRADITIONS AND REALITIES 59 (1946).

128. *See* Nancy F. Cott, *Putting Women on the Record: Mary Ritter Beard's Accomplishment, in* A WOMAN MAKING HISTORY: MARY RITTER BEARD THROUGH HER LETTERS 1, 1–2, 14, 19–62 (Nancy F. Cott ed., 1991).

129. CHARLES A. BEARD & MARY R. BEARD, HISTORY OF THE UNITED STATES 554–55 (1921).

130. BEARD, *supra* note 127, at vi.

131. *Id.* at 59.

132. J.H. "Jack" Hexter, YALE BULL. & CALENDAR, Jan. 13–20, 1997, at 8, 8.

133. J.H. Hexter, *The Ladies Were There All the Time*, N.Y. TIMES, Mar. 17, 1946 (§ 7), at 5 (book review).

134. *See Ralph H. Gabriel, 96, Dies; Taught at Yale for 43 Years*, N.Y. TIMES, Apr. 25, 1987, at 10.

135. E.H. Eby, Book Review, 31 PAC. NW. Q. 361, 363 (1940).

136. *See* RALPH HENRY GABRIEL, THE COURSE OF AMERICAN DEMOCRATIC THOUGHT: AN INTELLECTUAL HISTORY SINCE 1815 (1940).

137. *See* Sam Roberts, *William H. McNeill, 98, Author and Scholar*, N.Y. TIMES, July 13, 2016, at B15; L.S. Stavrianos, Book Review, 69 AM. HIST. REV. 713, 713–15 (1964).

138. H.R. Trevor-Roper, *Barbarians Were Often at the Gate*, N.Y. TIMES, Oct. 6, 1963 (§ 7), at 1 (book review) (emphasis added).

139. *See* WILLIAM H. MCNEILL, THE RISE OF THE WEST: A HISTORY OF THE HUMAN COMMUNITY 809–29 (1963).

140. *See* P.A.M. Taylor, *Samuel Eliot Morison: Historian*, 11 J. AM. STUD. 13, 13 (1977); Wilcomb E. Washburn, *Samuel Eliot Morison, Historian*, 36 WM. & MARY Q. 325, 325 (1979).

141. On Morison's teaching at Harvard, see Bernard Bailyn, *Morison: An Appreciation*, 89 PROC. MASS. HIST. SOC'Y 112, 112, 117, 121–22 (1977).

142. On women's exclusion from Harvard College, see NANCY WEISS MALKIEL, "KEEP THE DAMNED WOMEN OUT": THE STRUGGLE FOR COEDUCATION 31–38 (2016). On Morison's retirement, see *Historian Morison to Retire*, HARV. CRIMSON, Mar. 12, 1955, at 1.

143. Jill Lepore, *Plymouth Rocked*, NEW YORKER, Apr. 24, 2006, at 164, 166.

144. Alden Whitman, *Adm. Morison, 88, Historian, Is Dead*, N.Y. TIMES, May 16, 1976, at 1 (quoting Samuel Eliot Morison) (internal quotation marks omitted).

145. *See* SAMUEL ELIOT MORISON, THE OXFORD HISTORY OF THE AMERICAN PEOPLE 516–17, 899 (1965).

146. *Id.* at 516.

147. *See, e.g.*, AFRICAN AMERICAN WOMEN AND THE VOTE, 1837–1965 (Ann D. Gordon et al. eds., 1997); ADELE LOGAN ALEXANDER, PRINCESS OF THE HITHER ISLES: A BLACK SUFFRAGIST'S STORY FROM THE JIM CROW SOUTH (2019); CATHLEEN D. CAHILL, RECASTING THE VOTE: HOW WOMEN OF COLOR TRANSFORMED THE SUFFRAGE MOVEMENT (2020); NANCY F. COTT, THE GROUNDING OF MODERN FEMINISM (1987); ELLEN CAROL DUBOIS, SUFFRAGE: WOMEN'S LONG BATTLE FOR THE VOTE (2020); PAULA GIDDINGS, WHEN AND WHERE I ENTER: THE IMPACT OF BLACK WOMEN ON RACE AND SEX IN AMERICA (1984); MARTHA S. JONES, VANGUARD: HOW BLACK WOMEN BROKE BARRIERS, WON THE VOTE, AND INSISTED ON EQUALITY FOR ALL (2020); LINDA K. KERBER, NO CONSTITUTIONAL RIGHT TO BE LADIES: WOMEN AND THE OBLIGATIONS OF CITIZENSHIP (1998); JANE J. MANSBRIDGE, WHY WE LOST THE ERA (1986); RUTH ROSEN, THE WORLD SPLIT OPEN: HOW THE MODERN WOMEN'S MOVEMENT CHANGED AMERICA (2000); JULIE C. SUK, WE THE WOMEN: THE UNSTOPPABLE MOTHERS OF THE EQUAL RIGHTS AMENDMENT (2020); ROSALYN TERBORG-PENN, AFRICAN AMERICAN WOMEN IN THE STRUGGLE FOR THE VOTE, 1850–1920 (1998); LISA TETRAULT, THE MYTH OF SENECA FALLS: MEMORY AND THE WOMEN'S SUFFRAGE MOVEMENT, 1848–1898 (2014); Reva B. Siegel, *She the People: The Nineteenth Amendment, Sex Equality, Federalism, and the Family*, 115 HARV. L. REV. 947 (2002); Reva B. Siegel, *The Politics of Constitutional Memory*, 20 GEO. J.L. & PUB. POL'Y 19 (2022); Barbara Y. Welke, *When All the Women Were White, and All the Blacks Were*

Men: Gender, Class, Race, and the Road to Plessy, *1855–1914*, 13 Law & Hist. Rev. 261 (1995); sources cited *infra* note 324.

148. *See* Obergefell v. Hodges, 576 U.S. 644, 675–76 (2015).

149. *Id.* at 669; *see also id.* at 659–60, 673–74.

150. *Id.* at 660.

151. For Ginsburg's vote, see *id.* at 648.

152. *Id.* at 674.

153. 347 U.S. 483 (1954). On the NAACP's strategy, see Richard Kluger, Simple Justice: The History of *Brown v. Board of Education* and Black America's Struggle for Equality (1975).

154. *Obergefell*, 576 U.S. at 676.

155. *See* Declaration of Sentiments (1848), *reprinted in* 1 History of Woman Suffrage 70, 70–73 (Elizabeth Cady Stanton et al. eds., New York, Fowler & Wells 1881).

156. *See, e.g.,* Janet Dewart Bell, Lighting the Fires of Freedom: African American Women in the Civil Rights Movement 100–01 (2018) (interview with Diane Nash); *id.* at 112–15 (interview with Judy Richardson); Jones, *supra* note 147, at 175–265; *infra* text accompanying notes 193–226.

157. *See* 18 Cong. Rec. 980 (1887).

158. *Id.* at 983 (statement of Sen. Joseph Brown).

159. B.V. Hubbard, Socialism, Feminism, and Suffragism, the Terrible Triplets Connected by the Same Umbilical Cord, and Fed from the Same Nursing Bottle, at title page, 238 (1915) (capitalization omitted).

160. For an example of anti-suffragism in list form, see Nat'l Ass'n Opposed to Woman Suffrage, Some Reasons Why We Oppose Votes for Women (New York, 1894).

161. *See* Christiane Bird, *Alice Duer Miller, in* 3 American Women Writers: A Critical Reference Guide from Colonial Times to the Present 177, 177–78 (Lina Mainiero ed., 1981); Mary Chapman, *"Are Women People?": Alice Duer Miller's Poetry and Politics,* 18 Am. Literary Hist. 59, 67 (2006).

162. Alice Duer Miller, *Our Own Twelve Anti-Suffrage Reasons,* N.Y. Trib., Mar. 29, 1914 (pt. III), at 10; *see also* Alice Duer Miller, Are Women People? A Book of Rhymes for Suffrage Times 43 (1915) (reprinting poem with minor editing).

163. *See, e.g., Progress of the Suffragists,* N.Y. Times, Jan. 25, 1913, at 14; *Do the Women Want to Vote?,* N.Y. Times, Apr. 4, 1913, at 8; *Forcing Women to Vote,* N.Y. Times, Nov. 12, 1914, at 12; *Getting Back to Facts,* N.Y. Times, Nov. 23, 1914, at 10; *Silent, Silly, and Offensive,* N.Y. Times, Jan. 11, 1917, at 14; *Militants Get 3 Days; Lack Time to Starve,* N.Y. Times, June 28, 1917, at 6; *Suffragist Disorders Again,* N.Y. Times, Aug. 8, 1918, at 10.

164. Jennifer Schuessler, *The Women Who Fought Against the Vote,* N.Y. Times, Aug. 16, 2020 (Special Section), at 28.

165. *The Woman Suffrage Crisis,* N.Y. Times, Feb. 7, 1915, at C2.

166. *Defeat of Woman Suffrage,* N.Y. Times, Nov. 3, 1915, at 14.

167. *See* Carrie Chapman Catt & Nettie Rogers Shuler, Woman Suffrage and Politics: The Inner Story of the Suffrage Movement 266–69 (1923).

168. *Id.* at 107–08.

169. Charles Willis Thompson, *Now the Story of Woman Suffrage Has Been Told,* N.Y. Times, May 13, 1923 (§ 3), at 3 (book review).

170. Frontiero v. Richardson, 411 U.S. 677, 684 (1973) (plurality opinion) (internal quotation marks omitted).

171. *Cavalry Troop to Rescue of Paraders*, Bos. HERALD, Mar. 4, 1913, at 1; *Mobs Insult Women While on Parade in Capital City*, CALL (San Francisco), Mar. 4, 1913, at 1. On the race of the offenders, see J.P.G., *Capital's Shame*, EVENING POST (New York), Mar. 4, 1913, at 1.

172. *Mobs Insult Women While on Parade in Capital City, supra* note 171, at 1; *see also Cavalry Troop to Rescue of Paraders, supra* note 171, at 1 (same with minor editing); *Woman's Beauty, Grace, and Art Bewilder the Capital*, WASH. POST, Mar. 4, 1913, at 1 (same with minor editing).

173. J.P.G., *supra* note 171, at 1.

174. A.E.R., *Parade Struggles to Victory Despite Disgraceful Scenes*, 44 WOMAN'S J. 73, 73 (1913).

175. *Id.*

176. J.P.G., *supra* note 171, at 1.

177. *See* DORIS STEVENS, JAILED FOR FREEDOM 63–67 (1920).

178. *See id.* at 83–85; *President Onlooker at Mob Attack on Suffragists*, SUFFRAGIST, Aug. 18, 1917, at 7, 7; *The Administration Versus the Woman's Party*, SUFFRAGIST, Aug. 25, 1917, at 6, 6–7.

179. *See* H.R. Res. 130, 65th Cong. (1917); *President Onlooker at Mob Attack on Suffragists, supra* note 178, at 7; *The Government Versus the Woman's Party*, SUFFRAGIST, Aug. 25, 1917, at 5, 5.

180. *See* H.R. Res. 130; *The Government Versus the Woman's Party, supra* note 179, at 5.

181. *See* H.R. Res. 130; *President Onlooker at Mob Attack on Suffragists, supra* note 178, at 7; *The Government Versus the Woman's Party, supra* note 179, at 5.

182. *See President Onlooker at Mob Attack on Suffragists, supra* note 178, at 7; *see also* H.R. Res. 130; *The Administration Versus the Woman's Party, supra* note 178, at 6; *The Government Versus the Woman's Party, supra* note 179, at 5.

183. *President Onlooker at Mob Attack on Suffragists, supra* note 178, at 7 (internal quotation marks omitted).

184. *See id.*

185. *The Administration Versus the Woman's Party, supra* note 178, at 6.

186. INEZ HAYNES IRWIN, THE STORY OF THE WOMAN'S PARTY 232 (1921); *see also* STEVENS, *supra* note 177, at 128; *The Administration Versus the Woman's Party, supra* note 178, at 6; *The Government Versus the Woman's Party, supra* note 179, at 5.

187. STEVENS, *supra* note 177, at 128; *see also The Administration Versus the Woman's Party, supra* note 178, at 6; *The Government Versus the Woman's Party, supra* note 179, at 5.

188. STEVENS, *supra* note 177, at 129; *see also The Administration Versus the Woman's Party, supra* note 178, at 6–7; *The Government Versus the Woman's Party, supra* note 179, at 5.

189. *Cf.* United States v. Morrison, 529 U.S. 598, 601–02 (2000) (refusing to quote alleged rapist's "vulgar," misogynistic language made it easier for Court to deny redress).

190. *See Cartooning for Suffrage*, SUFFRAGIST, Mar. 2, 1918, at 8; *Cartoons Wilson*, CHI. DAILY TRIB., Oct. 23, 1916, at 11; *Only Woman Cartoonist in America Draws for Suffrage*, WASH. TIMES, Aug. 22, 1916, at 8.

191. *Training for the Draft*, SUFFRAGIST, Sept. 29, 1917, at 1 (capitalization omitted). For the original drawing, see National Woman's Party, Nina Allender Political Cartoon Collection (copy on file with author).

192. On the World War I draft, see Act of May 18, 1917, Pub. L. No. 65-12, 40 Stat. 76.

193. Frontiero v. Richardson, 411 U.S. 677, 684 (1973) (plurality opinion) (internal quotation marks omitted).

194. *See* FANNY LOU HAMER, TO PRAISE OUR BRIDGES: AN AUTOBIOGRAPHY 5 (Julius Lester & Mary Varela eds., 1967).

195. *See id.* at 5, 11–12; FANNIE LOU HAMER, Testimony Before the Credentials Committee at the Democratic National Convention, Atlantic City, New Jersey, August 22, 1964, *in* THE SPEECHES OF FANNIE LOU HAMER: TO TELL IT LIKE IT IS 42, 43 (Maegan Parker Brooks & Davis W. Houck eds., 2011).

196. *See* HAMER, *supra* note 194, at 11–12; HOWELL RAINES, MY SOUL IS RESTED: MOVEMENT DAYS IN THE DEEP SOUTH REMEMBERED 249 (1977) (quoting interview with Fannie Lou Hamer).

197. HAMER, *supra* note 194, at 12.

198. *See* U.S. CONST. amends. XV, XIX.

199. *See* sources cited *supra* note 84.

200. *See* U.S. COMM'N ON C.R., POLITICAL PARTICIPATION 246 tbl.9 (1968).

201. *See* HAMER, *supra* note 195, at 43.

202. 90 CONG. REC. 911 (1944) (statement of Sen. James Eastland).

203. *See* U.S. COMM'N ON C.R., *supra* note 200, at 246 tbl.9.

204. *See* HAMER, *supra* note 195, at 43; HAMER, *supra* note 194, at 11–12.

205. *See* HAMER, *supra* note 195, at 43.

206. *See* RAINES, *supra* note 196, at 250 (quoting interview with Fannie Lou Hamer); Jerry DeMuth, *'Tired of Being Sick and Tired,'* 198 NATION 548, 551 (1964) (quoting interview with Fannie Lou Hamer).

207. *See* HAMER, *supra* note 194, at 12; *see also* JOHN EGERTON, A MIND TO STAY HERE: PROFILES FROM THE SOUTH 97 (1970) (quoting interview with Fannie Lou Hamer); HAMER, *supra* note 195, at 43; RAINES, *supra* note 196, at 250 (quoting interview with Fannie Lou Hamer).

208. *See* EGERTON, *supra* note 207, at 97 (quoting interview with Fannie Lou Hamer); RAINES, *supra* note 196, at 250 (quoting interview with Fannie Lou Hamer).

209. RAINES, *supra* note 196, at 250 (quoting interview with Fannie Lou Hamer).

210. *See* 110 CONG. REC. 14,001 (1964) (statement of Fannie Lou Hamer); EGERTON, *supra* note 207, at 97 (quoting interview with Fannie Lou Hamer); HAMER, *supra* note 195, at 43; HAMER, *supra* note 194, at 12; RAINES, *supra* note 196, at 250–51 (quoting interview with Fannie Lou Hamer).

211. *See* 110 CONG. REC. 14,001 (statement of Fannie Lou Hamer); HAMER, *supra* note 195, at 43; HAMER, *supra* note 194, at 12–13; RAINES, *supra* note 196, at 251 (quoting interview with Fannie Lou Hamer).

212. *See* 110 CONG. REC. 14,001 (statement of Fannie Lou Hamer); EGERTON, *supra* note 207, at 98 (quoting interview with Fannie Lou Hamer); HAMER, *supra* note 195, at 44; RAINES, *supra* note 196, at 251 (quoting interview with Fannie Lou Hamer); DeMuth, *supra* note 206, at 550 (quoting interview with Fannie Lou Hamer).

213. *See* HAMER, *supra* note 194, at 13; RAINES, *supra* note 196, at 251 (quoting interview with Fannie Lou Hamer).

214. *See* 110 CONG. REC. 14,001 (statement of Fannie Lou Hamer); HAMER, *supra* note 195, at 44; HAMER, *supra* note 194, at 13; RAINES, *supra* note 196, at 251 (quoting interview with Fannie Lou Hamer).

215. *See* RAINES, *supra* note 196, at 252 (quoting interview with Fannie Lou Hamer).

216. *See* HAMER, *supra* note 194, at 16; RAINES, *supra* note 196, at 252 (quoting interview with Fannie Lou Hamer).

217. *See* 110 CONG. REC. 14,001–02 (statement of Fannie Lou Hamer); HAMER, *supra* note 195, at 44; June Johnson, *Broken Barriers and Billy Sticks*, SOJOURNERS, Dec. 1982, at 16, 16.

218. *See* 110 CONG. REC. 14,001–02 (statement of Fannie Lou Hamer); HAMER, *supra* note 195, at 44; RAINES, *supra* note 196, at 252–53 (quoting interview with Fannie Lou Hamer); Johnson, *supra* note 217, at 16.

219. *See* HAMER, *supra* note 195, at 44; HAMER, *supra* note 194, at 14; RAINES, *supra* note 196, at 253 (quoting interview with Fannie Lou Hamer); The Winona Incident: An Interview with Annelle Ponder and Fannie Lou Hamer, June 1963, *in* PAT WATTERS & REESE CLEGHORN, CLIMBING JACOB'S LADDER: THE ARRIVAL OF NEGROES IN SOUTHERN POLITICS 363, 370 (1967) (statement of Fannie Lou Hamer).

220. HAMER, *supra* note 195, at 44–45 (internal quotation marks omitted); *see also* 110 CONG. REC. 14,002 (statement of Fannie Lou Hamer); EGERTON, *supra* note 207, at 100 (quoting interview with Fannie Lou Hamer); RAINES, *supra* note 196, at 253 (quoting interview with Fannie Lou Hamer); The Winona Incident, *supra* note 219, at 370–71 (statement of Fannie Lou Hamer).

221. HAMER, *supra* note 195, at 45.

222. EGERTON, *supra* note 207, at 100 (quoting interview with Fannie Lou Hamer); *see also* RAINES, *supra* note 196, at 254 (quoting interview with Fannie Lou Hamer).

223. The Winona Incident, *supra* note 219, at 364, 371 (statement of Fannie Lou Hamer).

224. *See* HAMER, *supra* note 195, at 42–43. For examples of the media coverage, see Saul Kohler, *Mississippi Is Accused of Disloyalty: 2 Women Steal Show at Credentials Hearings on Seating*, PHILA. INQUIRER, Aug. 23, 1964, at 1; Catherine Mackin, *She Steals LBJ's Thunder*, S.F. EXAM'R, Aug. 26, 1964, at 9.

225. HAMER, *supra* note 195, at 45. For the official designation of "The Star-Spangled Banner" as "the national anthem of the United States of America," see Act of Mar. 3, 1931, ch. 436, 46 Stat. 1508. For the song's lyrics, see Francis Scott Key, *The Star Spangled Banner*, *in* ARMY SONG BOOK 2, 2–3 (Adjutant General's Office comp., 2d ed. 1941).

226. Stanley S. Scott, *2 Women Charge Police Beating in Winona, Mississippi Arrest*, ATLANTA DAILY WORLD, June 14, 1963, at 1 (quoting Fannie Lou Hamer) (internal quotation marks omitted).

227. *See* H.R. 7152, 88th Cong. § 701 (as introduced in House, June 20, 1963).

228. *See* 110 CONG. REC. 2584 (1964).

229. *See* Civil Rights Act of 1964, Pub. L. No. 88-352, § 703, 78 Stat. 241, 255.

230. Bostock v. Clayton County, 590 U.S. 644, 678 (2020); *see also id.* at 682–83.

231. Bradford v. Peoples Nat. Gas Co., 60 F.R.D. 432, 434–35 (W.D. Pa. 1973) (footnote omitted); *see also id.* at 434 n.1.

232. Rabidue v. Osceola Refin. Co., 584 F. Supp. 419, 428 n.36 (E.D. Mich. 1984).

233. Erickson v. Bartell Drug Co., 141 F. Supp. 2d 1266, 1269 (W.D. Wash. 2001).

234. EEOC v. Walden Book Co., 885 F. Supp. 1100, 1103 n.6 (M.D. Tenn. 1995); *see also* Meritor Sav. Bank, FSB v. Vinson, 477 U.S. 57, 63–64 (1986); County of Washington v. Gunther, 452 U.S. 161, 190 n.4 (1981) (Rehnquist, J., dissenting); Int'l Union of Elec., Radio & Mach. Workers v. Westinghouse Elec. Corp., 631 F.2d 1094, 1101 (3d Cir. 1980);

Barnes v. Costle, 561 F.2d 983, 986–87 (D.C. Cir. 1977); Wetzel v. Liberty Mut. Ins. Co., 511 F.2d 199, 204 (3d Cir. 1975), *vacated and remanded*, 424 U.S. 737 (1976); Dodge v. Giant Food, Inc., 488 F.2d 1333, 1336 n.17 (D.C. Cir. 1973) (per curiam); Rasmusson v. Copeland Lumber Yards, Inc., 988 F. Supp. 1294, 1297 (D. Nev. 1997); Wilson v. Sw. Airlines Co., 517 F. Supp. 292, 297 n.12 (N.D. Tex. 1981); Sale v. Waverly-Shell Rock Bd. of Educ., 390 F. Supp. 784, 787 (N.D. Iowa 1975); Bujel v. Borman Food Stores, Inc., 384 F. Supp. 141, 144 n.4 (E.D. Mich. 1974); Cooper v. Delta Air Lines, Inc., 274 F. Supp. 781, 782–83 (E.D. La. 1967).

235. Willingham v. Macon Tel. Publ'g Co., 507 F.2d 1084, 1090 (5th Cir. 1975); *see also id.* at 1086–88, 1091–93.

236. *See* Ulane v. E. Airlines, Inc., 742 F.2d 1081, 1084–86 (7th Cir. 1984).

237. *Id.* at 1085; *see also* Taken v. Okla. Corp. Comm'n, 125 F.3d 1366, 1369–70 (10th Cir. 1997).

238. *See* John Herbers, *Problems Face Job Rights Unit as Roosevelt Assumes Office*, N.Y. TIMES, June 3, 1965, at 2.

239. Edith Evans Asbury, *Protest Proposed on Women's Jobs*, N.Y. TIMES, Oct. 13, 1965, at 32 (quoting Franklin D. Roosevelt Jr.).

240. *Sex Discrimination Laws Debated*, 61 LAB. RELS. REP. 253, 253, 255 (1966) (quoting Herman Edelsberg) (internal quotation marks omitted).

241. *See Roosevelt Finds Sex Discrimination in Jobs Is Big Problem; Appoints Seven Key Aides*, N.Y. TIMES, July 21, 1965, at 25.

242. *See* Richard K. Berg, *Equal Employment Opportunity Under the Civil Rights Act of 1964*, 31 BROOK. L. REV. 62, 62 n.* (1964).

243. *Id.* at 78–79.

244. *See* Norbert A. Schlei, *Foreword* to BARBARA LINDEMANN SCHLEI & PAUL GROSSMAN, EMPLOYMENT DISCRIMINATION LAW, at vii, vii, xii (1976).

245. *Id.* at xi.

246. *See* P. SCOTT CORBETT ET AL., U.S. HISTORY 881 (2017); RICHARD A. EPSTEIN, FORBIDDEN GROUNDS: THE CASE AGAINST EMPLOYMENT DISCRIMINATION LAWS 278–79 (1992); JAMAL GREENE, HOW RIGHTS WENT WRONG: WHY OUR OBSESSION WITH RIGHTS IS TEARING AMERICA APART 72 (2021); EMMA J. LAPSANSKY-WERNER ET AL., UNITED STATES HISTORY 1025 (2009); EMMA J. LAPSANSKY-WERNER ET AL., UNITED STATES HISTORY: MODERN AMERICA 577 (2009); J. RALPH LINDGREN & NADINE TAUB, THE LAW OF SEX DISCRIMINATION 110–11 (1988); SANDRA DAY O'CONNOR, THE MAJESTY OF THE LAW: REFLECTIONS OF A SUPREME COURT JUSTICE 161–62 (Craig Jones ed., 2003); WILLIAM F. PEPPER & FLORYNCE R. KENNEDY, SEX DISCRIMINATION IN EMPLOYMENT: AN ANALYSIS AND GUIDE FOR PRACTITIONER AND STUDENT 18 (1981); GEORGE A. RUTHERGLEN & JOHN J. DONOHUE III, EMPLOYMENT DISCRIMINATION: LAW AND THEORY 222 (2005); ARTHUR B. SMITH, JR., EMPLOYMENT DISCRIMINATION LAW: CASES AND MATERIALS 327 (1978); CLAIRE SHERMAN THOMAS, SEX DISCRIMINATION IN A NUTSHELL 217 (2d ed. 1991).

247. *See* Robert Belton, *A Comparative Review of Public and Private Enforcement of Title VII of the Civil Rights Act of 1964*, 31 VAND. L. REV. 905, 917 (1978); Merton C. Bernstein & Lois G. Williams, *Title VII and the Problem of Sex Classifications in Pension Programs*, 74 COLUM. L. REV. 1203, 1216–17 (1974); Brietta R. Clark, Erickson v. Bartell Drug Co.: *A Roadmap for Gender Equality in Reproductive Health Care or an Empty Promise?*, 23 LAW

& INEQ. 299, 305–06 (2005); John J. Donohue III, *Prohibiting Sex Discrimination in the Workplace: An Economic Perspective*, 56 U. CHI. L. REV. 1337, 1337–38 (1989); Beverley H. Earle & Gerald A. Madek, *An International Perspective on Sexual Harassment Law*, 12 LAW & INEQ. 43, 48 (1993); Deborah Epstein, *Can a "Dumb Ass Woman" Achieve Equality in the Workplace? Running the Gauntlet of Hostile Environment Harassing Speech*, 84 GEO. L.J. 399, 409 n.62 (1996); Susan Estrich, *Sex at Work*, 43 STAN. L. REV. 813, 816–17 (1991); Hannah Arterian Furnish, *Prenatal Exposure to Fetally Toxic Work Environments: The Dilemma of the 1978 Pregnancy Amendment to Title VII of the Civil Rights Act of 1964*, 66 IOWA L. REV. 63, 74 (1980); B. Glenn George, *The Back Door: Legitimizing Sexual Harassment Claims*, 73 B.U. L. REV. 1, 4 (1993); Marcia L. Greenbaum & Bruce Fraser, *Sexual Harassment in the Workplace*, 36 ARB. J. 30, 31 (1981); Andrew P. Morriss, *Private Amici Curiae and the Supreme Court's 1997–1998 Term Employment Law Jurisprudence*, 7 WM. & MARY BILL RTS. J. 823, 847 (1999); Ellen Frankel Paul, *Sexual Harassment as Sex Discrimination: A Defective Paradigm*, 8 YALE L. & POL'Y REV. 333, 346 (1990); Suzanne Sangree, *Title VII Prohibitions Against Hostile Environment Sexual Harassment and the First Amendment: No Collision in Sight*, 47 RUTGERS L. REV. 461, 481–83 (1995); Arthur B. Smith, Jr., *The Law and Equal Employment Opportunity: What's Past Should Not Be Prologue*, 33 INDUS. & LAB. RELS. REV. 493, 504 (1980); N. Morrison Torrey, *Indirect Discrimination Under Title VII: Expanding Male Standing to Sue for Injuries Received as a Result of Employer Discrimination Against Females*, 64 WASH. L. REV. 365, 385–86 (1989); Ruth C. Vance, *Workers' Compensation and Sexual Harassment in the Workplace: A Remedy for Employees, or a Shield for Employers?*, 11 HOFSTRA LAB. L.J. 141, 147 (1993); William L. Woerner & Sharon L. Oswald, *Sexual Harassment in the Workplace: A View Through the Eyes of the Courts*, 41 LAB. L.J. 786, 786 (1990); *Developments in the Law: Employment Discrimination and Title VII of the Civil Rights Act of 1964*, 84 HARV. L. REV. 1109, 1167 (1971); Peter F. Ziegler, Note, *Employer Dress and Appearance Codes and Title VII of the Civil Rights Act of 1964*, 46 S. CAL. L. REV. 965, 968–69 (1973).

248. For news reports, see Harry Bernstein, *Debate Grows over Job Discrimination Due to Sex*, L.A. TIMES, Mar. 7, 1966 (pt. II), at 1; Ruth Brine, *The New Feminists: Revolt Against 'Sexism,'* TIME, Nov. 21, 1969, at 53, 54; John Herbers, *Bans on Job Bias Effective Today*, N.Y. TIMES, July 2, 1965, at 1; Diana Kunde, *Women at Work: A March Through Time*, DALL. MORNING NEWS, July 4, 1995, at 1D; Editorial, *No Laughing Matter*, WASH. POST, Oct. 12, 1965, at A16; Frances Stead Sellers, *A History: Harassment and the Law*, WASH. POST, Feb. 28, 1999, at B4; *Sex and Nonsense*, NEW REPUBLIC, Sept. 4, 1965, at 10, 10; Gerald D. Skoning, *Twists and Turns on Road to Equal Opportunity*, CHI. TRIB., July 2, 2014 (§ 1), at 17; *Women's Liberation Revisited*, TIME, Mar. 20, 1972, at 29, 29.

249. Earle & Madek, *supra* note 247, at 48.

250. SMITH, *supra* note 246, at 327 (internal quotation marks omitted); Belton, *supra* note 247, at 917; Brine, *supra* note 248, at 54; *Sex and Nonsense, supra* note 248, at 10.

251. Estrich, *supra* note 247, at 816; Vance, *supra* note 247, at 147; *see also* GREENE, *supra* note 246, at 72; Bernstein & Williams, *supra* note 247, at 1216.

252. Morriss, *supra* note 247, at 847.

253. LINDGREN & TAUB, *supra* note 246, at 111.

254. *See* Resolution Adopted Unanimously by the National Council of the National Woman's Party Dec. 16, 1963 Washington, D.C. Regarding the Proposed Civil Rights Bill (H.R.

7152) (copy on file with author; National Woman's Party Papers, 1913–1972, reel 108); Letter from Emma Guffey Miller, Nat'l Chairman, Nat'l Woman's Party, to Rep. Martha W. Griffiths (Jan. 20, 1964) (copy on file with author; National Woman's Party Papers, 1913–1972, reel 108); Letter from Emma Guffey Miller, Nat'l Chairman, Nat'l Woman's Party, to Rep. James W. Trimble (Jan. 22, 1964) (copy on file with author; National Woman's Party Papers, 1913–1972, reel 108).

255. *See* 110 Cong. Rec. 2583 (1964) (statement of Rep. Howard Smith).

256. Letter from Nina Horton Avery, Chairman, Virginia Comm. of Nat'l Woman's Party, to Howard W. Smith, Chairman, House Rules Comm. 1 (Dec. 15, 1963) (copy on file with author; University of Virginia Library, Papers of Howard W. Smith, box 108, folder 5); *see also* Letter from Lynn B. Franklin to Howard W. Smith, Chairman, House Rules Comm. (Dec. 10, 1963) (copy on file with author; National Woman's Party Papers, 1913–1972, reel 108); Letter from Emma Guffey Miller, President, Nat'l Woman's Party, to Howard W. Smith, Chairman, House Rules Comm. (Jan. 6, 1964) (copy on file with author; University of Virginia Library, Papers of Howard W. Smith, box 107, folder 3); Letter from Lynn Franklin to Howard W. Smith (Jan. 29, 1964) (copy on file with author; National Woman's Party Papers, 1913–1972, reel 108).

257. *See* 110 Cong. Rec. 2804.

258. *See* Don Oberdorfer, *'Judge' Smith Moves with Deliberate Drag*, N.Y. Times, Jan. 12, 1964 (§ 6), at 13.

259. Letter from Howard W. Smith, Chairman, House Rules Comm., to Nina Horton Avery, Chairman, Virginia Comm. of Nat'l Woman's Party (Dec. 26, 1963) (copy on file with author; National Woman's Party Papers, 1913–1972, reel 108; University of Virginia Library, Papers of Howard W. Smith, box 108, folder 5).

260. *See A Tribute to Those Who Will Not Return to the 90th Congress*, Nat'l Woman's Party Bull., Nov.–Dec. 1966, at 3, 3–4.

261. *See* 91 Cong. Rec. 30–31 (1945).

262. *See* 102 Cong. Rec. 13,124–25 (1956) (statement of Rep. Gordon McDonough).

263. *Id.* at 13,125 (statement of Rep. Howard Smith).

264. *Civil Rights: Hearings on H.R. 7152 Before the H. Comm. on Rules*, 88th Cong. 125 (1964) (statement of Rep. Emanuel Celler).

265. *See Equal Rights Amendment to the Constitution and Commission on the Legal Status of Women: Hearings Before Subcomm. No. 1 of the H. Comm. on the Judiciary*, 80th Cong. 6–8 (1948) [hereinafter *ERA Hearings*] (statement of Rep. Katharine St. George); Fern S. Ingersoll, *Former Congresswomen Look Back*, in Women in Washington: Advocates for Public Policy 191, 193–95 (Irene Tinker ed., 1983) (quoting interview with Katharine St. George); *Mrs. St. George Asks Equality in Work and Pay for Women*, Wash. Post, June 14, 1953, at 11M.

266. *Civil Rights*, *supra* note 264, at 125 (statement of Rep. Katharine St. George).

267. *Id.* (statement of Rep. Howard Smith).

268. Letter from Howard W. Smith to Emma Guffey Miller, President, Nat'l Woman's Party (Jan. 10, 1964) (copy on file with author; University of Virginia Library, Papers of Howard W. Smith, box 107, folder 3).

269. *See* Eleanor Harris, *May Craig: TV's Most Unusual Star*, Look, Apr. 24, 1962, at 109, 110; Ruth Montgomery, *"Little Woman in Blue" Who Outquips President*, Times-Herald

(D.C.), Jan. 7, 1945, at D3; Patricia Schroth, *Meet May Craig Newshen Extraordinary*, Down E., Aug. 1959, at 32, 32; Helen M. Staunton, *Mrs. Craig "Hell Fire" on Women's Equality*, Ed. & Publisher, June 17, 1944, at 46.

270. *See* May Craig, Unpublished Autobiography, Prologue at 12, Chapter 1 at 7, Chapter 3 at 10 (n.d.) (copy on file with author; Library of Congress, Manuscript Division, May Craig Papers, box 2); Montgomery, *supra* note 269, at D3.

271. *See* Robert Day, *"Well, There You Are, Senator. You Would Snap Back at May Craig!,"* New Yorker, Jan. 17, 1959, at 36.

272. *See* Norman Parkinson, *People Are Talking About . . .*, Vogue, June 1955, at 78.

273. *See Life Calls on a Washington Newspaperwoman*, Life, Feb. 19, 1945, at 110.

274. *See* Harris, *supra* note 269, at 110; Montgomery, *supra* note 269, at D3; Schroth, *supra* note 269, at 33; Staunton, *supra* note 269, at 46.

275. Staunton, *supra* note 269, at 46 (quoting May Craig) (internal quotation marks omitted).

276. Parkinson, *supra* note 272, at 78 (quoting May Craig) (internal quotation marks omitted); *see also* Craig, *supra* note 270, at Chapter 4 at 2.

277. *Meet the Press* (NBC television broadcast Jan. 26, 1964) (transcript at 9; copy on file with author).

278. *See Civil Rights: Hearings on H.R. 7152 Before the H. Comm. on Rules (pt. 2)*, 88th Cong. 558 (1964) (statement of Rep. Katharine St. George).

279. *See* 110 Cong. Rec. 2577 (1964) (statement of Rep. Howard Smith).

280. *See id.* at 2584.

281. *See* Off. of the Historian, U.S. House of Representatives, Women in Congress, 1917–1990, at 21–22, 57–58, 85–86, 89–90, 93–94, 125–28, 163–64, 177–78, 213–14, 227–28, 237–39, 249–50 (1991).

282. *See* 110 Cong. Rec. 2578 (statement of Rep. Frances Bolton); *id.* at 2578–80 (statement of Rep. Martha Griffiths); *id.* at 2580–81 (statement of Rep. Katharine St. George); *id.* at 2582 (statement of Rep. Catherine May); *id.* at 2582–83 (statement of Rep. Edna Kelly).

283. *See id.* at 2578 (statement of Rep. Frances Bolton).

284. *Id.* at 2581 (statement of Rep. Katharine St. George).

285. *Id.* at 2582 (statement of Rep. Catherine May).

286. *Id.* at 2583 (statement of Rep. Edna Kelly).

287. *See id.* at 2578–80 (statement of Rep. Martha Griffiths); *id.* at 2582 (statement of Rep. Catherine May).

288. *Id.* at 2580 (statement of Rep. Martha Griffiths).

289. *Id.* (statement of Rep. Katharine St. George).

290. *Id.* at 2581 (statement of Rep. Katharine St. George).

291. *See* Sue Cronk, *Battle to Better Women's Wages Still Goes on*, Wash. Post, June 14, 1964, at F9.

292. 110 Cong. Rec. 2581 (statement of Rep. Edith Green).

293. *Now the Talking Begins*, Time, Feb. 21, 1964, at 22, 22 (internal quotation marks omitted).

294. *See* 110 Cong. Rec. 2804.

295. *See* Letter from Emma Guffey Miller, Nat'l Chairman, Nat'l Woman's Party, to Fellow Member (Feb. 14, 1964) (copy on file with author; National Woman's Party Papers, 1913–1972, reel 108) [hereinafter Letter from Emma Guffey Miller (Feb. 14, 1964)]; Letter

from Emma Guffey Miller, Nat'l Chairman, Nat'l Woman's Party, to Ruth Gage Colby (Feb. 22, 1964) (copy on file with author; National Woman's Party Papers, 1913–1972, reel 108).

296. Martha Griffiths, *Women and Legislation*, *in* VOICES OF THE NEW FEMINISM 103, 113 (Mary Lou Thompson ed., 1970); *see also* Ingersoll, *supra* note 265, at 197 (quoting interview with Martha Griffiths).

297. *See* May Craig, *Civil Rights Bill Is Fraught with Change*, PORTLAND SUNDAY TELEGRAM (Maine), Feb. 16, 1964, at 20B.

298. *Meet the Press* (NBC television broadcast Mar. 8, 1964) (transcript at 9–10; copy on file with author).

299. For coverage of Dirksen's announcement, see Robert C. Albright, *Dirksen Unveils Sheaf of Rights Amendments*, WASH. POST, Apr. 8, 1964, at A1; Joseph Hearst, *Dirksen Seeks Compromises on Rights Bill*, CHI. TRIB., Apr. 8, 1964 (§ 1), at 2.

300. *See* Mary Ann Callan, *Sen. Smith—A Step into History*, L.A. TIMES, July 16, 1964 (pt. IV), at 1.

301. *See* PAULI MURRAY, SONG IN A WEARY THROAT: AN AMERICAN PILGRIMAGE 357 (1987) (quoting Letter from Margaret Chase Smith to Pauli Murray (1964)); Donald Allen Robinson, *Two Movements in Pursuit of Equal Employment Opportunity*, 4 SIGNS 413, 418 (1979) (quoting Letter from Margaret Chase Smith to Donald Allen Robinson (July 1, 1975)).

302. *See* ERA Hearings, *supra* note 265, at 75–76 (statement of Rep. Margaret Chase Smith); Statement by Senator Margaret Chase Smith to National Woman's Party (Dec. 23, 1963) (copy on file with author; National Woman's Party Papers, 1913–1972, reel 108).

303. *See* 2 MARGUERITE RAWALT, A HISTORY OF THE NATIONAL FEDERATION OF BUSINESS AND PROFESSIONAL WOMEN'S CLUBS, INC., 1944–1960, at 157–58 (1969).

304. The Reminiscences of Marguerite Rawalt 365 (1983) (copy on file with author; Columbia University, Oral History Research Office).

305. *Id.* at 396.

306. *Id.* at 365.

307. For the membership of the commission's Committee on Civil and Political Rights, see AMERICAN WOMEN: REPORT OF THE PRESIDENT'S COMMISSION ON THE STATUS OF WOMEN 77–78 (1963).

308. *See* MURRAY, *supra* note 301, at 355–56; JUDITH PATERSON, BE SOMEBODY: A BIOGRAPHY OF MARGUERITE RAWALT 153–54 (1986).

309. *See* Pauli Murray & Mary O. Eastwood, *Jane Crow and the Law: Sex Discrimination and Title VII*, 34 GEO. WASH. L. REV. 232, 242–56 (1965).

310. *See* MURRAY, *supra* note 301, at 355, 359.

311. *See* Pauli Murray, Memorandum in Support of Retaining the Amendment to H.R. 7152, Title VII (Equal Employment Opportunity) to Prohibit Discrimination in Employment Because of Sex (Apr. 14, 1964) (copy on file with author; Harvard University, Radcliffe Institute, Schlesinger Library, Pauli Murray Papers, box 85, folder 1485).

312. *Id.* at 20.

313. *See* MURRAY, *supra* note 301, at 357; PATERSON, *supra* note 308, at 154.

314. MURRAY, *supra* note 301, at 357–58 (quoting Bess Abell) (internal quotation marks omitted); *see also* PATERSON, *supra* note 308, at 154.

315. *See* sources cited *supra* note 282.

316. *See* source cited *supra* note 267.

317. Letter from Mary A. Birckhead, Nat'l Chairman & Emma Guffey Miller, President, Nat'l Woman's Party, to Members of the Nat'l Woman's Party & Friends (Sept. 1, 1965) (copy on file with author; National Woman's Party Papers, 1913–1972, reel 109); *see also* Letter from Emma Guffey Miller (Feb. 14, 1964), *supra* note 295; Letter from Nat'l Woman's Party to Ed., Washington Post (Oct. 1965) (copy on file with author; ProQuest History Vault, Struggle for Women's Rights, Organizational Records, 1880–1990); Letter from Ruth Gage-Colby, Nat'l Council Member, Nat'l Woman's Party, to Franklin D. Roosevelt, Jr., Chairman, Equal Emp. Opportunity Comm'n (Nov. 6, 1965) (copy on file with author; National Woman's Party Papers, 1913–1972, reel 109; ProQuest History Vault, Struggle for Women's Rights, Organizational Records, 1880–1990); Letter from Ruth Gage-Colby, Nat'l Council Member, Nat'l Woman's Party, to Anne Draper, Rsch. Dep't, Am. Fed'n of Lab. & Cong. of Indus. Orgs. (Nov. 6, 1965) (copy on file with author; National Woman's Party Papers, 1913–1972, reel 109); *A Tribute to Those Who Will Not Return to the 90th Congress*, *supra* note 260, at 4; Caruthers Gholson Berger, *Equal Pay, Equal Employment Opportunity and Equal Enforcement of the Law for Women*, 5 VAL. U. L. REV. 326, 332–37, 332 n.35 (1971).

318. Lucinda Klemeyer, *'Equal Rights' Is Battle Cry*, COLUMBUS DISPATCH, Feb. 12, 1967, at 2C (quoting Ernestine Powell) (internal quotation marks omitted).

319. 112 CONG. REC. 13,693 (1966) (statement of Rep. Martha Griffiths); 113 CONG. REC. 13,108 (1967) (statement of Rep. Martha Griffiths); *see also* sources cited *infra* note 321.

320. *See* 113 CONG. REC. 13,109 (statement of Rep. Martha Griffiths).

321. *See* Griffiths, *supra* note 296, at 112–13; Ingersoll, *supra* note 265, at 191, 196 (quoting 1979 interview with Martha Griffiths); Robinson, *supra* note 301, at 415 (citing April 22, 1975, interview with Martha Griffiths).

322. *See* Marguerite Rawalt, *The Equal Rights Amendment*, *in* WOMEN IN WASHINGTON, *supra* note 265, at 49, 59.

323. *See* MURRAY, *supra* note 301, at 355–58.

324. *See* JUDITH A. BAER, THE CHAINS OF PROTECTION: THE JUDICIAL RESPONSE TO WOMEN'S LABOR LEGISLATION 136 (1978); CAROLINE BIRD WITH SARA WELLES BRILLER, BORN FEMALE: THE HIGH COST OF KEEPING WOMEN DOWN 1–14 (1968); DOROTHY SUE COBBLE, THE OTHER WOMEN'S MOVEMENT: WORKPLACE JUSTICE AND SOCIAL RIGHTS IN MODERN AMERICA 175–77 (2004); JO FREEMAN, THE POLITICS OF WOMEN'S LIBERATION: A CASE STUDY OF AN EMERGING SOCIAL MOVEMENT AND ITS RELATION TO THE POLICY PROCESS 53–54 (1975); EMILY GEORGE, MARTHA W. GRIFFITHS 149–52 (1982); HUGH DAVIS GRAHAM, THE CIVIL RIGHTS ERA: ORIGINS AND DEVELOPMENT OF NATIONAL POLICY, 1960–1972, at 136–38 (1990); CYNTHIA HARRISON, ON ACCOUNT OF SEX: THE POLITICS OF WOMEN'S ISSUES, 1945–1968, at 176–81 (1988); ALICE KESSLER-HARRIS, IN PURSUIT OF EQUITY: WOMEN, MEN, AND THE QUEST FOR ECONOMIC CITIZENSHIP IN 20TH-CENTURY AMERICA 239–45 (2001); KESSLER-HARRIS, *supra* note 19, at 314; ROBERT D. LOEVY, TO END ALL SEGREGATION: THE POLITICS OF THE PASSAGE OF THE CIVIL RIGHTS ACT OF 1964, at 120–22 (1990); NANCY MACLEAN, FREEDOM IS NOT ENOUGH: THE OPENING OF THE AMERICAN WORKPLACE 118–21 (2006); SERENA MAYERI, REASONING FROM RACE: FEMINISM, LAW, AND THE CIVIL RIGHTS REVOLUTION 20–22 (2011); LEILA J. RUPP & VERTA TAYLOR, SURVIVAL IN THE DOLDRUMS: THE AMERICAN WOMEN'S

Rights Movement, 1945 to the 1960s, at 176–79 (1987); Patricia G. Zelman, Women, Work, and National Policy: The Kennedy-Johnson Years 57–71 (1982); Arianne Renan Barzilay, *Parenting Title VII: Rethinking the History of the Sex Discrimination Provision*, 28 Yale J.L. & Feminism 55, 68–70, 93–95 (2016); Robert C. Bird, *More than a Congressional Joke: A Fresh Look at the Legislative History of Sex Discrimination of the 1964 Civil Rights Act*, 3 Wm. & Mary J. Women & L. 137, 149–50, 155–56 (1997); Carl M. Brauer, *Women Activists, Southern Conservatives, and the Prohibition of Sex Discrimination in Title VII of the 1964 Civil Rights Act*, 49 J.S. Hist. 37, 38–56 (1983); Cynthia Deitch, *Gender, Race, and Class Politics and the Inclusion of Women in Title VII of the 1964 Civil Rights Act*, 7 Gender & Soc'y 183, 193–97 (1993); Cary Franklin, *Inventing the "Traditional Concept" of Sex Discrimination*, 125 Harv. L. Rev. 1307, 1326–28 (2012); Jo Freeman, *How "Sex" Got into Title VII: Persistent Opportunism as a Maker of Public Policy*, 9 Law & Ineq. 163, 174–84 (1991); Michael Evan Gold, *A Tale of Two Amendments: The Reasons Congress Added Sex to Title VII and Their Implication for the Issue of Comparable Worth*, 19 Duq. L. Rev. 453, 463–66 (1981); Robinson, *supra* note 301, at 415–20; Gola E. Waters, *Sex, State Protective Laws and the Civil Rights Act of 1964*, 18 Lab. L.J. 344, 346, 352 (1967).

Chapter 2

1. *See* 1 History of Woman Suffrage 67–73 (Elizabeth Cady Stanton et al. eds., New York, Fowler & Wells 1881).

2. Declaration of Sentiments (1848), *reprinted in id.* at 70, 70–71.

3. *Id.* at 70–73.

4. Elizabeth Cady Stanton, Address to the Legislature of New-York 3 (Albany, Weed, Parsons & Co. 1854); *see also* Letter from Elizabeth Cady Stanton to the Convention (Apr. 7, 1850), *in* Proceedings of the Ohio Women's Convention 15, 16 (Cleveland, Smead & Cowles' Press 1850).

5. *Tea and Taxes*, Chi. Daily Trib., Dec. 17, 1873, at 3 (quoting resolution of women's "anti-tax league").

6. *Id.*

7. *See The Tea Party*, N.Y. Times, Dec. 16, 1873, at 5.

8. *See* Benjamin L. Carp, Defiance of the Patriots: The Boston Tea Party & the Making of America 89–90, 98–100 (2010).

9. *Tea Party Teachings*, N.Y. Herald, Dec. 17, 1873, at 10 (quoting Clemence S. Lozier) (internal quotation marks omitted); *see also The New-York Woman's Suffrage Society*, N.Y. Times, Dec. 17, 1873, at 5.

10. H.R. Misc. Doc. No. 44-45, at 1 (1876).

11. Mary Olney Brown, *Centennial Protest of the Women of Washington Territory*, New Nw. (Portland), July 14, 1876, at 2; *see also* H.A. Loughary, *The Fourth at M'Minnville*, New Nw. (Portland), July 14, 1876, at 2.

12. *See* Joslyn, *An Incident of the Centennial Fourth*, Evening Post (New York), July 6, 1876, at 3; L.D.B., *Woman Suffrage in Philadelphia*, 7 Woman's J. 258, 258 (1876).

13. *See* James D. McCabe, The Illustrated History of the Centennial Exhibition 727–31 (Philadelphia, Nat'l Publ'g Co. 1876).

14. *See* Joslyn, *supra* note 12, at 3; *The Woman's Suffrage Movement*, Phila. Evening Bull., July 5, 1876, at 8.

15. Letter from Susan B. Anthony to Isabella Beecher Hooker (Jan. 20, 1875), *in* 3 The Selected Papers of Elizabeth Cady Stanton and Susan B. Anthony 144, 145 (Ann D. Gordon ed., 2003) (emphasis omitted).

16. *See* 3 History of Woman Suffrage 28–30 (Elizabeth Cady Stanton et al. eds., Rochester, Susan B. Anthony 1886); Joslyn, *supra* note 12, at 3; L.D.B., *supra* note 12, at 258; *The Woman's Suffrage Movement*, *supra* note 14, at 8.

17. *Citizen Suffrage*, Phila. Inquirer, July 20, 1876, at 2; *see also* History of Woman Suffrage, *supra* note 16, at 31; Joslyn, *supra* note 12, at 3; L.D.B., *supra* note 12, at 258; *The Woman's Suffrage Movement*, *supra* note 14, at 8.

18. Nat'l Woman Suffrage Ass'n, Declaration of Rights of the Women of the United States 1 (1876).

19. The Declaration of Independence para. 2 (U.S. 1776).

20. Nat'l Woman Suffrage Ass'n, *supra* note 18, at 4.

21. *The New Declaration of Independence*, Evening Post (New York), July 6, 1876, at 2.

22. *The Woman's Suffrage Movement*, *supra* note 14, at 8.

23. Joslyn, *supra* note 12, at 3.

24. L.D.B., *supra* note 12, at 258; *see also* Joslyn, *supra* note 12, at 3.

25. Susan B. Anthony, Letter to the Editor (Aug. 24, 1876), Ballot Box (Toledo), Oct. 1876, at 1; *see also* Elizabeth Cady Stanton, Letter to the Editor, Ballot Box (Toledo), Oct. 1876, at 1.

26. Lillie Devereux Blake, Letter to the Editor (Sept. 20, 1887), 18 Woman's J. 308, 308–09 (1887).

27. *See id.* at 309.

28. *See* Joslyn, *supra* note 12, at 3; L.D.B., *supra* note 12, at 258; *The Woman's Suffrage Movement*, *supra* note 14, at 8.

29. *See* Blake, *supra* note 26, at 309.

30. U.S. Const. pmbl.

31. *A Centennial Protest*, 18 Woman's J. 308, 308 (1887).

32. Lillie Devereux Blake, Letter to the Editor (Oct. 13, 1886), 17 Woman's J. 333, 333 (1886).

33. *They Enter a Protest*, N.Y. Times, Oct. 29, 1886, at 8.

34. *See id.*; Lillie Devereux Blake, Letter to the Editor (Nov. 1, 1886), 17 Woman's J. 357, 357 (1886).

35. *See Editorial Notes*, 17 Woman's J. 337, 337 (1886).

36. Lillie Devereux Blake, Letter to the Editor (Oct. 19, 1886), 17 Woman's J. 341, 341 (1886).

37. *They Enter a Protest*, *supra* note 33 at 8 (quoting Lillie Devereux Blake) (internal quotation marks omitted).

38. *See* Catharine A.F. Stebbins, *New Battle Hymn of the Republic*, *in* Woman Suffrage Campaign Song Book 13 (Ada M. Bittenbender arranger, Lincoln, Trib. Printing Co. 1882).

39. *See* Eugénie M. Rayé-Smith, *"Votes for Women," Sure to Win*, *in* Equal Suffrage Song Sheaf 7 (2d ed 1912); Louise V. Boyd, *Yankee Doodle Revised*, *in* Woman Suffrage Campaign Song Book, *supra* note 38, at 12; L. May Wheeler, *Yankee Doodle*, *in* Booklet of

SONG: A COLLECTION OF SUFFRAGE AND TEMPERANCE MELODIES 43 (L. May Wheeler comp., Minneapolis, Co-op. Printing Co. 1884).

40. *See Fore-Mother's Hymn*, 1 NEW ERA 307 (1885); Elizabeth Boynton Harbert, *The New America*, *in* BOOKLET OF SONG, *supra* note 39, at 14; L. May Wheeler, *My Native Country*, *in* BOOKLET OF SONG, *supra* note 39, at 16.

41. For the first publication, see CELEBRATION OF AMERICAN INDEPENDENCE, BY THE BOSTON SABBATH SCHOOL UNION (1831). On Smith's authorship, see *His Country Honors Him*, BOS. HERALD, Apr. 4, 1895, at 1.

42. *See* Harbert, *supra* note 40, at 14.

43. *See, e.g.*, HARRIET MAY MILLS & ISABEL HOWLAND, MANUAL FOR POLITICAL EQUAL- ITY CLUBS 16 (Philadelphia, Nat'l Am. Woman Suffrage Ass'n 1896); NAT'L WOMAN SUFFRAGE ASS'N, REPORT OF THE INTERNATIONAL COUNCIL OF WOMEN 23, 109 (D.C., Rufus H. Darby 1888); *Equal Suffrage Convention*, EVENING TEL. (Dixon), Apr. 13, 1897, at 4; *E.S.A. Public Meeting*, LINCOLN BEACON, Jan. 25, 1894, at 1; *Woman Suffragists*, HARTFORD COURANT, Oct. 31, 1894, at 9.

44. Harbert, *supra* note 40, at 14–15.

45. Lavinia Dock, *A Sub-Caste*, 11 EQUAL RTS. 125, 126 (1924).

46. *The Boston Tea Party*, 17 EQUAL RTS. 34, 34 (1931).

47. *Mother of U.S. Equal-Rights Measure Nearly Penniless in Nursing Home at 90*, N.Y. TIMES, Nov. 4, 1975, at 21 (quoting Alice Paul) (internal quotation marks omitted).

48. *See* BETTY FRIEDAN, IT CHANGED MY LIFE: WRITINGS ON THE WOMEN'S MOVEMENT 75–86 (1976).

49. Viola Osgood, *NOW Stages Hub March on Eve of Tea Party*, BOS. SUNDAY GLOBE, Dec. 16, 1973, at 30 (internal quotation marks omitted).

50. *See* John Kifner, *2 Counterrallies in Philadelphia*, N.Y. TIMES, July 5, 1976, at 18; Donald Sanders, *Washington Erupts; A Million Join Party*, FRESNO BEE, July 5, 1976, at A1.

51. Grace Lichtenstein, *McSorley's Admits Women Under a New City Law*, N.Y. TIMES, Aug. 11, 1970, at 1 (internal quotation marks omitted).

52. *See* 116 CONG. REC. 28,036–37 (1970).

53. *Day of Protest, Power, Promise for 'Lib' in N.Y.*, DES MOINES REG., Aug. 11, 1970, at 5 (internal quotation marks omitted); *see also* Lichtenstein, *supra* note 51, at 1.

54. Lichtenstein, *supra* note 51, at 1 (quoting Cindy Cisler) (internal quotation marks omitted).

55. *See infra* Chapter 6.

56. *NOW Acts*, NAT'L NOW TIMES, Apr. 1987, at 10.

57. 1 HISTORY OF WOMAN SUFFRAGE, *supra* note 1. The sixth volume appeared in 1922. *See* 6 THE HISTORY OF WOMAN SUFFRAGE (Ida Husted Harper ed., 1922).

58. For more discussion, see LISA TETRAULT, THE MYTH OF SENECA FALLS: MEMORY AND THE WOMEN'S SUFFRAGE MOVEMENT, 1848–1898, at 120–44 (2014).

59. 1 HISTORY OF WOMAN SUFFRAGE, *supra* note 1, at 7.

60. I.H.H., *Preface* to 4 THE HISTORY OF WOMAN SUFFRAGE, at v, viii (Susan B. Anthony & Ida Husted Harper eds., 1902).

61. Hallie Q. Brown, *Introduction* to HOMESPUN HEROINES AND OTHER WOMEN OF DISTINC- TION, at vii, vii (Hallie Q. Brown ed., 1926).

62. *See President National Federation of Colored Women's Clubs to Visit Tampa*, TAMPA DAILY TIMES, Jan. 20, 1923, at 3B; Lester A. Walton, *Women's National Assoc'n Holds Meeting at Tuskegee*, N.Y. AGE, July 24, 1920, at 1.

63. Brown, *supra* note 61, at vii.

64. *See* CARRIE CHAPMAN CATT & NETTIE ROGERS SHULER, WOMAN SUFFRAGE AND POLITICS: THE INNER STORY OF THE SUFFRAGE MOVEMENT, at viii–ix (1923).

65. *Id.* at ix.

66. *See* INEZ HAYNES IRWIN, THE STORY OF THE WOMAN'S PARTY (1921); DORIS STEVENS, JAILED FOR FREEDOM (1920).

67. *See "Jailed for Freedom" Studied in Colleges*, 15 EQUAL RTS. 68, 68 (1929).

68. For media coverage of the conference, see Emma Bugbee, *Women Open Campaign for Equal Rights*, N.Y. TRIB., July 22, 1923 (pt. I), at 1; Editorial, 117 NATION 128 (1923); *Women Adopt Form for Equal Rights*, N.Y. TIMES, July 22, 1923 (§ 1), at 1; *Women Open Fight for Equal Rights*, N.Y. TIMES, July 21, 1923, at 8.

69. *Seneca Falls: Then—and Now*, 1 EQUAL RTS. 110, 110 (1923).

70. Bugbee, *supra* note 68, at 1 (quoting National Woman's Party resolution) (internal quotation marks omitted).

71. *Women Adopt Form for Equal Rights*, *supra* note 68, at 1 (quoting Alice Paul) (internal quotation marks omitted).

72. *See* HISTORY OF WOMAN SUFFRAGE, *supra* note 1, at 67.

73. *Women Adopt Form for Equal Rights*, *supra* note 68, at 1 (quoting Alice Paul) (internal quotation marks omitted).

74. Emma Bugbee, *Women Open Campaign for Equal Rights*, 1 EQUAL RTS. 189, 189 (1923) (quoting Alice Paul) (internal quotation marks omitted).

75. Martha Weinman Lear, *The Second Feminist Wave*, N.Y. TIMES, Mar. 10, 1968 (§ 6), at 24.

76. *See* FRIEDAN, *supra* note 48, at 75–86, 141–42; Linda Charlton, *Women March Down Fifth in Equality Drive*, N.Y. TIMES, Aug. 27, 1970, at 1; *Women March on Fifth Avenue*, ST. LOUIS POST-DISPATCH, Aug. 27, 1970, at 4A.

77. *Jewish Roots: An Interview with Betty Friedan*, TIKKUN, Jan./Feb. 1988, at 25, 25 (statement of Betty Friedan). For more discussion of Friedan's college years, see BETTY FRIEDAN, LIFE SO FAR 34–52, 97, 114–15 (2000).

78. On the strike's demands, see Haynes Johnson, *'Equal Rights Now,' Exhort Women Protesters*, WASH. POST, Aug. 27, 1970, at A1; *Liberation*, NEW YORKER, Sept. 5, 1970, at 26, 26; *The Women Who Know Their Place*, NEWSWEEK, Sept. 7, 1970, at 16, 16, 18.

79. *See* Judy Klemesrud, *It Was a Great Day for Women on the March*, N.Y. TIMES, Aug. 30, 1970 (§ 4), at 4; *see also Women March on Fifth Avenue*, *supra* note 76, at 4A; *Women on the March*, TIME, Sept. 7, 1970, at 12.

80. *Liberation*, *supra* note 78, at 26, 28; *see also* Klemesrud, *supra* note 79, at 4.

81. Claudia Levy & Alex Ward, *Women Rally to Publicize Grievances*, WASH. POST, Aug. 27, 1970, at A1.

82. *See* FRIEDAN, *supra* note 48, at 151; Charlton, *supra* note 76, at 1; *The Women Who Know Their Place*, *supra* note 78, at 16–17; *Women March on Fifth Avenue*, *supra* note 76, at 4A.

83. *See* NAT'L COMM'N ON THE OBSERVANCE OF INT'L WOMEN'S YEAR, THE SPIRIT OF HOUSTON: THE FIRST NATIONAL WOMEN'S CONFERENCE 9–10 (1978) [hereinafter SPIRIT OF HOUSTON]. For the congressional authorization, see Act of Dec. 23, 1975, Pub. L. No. 94-167, 89 Stat. 1003.

84. SPIRIT OF HOUSTON, *supra* note 83, at 11.

85. *See id.* at 128, 193.

86. *See id.* at 193; Carol Ritter, *Women Light Torch for Run to Equality*, DEMOCRAT & CHRON. (Rochester), Sept. 29, 1977, at 8B; Carol Ritter, *Women's Torch on Road to Houston*, DEMOCRAT & CHRON. (Rochester), Sept. 30, 1977, at 4B.

87. *See* Steve McGonigle, *Women Prepare to Battle Barriers to Equal Rights*, ABILENE REP.-NEWS, Nov. 19, 1977, at 10A.

88. *See* Leigh Cook, *6,000 Women Cheer Their National Leaders*, ASBURY PARK PRESS, Nov. 20, 1977, at A2. For the length of the journey, see SPIRIT OF HOUSTON, *supra* note 83, at 128.

89. Cook, *supra* note 88, at A2 (quoting Bella Abzug) (internal quotation marks omitted).

90. On suffragists wearing white, see *Congressional Union for Woman Suffrage*, 1 SUFFRAGIST 27, 27 (1913); *Suffrage Army out on Parade*, N.Y. TIMES, May 5, 1912, at 1.

91. *See, e.g., Abortion-Rights Supporters Rally*, PHILA. INQUIRER, Mar. 10, 1986, at 10A; Karen De Witt, *100,000 Join March for Extension of Rights Amendment Deadline*, N.Y. TIMES, July 10, 1978, at A1; Karen De Witt, *Huge Crowd Backs Right to Abortion in Capital March*, N.Y. TIMES, Apr. 6, 1992, at A1; *ERA Supporters Rally in 4 States*, ATLANTA CONST., June 7, 1982, at 2A; Paul Houston & Brian Couturier, *Massive Demonstration Backs Legal Abortions*, L.A. TIMES, Apr. 10, 1989 (pt. I), at 1; Mike Williams, *Fla. Senate Halts Limits on Abortion*, ATLANTA CONST., Oct. 11, 1989, at A1; *Women: A New ERA*, NEWSWEEK, Oct. 16, 1978, at 38, 38.

92. *See* 167 CONG. REC. H1422 (daily ed. Mar. 17, 2021) (statement of Speaker Nancy Pelosi); Kevin Freking, *Domestic Violence Bill Now Heads to Senate*, HOUS. CHRON., Mar. 18, 2021, at A5; Vanessa Friedman, *A Sea of White, Lit by History*, N.Y. TIMES, Feb. 7, 2019, at D5; Vanessa Friedman, *The Inescapable Messaging of Clothing*, N.Y. TIMES, Feb. 6, 2020, at D2; Connie Schultz, *Making a Stand for Women Everywhere*, ROCHESTER DEMOCRAT & CHRON., Mar. 4, 2017, at 16A.

93. *See* Jane Perlez, *'Gerry, Gerry,' the Convention Chants*, N.Y. TIMES, July 20, 1984, at A1.

94. *See* Amy S. Rosenberg et al., *A Mother-and-Daughter Moment*, PHILA. INQUIRER, July 29, 2016, at E4.

95. *See* Victoria McGrane, *A Women's Whites Movement, Cast for Clinton*, BOS. GLOBE, Nov. 3, 2016, at A1.

96. *See* Vanessa Friedman, *Message About the Past and the Future of Politics in a Fashion Statement*, N.Y. TIMES, Nov. 9, 2020, at P14.

97. *See, e.g.,* Michele Vowell, *'Votes for Women,'* KY. NEW ERA, Aug. 19, 2000, at A1; *Women's Groups Host Events Featuring ERA Co-President Neuwirth*, POST-CRESCENT (Appleton), Feb. 15, 2020, at 6A.

98. *See* Beth Musgrave, *Lexington Breaks Bronze Ceiling with Statue of Suffragists*, LEXINGTON HERALD-LEADER, Aug. 21, 2020, at 1A.

99. *See* Fritz Hahn, *Museum Celebrates Journey to Women's Suffrage*, WASH. POST, Aug. 14, 2020 (Weekend), at 6.

100. *See* IRWIN, *supra* note 66, at 261–91; STEVENS, *supra* note 66, at 192–209. For more on the museum, see *infra* Chapter 7.

101. *See* IRWIN, *supra* note 66, at 16–17; STEVENS, *supra* note 66, at 175–77, 356.

102. *See* Brandy Centolanza, *Celebrating 100 Years of 19th Amendment*, VA. GAZETTE, Feb. 19, 2020, at 8A.

103. *See* MARY CHURCH TERRELL, A COLORED WOMAN IN A WHITE WORLD 151, 194 (1940).

104. *See id.* at 316–17.

105. *See* Alisha Haridasani Gupta, *For 3 Suffragists, an Honor Long Past Due*, N.Y. TIMES, Aug. 7, 2020, at C5; Morgan Hines, *Central Park Marker Honors Suffragists*, ROCHESTER DEMOCRAT & CHRON., Aug. 27, 2020, at 4A.

106. Ulysses S. Grant, Seventh Annual Message (Dec. 7, 1875), *in* 7 A COMPILATION OF THE MESSAGES AND PAPERS OF THE PRESIDENTS, 1789–1897, at 332, 332 (James D. Richardson ed., D.C., Gov't Printing Off. 1898).

107. Thomas W. Ferry, Speech of Hon. Thos. W. Ferry, Vice President of the United States (July 4, 1876), *in* OUR NATIONAL CENTENNIAL JUBILEE 17, 17–18 (Frederick Saunders ed., New York, E.B. Treat 1877).

108. Grant, *supra* note 106, at 333.

109. Ferry, *supra* note 107, at 18.

110. Grover Cleveland, Remarks Accepting the Bartholdi Statue of "Liberty Enlightening the World," PUB. PAPERS 176, 176–177 (Oct. 28, 1886).

111. Grover Cleveland, Remarks at the Centennial Celebration of the Adoption of the Constitution, Philadelphia, PUB. PAPERS 263, 264 (Sept. 17, 1887).

112. *See infra* Chapter 3.

113. Cleveland, *supra* note 111, at 264 (internal quotation marks omitted).

114. Grover Cleveland, *Would Woman Suffrage Be Unwise?*, LADIES' HOME J., Oct. 1905, at 7, 7.

115. Grover Cleveland, *Woman's Mission and Woman's Clubs*, LADIES' HOME J., May 1905, at 3, 3 (internal quotation marks omitted).

116. *Vigorous Reply to Grover Cleveland*, EVENING TIMES (Rochester), Apr. 25, 1905, at 6 (quoting Susan B. Anthony) (internal quotation marks omitted).

117. *What Shall We Do with Our Ex-Presidents?—Susan B. Anthony Knows.*, MINNEAPOLIS J., Apr. 26, 1905, at 1 (capitalization omitted). For the original drawing, see Library of Congress, Prints and Photographs Division (item 2016678242; copy on file with author).

118. Gerald R. Ford, Proclamation No. 4411, 3 C.F.R. 524, 524 (1971–1975).

119. Gerald R. Ford, Remarks in Philadelphia, Pennsylvania, 2 PUB. PAPERS 1966, 1967 (July 4, 1976).

120. *Id.* at 1969.

121. Ronald Reagan, Remarks at the "We the People" Bicentennial Celebration in Philadelphia, Pennsylvania, 2 PUB. PAPERS 1040, 1042 (Sept. 17, 1987); *see also* Ronald Reagan, Remarks at the Bicentennial Celebration of the United States Constitution, 2 PUB. PAPERS 1040, 1040 (Sept. 16, 1987).

122. Warren E. Burger, *Tell the Story of Freedom*, A.B.A. J., May 1, 1986, at 54, 54; *see also* Warren E. Burger, *Address*, 1991 DET. C.L. REV. 1141, 1143; Warren E. Burger, *Foreword* to CATHERINE DRINKER BOWEN, MIRACLE AT PHILADELPHIA: THE STORY OF THE CONSTITUTIONAL CONVENTION MAY TO SEPTEMBER 1787, at ix, ix–x (1986).

123. *See* WE THE PEOPLE: THE COMMISSION ON THE BICENTENNIAL OF THE UNITED STATES CONSTITUTION, 1985–1992: FINAL REPORT 214, 256 (1992).

124. *See* 5 U.S.C. § 6103.

125. ARCHITECT OF THE CAPITOL, THOSE WHO HAVE LAIN IN STATE OR IN HONOR IN THE UNITED STATES CAPITOL 1 (2024).

126. *See id.* at 1–5.

127. *See* Lynette Long, *Stamp out Gender Bias in Postal Service Commemoratives*, Sun (Baltimore), Jan. 13, 2006, at 11A. For a list of women featured on postage stamps, see Historian, U.S. Postal Serv., Women Subjects on United States Postage Stamps (2024).

128. Neil MacFarquhar, *Stars and Stripes, Wrapped in the Same Old Blue*, N.Y. Times, Apr. 29, 2007 (§ 4), at 5 (quoting Ann Barrett) (internal quotation marks omitted).

129. *See* Lauren Prestileo, *A Ticket to the World, Full of Men's Words*, N.Y. Times, Mar. 1, 2020 (Travel), at 3.

130. *See* Postal Facilities Dedicated by Congress in Honor of Individuals 1 (2022).

131. *See* 165 Cong. Rec. H5955 (daily ed. July 17, 2019) (statement of Rep. Denny Heck).

132. *See* E-mail from Christi Chidester Votisek, Commc'ns Specialist, U.S. Gen. Servs. Admin., to author (July 28, 2021) (copy on file with author).

133. *See* Maya Rhodan, *Will Women Ever Break the Bronze Ceiling?*, Time, Sept. 4, 2017, at 28, 28.

134. Carol D. Shull, *Searching for Women in the National Register of Historic Places*, *in* Restoring Women's History Through Historic Preservation 303, 303–05, 423 n.11 (Gail Lee Dubrow & Jennifer B. Goodman eds., 2003).

135. Janet Scudder, Modeling My Life 153–56 (1925) (internal quotation marks omitted).

136. *See* Cari Shane, *5,193 Public Sculptures. 4,799 Are Men. 394 Are Women. Why?*, Wash. Post, Apr. 17, 2011, at E1.

137. *See* Monument Lab, National Monument Audit 10, 12 (2021).

138. *See id.* at 12, 17, 19.

139. Barack Obama, Inaugural Address, 1 Pub. Papers 45, 47 (Jan. 21, 2013).

140. Joseph R. Biden, Jr., Inaugural Address, 2021 Daily Comp. Pres. Doc. 1, 2 (Jan. 20, 2021).

141. Kamala Harris, A Vision of Our Nation as a Beloved Community (Aug. 19, 2020), *in* 86 Vital Speeches of the Day 265, 265 (2020).

142. *See* Elizabeth L. Maurer et al., Nat'l Women's Hist. Museum, Where Are the Women? A Report on the Status of Women in the United States Social Studies Standards 1–4, app. 1 at 234–41 (2017).

143. For recent examples from the vast literature focused on race and commemoration conflicts, see Karen L. Cox, No Common Ground: Confederate Monuments and the Ongoing Fight for Racial Justice (2021); Connor Towne O'Neill, Down Along with that Devil's Bones: A Reckoning with Monuments, Memory, and the Legacy of White Supremacy (2020).

144. On the commission, see Ida Husted Harper, *The History of the Suffrage Statues*, 8 Suffragist 315, 316 (1920); Hannah Mitchell, *A Suffrage Group for the Capitol*, N.Y. Trib., Jan. 30, 1921 (pt. VII), at 6.

145. *Mrs. Adelaide Johnson Is the Sculptor of Suffrage*, Wash. Post, Apr. 4, 1909 (Miscellany), at 9.

146. *See* Emma Bugbee, *Suffrage Busts Dispute Ended After 30 Years*, N.Y. Trib., Feb. 16, 1921, at 9; *Sculptress Will Reach Here Today*, Wash. Times, Jan. 31, 1921, at 13.

147. On Johnson's work in Italy, see Harper, *supra* note 144, at 316; Mitchell, *supra* note 144, at 6; *Woman Sculptor Brings Suffrage Memorial Home*, N.Y. Herald, Jan. 21, 1921, at 7.

148. Several newspapers reprinted the complete inscription, with minor variations. *See Adelaide Johnson's Inscription Cut on the Suffrage Memorial*, Evening World (New York), Jan. 22, 1921, at 3; *Engrave Tribute to Pioneers on Suffrage Statue*, Wash. Herald, Sept.

25, 1921, at 1; *Monument to Women Unveiled at Capitol*, OAKLAND TRIB., Feb. 20, 1921, at W-5; *Why Whitewashed Inscription Was Turned to the Wall*, WOMAN PATRIOT, Feb. 26, 1921, at 8.

149. *See* Mitchell, *supra* note 144, at 6.

150. *See* Alice Paul, *An Appeal from Alice Paul*, 8 SUFFRAGIST 303, 303 (1920); Mitchell, *supra* note 144, at 6.

151. *See Memorial for Suffrage Arrives at the Capitol*, EVENING STAR (D.C.), Feb. 5, 1921 (pt. 1), at 2; *View Suffrage Memorial Art*, WASH. HERALD, Feb. 7, 1921, at 2.

152. *See* Mitchell, *supra* note 144, at 6.

153. THE UNITED STATES CAPITOL AND CONGRESS, S. DOC. NO. 106-24, at 2 (2001).

154. *See Suffrage Memorial Halted at Capital*, N.Y. TIMES, Feb. 9, 1921, at 28; *Suffrage Memorial May Be Declined*, CHRISTIAN SCI. MONITOR (Boston), Feb. 9, 1921, at 2; *Suffrage Statue Is Still Without a Resting Place*, N.Y. TRIB., Feb. 10, 1921, at 4; *Three Famous Suffragists Sit on the Capitol Steps All Night*, SUN (Baltimore), Feb. 10, 1921, at 1; *Women's Memorial Waits*, N.Y. TIMES, Feb. 10, 1921, at 4.

155. *See* RECOLLECTIONS OF THOMAS R. MARSHALL VICE-PRESIDENT AND HOOSIER PHILOSO-PHER: A HOOSIER SALAD 234–37 (1925).

156. *See The Capitol Surrendered to Militants*, WOMAN PATRIOT, Feb. 26, 1921, at 7.

157. *See Statues Win Capital Niche*, WASH. TIMES, Feb. 12, 1921, at 8. For Christine's first name, see *Gillett Chosen for Speakership of Next House*, N.Y. TIMES, Feb. 28, 1919, at 1.

158. *See* Marble Busts of Lucretia Mott, Elizabeth Cady Stanton and Susan B. Anthony: Memorandum of Action of Joint Committee on the Library Accepting the Same at a Meeting Held Thursday Feb. 10, 1921, at 1 (copy on file with author; archives of the Architect of the Capitol) [hereinafter Memorandum of Action].

159. *See Congress Gets Marble Busts of Feminists*, WASH. HERALD, Feb. 16, 1921, at 1; *Honor Pioneer Suffragists at Nation's Capitol*, CHI. DAILY TRIB., Feb. 16, 1921, at 20; *Suffrage Statue Given to Nation*, N.Y. TIMES, Feb. 16, 1921, at 9.

160. Memorandum of Action, *supra* note 158, at 1.

161. CHARLES E. FAIRMAN, ART AND ARTISTS OF THE CAPITOL OF THE UNITED STATES OF AMERICA 386 (1927); *see also Put Statue in Basement*, EVENING STAR (D.C.), Feb. 17, 1921, at 2.

162. *See* Marjorie Dorman, *Girl Reporter Describes White House Scenes on Wilson's Last Day There*, BROOKLYN DAILY EAGLE, Mar. 4, 1921, at 2.

163. *See id.; Ask Choice Site for Group*, WASH. HERALD, Apr. 3, 1921 (§ 6), at 4.

164. *See Erases Inscription on 'Suffrage Group'*, N.Y. TIMES, Oct. 15, 1921, at 6; *Pompous Title Erased from Suffrage Statue*, SUN (Baltimore), Oct. 15, 1921, at 1; *Whitewash Covers Legend on Suffrage Mother Statue*, WASH. HERALD, Oct. 15, 1921 (§ 2), at 13.

165. Mary Pakenham, *About Women in Washington*, CHI. TRIB., May 15, 1965 (§ 1), at 5.

166. Marble Statue of Three Suffragists by Adelaide Johnson in the Capitol Crypt, Washington, D.C. (Feb. 12, 1965) (copy on file with author; Library of Congress, Prints and Photographs Division, item 97510834).

167. *See Equal Rights Meeting Held in Capitol Crypt*, N.Y. TIMES, Nov. 19, 1923, at 3; Genevieve Reynolds, *Woman's Party Leaders Here for 3-Day National Conclave*, WASH. POST, Apr. 1, 1949, at 4C; *Seventy-Fifth Anniversary Year Closes*, 1 EQUAL RTS. 327, 327 (1923); *Suffragettes Meet*, N.Y. TIMES, Aug. 27, 1953, at 27; *Women Plan Fight for Equal Rights*, EVENING STAR (D.C.), Jan. 4, 1928, at 42.

168. Solveig Eggersz, *Susan, George and Abe, Unite*, WASH. DAILY NEWS, Feb. 16, 1971, at 31 (internal quotation marks omitted).

169. *See Anniversary Roses*, KOKOMO TRIB., Aug. 28, 1973, at 7. For more on the rally, see *Area Woman Attends Rally*, DECATUR HERALD, Aug. 30, 1973, at 11; *Suffrage Day Celebrants Hear Talks*, LAS VEGAS DAILY OPTIC, Aug. 29, 1973, at 3.

170. *See* Raj Kamal Jha, *Cry of Liberation for Suffragists*, WASH. POST, Aug. 27, 1990, at B1.

171. *See Feminists Map New ERA Strategy*, IND. GAZETTE, Dec. 11, 1993, at 12.

172. *See Women Mark 75 Years of Voting Rights*, N.Y. TIMES, Aug. 27, 1995, at 14.

173. *See* Jha, *supra* note 170, at B1; *Women Mark 75 Years of Voting Rights, supra* note 172, at 14.

174. *See* James Brooke, *3 Suffragists (in Marble) to Move up in the Capitol*, N.Y. TIMES, Sept. 27, 1996, at A18.

175. *See, e.g.*, 141 CONG. REC. 27,251 (1995) (statement of Rep. Patricia Schroeder); *Ask Choice Site for Group, supra* note 163, at 4; Jha, *supra* note 170, at B1; Cindy Loose, *They Got the Vote, but Not the Rotunda*, WASH. POST, Aug. 19, 1995, at A1; *Women Mark 75 Years of Voting Rights, supra* note 172, at 14; Gregg Zoroya, *Ladies Who Languish in a Basement*, L.A. TIMES, May 27, 1996, at E1.

176. *See* S. Con. Res. 21, 104th Cong. (1995) (passed the Senate); 141 CONG. REC. 26,959–61 (1995); H.R.J. Res. 528, 72d Cong. (1932); H.R. Res. 115, 70th Cong. (1928); H.R. Con. Res. 43, 67th Cong. (1922).

177. *See* H.R. 192, 83d Cong. (1953); H.R. 8036, 81st Cong. (1950); S. 3328, 81st Cong. (1950).

178. Rodney Dutcher, *"Three Old Ladies in Bathtub"—A Puzzling Problem for Congress*, READING TIMES, Mar. 15, 1928, at 16.

179. Barbara Yost, *Newt: 'Keep the Women Hidden,'* TENNESSEAN, Aug. 7, 1995, at 11A (quoting Newt Gingrich) (internal quotation marks omitted).

180. On the sculpture's return to the Rotunda, see 143 CONG. REC. 13,020 (1997) (statement of Sen. Olympia Snowe at rededication ceremony).

181. H.R. Con. Res. 216, 104th Cong. § 1 (1996) (enacted).

182. 142 CONG. REC. 25,245 (1996) (statement of Rep. Carolyn Maloney).

183. *See* Kevin Eckstrom, *Women's Statue Back Among U.S. Heroes*, ATLANTA CONST., June 27, 1997, at A12 (quoting Rep. Louise Slaughter); Michael Kilian, *Out of Capitol Cellar, Statue of Feminists Returns to Glory*, CHI. TRIB., June 27, 1997 (§ 1), at 3 (quoting Rep. Constance Morella).

184. *See* Photographs of Portrait Monument (copy on file with author).

185. *See* CARRIE CHAPMAN CATT, WOMAN SUFFRAGE BY FEDERAL CONSTITUTIONAL AMENDMENT 74–77 (1917); *National Suffrage and the Race Problem*, SUFFRAGIST, Nov. 14, 1914, at 3. For Paul's statement that she "probably wrote" this *Suffragist* editorial, see Amelia R. Fry, Conversations with Alice Paul: Woman Suffrage and the Equal Rights Amendment 135 (1976) (copy on file with author; University of California, Berkeley, Bancroft Library, Suffragists Oral History Project) (statement of Alice Paul).

186. *See* CATT, *supra* note 185, at 76–79; *National Suffrage and the Race Problem, supra* note 185, at 3. For the same argument from Cordelia Powell Odenheimer, past President-General of the United Daughters of the Confederacy, see *Southern Suffragists Roused over Slacker Vote*, 2 WOMAN CITIZEN 132, 132, 137 (1918).

187. *See City Governments Place for Women*, EVENING STAR (D.C.), Feb. 16, 1921, at 2; Alice Paul, *Editorial*, 9 SUFFRAGIST 339, 339 (1921).

188. Freda Kirchwey, *Alice Paul Pulls the Strings*, 112 NATION 332, 333 (1921) (quoting the delegation's memorial); *see also* Ella Rush Murray, *The Woman's Party and the Violation of the 19th Amendment*, 21 CRISIS 259, 260 (1921).

189. *See* Kirchwey, *supra* note 188, at 333; Murray, *supra* note 188, at 260.

190. For a letter urging Talbert's invitation, see Letter from Mary W. Ovington to Alice Paul, Chairman, Nat'l Woman's Party (Jan. 4, 1921) (copy on file with author; ProQuest History Vault, NAACP Papers, folder 001517-002-0484). For more on Talbert, see *Mary B. Talbert*, APPEAL (St. Paul & Minneapolis), June 17, 1922, at 2.

191. *See* Letter from Florence Kelley, Gen. Sec'y, Nat'l Consumers' League, to Mary W. Ovington, NAACP 1 (Dec. 22, 1920) (copy on file with author; ProQuest History Vault, NAACP Papers, folder 001517-002-0484) [hereinafter Letter from Kelley].

192. *See* EQUAL JUST. INITIATIVE, LYNCHING IN AMERICA: CONFRONTING THE LEGACY OF RACIAL TERROR 3–4 (3d ed. 2017).

193. Letter from Kelley, *supra* note 191, at 1–2; *see also* Letter from Emma Wold, Headquarters Sec'y, Nat'l Woman's Party, to Harriet Stanton Blatch (Dec. 29, 1920) (copy on file with author; ProQuest History Vault, NAACP Papers, folder 001517-002-0484).

194. S. 4119, 67th Cong. (as passed by Senate, Feb. 28, 1923). For the Senate vote, see 64 CONG. REC. 4839 (1923).

195. Gertrude Richardson Brigham, *Considered Zolnay Alone for Statue*, WASH. POST, June 30, 1923, at 6 (quoting Jane W. Blackburn Moran) (internal quotation marks omitted).

196. *See* VIRGINIUS DABNEY, THE LAST REVIEW: THE CONFEDERATE REUNION, RICHMOND, 1932, at 26 (1984).

197. 64 CONG. REC. 1509 (1923) (statement of Rep. Charles Stedman).

198. *See, e.g.*, *Senate Okeyed Mammy Statue over Protests*, AFRO-AM. (Baltimore), Mar. 9, 1923, at 1; *The "Mammies" Monument*, AFRO-AM. (Baltimore), Feb. 9, 1923 (§ 2), at 9; *Want No Black Mammy Monument*, CAL. EAGLE, Feb. 17, 1923, at 1.

199. *See Mammy Statue Topples After Defender Attack*, CHI. DEF., Apr. 26, 1924 (pt. 1), at 3.

200. *See, e.g.*, A.L. Jackson, *The Black Mammy Statue*, CHI. DEF., Apr. 21, 1923, at 12; *Right Kind of Memorial*, N.Y. AGE, Feb. 3, 1923, at 4; *Voice Protest Against "Mammy" Statue*, WASH. TRIB., Feb. 10, 1923, at 1.

201. Mary Church Terrell, Letter to the Editor, EVENING STAR (D.C.), Feb. 10, 1923, at 6. For reprintings, see *For and Against the "Black Mammy's" Monument*, LITERARY DIG., Apr. 28, 1923, at 48, 50; Mary Church Terrell, Letter to the Editor (Feb. 12, 1923), BOS. HERALD, Feb. 15, 1923, at 16; *The Black Mammy Monument*, BROAD AX (Chicago), Mar. 17, 1923, at 2. For additional advocacy, see MARY CHURCH TERRELL, SOME FACTS FOR COLORED WOMEN TO THINK ABOUT 4 (circa Nov. 1924) (copy on file with author; Howard University, Moorland-Spingarn Research Center, Mary Church Terrell Papers, box 102-5, folder 150).

202. *See A Black Group Assails Statue of Suffragists*, N.Y. TIMES, Mar. 9, 1997, at 28; Dorothy Gilliam, *Measuring a Statue by Its Truth*, WASH. POST, Mar. 22, 1997, at C1; Chester A. Higgins Sr., *Black Women Cry! Put Truth in the Suffrage Statue!*, ATLANTA DAILY WORLD, Feb. 20, 1997, at 4; Robin Leary, *Black Groups Want Sojourner Truth on Statue*, PHILA. TRIB., May 2, 1997, at 1A; Kevin Merida, *A Vote Against Suffrage Statue*, WASH. POST, Apr. 14, 1997, at A1; Darlene Superville, *Black Women's Group Wants Truth Added to Suffrage Statue*, NEW PITTSBURGH COURIER, Mar. 29, 1997, at 2.

203. *Tucker Leads War Against Woman Suffrage Statue Without 'Truth,'* New Pittsburgh Courier, Feb. 8, 1997, at 2 (quoting C. DeLores Tucker) (internal quotation marks omitted).

204. *See* S. 3910, 109th Cong. (2006); S. 2600, 108th Cong. (2004); H.R. 601, 108th Cong. (2003); H.R. 5679, 107th Cong. (2002); H.R. Con. Res. 72, 105th Cong. (1997); H.R. Con. Res. 62, 105th Cong. (1997); Suzette Hackney, *Sojourner Truth*, Detroit Free Press, Oct. 15, 2006, at 1B; Brandace Simmons, *Brunch Celebrates Truth Victory*, Roll Call, Sept. 27, 2007, at 49.

205. *See* Act of Dec. 20, 2006, Pub. L. No. 109-427, § 2, 120 Stat. 2912, 2912.

206. *See* Ari B. Bloomekatz, *L.A. Artist's 'Truth' to Be Unveiled*, L.A. Times, Apr. 28, 2009, at A5; Neely Tucker, *Truth's Rightful Place on the Hill*, Wash. Post, Apr. 29, 2009, at C1.

207. For histories of this advocacy, see Adele Logan Alexander, Princess of the Hither Isles: A Black Suffragist's Story from the Jim Crow South 140–46, 170–75, 213–15, 255–57 (2019); Cathleen D. Cahill, Recasting the Vote: How Women of Color Transformed the Suffrage Movement (2020); Paula Giddings, When and Where I Enter: The Impact of Black Women on Race and Sex in America 49–55, 119–31 (1984); Nell Irvin Painter, Sojourner Truth: A Life, a Symbol 113–42, 220–33 (1996); Rosalyn Terborg-Penn, African American Women in the Struggle for the Vote, 1850–1920 (1998); Liette Gidlow, *The Sequel: The Fifteenth Amendment, the Nineteenth Amendment, and Southern Black Women's Struggle to Vote*, 17 J. Gilded Age & Progressive Era 433, 437–38 (2018).

208. *See* Bloomekatz, *supra* note 206, at A5; Tucker, *supra* note 206, at C1.

209. *See* Mattie Kahn, *All the Light They Cannot See*, Elle, June 2017, at 140, 142.

210. H.R. 4722, 105th Cong. § 1 (1998).

211. *Establishing a Commission to Study the Potential Creation of a National Women's History Museum: Hearing Before the H. Comm. on H. Admin.*, 113th Cong. 5 (2013) (statement of Rep. Carolyn Maloney); *see also id.* at 34 (statement of Joan Bradley Wages, President and CEO, National Women's History Museum).

212. 160 Cong. Rec. 4406 (2014) (statement of Rep. Carolyn Maloney); *see also id.* at 4412 (statement of Rep. Marcia Kaptur); *id.* at 7059–60 (statement of Rep. Carolyn Maloney); 166 Cong. Rec. H1032 (daily ed. Feb. 11, 2020) (statement of Rep. Carolyn Maloney).

213. *See* Gregory Korte, *Two Senators Put Hold on Women's Museum*, USA Today, Sept. 29, 2010, at 7A.

214. *See* H.R. 1700, 111th Cong. (as passed by House, Oct. 14, 2009).

215. Korte, *supra* note 213, at 7A (quoting Letter from Tom Coburn and Jim DeMint to Mitch McConnell, Senate Minority Leader (2010)) (internal quotation marks omitted).

216. Gail Collins, *Unhold Us, Senators*, N.Y. Times, Sept. 25, 2010, at A21 (quoting office of Senator Tom Coburn) (internal quotation marks omitted).

217. *See* Korte, *supra* note 213, at 7A.

218. *See infra* Chapter 6.

219. Penny Nance, *National Women's Boondoggle*, Wash. Times, Oct. 15, 2010, at B3.

220. *See* Letter from Penny Nance, CEO & President, Concerned Women for Am. Legis. Action Comm. et al., to Representative (Dec. 3, 2014) (copy on file with author) [hereinafter Letter from Nance et al.].

221. *See supra* text accompanying note 89.

222. *See infra* Chapter 6.

223. *See* Letter from Nance et al., *supra* note 220.

224. Eagle F., 2014 Year-End Report: 113th United States Congress, Second Session 2–3 (2014).

225. *Id.* at 3.

226. 160 Cong. Rec. 7060 (2014) (statement of Rep. Michele Bachmann).

227. *See* Carl Levin and Howard P. "Buck" McKeon National Defense Authorization Act for Fiscal Year 2015, Pub. L. No. 113-291, § 3056, 128 Stat. 3292, 3810–13 (2014).

228. The American Museum of Women's History: Congressional Commission Report to the President of the United States and Congress 18–19 (2016).

229. *See* H.R. 1980, 116th Cong. (as passed by House, Feb. 11, 2020).

230. 166 Cong. Rec. S7416 (daily ed. Dec. 10, 2020) (statement of Sen. Mike Lee).

231. *Id.* at S7414 (statement of Sen. Mike Lee).

232. *See* Consolidated Appropriations Act, 2021, Pub. L. No. 116-260, Div. T, 134 Stat. 1182, 2272–78 (2020).

233. *See* Zachary Small, *The Smithsonian Picks the Sites for Two New Museums*, N.Y. Times, Oct. 29, 2022, at C6.

234. *See* U.S. Dep't of the Interior, Foundation Document: National Mall and Memorial Parks District of Columbia 4, 15–16 (2017).

235. For the legislation that Congress would have to amend to authorize construction on the Mall, see Commemorative Works Clarification and Revision Act of 2003, Pub. L. No. 108-126, Tit. II, 117 Stat. 1348, 1349–53.

236. *See To Please the Ladies*, Kearney Cnty. Advoc., Oct. 30, 1886, at 1; Edward Dauer & Joanne Dauer, American History as Seen Through Currency: A Pictorial History of United States Currency as Seen Throughout Important Historical Events 146–47, 149 (2003); Arthur L. Friedberg & Ira S. Friedberg, A Guide Book of United States Paper Money: Complete Source for History, Grading, and Values 32–34 (5th ed. 2016).

237. *See* Helen C. Rountree, Pocahontas, Powhatan, Opechancanough: Three Indian Lives Changed by Jamestown 156–67 (2005); Camilla Townsend, Pocahontas and the Powhatan Dilemma, at x–xi, 103–28 (2004).

238. *See* Dauer & Dauer, *supra* note 236, at 146; Friedberg & Friedberg, *supra* note 236, at 179–80.

239. Barack Obama, Remarks in Kansas City, Missouri, 2 Pub. Papers 1037, 1037 (July 30, 2014).

240. Dianna M. Náñez, *Do You Vote for Harriet Tubman on the $20 Bill?*, Ariz. Republic, May 16, 2015, at 16A (internal quotation marks omitted). For more on this campaign, see *infra* Chapter 7.

241. *See* S. 925, 114th Cong. (2015); Letter from Jeanne Shaheen et al., U.S. Sens., to Barack Obama, President of the U.S. (June 4, 2015) (copy on file with author).

242. Jackie Calmes, *Treasury Says a Woman's Portrait Will Join Hamilton's on the $10 Bill*, N.Y. Times, June 18, 2015, at A20 (quoting Treasury Department) (internal quotation marks omitted).

243. *See* Jackie Calmes, *A Woman on the $10 Bill? Everyone Has 2 Cents to Contribute*, N.Y. Times, Jan. 27, 2016, at A1; Jackie Calmes, *Broadway Success of 'Hamilton' May Have Saved Hamilton on the $10 Bill*, N.Y. Times, Apr. 16, 2016, at A11; Michael Paulson, *A Must-See for Treasury Chiefs, Too*, N.Y. Times, Aug. 28, 2015, at C1; Michael Paulson, *'Hamilton' Cast Talks About Money*, N.Y. Times, June 19, 2015, at C2.

244. *See* Jackie Calmes, *$20 Billing: Tubman Is in, Jackson Is out*, N.Y. TIMES, Apr. 21, 2016, at A1.

245. *See* JON MEACHAM, AMERICAN LION: ANDREW JACKSON IN THE WHITE HOUSE 91–97, 302–04, 316–18 (2008).

246. *See* CATHERINE CLINTON, HARRIET TUBMAN: THE ROAD TO FREEDOM 33–45, 73–97, 140–88, 191–93, 211–12 (2004).

247. *See* Jonathan Martin & Nate Cohn, *Electoral Map a Reality Check to a Trump Bid*, N.Y. TIMES, Apr. 3, 2016, at 1.

248. *Today* (NBC television broadcast Apr. 21, 2016) (statement of Donald Trump).

249. *See* BD. OF GOVERNORS OF THE FED. RSRV. SYS., VOLUME OF CURRENCY IN CIRCULATION (2024).

250. William Petroski, *King Tries to Block Tubman from the $20 Bill*, DES MOINES REG., June 22, 2016, at 4A (quoting Steve King) (internal quotation marks omitted).

251. *See The Annual Testimony of the Secretary of the Treasury on the State of the International Financial System, Parts I and II: Hearings Before the H. Comm. on Fin. Servs.*, 116th Cong. 91–92 (2020) (statement of Steven T. Mnuchin, Secretary, U.S. Department of the Treasury); Letter from Drew Maloney, Assistant Sec'y for Legis. Affs., Dep't of the Treasury, to Jeanne Shaheen, U.S. Sen. (May 15, 2018) (copy on file with author); Binyamin Appelbaum, *Stepping Back from Plan for a Tubman $20 Bill*, N.Y. TIMES, Sept. 1, 2017, at A16; Alan Rappeport, *Is Tubman on $20 Bill? Treasury Won't Say*, N.Y. TIMES, June 6, 2018, at A15 [hereinafter Rappeport, *Is Tubman on $20 Bill?*]; Alan Rappeport, *Tubman as New Face of $20 Bill? Not Before President Exits Office*, N.Y. TIMES, May 23, 2019, at A1 [hereinafter Rappeport, *Tubman as New Face of $20 Bill?*]; Alan Rappeport, *Inquiry Sought into Delay in Designing $20 Bill*, N.Y. TIMES, June 20, 2019, at B3 [hereinafter Rappeport, *Inquiry Sought*]; Alan Rappeport, *Mnuchin Says No New $20 Bill Until '30*, N.Y. TIMES, June 12, 2020, at B2.

252. *See* Appelbaum, *supra* note 251, at A16; Rappeport, *Is Tubman on $20 Bill?*, *supra* note 251, at A15; Rappeport, *Tubman as New Face of $20 Bill?*, *supra* note 251, at A1; Alan Rappeport, *Unreal Sight of a Nearly Real $20 Bill*, N.Y. TIMES, June 15, 2019, at B1; Rappeport, *Inquiry Sought*, *supra* note 251, at B3.

253. Jenna Johnson & Karen Tumulty, *Trump Touts Andrew Jackson as His Hero, and Reflection*, WASH. POST, Mar. 16, 2017, at A24 (quoting Donald Trump) (internal quotation marks omitted).

254. OMAROSA MANIGAULT NEWMAN, UNHINGED: AN INSIDER'S ACCOUNT OF THE TRUMP WHITE HOUSE 295 (2018) (quoting Donald Trump) (internal quotation marks omitted).

255. *See* Jacob Bogage, *Effort to Put Tubman on $20 Bill Is Revived*, WASH. POST, Jan. 26, 2021, at A13; N'dea Yancey-Bragg, *Biden Revives Push for Tubman on $20 Bill*, USA TODAY, Jan. 27, 2021, at 2A.

Chapter 3

1. *See* Minor v. Happersett, 88 U.S. (21 Wall.) 162, 163–64 (1875).

2. *See* Francis Minor, Letter to the Editor (Dec. 30, 1869), 5 REVOLUTION 38, 38 (1870); *Mrs. Francis Minor*, 4 REVOLUTION 258, 258–59 (1869); *The St. Louis Convention*, 4 REVOLUTION 250, 250 (1869); *The St. Louis Resolutions*, 4 REVOLUTION 259, 259 (1869).

3. *See Minor*, 88 U.S. at 163–64.

4. *See id.* For the Missouri decision, see Minor v. Happersett, 53 Mo. 58, 64–65 (1873).

5. *Minor*, 88 U.S. at 165, 178.

6. *See, e.g.*, Rodriguez v. Popular Democratic Party, 457 U.S. 1, 9 (1982).

7. For the newspaper's first issue, see Myra Bradwell, *Prospectus*, CHI. LEGAL NEWS, Oct. 3, 1868, at 4. By 1872, the clerk of the House of Representatives had made the *Chicago Legal News* an authorized publisher of federal legislation. *See* H.R. EX. DOC. NO. 42-219, at 1–2 (1872).

8. *Woman's Right to Vote*, 1 CHI. LEGAL NEWS 45, 45 (1868).

9. *See* Bradwell v. Illinois, 83 U.S. (16 Wall.) 130, 130–33 (1873). Bradwell reported on her own case, reprinting her application for bar admission during the Illinois Supreme Court's September 1869 term, the Illinois Supreme Court's October 1869 letter refusing to admit her, and the court's subsequent written opinion issued in late January or early February 1870. *See A Woman Cannot Practice Law or Hold Any Office in Illinois*, 2 CHI. LEGAL NEWS 145, 145–47 (1870).

10. *In re* Bradwell, 55 Ill. 535, 536–38 (1870).

11. *Id.* at 539.

12. *See Bradwell*, 83 U.S. at 139.

13. *See* Belva A. Lockwood, *My Efforts to Become a Lawyer*, 41 LIPPINCOTT'S 215, 224 (1888).

14. *See id.* at 227–29. For the legislation, see Act of Feb. 15, 1879, ch. 81, 20 Stat. 292.

15. *See* Belva A. Lockwood, *How I Ran for the Presidency*, 17 NATIONAL 728, 728–33 (1903).

16. *In re* Lockwood, 154 U.S. 116, 116 (1894) (citation and internal quotation marks omitted).

17. *See id.* at 118.

18. For the classic definition of coverture, see 1 WILLIAM BLACKSTONE, COMMENTARIES *430.

19. *See* 62 U.S. (21 How.) 582, 588–93 (1859); *id.* at 600–03 (Daniel, J., dissenting); *see also* Quong Wing v. Kirkendall, 223 U.S. 59, 63 (1912); De la Rama v. De la Rama, 201 U.S. 303, 307 (1906); Anderson v. Watt, 138 U.S. 694, 706 (1891); Cheely v. Clayton, 110 U.S. 701, 705 (1884); Kelly v. Owen, 74 U.S. (7 Wall.) 496, 497–99 (1869).

20. *See* Bradwell v. Illinois, 83 U.S. (16 Wall.) 130, 139 (1873) (Bradley, J., concurring).

21. *Id.* at 141.

22. On *Muller*, see *supra* Chapter 1.

23. *Bradwell*, 83 U.S. at 141 (Bradley, J., concurring).

24. 98 U.S. 145, 166 (1879).

25. *See id.* at 146, 161–67.

26. For federal anti-polygamy legislation, see Act of Mar. 3, 1887, ch. 397, 24 Stat. 635; Act of Mar. 22, 1882, ch. 47, 22 Stat. 30; Act of June 23, 1874, ch. 469, 18 Stat. 253; Act of July 1, 1862, ch. 126, 12 Stat. 501. For the Mormon Church's announcement of its commitment to polygamy, see *A Special Conference of the Elders of the Church of Jesus Christ of Latter-Day-Saints*, DESERET NEWS—EXTRA (Great Salt Lake City), Sept. 14, 1852, at 1, 14, 19–20.

27. *Reynolds*, 98 U.S. at 165–66.

28. *See* An Act Conferring upon Women the Elective Franchise, § 1, 1870 Utah Laws 8, 8.

29. *See* Act of Mar. 3, 1887 § 20.

30. *Reynolds*, 98 U.S. at 164.

31. *Id.* at 165–66.

32. 169 U.S. 366, 380, 391–98 (1898).

33. *Id.* at 386.

34. *See* AMERICAN WOMEN: THE REPORT OF THE PRESIDENT'S COMMISSION ON THE STA-TUS OF WOMEN AND OTHER PUBLICATIONS OF THE COMMISSION 152–54 (1965); LEO KANOWITZ, WOMEN AND THE LAW: THE UNFINISHED REVOLUTION 59–61 (1969).

35. Frankenthal v. Gilbert, 34 F. 5, 7 (S.D. Miss. 1888); Stiles v. Lord, 11 P. 314, 315 (Ariz. 1886); Byington v. Carlin, 125 N.W. 233, 234 (Iowa 1910); Niemeyer v. Niemeyer, 70 Mo. App. 609, 612 (1897); Shute v. Sargent, 36 A. 282, 282 (N.H. 1893); Morton v. State, 209 S.W. 644, 645 (Tenn. 1919); Gould v. Frost, 196 S.W. 949, 950 (Tenn. 1917). For references to "complete emancipation," see Cap. Traction Co. v. Rockwell, 17 App. D.C. 369, 378–79 (1901); Hastings v. Day, 130 N.W. 134, 136 (Iowa 1911); Musselman v. Galligher, 32 Iowa 383, 385 (1871); Wyatt v. Wyatt, 32 So. 317, 318 (Miss. 1902); Grimes v. Reynolds, 83 S.W. 1132, 1132 (Mo. 1904).

36. Bynum v. Johnston, 222 F. 659, 663 (8th Cir. 1915); Thompson v. Minnich, 81 N.E. 336, 338 (Ill. 1907); Spivey v. Walton, 64 So. 937, 938 (Miss. 1914); Day v. Burgess, 202 S.W. 911, 911 (Tenn. 1918).

37. Schuler v. Henry, 94 P. 360, 361 (Colo. 1908); Buzby Soap Co. v. Phelps, 5 Pa. D. 756, 756 (Ct. Com. Pl. Delaware County 1895). For variations on this theme, see Bronson v. Brady, 28 App. D.C. 250, 256 (1906); Wills v. Jones, 13 App. D.C. 482, 495 (1898); *In re* Booth's Will, 66 P. 710, 711–12 (Or. 1901); Fredericks v. Hanover Fire Ins. Co., 7 Pa. D. 79, 80 (Ct. Com. Pl. Allegheny County 1898); Loftus v. Farmers' & Mechs.' Nat'l Bank of Phila., 6 Pa. C. 340, 342 (Ct. Com. Pl. Philadelphia County 1889).

38. Martin v. Robson, 65 Ill. 129, 139 (1872).

39. Wells v. Caywood, 3 Colo. 487, 490 (1877).

40. Helvie v. Hoover, 69 P. 958, 961 (Okla. 1902).

41. For some examples, see N.H. GEN. LAWS ch. 82, § 5 (1878); *id.* at ch. 95, § 2; *id.* at ch. 148, § 24; *id.* at ch. 180, § 14; *id.* at ch. 187, § 2; *id.* at ch. 204, § 6; *id.* at ch. 225, § 1; *id.* at ch. 226, § 14; *id.* at ch. 270, § 7; *id.* at ch. 274, § 10; *id.* at ch. 282, § 17.

42. On the struggle for woman suffrage in New Hampshire, see A BRIEF HISTORY OF THE NEW HAMPSHIRE WOMAN SUFFRAGE ASSOCIATION 6–20 (1907). For the 1878 law, see Act of Aug. 13, 1878, ch. 46, 1878 N.H. Laws 176.

43. Harris v. Webster, 58 N.H. 481, 483 (1878); *see also* Hammond v. Corbett, 50 N.H. 501, 507 (1871).

44. *See* Missouri Equal Suffrage League, *Put Yourself in Woman's Place*, ST. LOUIS POST-DISPATCH, Oct. 28, 1914 (pt. 2), at 13 (advertisement).

45. *See Woman Suffrage Loses in 6 States, Wins in Montana*, ST. LOUIS POST-DISPATCH, Nov. 4, 1914, at 2.

46. Claxton v. Pool, 167 S.W. 623, 629 (Mo. Ct. App. 1914).

47. *See* MO. CONST. art. I, § 22 (adopted Feb. 27, 1945); Curtis A. Betts, *Ten Alterations in Bill of Rights Proposed by Constitution, but It Guards Fundamental Guarantees*, ST. LOUIS POST-DISPATCH, Feb. 13, 1945, at 1B.

48. *See* Duren v. Missouri, 439 U.S. 357, 359–60 (1979).

49. *See* Adkins v. Children's Hosp., 261 U.S. 525, 539, 553, 562 (1923).

50. *Id.* at 553 (citation omitted).

51. Boyd v. Gwyn, 6 Pa. D. & C. 275, 277–78 (Ct. Com. Pl. Philadelphia County 1925).

52. McNeil v. Conn. Fire Ins. Co., 24 F.2d 221, 223 (W.D. Tenn. 1928).

53. Ziegenbein v. Damme, 292 N.W. 921, 923 (Neb. 1940).

54. Rutecki v. Lukaszewski, 79 N.Y.S.2d 341, 344 (App. Div. 1948); *see also* Andris v. Andris, 109 S.W.2d 707, 716 (Mo. Ct. App. 1937); Opritza v. City of Youngstown, 6 Ohio Law Abs. 475, 475 (Ct. App. 1928); Myers v. Myers, 17 Pa. D. & C. 236, 238 (Ct. Com. Pl. Clinton County 1931); Times Printing Co. v. Mulkey, 2 Tenn. App. 312, 319 (1926); Hinson v. Hinson, 461 P.2d 560, 563 (Wash. Ct. App. 1969).
55. United States v. Dege, 364 U.S. 51, 54 (1960).
56. United States v. Yazell, 382 U.S. 341, 343, 351 (1966).
57. *Ex parte* Estep, 129 F. Supp. 557, 558 (N.D. Tex. 1955).
58. Apostle v. Pappas, 277 N.Y.S. 400, 404 (Sup. Ct. 1935).
59. Young v. Young, 184 So. 187, 190 (Ala. 1938).
60. Merch.'s Hostess Serv. of Fla., Inc. v. Cain, 9 So. 2d 373, 375 (Fla. 1942) (en banc); *see also* United States v. Anthony, 145 F. Supp. 323, 341 (M.D. Pa. 1956); Cosper v. Valley Bank, 237 P. 175, 176 (Ariz. 1925); Follansbee v. Benzenberg, 265 P.2d 183, 189 (Cal. Dist. Ct. App. 1954); Rains v. Rains, 46 P.2d 740, 742 (Colo. 1935); Curtis v. Ashworth, 142 S.E. 111, 113 (Ga. 1928); Lincoln v. Mills, 3 So. 2d 835, 835 (Miss. 1941); Hodson v. Picker, 287 N.Y.S. 642, 646 (Dom. Rel. Ct. 1936).
61. *See* AMERICAN WOMEN, *supra* note 34, at 68–70, 152–57; KANOWITZ, *supra* note 34, at 46–99.
62. *See* AMERICAN WOMEN, *supra* note 34, at 46–48, 57, 131–32; Pauli Murray & Mary O. Eastwood, *Jane Crow and the Law: Sex Discrimination and Title VII*, 34 GEO. WASH. L. REV. 232, 246–48 (1965).
63. *See* AMERICAN WOMEN, *supra* note 34, at 55, 151; WOMEN'S BUREAU, U.S. DEP'T OF LAB., BULLETIN NO. 294, 1969 HANDBOOK ON WOMEN WORKERS 271, 277–28 (1969).
64. *See* Goesaert v. Cleary, 335 U.S. 464, 465–67 (1948); Radice v. New York, 264 U.S. 292, 293–98 (1924); *infra* text accompanying notes 87–121.
65. *See* Hoyt v. Florida, 368 U.S. 57, 61–62 (1961); Fay v. New York, 332 U.S. 261, 267, 289–90 (1947); Breedlove v. Suttles, 302 U.S. 277, 282–84 (1937); *infra* text accompanying notes 66–71, 124–147.
66. *See supra* text accompanying notes 49–50.
67. *See Breedlove*, 302 U.S. at 279–84.
68. On poll taxes, see CAROL ANDERSON, ONE PERSON, NO VOTE: HOW VOTER SUPPRESSION IS DESTROYING OUR DEMOCRACY 7–10 (2018); DAVID MONTEJANO, ANGLOS AND MEXICANS IN THE MAKING OF TEXAS, 1836–1986, at 143, 146, 252, 279, 292 (1987); MICHAEL WALDMAN, THE FIGHT TO VOTE 161–63 (2016); Ralph J. Bunche, *The Negro in the Political Life of the United States*, 10 J. NEGRO EDUC. 567, 569–73 (1941); Harvey Walker, *The Poll Tax in the United States*, 9 BULL. NAT'L TAX ASS'N 46, 47–50 (1923).
69. *See Breedlove*, 302 U.S. at 279–80.
70. *Id.* at 282.
71. *Id.*
72. *See* Reed v. Reed, 404 U.S. 71, 71–77 (1971).
73. *See infra* Chapter 5 and text accompanying notes 172–182.
74. Trammel v. United States, 445 U.S. 40, 52 (1980) (alteration, citation, and internal quotation marks omitted).
75. Obergefell v. Hodges, 576 U.S. 644, 660 (2015).

76. Smith v. Tri-State Culvert Mfg. Co., 191 S.E.2d 92, 93 (Ga. Ct. App. 1972) (internal quotation marks omitted); *see also In re* Wincorp, Inc., 185 B.R. 914, 919 (Bankr. S.D. Fla. 1995); Parniawski v. Parniawski, 359 A.2d 719, 721 (Conn. Super. Ct. 1976).

77. 163 U.S. 537, 543 (1896); *see also id.* at 544–45; Civil Rights Cases, 109 U.S. 3, 25 (1883); Shelby County v. Holder, 570 U.S. 529, 547–57 (2013).

78. Sevcik v. Sandoval, 911 F. Supp. 2d 996, 997, 1008 (D. Nev. 2012), *rev'd*, Latta v. Otter, 771 F.3d 456 (9th Cir. 2014).

79. *See* 208 U.S. 412, 416–23 (1908).

80. *See id.* at 422.

81. *Id.* at 418 (quoting First Nat'l Bank of S. Or. v. Leonard, 59 P. 873, 875 (Or. 1900)) (internal quotation marks omitted).

82. For the plaintiff's arguments, see *id.* at 413–14, 417–19.

83. 91 N.E. 695, 701 (Ill. 1910).

84. *Id.* at 696–97.

85. *Id.* at 697.

86. *Id.* at 696.

87. *See* 335 U.S. 464, 465–67 (1948).

88. *Id.* at 465 (citation and internal quotation marks omitted).

89. For the start of Prohibition, see U.S. CONST. amend. XVIII. For decisions upholding restrictions on female bartending before Prohibition, see Cronin v. Adams, 192 U.S. 108, 113–15 (1904); *In re* Considine, 83 F. 157, 157–59 (C.C.D. Wash. 1897); State *ex rel.* Marion v. Reynolds, 36 P. 449, 449–50 (Mont. 1894) (per curiam); Mayor of Hoboken v. Goodman, 51 A. 1092, 1092–94 (N.J. 1902); Bergman v. Cleveland, 39 Ohio St. 651, 652–53 (1884); Walter v. Commonwealth, 88 Pa. 137, 140–43 (1878); State v. Considine, 47 P. 755, 756–57 (Wash. 1897).

90. For the end of Prohibition, see U.S. CONST. amend. XXI. On the union's lobbying for the Michigan law, see Frank Morris, *Ban Women Bartenders*, DETROIT EVENING TIMES, Apr. 26, 1945, at C5; Malcolm W. Bingay, *Barring Barmaids*, DETROIT FREE PRESS, Dec. 29, 1948, at 6; Transcript of Record at 48, Goesaert v. Cleary, 335 U.S. 464 (1948) (No. 49) (statement of Anne R. Davidow); *Court Studies Ban on Women Bartenders*, PORT HURON TIMES HERALD, Nov. 20, 1948, at 3 (quoting Anne R. Davidow's oral argument before the Supreme Court); *Nation's Highest Court Gets Controversial Bar Maid Law*, BATTLE CREEK ENQUIRER & NEWS, Nov. 20, 1948, at 1 (same). On the union's efforts to ban female bartending in other states, see *Anti-Communist Vote Wins in Hotel Union*, N.Y. TIMES, Aug. 19, 1946, at 16; *Chat of the Craft*, CATERING INDUS. EMP., Mar. 1945, at 17, 18; *Greetings from San Francisco, California—Convention City, 1938*, CATERING INDUS. EMP., Sept. 1936, at 28, 28; *Massachusetts State Council Hold Annual Session at Boston*, CATERING INDUS. EMP., July 1936, at 37, 37; *Our Minnesota Locals Meet at State Labor Convention*, CATERING INDUS. EMP., Oct. 1936, at 33, 33–34; *Our Ohio State Branch Draft Legislative Program*, CATERING INDUS. EMP., Dec. 1936, at 35, 35. The bartenders' union was founded in the nineteenth century and consistently excluded women until male labor shortages during World War II made admitting some female members advisable. *See* Edward Flore, *A World Upside Down*, CATERING INDUS. EMP., Dec. 1942, at 3, 3–4; Edward Flore, *Bartenderettes*, CATERING INDUS. EMP., May 1943, at 4, 4. The union reinstated its exclusion policy in 1946. *See* Hugo Ernst, *Bartending Must Revert to Bartenders*,

Says the G.E.B., CATERING INDUS. EMP., Apr. 1946, at 4, 5; *Minutes of the Meetings of the General Executive Board*, CATERING INDUS. EMP., Apr. 1946, at 9, 15.

91. Anti-Prohibition Div., Hotel & Rest. Emps. & Bartenders Int'l Union (AFL), Anti-Barmaid Laws: A Survey of Laws, Ordinances and Regulations in States and Municipalities Governing the Employment of Women as Bartenders 2–3 (Dec. 1948) (copy on file with author; Cornell University Library, Kheel Center for Labor-Management Documentation and Archives, HERE General Office Legal Files, reel 30). The union leadership mailed this report to local unions in December 1948. *See* OFFICERS REPORT AND PROCEEDINGS OF THE THIRTY-SECOND GENERAL CONVENTION OF THE HOTEL & RESTAURANT EMPLOYEES AND BARTENDERS INTERNATIONAL UNION 57 (1949) [hereinafter OFFICERS REPORT] (statement of Fred Sweet, Director, Anti-Prohibition Department); Frederick B. Sweet, *On the Anti-Prohibition Front High Court Okays Anti-Prohibition Laws*, CATERING INDUS. EMP., Jan. 1949, at 19, 19.

92. *See Anti-Communist Vote Wins in Hotel Union, supra* note 90, at 16; *Chat of the Craft, supra* note 90, at 18; Edward Flore, *Snaps from the General President's Report to the Twenty-Eighth General Convention—Rochester*, CATERING INDUS. EMP., Sept. 1936, at 4, 4.

93. *Bartenders Urge Ban on Barmaids*, N.Y. TIMES, Oct. 13, 1936, at 29 (quoting Louis W. Wulff) (internal quotation marks omitted). This interview appeared in newspapers around the country. *See, e.g., Barmaids Defy Men and Union*, PITTSBURGH PRESS, Nov. 2, 1936, at 32; *Barmen Fear Winks by Lady Drink Mixers*, EVENING SUN (Baltimore), Oct. 13, 1936, at 3; City of De Ridder v. Mangano, 171 So. 826, 828 (La. 1936).

94. *Barmaids*, ST. LOUIS POST-DISPATCH, Dec. 9, 1945 (Pictures), at 6.

95. *Union Opposes Barmaids*, EVENING SUN (Baltimore), May 25, 1942, at 15 (quoting Anthony Glorioso) (internal quotation marks omitted).

96. *See* Edith Carroll, *Barmaids Come Back*, N.Y. TIMES, Mar. 18, 1945 (§ 6), at 27; *Chat of the Craft, supra* note 90, at 18; *Judge Upholds St. Paul Ban on Barmaids*, MINNEAPOLIS MORNING TRIB., Feb. 6, 1946, at 11; *Our Ohio State Branch Draft Legislative Program, supra* note 90, at 35.

97. *See* Act No. 133, § 19a, 1945 Mich. Pub. Acts 139, 146–47.

98. *See* Goesaert v. Cleary, 335 U.S. 464, 467 (1948).

99. *The Embattled Barmaids*, LIFE, Apr. 13, 1953, at 40, 40 (quoting unnamed source) (internal quotation marks omitted).

100. *See* Radice v. New York, 264 U.S. 292, 293–98 (1924); Dominion Hotel v. Arizona, 249 U.S. 265, 267–69 (1919); Bosley v. McLaughlin, 236 U.S. 385, 388–96 (1915); Miller v. Wilson, 236 U.S. 373, 379–84 (1915); Hawley v. Walker, 232 U.S. 718, 718 (1914) (per curiam), *aff'g Ex Parte* Hawley, 85 Ohio St. 494 (1912) (mem.), *aff'g* 22 Ohio Dec. 39 (Ct. Com. Pl. 1911); Riley v. Massachusetts, 232 U.S. 671, 678–81 (1914).

101. *See* People v. Jemnez, 121 P.2d 543, 543–45 (Cal. App. Dep't Super. Ct. 1942); City of De Ridder v. Mangano, 171 So. 826, 827–29 (La. 1936); Anderson v. City of St. Paul, 32 N.W.2d 538, 548 (Minn. 1948); *In re* Shahade's License, 57 Pa. D. & C. 573, 573–80 (Ct. Quarter Sess. Cambria County 1946); Commonwealth v. Kline, 40 Pa. D. & C. 604, 604–08 (Ct. Quarter Sess. Washington County 1941). For an exception, see Brown v. Foley, 29 So. 2d 870, 871 (Fla. 1947) (en banc).

102. *See* Fitzpatrick v. Liquor Control Comm'n, 25 N.W.2d 118, 119, 127 (Mich. 1946).

103. *See* Transcript of Record, *supra* note 90, at 2, 9.

104. *See id.* at 9.

105. *See id.* at 2.
106. For an interview Davidow gave from her Detroit law office in 1979, see Susan Morse, *Age Hasn't Mellowed Brother-Sister Team*, Boca Raton News, Jan. 24, 1979, at 5C. For a 1978 interview, see source cited *infra* note 110.
107. *See* Goesaert v. Cleary, 335 U.S. 464, 464 (1948).
108. *See* Transcript of Record, *supra* note 90, at 18–39.
109. *See* Goesaert v. Cleary, 74 F. Supp. 735 (E.D. Mich. 1947), *aff'd*, 335 U.S. 464 (1948).
110. Interview by Ann Schlitt with Anne R. Davidow in Detroit, Mich. (Dec. 1978) (copy on file with Harvard University, Radcliffe Institute, Schlesinger Library, identifier T-084_01).
111. *Id.*
112. *See Goesaert*, 335 U.S. at 465–67.
113. *Id.* at 465.
114. *Id.* at 467.
115. *Id.* at 466.
116. *Id.*
117. *Id.* at 465–66.
118. Officers Report, *supra* note 91, at 57 (statement of Fred Sweet, Director, Anti-Prohibition Department); *see also* Sweet, *supra* note 91, at 19; Alexander Feinberg, *Cafe Staffed by Barmaids Picketed by Union that Won't Admit Them*, N.Y. Times, Apr. 4, 1950, at 1; *To Ask City Barmaid Ban*, N.Y. Times, Apr. 6, 1950, at 32; *Union to Seek Law Banning Barmaids*, N.Y. Times, Apr. 5, 1950, at 38.
119. *See* Women's Bureau, *supra* note 63, at 277.
120. *See Equal Rights 1970: Hearings on S.J. Res. 61 and S.J. Res. 231 Before the S. Comm. on the Judiciary*, 91st Cong. 68–69 (1970) (statement of Sen. Marlow Cook).
121. *See id.* at 28–45 (statement of Myra Wolfgang, Vice President, Hotel & Restaurant Employees and Bartenders International Union).
122. *Id.* at 33 (statement of Myra Wolfgang, Vice President, Hotel & Restaurant Employees and Bartenders International Union). For more on Wolfgang's mobilization against the ERA, see Elizabeth Shelton, *Amendment Backers*, Wash. Post, Sept. 3, 1970, at C3.
123. *See* Craig v. Boren, 429 U.S. 190, 210 n.23 (1976).
124. 332 U.S. 261 (1947).
125. 100 U.S. 303, 310 (1880).
126. *See Fay*, 332 U.S. at 264, 266–67, 289.
127. *Id.* at 289.
128. *Id.* at 290.
129. *Id.* at 289–90.
130. *Id.*
131. *Id.* at 290.
132. *Id.*
133. 368 U.S. 57, 61–62 (1961).
134. *Id.* at 58–59 (internal quotation marks omitted). For Gwendolyn's first name, see Hoyt v. State, 119 So. 2d 691, 692 (Fla. 1959).
135. *See Hoyt*, 368 U.S. at 58–59.
136. *See id.* at 58, 61, 64.
137. *Id.* at 64–65.
138. *See id.* at 65.

139. *See* Brief on Behalf of Appellant at 3–4, 40, Hoyt v. State, 119 So. 2d 691 (Fla. 1959).

140. *Id.* at 4.

141. *Id.* at 3; *see also id.* at 24, 41; Brief for Appellant at 5, Hoyt v. Florida, 368 U.S. 57 (1961) (No. 31).

142. Brief on Behalf of Appellant, *supra* note 139, at 4; *see also id.* at 41; Brief for Appellant, *supra* note 141, at 5.

143. Brief on Behalf of Appellant, *supra* note 139, at 4.

144. *Hoyt*, 368 U.S. at 59. For a similar description from the Florida Supreme Court, see *Hoyt*, 119 So. 2d at 692–93.

145. *Hoyt*, 368 U.S. at 61 (internal quotation marks omitted).

146. *Id.* at 61–62.

147. *Id.* at 62.

148. *See* Taylor v. Louisiana, 419 U.S. 522, 523–26, 531–37 (1975).

149. 194 S.E.2d 707, 709–11 (Va. 1973) (citation and internal quotation marks omitted).

150. *Id.* at 710.

151. 218 U.S. 611, 614–19 (1910).

152. *See id.* at 614–16.

153. *Id.* at 615–16 (citation and internal quotation marks omitted).

154. *See* Thompson v. Thompson, 31 App. D.C. 557, 558 (1908); *see also Thompson*, 218 U.S. at 614.

155. *Thompson*, 218 U.S. at 615.

156. *Id.* at 619.

157. *Id.* at 618.

158. *Id.* at 616 (citation and internal quotation marks omitted).

159. *Id.* at 618; *see also id.* at 617.

160. Schultz v. Christopher, 118 P. 629, 629–30 (Wash. 1911).

161. *See* Lillienkamp v. Rippetoe, 179 S.W. 628, 628–29 (Tenn. 1915).

162. *Id.* (citation and internal quotation marks omitted).

163. *Id.* at 629; *see also* Palmer v. Edwards, 155 So. 483, 484 (La. Ct. App. 1934); Austin v. Austin, 100 So. 591, 591–93 (Miss. 1924).

164. Becker v. Janinski, 15 N.Y.S. 675, 678 (Ct. Com. Pl. New York City and County 1891).

165. *In re* Davidson, 233 F. 462, 463 (M.D. Ala. 1916).

166. *Id.* at 463, 466.

167. *Id.* at 466; *see also* Fain v. Minge, 43 S.W.2d 504, 505 (Ky. Ct. App. 1931); Nelson v. Metro. St. Ry. Co., 88 S.W. 781, 783 (Mo. Ct. App. 1905).

168. *See* 1 FOWLER V. HARPER & FLEMING JAMES, JR., THE LAW OF TORTS 635–38 (1956).

169. *See id.* at 641–42; Note, *Judicial Treatment of Negligent Invasion of Consortium*, 61 COLUM. L. REV. 1341, 1349–50 (1961).

170. Dupe v. Hunsberger, 58 Pa. D. & C. 483, 485 (Ct. Com. Pl. Montgomery County 1946).

171. Kronenbitter v. Washburn Wire Co., 159 N.Y.S.2d 739, 739–40 (Sup. Ct. 1957); *see also* Nash v. Mobile & O.R. Co., 116 So. 100, 101 (Miss. 1928); Maloy v. Foster, 8 N.Y.S.2d 608, 611 (Sup. Ct. 1938); Howard v. Verdigris Valley Elec. Coop., 207 P.2d 784, 787–88 (Okla. 1949); Neuberg v. Bobowicz, 162 A.2d 662, 663–67 (Pa. 1960); Nickel v. Hardware Mut. Cas. Co., 70 N.W.2d 205, 206–08 (Wis. 1955).

172. *See* 505 U.S. 833, 881 (1992) (plurality opinion).

173. *See id.* at 885–86.

174. *See id.* at 881–87.
175. *Id.* at 887.
176. *Id.* at 883.
177. *Id.* at 872; *see also id.* at 878, 885.
178. *Id.* at 882.
179. *Id.* at 887.
180. *Id.* at 856 (majority opinion).
181. *Id.* at 897–98.
182. *Id.* at 898.

Chapter 4

1. *See, e.g.,* Jim Hoagland, *The Post-Racial Election*, WASH. POST, Nov. 2, 2008, at B7; Joan Vennochi, *Closing the Door on Victimhood*, BOS. GLOBE, Nov. 6, 2008, at A23.
2. Phillip Morris, *America Begins Its Journey into a Post-Racial Era*, PLAIN DEALER (Cleveland), Nov. 6, 2008, at A1.
3. *President-Elect Obama*, WALL ST. J., Nov. 5, 2008, at A22.
4. *See, e.g., A Bishop Declares for Woman's Rights*, EVENING STAR (D.C.), June 26, 1890, at 2; *Female Pickpockets*, N.Y. DAILY TRIB., Sept. 4, 1910, at 6; *Old Fashions in Styles*, KAN. CITY TIMES, Dec. 9, 1894 (pt. 2), at 16; *Our Club Women*, ENID EVENTS, May 8, 1902, at 1; *Revising the Marriage Service*, PHILA. INQUIRER, Oct. 8, 1916 (News), at 10; Lurana W. She, *The Overturning of Woman's Sphere*, N.Y. TIMES, Dec. 29, 1908, at 8; *Starch*, BROOKLYN DAILY EAGLE, Mar. 29, 1905, at 4.
5. On women's disenfranchisement, see MINUTES OF THE FIRST SESSION OF THE TEXAS EQUAL RIGHTS ASSOCIATION (Beaumont, 1893); *Want Equal Suffrage*, GALVESTON DAILY NEWS, Apr. 30, 1893, at 5. For jobs reserved for men, or white men, see *Help Wanted— Male*, GALVESTON DAILY NEWS, Sept. 8, 1892, at 5.
6. *The Emancipation of Women*, AUSTIN DAILY STATESMAN, Sept. 9, 1892, at 2.
7. ST. LOUIS GLOBE-DEMOCRAT, Feb. 28, 1897, at 6.
8. For examples of reprintings, see *World Grows Better*, SUNDAY STAR (D.C.), Feb. 4, 1912 (pt. II), at 7; *World's Progress Morally*, L.A. TIMES, Mar. 17, 1912 (pt. III), at 17; *see also* Marcel Prevost, *Women Afraid of Liberty*, WASH. POST, May 28, 1905 (pt. 4), at 7.
9. *See supra* Chapter 1.
10. *See Woman Not Eligible to Be County Examiner*, ARK. DEMOCRAT, Aug. 20, 1904, at 6.
11. Ida Bariden Frauenthal, *Good Citizenship*, ARK. GAZETTE, Oct. 9, 1904 (pt. II), at 6.
12. Mrs. H.N. M'Kusick, *Club Women and Club Life*, SUNDAY TRIB. (Minneapolis), Feb. 21, 1904, at 14. For a contemporary history of women's efforts to win full voting rights in Minnesota, see ETHEL EDGERTON HURD, WOMAN SUFFRAGE IN MINNESOTA: A RECORD OF THE ACTIVITIES IN ITS BEHALF SINCE 1847, at 25–29 (1916).
13. Hugh S. Fullerton, *Wife Should Be a Partner; She Will Help Save Money*, CHI. SUNDAY TRIB., Oct. 7, 1906 (Worker's Magazine), at 3.
14. *Are American Women Too Emancipated?*, SPOKESMAN-REVIEW (Spokane), July 9, 1910, at 4; *see also Equal Suffrage in New York*, CHI. DAILY TRIB., Nov. 8, 1917, at 6; *Other Side of Divorce Problem*, WASH. POST, Dec. 29, 1908, at 6.

15. *See* 4 THE HISTORY OF WOMAN SUFFRAGE 1026 (Susan B. Anthony & Ida Husted Harper eds., 1902); THE INT'L WOMAN SUFFRAGE ALL., WOMAN SUFFRAGE IN PRACTICE 2–3 (1913).

16. *See* 5 THE HISTORY OF WOMAN SUFFRAGE 193 n.1, 200 (Ida Husted Harper ed., 1922); THE INT'L WOMAN SUFFRAGE ALL., *supra* note 15, at 56.

17. For discussion of these disabilities and the judicial victory announcements that ignored coverture's persistence, see *supra* Chapter 3.

18. *Matrimony on Business Principles*, BROOKLYN DAILY EAGLE, May 13, 1888, at 8.

19. CHI. DAILY TRIB., Feb. 6, 1895, at 6; *see also Married Women's Emancipation*, READING TIMES, Mar. 21, 1893, at 2.

20. *Married Women Are Emancipated*, NEWS & OBSERVER (Raleigh), Nov. 10, 1911, at 3.

21. Joseph H. Beale, Jr., *The Development of Jurisprudence During the Past Century*, 18 HARV. L. REV. 271, 279 (1905). On Beale's professorship, see Roscoe Pound, *Preface* to HARVARD LEGAL ESSAYS: WRITTEN IN HONOR OF AND PRESENTED TO JOSEPH HENRY BEALE AND SAMUEL WILLISTON, at vii, vii (Roscoe Pound ed., 1934).

22. *See Judge Peck Dead; Author, Teacher*, N.Y. TIMES, Oct. 30, 1938, at L41.

23. Epaphroditus Peck, *Women's Rights in a Male-Suffrage State*, 25 YALE L.J. 459, 459 (1916); *see also id.* at 460.

24. *Id.* at 466.

25. *Downtrodden Man*, BUFFALO MORNING EXPRESS, June 1, 1921, at 10.

26. Harry A. Franck, *Woman's Role Changes, the World Over*, N.Y. TIMES, Nov. 4, 1928 (§ 5), at 12.

27. Samuel D. Schmalhausen & V.F. Calverton, *Introduction* to WOMAN'S COMING OF AGE: A SYMPOSIUM, at xi, xvi (Samuel D. Schmalhausen & V.F. Calverton eds., 1931).

28. Lillian G. Genn, *Modern Woman FAILURE as a Wife?*, OAKLAND TRIB., Aug. 14, 1932 (Magazine & Fiction), at 5 (quoting Grace Adams) (internal quotation marks omitted).

29. *New Guild*, DAYTON DAILY NEWS, Apr. 14, 1949, at 28.

30. Editorial, *Is It Really a Woman's World?*, BIRMINGHAM NEWS, July 14, 1958, at 6; *see also* SUZANNE LA FOLLETTE, CONCERNING WOMEN 10 (1926); *Banish the Rolling Pin*, FORT WORTH STAR-TELEGRAM, Sept. 17, 1923, at 8; Eunice Fuller Barnard, *A Cry of Freedom for the Debutante*, N.Y. TIMES, May 3, 1931 (§ 5), at 7; Evelyn Cunningham, *How Far Should a Woman Go Toward Being Independent?*, PITTSBURGH COURIER, Aug. 11, 1956 (§ 2), at 14; James R. Dalton, Letter to the Editor, DAILY NEWS (New York), Mar. 22, 1923, at 13; Eleanor Darnton, *19,000 Women of Distinction*, OAKLAND TRIB., June 8, 1958 (Parade), at 4; *Double Takes*, EVANSVILLE COURIER, Mar. 17, 1964, at 6; *Heard Dean Justin*, COUNCIL GROVE REPUBLICAN, May 17, 1935, at 1; Katherine Heidinger, *Women Have Legal Rights*, CLARION-LEDGER / JACKSON DAILY NEWS, Nov. 26, 1967, at F3; Nancy Barr Mavity, *The Two-Income Family*, HARPER'S, Dec. 1951, at 57, 57; H. Frederick Moeller, Letter to the Editor, CINCINNATI ENQUIRER, May 13, 1956 (§ 3), at 2; Elsie Robinson, *Should Girls Leave Home?*, DETROIT TIMES, Nov. 22, 1942 (Metropolitan Magazine), at 8; Elizabeth Bancroft Schlesinger, *They Say Women Are Emancipated*, 77 NEW REPUBLIC 125, 127 (1933); R.A. Webster, Letter to the Editor, TUCSON DAILY CITIZEN, July 31, 1942, at 10.

31. On women of color's disenfranchisement, see *supra* Chapter 1. On sex stratification in employment, see *supra* Chapters 1 & 3. On unequal rules governing marriage, see *supra* Chapter 3. On women's exclusion from Ivy League colleges until the late 1960s and early

1970s, see NANCY WEISS MALKIEL, "KEEP THE DAMNED WOMEN OUT": THE STRUGGLE FOR COEDUCATION 31–306, 441–88 (2016).

32. *The Lucy Stone Age Dawns*, KAN. CITY STAR, July 31, 1921, at 15C.

33. FREDERICK LEWIS ALLEN, ONLY YESTERDAY: AN INFORMAL HISTORY OF THE NINETEEN-TWENTIES 96 (1931); *see also id.* at 88–122. On sales, see *Frederick Lewis Allen Is Dead; Editor Wrote 'Only Yesterday,'* N.Y. TIMES, Feb. 14, 1954, at 1. For Allen's self-description, see *F.L.A. (1890–1954)*, HARPER'S, Apr. 1954, at 74, 74 (internal quotation marks omitted).

34. Arnold J. Toynbee, *We Must Pay for Freedom*, WOMAN'S HOME COMPANION, Mar. 1955, at 52, 134.

35. Harold Hyman, *Enlightened View*, IOWA CITY PRESS-CITIZEN, Jan. 20, 1960, at 15.

36. Mary Merryfield, *The New Woman: The Housewife*, CHI. SUNDAY TRIB., June 17, 1962 (pt. 3), at 40 (emphasis omitted).

37. Robert Quillen, *Letters from a Bald-Headed Dad to a Flapper Daughter*, ATLANTA CONST., Jan. 30, 1932, at 8.

38. *Scrub It Out!*, MIDLAND J. (Rising Sun), Aug. 30, 1940, at 4.

39. Mary Agnes Starr, *Preparing College Women as Homemakers to Be Tried at Earlham; Jones House Readied*, PALLADIUM-ITEM & SUN-TELEGRAM (Richmond), Mar. 1, 1959, at 7 (quoting Landrum Bolling) (internal quotation marks omitted).

40. Mary I. Bunting, *The Radcliffe Institute for Independent Study*, 42 EDUC. REC. 279, 280 (1961). On Bunting's presidency, see *Contributors to This Issue*, 42 EDUC. REC. 260, 260 (1961).

41. Paul Woodring, *Educating Women*, SATURDAY REV., May 18, 1963, at 61, 61; *see also* Eunice Fuller Barnard, *Feminism Now Battles on a New Front*, N.Y. TIMES, July 3, 1932 (§ 6), at 11; Editorial, *The Feminists Win Their Rights Fight*, BERKSHIRE EAGLE, June 18, 1964, at 20; Don Galore, *Observations*, SUMMERFIELD SUN, May 7, 1936, at 2; Robert Quillen, *It Isn't Equality Woman Wants; She Wants Her Wages*, WASH. POST, Aug. 13, 1928, at 4.

42. *See Historian Will Durant Dies; Author of 'Civilization' Series*, N.Y. TIMES, Nov. 9, 1981, at A1.

43. *Durant Discusses Woman*, N.Y. TIMES, Oct. 11, 1926, at 4 (quoting Will Durant) (internal quotation marks omitted).

44. Gladys Shultz, *Career Girls, Then and Now*, GLAMOUR, Mar. 1942, at 35, 35.

45. *Id.* at 36; *see also On the Side*, BREMEN ENQUIRER, Jan. 10, 1952, at 1.

46. *John A. Macy Dead; Was Noted Critic*, N.Y. TIMES, Aug. 27, 1932, at 15; *see also* GEORGE E. DE MILLE, LITERARY CRITICISM IN AMERICA: A PRELIMINARY SURVEY 246, 279–80 (1931).

47. John Macy, *Equality of Woman with Man: A Myth*, 153 HARPER'S 705, 706 (1926).

48. *Id.* at 707.

49. *See John Erskine Dies in His Home at 71*, N.Y. TIMES, June 3, 1951, at 92.

50. JOHN ERSKINE, THE INFLUENCE OF WOMEN AND ITS CURE 17, 130 (1936).

51. *See* Richard Severo, *Russell Lynes, 80, an Editor and Arbiter of Taste*, N.Y. TIMES, Sept. 16, 1991, at B12.

52. RUSSELL LYNES, A SURFEIT OF HONEY 51 (1957).

53. *Id.* at 53; *see also* Mary Dyer Lemon, *Some Colorful Books Ensnare Summer Reader*, INDIANAPOLIS SUNDAY STAR, Aug. 23, 1936 (pt. 6), at 4; *Seven 'Jury Widowers' Are Hoping for Early Verdict*, LONG BEACH SUN, Mar. 29, 1931, at A7.

54. *See infra* Chapter 6.

55. Edward Hoagland, *The Liberation of Women—and Men*, N.Y. TIMES, Dec. 31, 1981, at A23. For the book, see EDWARD HOAGLAND, THE TUGMAN'S PASSAGE 147–48 (1982).

56. For the extended deadline, see H.R.J. Res. 638, 95th Cong., 92 Stat. 3799 (1978).

57. Don R. Collum, *Men Are Surviving Despite Women's Lib*, SPOKESMAN-REVIEW (Spokane), Apr. 11, 1982, at B3; *see also* Lisa Anderson, *Beyond Feminism*, CHI. TRIB., Apr. 5, 1987 (§ 19), at 13; Leslie Brown, *For Young Women, Feminism Doesn't Seem Germane*, BURLING-TON FREE PRESS, Mar. 6, 1984, at 1D; Lacey Fosburgh, *Traditional Groups Prefer to Ignore Women's Lib*, N.Y. TIMES, Aug. 26, 1970, at 44.

58. Claudia Wallis, *Onward, Women!*, TIME, Dec. 4, 1989, at 80, 82 (quoting Carol Gilligan) (internal quotation marks omitted).

59. Nancy Gibbs, *The Dreams of Youth*, TIME, Fall 1990, at 10, 12.

60. *See* EMILY A. SHRIDER ET AL., U.S. DEP'T OF COM., INCOME AND POVERTY IN THE UNITED STATES: 2020, at 47 tbl.A-7 (2021).

61. *See* Jaclyn Fierman, *Why Women Still Don't Hit the Top*, FORTUNE, July 30, 1990, at 40, 40.

62. *See* JENNIFER E. MANNING & IDA A. BRUDNICK, CONG. RSCH. SERV., WOMEN IN CONGRESS: STATISTICS AND BRIEF OVERVIEW 18 tbl.A-1 (2021).

63. *See Man of the Year*, TIME, Jan. 5, 1981, at cover (Ronald Reagan); *Man of the Year: Poland's Lech Walesa*, TIME, Jan. 4, 1982, at cover; *Machine of the Year: The Computer Moves in*, TIME, Jan. 3, 1983, at cover; *Men of the Year: Ronald Reagan, Yuri Andropov*, TIME, Jan. 2, 1984, at cover; *Man of the Year: Peter Ueberroth: The Achievement Was Olympian*, TIME, Jan. 7, 1985, at cover; *Man of the Year: Deng Xiaoping*, TIME, Jan. 6, 1986, at cover; *Woman of the Year: Philippine President Corazon Aquino*, TIME, Jan. 5, 1987, at cover; *Man of the Year: The Education of Mikhail Sergeyevich Gorbachev*, TIME, Jan. 4, 1988, at cover; *Planet of the Year: Endangered Earth*, TIME, Jan. 2, 1989, at cover; *Man of the Decade: Mikhail Gorbachev*, TIME, Jan. 1, 1990, at cover.

64. MARVIN HARRIS, AMERICA NOW: THE ANTHROPOLOGY OF A CHANGING CULTURE 89 (1981).

65. Ben Wattenberg, *What Women Wanted*, SUN (Baltimore), May 18, 1983, at A11.

66. *See* Ginia Bellafante, *Feminism: It's All About Me!*, TIME, June 29, 1998, at 54, 58; Eliza-beth Cohen, *When Sex and Feminism Mix*, N.Y. POST, May 5, 1998, at 23; Paula Geyh, *Feminism Fatale? 'Bad Girls' Adapt Women's Movement to Suit Themselves*, CHI. TRIB., July 26, 1998 (§ 13), at 1; Joanne Jacobs, *Baby Boomers Busy with Opportunities Won by Feminism*, EVANSVILLE PRESS, July 9, 1998, at 7; Daphne Merkin, *The Marriage Mystique*, NEW YORKER, Aug. 3, 1998, at 70, 71; Kathleen Parker, *Feminism Isn't Dead, Just Bored and Confused*, SUN-SENTINEL (South Florida), June 27, 1998, at 15A; *see also* Steve Strauss, *Women in Business Have Come a Long Way*, NEWS J. (Delaware), May 21, 2012, at A11.

67. Bellafante, *supra* note 66, at 58.

68. Geyh, *supra* note 66, at 1.

69. Michael Skube, *Crittenden's Credo: Only Unhappy Victors in Battle of the Sexes*, ATLANTA J.–CONST., Jan. 31, 1999, at L10 (book review).

70. Kathleen Parker, *Feminism: A Cup that Is Half Full?*, ORLANDO SENTINEL, Oct. 4, 2000, at E1.

71. Kathleen Parker, *Sorry, Gloria, We've Moved on*, WASH. POST, Feb. 10, 2016, at A23; *see also* PAULA KAMEN, FEMINIST FATALE: VOICES FROM THE "TWENTYSOMETHING" GENERATION EXPLORE THE FUTURE OF THE "WOMEN'S MOVEMENT" 2 (1991); Bonnie Erbe, *Women's Work*, ATLANTA CONST., Feb. 6, 1996, at A9.

72. On Boyd's career, see *Ernest Boyd, 59, a Literary Critic*, N.Y. TIMES, Dec. 31, 1946, at 17.

73. Lillian G. Genn, *Woman's Emancipation a False Alarm!*, DAILY HOME NEWS (New Brunswick), Nov. 5, 1931, at 26 (quoting Ernest Boyd) (internal quotation marks omitted).

74. Leland Stowe, *What's Wrong with Our Women?*, ESQUIRE, Sept. 1948, at 31, 93; *see also* "Mr. X," *The Trouble with Women*, PITTSBURGH SUN-TEL., Aug. 30, 1953 (pt. 4), at 2.

75. Olive Carruthers, *A Man's Guide to Curing What's Wrong with Women*, CHI. SUNDAY TRIB., Oct. 21, 1951 (pt. 4), at 8 (book review).

76. For the title of the issue, see *The American Woman: Her Achievements and Troubles*, LIFE, Dec. 24, 1956, at cover (capitalization omitted).

77. Catherine Marshall, *An Introduction by Mrs. Peter Marshall*, LIFE, Dec. 24, 1956, at 2, 2; *see also* Gina Lombroso Ferrero, *Feminism Destructive of Woman's Happiness*, 25 CURRENT HIST. 486 (1927); Eleanor Hart, '*U.S. Wife Can't Match European*,' MIA. HERALD, Jan. 18, 1959, at 32E; Samuel G. Kling, *A Divorce Lawyer on Marriage*, SUNDAY SUN (Baltimore), Nov. 20, 1966 (This Week), at 4; Dolly Reitz, *Mom's Place Is in the Home*, SPOKESMAN-REVIEW (Spokane), Mar. 28, 1956, at 8; Sanford Zalburg, *Do You Control Your Drinking or Does It Control You?*, HONOLULU SUNDAY ADVERTISER, Jan. 22, 1956, at A1.

78. FERDINAND LUNDBERG & MARYNIA F. FARNHAM, MODERN WOMAN: THE LOST SEX 143 (1947). For examples of the book's inclusion on bestseller lists, see *The Best Sellers*, N.Y. TIMES, Oct. 12, 1947 (§ 7), at 8; *The Best Sellers*, N.Y. TIMES, May 18, 1947 (§ 7), at 8.

79. LUNDBERG & FARNHAM, *supra* note 78, at 13.

80. *Id.* at 167.

81. HENDRIK DE LEEUW, WOMAN: THE DOMINANT SEX 10 (1957).

82. ERIC JOHN DINGWALL, THE AMERICAN WOMAN: A HISTORICAL STUDY 132 (1957).

83. Mary Prime, *Emancipation Has Woes; Lady Execs Getting Ulcers*, AUSTIN AM., July 31, 1959, at A9 (quoting Marie Murphy) (internal quotation marks omitted); *see also Women 40 to 60 Who Want to Live Longer Should Slow Down*, VALLEY NEWS & VALLEY GREEN SHEET (Van Nuys), Oct. 6, 1960, at 32C.

84. *See* SHRIDER ET AL., *supra* note 60, at 47 tbl.A-7.

85. *See supra* Chapters 1 & 3.

86. For the first such limits, see Roe v. Wade, 410 U.S. 113, 116–67 (1973), *overruled by* Dobbs v. Jackson Women's Health Org., 597 U.S. 215 (2022).

87. Meryle Secrest, *WANTED: Identity for Today's Woman*, WASH. POST, Apr. 21, 1968, at G17.

88. Ena Naunton, *Hippies' Doctor Now Fights Coke*, MIA. HERALD, Feb. 25, 1982, at 1E (quoting Dr. George Gay) (internal quotation marks omitted).

89. David B. Wilson, *Assessing the Damage When Bonds of Marriage, Home Are Broken*, BOS. GLOBE, Sept. 16, 1986, at 15.

90. *See* Eloise Salholz et al., *Too Late for Prince Charming?*, NEWSWEEK, June 2, 1986, at 54, 55.

91. *Id.* at 61; *see also* Marian Christy, *Shoes: A Woman's Way to Paint a Picture of Herself*, BOS. SUNDAY GLOBE, Mar. 9, 1969 (Women), at A9; Woody Laughnan, *Bachelor Pads: Easier Said Than Done*, FRESNO BEE, Aug. 17, 1976, at C1; Cal Thomas, *Twenty Years of NOW Has Been Far Too Many*, SUNDAY TENNESSEAN, Dec. 7, 1986, at 5H.

92. WILLIAM NOVAK, THE GREAT AMERICAN MAN SHORTAGE AND OTHER ROADBLOCKS TO ROMANCE (AND WHAT TO DO ABOUT IT) 100 (1983).

93. *Id.* at 85. For some of the media coverage, see Rhonda Day, *So the Love Boat Has Sailed Without You*, FRESNO BEE, Dec. 6, 1983, at A15; Jan Heintz, *Book Tells All About Men*, SUNDAY DISPATCH (Moline), Oct. 2, 1983, at 39; Laura Kavesh, *At Last, the Truth Is out: A Good Man Is Hard to Find*, CHI. TRIB., May 15, 1983 (§ 12), at 1; Beverly Stephen, *A Man Explains Why There's a 'Great American Man Shortage,'* CHARLOTTE NEWS, June 6, 1983, at 6B.

94. On the book's sales, see *Best Sellers*, N.Y. TIMES, Dec. 1, 1985 (§ 7), at 40 (reporting thirty-five weeks on bestseller list).

95. CONNELL COWAN & MELVYN KINDER, SMART WOMEN, FOOLISH CHOICES: FINDING THE RIGHT MEN AND AVOIDING THE WRONG ONES 59–60 (1985).

96. *See id.* at xv–xvi, 12–13, 50, 59–61.

97. *Id.* at xv–xvi; *see also* TONI GRANT, BEING A WOMAN: FULFILLING YOUR FEMININITY AND FINDING LOVE 3–10 (1988); MEGAN MARSHALL, THE COST OF LOVING: WOMEN AND THE NEW FEAR OF INTIMACY 217–22 (1984).

98. KAREN LEHRMAN, THE LIPSTICK PROVISO: WOMEN, SEX & POWER IN THE REAL WORLD 154 (1997); *see also id.* at 156–57, 187. For book reviews, see Deirdre English, *Sex, Lies & Feminism*, LA WKLY., July 4, 1997, at 51; Lynn Harris, *Living by the Book*, DAILY NEWS (New York), June 26, 1997, at 51; Paula Kamen, *New Roles*, CHI. TRIB., Aug. 3, 1997 (§ 14), at 5; Laura Miller, *Oppressed by Liberation*, N.Y. TIMES, May 11, 1997 (§ 7), at 11.

99. MICHAEL SEGELL, STANDUP GUY: MANHOOD AFTER FEMINISM 10 (1999).

100. *Id.* at xi.

101. Samantha Parent Walravens, *Introduction* to TORN: TRUE STORIES OF KIDS, CAREER & THE CONFLICT OF MODERN MOTHERHOOD 1, 1–2 (Samantha Parent Walravens ed., 2011).

102. *See* LORI GOTTLIEB, MARRY HIM: THE CASE FOR SETTLING FOR MR. GOOD ENOUGH 7–12 (2010).

103. *Id.* at 43.

104. On Waller's popular writing, see William J. Goode et al., *Willard W. Waller: A Portrait, Introduction* to WILLARD W. WALLER, ON THE FAMILY, EDUCATION, AND WAR: SELECTED WRITINGS 1, 74, 77–78, 99–103 (William J. Goode et al. eds., 1970).

105. For some of the newspapers publishing Waller's essay, see Willard Waller, *The Coming War on Women*, L.A. TIMES, Feb. 18, 1945 (Magazine), at 4; Willard Waller, *The Coming War on Women*, ST. LOUIS GLOBE-DEMOCRAT, Feb. 18, 1945 (Magazine), at 4; Willard Waller, *The Coming War on Women*, SUNDAY STAR (D.C.), Feb. 18, 1945 (Magazine), at 4. For discussion of historical precursors, see *supra* Chapter 1.

106. Agnes E. Meyer, *Women Aren't Men*, ATLANTIC, Aug. 1950, at 32, 32, 34–35.

107. *Id.* at 34.

108. HELEN SHERMAN & MARJORIE COE, THE CHALLENGE OF BEING A WOMAN: UNDERSTANDING OURSELVES AND OUR CHILDREN 16, 18 (1955).

109. *Id.* at 18.

110. *Id.* at 6.

111. *Id.* at 45.

112. David R. Mace with Evan McLeod Wylie, *What Do You Want from Your Marriage Today*, WOMAN'S HOME COMPANION, Apr. 1956, at 29, 79.

113. Editorial, *More Working Women*, SHREVEPORT TIMES, June 15, 1967, at 8A (internal quotation marks omitted).

114. *CBS Evening News* (CBS television broadcast Aug. 26, 1970). On the strike, see *supra* Chapter 2.

115. Max Lerner, *American Women Entering Postfeminist Period*, CAP. J. (Salem), Feb. 6, 1974 (§ 1), at 5.

116. Karen Lehrman, *Has Sexual Correctness Gone Too Far? Yes: Hang-ups over Flirting Only Trivialize Real Problems*, USA TODAY, Apr. 4, 1994, at 15A.

117. Ruben Navarrette Jr., *Review on Moms' Juggling Mixed*, ALBUQUERQUE J., July 29, 2002, at A6.

118. ROSCOE LEWIS ASHLEY, AMERICAN HISTORY: FOR USE IN SECONDARY SCHOOLS 543–44 (1907) (internal quotation marks omitted).

119. WILBUR F. GORDY, A HISTORY OF THE UNITED STATES FOR SCHOOLS 443 (new ed. 1913); *see also* REUBEN POST HALLECK, HISTORY OF OUR COUNTRY FOR HIGHER GRADES 472 (1923); ELEANOR E. RIGGS, AN AMERICAN HISTORY 295 (1916); CHARLES L. ROBBINS WITH ELMER GREEN, SCHOOL HISTORY OF THE AMERICAN PEOPLE 530 (1925). On Ivy League colleges with male-only admissions policies until the late 1960s or early 1970s, see MALKIEL, *supra* note 31, at 31–306, 441–88.

120. ALBERT BUSHNELL HART, NEW AMERICAN HISTORY 638 (1917); *see also* WILLIAM A. MOWRY & ARTHUR MAY MOWRY, FIRST STEPS IN THE HISTORY OF OUR COUNTRY 285, 290–91 (1899).

121. On suffrage, see *Victory Map of 1918*, 3 WOMAN CITIZEN 570, 570–71 (1918).

122. *See supra* Chapters 1 & 3.

123. GRACE A. TURKINGTON, MY COUNTRY: A TEXTBOOK IN CIVICS AND PATRIOTISM FOR YOUNG AMERICANS 336 (1918); *see also id.* at 85, 150.

124. WADDY THOMPSON, A HISTORY OF THE PEOPLE OF THE UNITED STATES 300 (1919); *see also* WILLIAM ESTABROOK CHANCELLOR, HISTORY AND GOVERNMENT OF THE UNITED STATES FOR EVENING SCHOOLS 63 (1905).

125. ROLLA M. TRYON ET AL., THE AMERICAN NATION YESTERDAY AND TODAY 267 (1930).

126. WILLIAM A. HAMM, THE AMERICAN PEOPLE 575–76 (1938); *see also id.* at 578–79; WILLIAM A. HAMM, FROM COLONY TO WORLD POWER: A HISTORY OF THE UNITED STATES 282, 443–46 (1947) [hereinafter HAMM, FROM COLONY TO WORLD POWER]. On sex discrimination in employment, see *supra* Chapters 1 & 3.

127. *See Employment of Married Women as Teachers*, 10 RSCH. BULL. NAT'L EDUC. ASS'N 14, 20 tbl.6 (1932).

128. *See* WOMEN WORKERS THROUGH THE DEPRESSION: A STUDY OF WHITE COLLAR EMPLOYMENT MADE BY THE AMERICAN WOMAN'S ASSOCIATION 104 (Lorine Pruette ed., 1934).

129. *See* Act of June 30, 1932, Pub. L. No. 72-212, § 213, 47 Stat. 382, 406, *repealed by* Act of July 26, 1937, Pub. L. No. 75-212, 50 Stat. 533.

130. *See* WOMEN'S BUREAU, U.S. DEP'T OF LAB., EFFECTS OF DISMISSING MARRIED PERSONS FROM THE CIVIL SERVICE 3 (1936); WOMEN'S BUREAU, U.S. DEP'T OF LAB., GAINFUL EMPLOYMENT OF MARRIED WOMEN 16 (1936).

131. *See The Fortune Quarterly Survey: VI*, 14 FORTUNE 130, 222, 224 (1936).

132. George Gallup, *America Speaks: Majority Against Married Women Having Jobs*, RICHMOND TIMES-DISPATCH, Nov. 15, 1936 (§ IV), at 1 (internal quotation marks omitted).

133. FREMONT P. WIRTH, UNITED STATES HISTORY 194 (1949); *see also id.* at 689–90; CARL RUSSELL FISH, HISTORY OF AMERICA 505, 556 (1925).

134. JOHN D. HICKS, A SHORT HISTORY OF AMERICAN DEMOCRACY 652 (1949); *see also* ARTHUR MEIER SCHLESINGER, POLITICAL AND SOCIAL HISTORY OF THE UNITED STATES, 1829–1925, at 316 (1925).

135. For more discussion of these decisions, see *supra* Chapter 3.

136. MELVILLE FREEMAN, THE STORY OF OUR REPUBLIC, pt. II, at 306 (Eston V. Tubbs ed., 1938) (emphasis omitted).

137. LEON H. CANFIELD ET AL., THE UNITED STATES IN THE MAKING 604–05 (1948) (capitalization omitted); *see also* LEON H. CANFIELD & HOWARD B. WILDER, THE MAKING OF MODERN AMERICA 592 (Howard R. Anderson et al. eds., 1964).

138. LELAND D. BALDWIN & MARY WARRING, HISTORY OF OUR REPUBLIC 508 (1965); *see also* SMITH BURNHAM, THE MAKING OF OUR COUNTRY: A HISTORY OF THE UNITED STATES FOR SCHOOLS 528–29, 597 (1920); LILLIAN P. CLARK, BUREAU OF NATURALIZATION, U.S. DEP'T OF LAB., FEDERAL TEXTBOOK ON CITIZENSHIP TRAINING, PART III: OUR NATION 92 (1926); LOUIS B. WRIGHT ET AL., THE DEMOCRATIC EXPERIENCE: A SHORT AMERICAN HISTORY 363 (1963).

139. WILLIAM J. LONG, AMERICA: A HISTORY OF OUR COUNTRY 302 (1923).

140. EUGENE C. BARKER ET AL., THE BUILDING OF OUR NATION 264 (1948); *see also id.* at 659–61.

141. Declaration of Sentiments (1848), *reprinted in* 1 HISTORY OF WOMAN SUFFRAGE 70, 70–73 (Elizabeth Cady Stanton et al. eds., New York, Fowler & Wells 1881).

142. PAUL F. BOLLER, JR. & E. JEAN TILFORD, THIS IS OUR NATION 259–60 (1961); *see also* CHARLES A. BEARD & WILLIAM C. BAGLEY, THE HISTORY OF THE AMERICAN PEOPLE 339 (rev. ed. 1924); CHARLES A. BEARD & MARY R. BEARD, HISTORY OF THE UNITED STATES 555, 560, 562–64 (1921); WILLIAM BACKUS GUITTEAU, THE HISTORY OF THE UNITED STATES: A TEXTBOOK FOR SECONDARY SCHOOLS 321 (1924); HAMM, FROM COLONY TO WORLD POWER, *supra* note 126, at 282; SCHLESINGER, *supra* note 134, at 75; SOCIAL AND ECONOMIC FORCES IN AMERICAN HISTORY 352 (Albert Bushnell Hart ed., 1915).

143. BARKER ET AL., *supra* note 140, at 660.

144. JAMES A. FROST ET AL., A HISTORY OF THE UNITED STATES: THE EVOLUTION OF A FREE PEOPLE 398 (1968); *see also* NATHANIEL WRIGHT STEPHENSON & MARTHA TUCKER STEPHENSON, A SCHOOL HISTORY OF THE UNITED STATES 510–11 (1921).

145. *See, e.g.,* Carrie Chapman Catt, *Ready for Citizenship,* 20 PUBLIC 817, 817–18 (1917).

146. *See, e.g.,* 56 CONG. REC. 10,928–29 (1918) (statement of President Woodrow Wilson).

147. *See* 58 CONG. REC. 635 (1919).

148. *See* MAUD WOOD PARK, FRONT DOOR LOBBY 19, 35 (Edna Lamprey Stantial ed., 1960).

149. *Id.* at 268.

150. *See id.* at 268, 270–71.

151. *See* SUBCOMM. ON THE CONSTITUTION OF THE S. COMM. ON THE JUDICIARY, AMENDMENTS TO THE CONSTITUTION: A BRIEF LEGISLATIVE HISTORY, S. PRINT NO. 99-87, at 57 (1985).

152. *See* ELAINE WEISS, THE WOMAN'S HOUR: THE GREAT FIGHT TO WIN THE VOTE 1–324 (2018); A. Elizabeth Taylor, *Tennessee: The Thirty-Sixth State, in* VOTES FOR WOMEN! THE WOMAN SUFFRAGE MOVEMENT IN TENNESSEE, THE SOUTH, AND THE NATION 53, 60–66 (Marjorie Spruill Wheeler ed., 1995); Carol Lynn Yellin, *Showdown in Tennessee, in* CAROL LYNN YELLIN & JANANN SHERMAN, THE PERFECT 36: TENNESSEE DELIVERS WOMAN SUFFRAGE 75, 81–108 (Ilene Jones-Cornwell ed., 1998).

153. *See* WEISS, *supra* note 152, at 297–308; Taylor, *supra* note 152, at 64; Yellin, *supra* note 152, at 106.

154. JOHN A. GARRATY, THE STORY OF AMERICA 163 (1991); *see also* WILFRED M. MCCLAY, LAND OF HOPE: AN INVITATION TO THE GREAT AMERICAN STORY 34 (2019).

155. 2 JAMES A. BANKS ET AL., UNITED STATES: ADVENTURES IN TIME AND PLACE 588 (Teacher's Multimedia ed. 2001) (internal quotation marks omitted). For the United Press news story the textbook quoted, see *Marchers for "the Cause" in Vast Pageant*, PITTSBURG PRESS, May 5, 1912, at 1. For discussion of mob violence at the 1913 suffrage parade, see *supra* Chapter 1.

156. DANIEL J. BOORSTIN ET AL., A HISTORY OF THE UNITED STATES 473 (1981).

157. ROBERT A. DIVINE ET AL., AMERICA PAST AND PRESENT 785 (9th ed. 2011).

158. *See* ARIANE HEGEWISCH ET AL., INST. FOR WOMEN'S POL'Y RSCH., PUB. NO. C527, GENDER AND RACIAL WAGE GAPS WORSENED IN 2023 AND PAY EQUITY STILL DECADES AWAY 1 (2024).

159. EMMA J. LAPSANSKY-WERNER ET AL., UNITED STATES HISTORY 425 (2009) [hereinafter LAPSANSKY-WERNER ET AL., UNITED STATES HISTORY]; *see also* EMMA J. LAPSANSKY-WERNER ET AL., UNITED STATES HISTORY: MODERN AMERICA 91 (2009) [hereinafter LAPSANSKY-WERNER ET AL., MODERN AMERICA].

160. BANKS ET AL., *supra* note 155, at 588.

161. P. SCOTT CORBETT ET AL., U.S. HISTORY 601 (2017); *see also id.* at 676, 709.

162. JAMES L. ROARK ET AL., THE AMERICAN PROMISE: A HISTORY OF THE UNITED STATES 725 (3d ed. 2005); *see also* JOYCE APPLEBY ET AL., DISCOVERING OUR PAST: A HISTORY OF THE UNITED STATES 417 (2014) [hereinafter APPLEBY ET AL., DISCOVERING OUR PAST]; JOYCE APPLEBY ET AL., THE AMERICAN VISION 204, 551, 927 (2003) [hereinafter APPLEBY ET AL., THE AMERICAN VISION]; SARAH BEDNARZ ET AL., BUILD OUR NATION 394, 538 (1997); ALAN BRINKLEY, AMERICAN HISTORY: CONNECTING WITH THE PAST 576 (14th ed. 2012); BENJAMIN GINSBERG ET AL., WE THE PEOPLE: AN INTRODUCTION TO AMERICAN POLITICS 55, 142, 267 (14th ed. 2023); MCCLAY, *supra* note 154, at 290; GEORGE MCKENNA, THE DRAMA OF DEMOCRACY: AMERICAN GOVERNMENT AND POLITICS 55 (3d ed. 1998); IMMIGR. & NATURALIZATION SERV., U.S. DEP'T OF JUST., UNITED STATES HISTORY, 1600–1987: LEVEL I, at 112 (1987); IMMIGR. & NATURALIZATION SERV., U.S. DEP'T OF JUST., UNITED STATES HISTORY, 1600–1987: LEVEL II, at 101 (1987).

163. BOORSTIN ET AL., *supra* note 156, at 473.

164. On voting, see *supra* Chapters 1 & 3; *infra* Chapter 5.

165. *See* APPLEBY ET AL., DISCOVERING OUR PAST, *supra* note 162, at 825; APPLEBY ET AL., THE AMERICAN VISION, *supra* note 162, at 927–28; BRINKLEY, *supra* note 162, at 845; RICHARD C. BROWN & HERBERT J. BASS, ONE FLAG, ONE LAND 695 (1985); CORBETT ET AL., *supra* note 161, at 866, 881; DIVINE ET AL., *supra* note 157, at 769; LAPSANSKY-WERNER ET AL., UNITED STATES HISTORY, *supra* note 159, at 526, 1025; LAPSANSKY-WERNER ET AL., MODERN AMERICA, *supra* note 159, at 91, 513, 577; MCKENNA, *supra* note 162, at 154, 157; NORMAN K. RISJORD, HISTORY OF THE AMERICAN PEOPLE 752 (1986); ROARK ET AL., *supra* note 162, at 1036.

166. BOORSTIN ET AL., *supra* note 156, at 709; *see also* ROARK ET AL., *supra* note 162, at 1055.

167. *See* 417 U.S. 484, 496 n.20 (1974).

168. *See* 442 U.S. 256, 274–81 (1979).

Chapter 5

1. Wills v. Jones, 13 App. D.C. 482, 495 (1898); Appeal of Robinson, 33 A. 652, 654 (Me. 1895); Cummings v. Everett, 19 A. 456, 456 (Me. 1890); Bradley v. State, 1 Miss. (1 Walker) 156, 158 (1824); Hammond v. Corbett, 50 N.H. 501, 506 (1872); *see also* Cap. Traction Co. v. Rockwell, 17 App. D.C. 369, 379 (1901); Yost v. Grand Trunk Ry. Co., 128 N.W. 784, 786 (Mich. 1910); Rivard v. Mo. Pac. Ry. Co., 165 S.W. 763, 767 (Mo. 1914) (in banc); Trinity Cnty. Lumber Co. v. Conner, 187 S.W. 1022, 1024 (Tex. Civ. App. 1916); Schultz v. Christopher, 118 P. 629, 629 (Wash. 1911).

2. Charauleau v. Woffenden, 25 P. 652, 656 (Ariz. 1876).

3. Sturgineger v. Hannah, 11 S.C.L. (2 Nott & McC.) 147, 148–49 (1819); *see also* Smith v. Meyers, 74 N.W. 277, 278 (Neb. 1898).

4. Ziady v. Curley, 396 F.2d 873, 876 (4th Cir. 1968); Brandt v. Keller, 109 N.E.2d 729, 730 (Ill. 1952); Deshotel v. Atchison, Topeka & Santa Fe Ry. Co., 319 P.2d 357, 358 (Cal. Dist. Ct. App. 1957) (word misspelled in original); *see also In re* Gutierrez, 33 F.2d 987, 989 (S.D. Tex. 1929); Conley v. Conley, 15 P.2d 922, 923 (Mont. 1932).

5. Werthan Bag Corp. v. Agnew, 202 F.2d 119, 124 (6th Cir. 1953); Thill v. Mod. Erecting Co., 170 N.W.2d 865, 868 (Minn. 1969); Ekalo v. Constructive Serv. Corp. of Am., 215 A.2d 1, 3 (N.J. 1965).

6. Gregg v. Gregg, 87 A.2d 581, 583 (Md. 1952).

7. Peters v. Alsup, 95 F. Supp. 684, 691 (D. Haw. 1951); Follansbee v. Benzenberg, 265 P.2d 183, 189 (Cal. Dist. Ct. App. 1954); Acuff v. Schmit, 78 N.W.2d 480, 484 (Iowa 1956); People v. Morton, 132 N.Y.S.2d 302, 306 (App. Div. 1954).

8. Taylor v. Milam, 89 F. Supp. 880, 882 (W.D. Ark. 1950); West v. City of San Diego, 353 P.2d 929, 933 (Cal. 1960) (in bank); *In re* Littauer's Estate, 135 N.Y.S.2d 582, 587 (App. Div. 1954); Courtney v. Courtney, 87 P.2d 660, 669 (Okla. 1938); McDonnell v. Miller, 133 S.W.2d 142, 144 (Tex. Civ. App. 1939).

9. Crowell v. Crowell, 105 S.E. 206, 210 (N.C. 1920).

10. United States v. Dege, 364 U.S. 51, 52, 54 (1960); *see also* Trammel v. United States, 445 U.S. 40, 44 (1980).

11. *See* Reed v. Reed, 404 U.S. 71, 71–77 (1971).

12. Schlesinger v. Ballard, 419 U.S. 498, 508 (1975).

13. Sessions v. Morales-Santana, 582 U.S. 47, 72 n.21 (2017) (citation and internal quotation marks omitted); J.E.B. v. Alabama, 511 U.S. 127, 131, 135 (1994) (citation and internal quotation marks omitted); Cal. Fed. Sav. & Loan Ass'n v. Guerra, 479 U.S. 272, 290 (1987); Roberts v. U.S. Jaycees, 468 U.S. 609, 625 (1984); Heckler v. Mathews, 465 U.S. 728, 739, 744–45, 750 (1984) (citations and internal quotation marks omitted); Miss. Univ. for Women v. Hogan, 458 U.S. 718, 725, 730 n.16 (1982); Rostker v. Goldberg, 453 U.S. 57, 67 (1981) (citation and internal quotation marks omitted); *Trammel*, 445 U.S. at 52; Califano v. Westcott, 443 U.S. 76, 81 (1979) (citation and internal quotation marks omitted); Parham v. Hughes, 441 U.S. 347, 355 (1979) (plurality opinion) (citation and internal quotation marks omitted); Califano v. Webster, 430 U.S. 313, 317 (1977) (per curiam) (citation and internal quotation marks omitted); Califano v. Goldfarb, 430 U.S. 199, 207, 211, 217 (1977) (plurality opinion) (citations and internal quotation marks omitted); Craig v. Boren, 429 U.S. 190, 198 (1976) (citation and internal quotation marks omitted); Weinberger v. Wiesenfeld, 420 U.S. 636, 643 (1975) (citation and internal quotation marks omitted).

14. *J.E.B.*, 511 U.S. at 135 (citation and internal quotation marks omitted); *Miss. Univ. for Women*, 458 U.S. at 726; *Craig*, 429 U.S. at 198.

15. *Parham*, 441 U.S. at 355 (plurality opinion).

16. *J.E.B.*, 511 U.S. at 135, 139 n.11 (citations and internal quotation marks omitted); City of Cleburne v. Cleburne Living Ctr., Inc., 473 U.S. 432, 441 (1985); Corning Glass Works v. Brennan, 417 U.S. 188, 195 (1974) (citation and internal quotation marks omitted).

17. *Heckler*, 465 U.S. at 745 (citation and internal quotation marks omitted); *Parham*, 441 U.S. at 354 (plurality opinion) (citation and internal quotation marks omitted); Orr v. Orr, 440 U.S. 268, 279 (1979) (citation and internal quotation marks omitted); *Goldfarb*, 430 U.S. at 207, 211 (plurality opinion) (citations and internal quotation marks omitted); *Craig*, 429 U.S. at 198 (citation and internal quotation marks omitted); Stanton v. Stanton, 421 U.S. 7, 14 (1975) (internal quotation marks omitted).

18. *See* Dobbs v. Jackson Women's Health Org., 597 U.S. 215, 231 (2022).

19. 453 U.S. 57, 83 (1981).

20. For the law establishing the modern registration system, see Selective Service Act of 1948, Pub. L. No. 80-759, § 3, 62 Stat. 604, 605.

21. For brief references to the issue, see *Sundry Legislation Affecting the Naval and Military Establishments: Hearings Before the H. Comm. on Armed Servs.*, 80th Cong. 6659–60 (1948) (discussion between Rep. Cecil Bishop, Secretary of Defense James Forrestal, and Secretary of the Army Kenneth Royall); 94 CONG. REC. 4717 (1948) (statement of Rep. Joseph Bryson); *id.* at 6970 (discussion between Rep. Francis Case and Rep. Edith Rogers); *id.* at 8358–59 (statement of Rep. Robert Doughton); *id.* at 8385 (statement of Rep. Helen Douglas); *id.* at 8659 (statement of Rep. Robert Rich).

22. *To Establish the Women's Army Corps in the Regular Army, to Authorize the Enlistment and Appointment of Women in the Regular Navy and Marine Corps and the Naval and Marine Corps Reserve, and for Other Purposes: Hearings on S. 1641 Before the Subcomm. on Org. & Mobilization of the H. Comm. on Armed Servs.*, 80th Cong. 5564 (1948) (statement of General Dwight D. Eisenhower). For congressmen quoting or paraphrasing Eisenhower, see 94 CONG. REC. 4694 (1948) (statement of Rep. Paul Shafer); *id.* at 4696 (statement of Rep. Overton Brooks); *id.* at 6967 (statement of Rep. William Cole).

23. *See Women's Armed Services Integration Act of 1947: Hearings on S. 1103, S. 1527, and S. 1641 Before the S. Comm. on Armed Servs.*, 80th Cong. 97–98 (1947) (statement of Sen. Leverett Saltonstall); 94 CONG. REC. 6968–69 (1948) (discussion between Rep. Ellsworth Buck and Rep. Overton Brooks).

24. *Women's Armed Services Integration Act of 1947, supra* note 23, at 67 (statement of Rear Admiral T.L. Sprague); *see also id.* at 98 (statement of Rear Admiral T.L. Sprague); *id.* at 67, 97–98 (statement of Colonel Mary Hallaren); *id.* at 98 (statement of Captain Joy Hancock).

25. For 1960s or 1970s opinions upholding women's exclusion from military registration and conscription while offering little or no explanation, see United States v. Reiser, 532 F.2d 673, 673 (9th Cir. 1976); United States v. Baechler, 509 F.2d 13, 14–15 (4th Cir. 1974) (per curiam); United States v. Bertram, 477 F.2d 1329, 1330 (10th Cir. 1973); United States v. Camara, 451 F.2d 1122, 1126 (1st Cir. 1971); United States v. Fallon, 407 F.2d 621, 623 (7th Cir. 1969); United States v. Offord, 373 F. Supp. 1117, 1118–19 (E.D. Wis. 1974); United States v. Dorris, 319 F. Supp. 1306, 1308 (W.D. Pa. 1970); United States v. Clinton, 310 F. Supp. 333, 336 (E.D. La. 1970); Suskin v. Nixon, 304 F. Supp. 71, 72 (N.D. Ill. 1969).

26. 291 F. Supp. 122, 124–25 (S.D.N.Y. 1968). For decisions quoting *St. Clair*, see United States v. Yingling, 368 F. Supp. 379, 386 (W.D. Pa. 1973); United States v. Cook, 311 F. Supp. 618, 621–22 (W.D. Pa. 1970).

27. *St. Clair*, 291 F. Supp. at 124 (quoting Hoyt v. Florida, 368 U.S. 57, 62 (1961)) (internal quotation marks omitted). For more discussion of *Hoyt*, see *supra* Chapter 3.

28. *St. Clair*, 291 F. Supp. at 125.

29. *Sex Discrimination by Draft Is Charged*, N.Y. TIMES, July 17, 1968, at 37 (quoting Dudley Bonsal) (internal quotation marks omitted).

30. *See* Act of Sept. 28, 1971, Pub. L. No. 92-129, § 101(a)(35), 85 Stat. 348, 353 (ending statutory authorization for the draft as of July 1, 1973); David E. Rosenbaum, *Nation Ends Draft, Turns to Volunteers*, N.Y. TIMES, Jan. 28, 1973, at 1 (Defense Secretary announcing draft's termination); Proclamation No. 4360, 3 C.F.R. 462 (1971–1975) (March 29, 1975, proclamation terminating registration).

31. *See* Jimmy Carter, Selective Service Revitalization: Statement on the Registration of Americans for the Draft, 1 PUB. PAPERS 289, 289–91 (Feb. 8, 1980).

32. On Carter's Navy career, see JONATHAN ALTER, HIS VERY BEST: JIMMY CARTER, A LIFE 52–91 (2020). On Carter's support for the ERA, see Jimmy Carter, Equal Rights Amendment: Remarks on Signing H.J. Res. 638, 2 PUB. PAPERS 1800, 1801 (Oct. 20, 1978).

33. *See* Carter, *supra* note 31, at 289; H. COMM. ON ARMED SERVS., 96TH CONG., PRESIDENTIAL RECOMMENDATIONS FOR SELECTIVE SERVICE REFORM: A REPORT TO CONGRESS PREPARED PURSUANT TO P.L. 96-107, at 20–23 (Comm. Print 1980).

34. Carter, *supra* note 31, at 290–91.

35. *See infra* Chapter 6.

36. *See* Act of June 27, 1980, Pub. L. No. 96-282, 94 Stat. 552, 552. For Carter's July 2, 1980, proclamation reinstating male-only registration, see Proclamation No. 4771, 3 C.F.R. 82 (1980).

37. *See* Rostker v. Goldberg, 453 U.S. 57, 59 (1981).

38. *See* Complaint at 2–11, Rowland v. Tarr, 341 F. Supp. 339 (E.D. Pa. 1972) (No. 71-1480) (complaint filed June 16, 1971). For more on the plaintiffs and their main lawyer, see Gregory J. Stone, *A One-Man Army Tackles the Draft*, NAT'L L.J., Aug. 11, 1980, at 1.

39. For the suit's procedural history from 1971 to 1980, see Goldberg v. Tarr, 510 F. Supp. 292, 292–94 (E.D. Pa. 1980).

40. *See* Rowland v. Tarr, 480 F.2d 545, 546–47 (3d Cir. 1973) (per curiam).

41. *See id.* at 547.

42. *See* Craig v. Boren, 429 U.S. 190, 197 (1976).

43. *See* Goldberg v. Rostker, 509 F. Supp. 586, 605 (E.D. Pa. 1980), *rev'd*, 453 U.S. 57 (1981).

44. *See* Rostker v. Goldberg, 453 U.S. 57, 83 (1981).

45. *See id.* at 59–72.

46. *Id.* at 72–74.

47. *Id.* at 75.

48. *Id.* at 74 (emphasis added) (citation and internal quotation marks omitted).

49. *Id.* at 72 (citation and internal quotation marks omitted).

50. *Id.* at 74 (citation and internal quotation marks omitted); *see also id.* at 61.

51. *See* S. REP. No. 96-826, at 156–61 (1980).

52. *See Rostker*, 453 U.S. at 60 n.1, 64–65, 68, 69 n.6, 73, 75–82, 78 n.14.

53. S. REP. No. 96-826, at 160–61 (capitalization omitted).

54. *Id.* at 159.

55. *Id.* Senator John Warner also read these passages into the *Congressional Record. See* 126 Cong. Rec. 13,880–81 (1980) (statement of Sen. John Warner).

56. 126 Cong. Rec. 13,894 (statement of Sen. Sam Nunn).

57. *Department of Defense Authorization for Appropriations for Fiscal Year 1981: Hearings on S. 2294 Before the S. Comm. on Armed Servs. (pt. 3),* 96th Cong. 1691–92 (1980) (statement of Sen. Sam Nunn); *see also id.* at 1694 (statement of Sen. Sam Nunn).

58. 126 Cong. Rec. 13,885 (statement of Sen. John Warner); *see also id.* at 13,885, 13,895 (statement of Sen. Carl Levin).

59. *Military Posture and Department of Defense Authorization for Appropriations for Fiscal Year 1981 and Armed Forces Educational Assistance Act of 1980: Hearings on H.R. 6495 [H.R. 6974] and H.R. 7266 Before the H. Comm. on Armed Servs. (pt. 5),* 96th Cong. 145 (1980) (statement of Rep. Marjorie Holt); *see also id.* at 143 (statement of Rep. Marjorie Holt).

60. 126 Cong. Rec. 13,888–89 (statement of Sen. Jake Garn).

61. *Id.* at 13,889 (statement of Sen. Jake Garn).

62. *See* 117 Cong. Rec. 46,197 (1971).

63. For publication of the memo, see *Rehnquist: ERA Would Threaten Family Unit,* Legal Times, Sept. 15, 1986, at 4, 4–5.

64. *See* Rostker v. Goldberg, 453 U.S. 57, 74 (1981).

65. *See* 450 U.S. 464, 466–67, 471 n.6 (1981) (plurality opinion).

66. *See* Act of Apr. 16, 1850, ch. 99, § 47, 1850 Cal. Stat. 229, 234.

67. *See id.;* Act of Mar. 16, 1889, ch. 191, § 1, 1889 Cal. Stat. 223, 223; Act of Mar. 27, 1897, ch. 139, § 1, 1897 Cal. Stat. 201, 201; Act of May 19, 1913, ch. 122, § 1, 1913 Cal. Stat. 212, 212; *Michael M.,* 450 U.S. at 466 (plurality opinion).

68. Cal. Penal Code § 261(1) note at 111 (Creed Haymond & John C. Burch annotators, San Francisco, A.L. Bancroft & Co. 1st ed. 1874).

69. 39 P. 607, 608 (Cal. 1895).

70. *Id.; see also* People v. Laurintz, 46 P. 613, 613 (Cal. 1896) (quoting these passages from *Verdegreen*).

71. 393 P.2d 673, 674 (Cal. 1964) (in bank).

72. *Id.; see also* People v. Courtney, 4 Cal. Rptr. 274, 276 (Dist. Ct. App. 1960).

73. People v. Mackey, 120 Cal. Rptr. 157, 160 (Ct. App. 1975).

74. *See* Petition for Hearing at 2 & n.1, 5, 11–19, McMillan v. Superior Court, 601 P.2d 572 (Cal. 1979) (in bank) (No. S.F. 23929).

75. For McMillan's lawyers using his full name, see *id.* at 1. For examples from the years of news reports identifying McMillan, see *Judge Won't Rule out Statutory Rape Law,* Press Democrat (Santa Rosa), Aug. 22, 1978, at 9A; *High Court to Argue RP Sex Case,* Argus-Courier (Petaluma), Oct. 22, 1980, at 9A.

76. *See* Transcript of Preliminary Hearing (Cal. Mun. Ct. July 13, 1978) (testimony of Sharon), *reprinted in* Joint Appendix at 19–23, 29–30, 32–33, Michael M. v. Superior Ct., 450 U.S. 464 (1981) (No. 79-1344).

77. *Id.* at 22 (testimony of Sharon).

78. *Id.* at 21 (testimony of Sharon).

79. *See* John Purroy, *Rape Suspect Fails to Show for Hearing,* Press Democrat (Santa Rosa), Apr. 14, 1981, at 1B.

80. Michael M. v. Superior Ct., 601 P.2d 572, 574 (Cal. 1979) (in bank), *aff'd*, 450 U.S. 464 (1981).
81. *Michael M.*, 450 U.S. at 467 (plurality opinion).
82. 410 U.S. 113, 116–67 (1973), *overruled by* Dobbs v. Jackson Women's Health Org., 597 U.S. 215 (2022). On Blackmun's reputation, see Joan Biskupic, *Justice Blackmun Dies, Leaving Rights Legacy*, WASH. POST, Mar. 5, 1999, at A1; Linda Greenhouse, *Justice Blackmun, Author of Abortion Right, Dies*, N.Y. TIMES, Mar. 5, 1999, at A1; David G. Savage, *Blackmun, Author of Roe Vs. Wade, Dies*, L.A. TIMES, Mar. 5, 1999, at A1.
83. *Michael M.*, 450 U.S. at 483 (Blackmun, J., concurring in the judgment).
84. *See id.* at 483 n.*.
85. *Id.* at 483–85.
86. *See Shop Clerk Attacked, RP Man, 18, Arrested*, PRESS DEMOCRAT (Santa Rosa), Dec. 21, 1978, at 11A.
87. *See* John Purroy, *Michael: Other Brushes with the Law*, PRESS DEMOCRAT (Santa Rosa), Oct. 12, 1980, at 1B.
88. *See Shop Clerk Attacked, RP Man, 18, Arrested*, *supra* note 86, at 11A.
89. *See* Purroy, *supra* note 87, at 1B.
90. *See* Michael M. v. Superior Ct., 601 P.2d 572, 573–76 (Cal. 1979) (in bank), *aff'd*, 450 U.S. 464, 466–76 (1981) (plurality opinion).
91. *See* 601 P.2d at 573.
92. Assemb. B. 1588 § 21, 1979–80 Reg. Sess. (Cal. 1979). For Knox's party affiliation, see 1 CAL. LEG., 1979–80 REG. SESS., ASSEMBLY FINAL HISTORY 4.
93. Coleman E. Stewart, *Thoughts of a Retired Judge*, NEWS MESSENGER (Lincoln), Oct. 11, 1979, at 2. On Stewart, see *Coleman E. Stewart*, LINCOLN NEWS MESSENGER, Oct. 10, 1991, at 7.
94. *See* W.B. Rood, *GOP, Democrats in 'War of Letters,'* L.A. TIMES, Dec. 5, 1979 (pt. I), at 3. On Nolan's career, see *Assembly Gets New GOP Leader*, SALINAS CALIFORNIAN, Nov. 9, 1984, at 5.
95. Rood, *supra* note 94, at 3 (quoting letter) (internal quotation marks omitted).
96. *See* Editorial, *Cheap Shot from the CRA*, SACRAMENTO BEE, Dec. 10, 1979, at B10.
97. *See id.*; Rood, *supra* note 94, at 3.
98. *See* CAL. LEG., *supra* note 92, at 988.
99. On Watson, see Claudia Luther, *Diane Watson: Seasoning of a Warrior*, L.A. TIMES, Apr. 7, 1980 (pt. I), at 3.
100. *See* S.B. 2045 § 1, 1979–80 Reg. Sess. (Cal. 1980).
101. *See* CAL. LEG., 1979–80 REG. SESS., SENATE FINAL HISTORY 1160.
102. On McCarthy, see CAL. LEG., *supra* note 92, at 5.
103. *See* Preprint Assemb. B. 20 § 24, 1979–80 Reg. Sess. (Cal. 1980).
104. *See* Editorial, *Revision of Sexual Assault Laws*, CHINO CHAMPION, July 18, 1980, at 13; Editorial, *Act of Violence*, CHULA VISTA STAR-NEWS, July 27, 1980, at C8; *see also* John Purroy, *Hearing Date Set for Sex Law*, PRESS DEMOCRAT (Santa Rosa), Oct. 20, 1980, at 2A.
105. *See* Editorial, *Sex and the Sexes*, SACRAMENTO BEE, Mar. 25, 1981, at B6.
106. *See* Michael M. v. Superior Ct., 450 U.S. 464, 476 (1981) (plurality opinion).
107. *Id.* at 471 n.6.
108. *Id.* (citation and internal quotation marks omitted).

109. *Id.* (internal quotation marks omitted).
110. For a 1978 case where California made this argument, see People v. McKellar, 146 Cal. Rptr. 327, 331 (Ct. App. 1978). For California advancing this argument in McMillan's case, see *Michael M.*, 450 U.S. at 470 (plurality opinion).
111. *See Michael M.*, 450 U.S. at 470–76 (plurality opinion).
112. *Id.* at 473 (emphasis added).
113. *Id.* at 476 (citation and internal quotation marks omitted).
114. *Id.* at 473.
115. *See Teen Sex Upheld as Male Crime*, PRESS DEMOCRAT (Santa Rosa), Mar. 23, 1981, at 1A.
116. *See R.P. Rape Case Figure Missing, Says Attorney*, PRESS DEMOCRAT (Santa Rosa), Mar. 31, 1981, at 2A; Purroy, *supra* note 79, at 1B.
117. *See* Bony Saludes, *Six-Year-Old Teen Rape Case May Fizzle Without Victim*, PRESS DEMO-CRAT (Santa Rosa), Oct. 12, 1984, at 2A.
118. *See* Bony Saludes, *Charge Dropped in Teen Sex Trial*, PRESS DEMOCRAT (Santa Rosa), Oct. 16, 1984, at 3A.
119. *See* Act of Sept. 29, 1993, ch. 596, § 1, 1993 Cal. Stat. 3139, 3139–40.
120. 467 U.S. 69 (1984).
121. *See id.* at 71–72; Brief of Petitioner at 2–3, Hishon v. King & Spalding, 467 U.S. 69 (1984) (No. 82-940).
122. *See Hishon*, 467 U.S. at 72; Complaint (Feb. 22, 1980), *reprinted in* Joint Appendix at 6–15, Hishon v. King & Spalding, 467 U.S. 69 (1984) (No. 82-940).
123. Connie Bruck, Hishon v. King & Spalding: *The Case No One Will Win*, AM. LAW., Nov. 1983, at 101, 106 (quoting Elizabeth Anderson Hishon) (internal quotation marks omitted). On Hishon's legal specialty, see *id.* at 102–03.
124. *See* Brief of Petitioner, *supra* note 121, at 3, 21.
125. *Id.* at 3 (internal quotation marks omitted).
126. *See id.* at 21.
127. *See* David Margolick, *Sex Bias Suit Perils Law Firms' Methods of Picking Partners*, N.Y. TIMES, Apr. 23, 1983, at 1; James B. Stewart, *Fairness Issue: Are Women Lawyers Discriminated Against at Large Law Firms?*, WALL ST. J., Dec. 20, 1983, at 1.
128. Margolick, *supra* note 127, at 1.
129. On the first Jewish associate, see Robert G. Kaiser, *Old South Bastion*, WASH. POST, Dec. 28, 1976, at A1. On the first African American associate, see Jim Merriner, *Back in the Blue Chips*, ATLANTA CONST., Aug. 16, 1979, at 1C.
130. *See* Hishon v. King & Spalding, 24 Fair Empl. Prac. Cas. (BNA) 1303, 1303–07 (N.D. Ga. 1980), *aff'd*, 678 F.2d 1022, 1024–30 (11th Cir. 1982), *rev'd*, 467 U.S. 69 (1984).
131. Brief of Petitioner, *supra* note 121, at 2–4 (internal quotation marks omitted).
132. For photographs of Hishon, see Tracy Thompson, *Lawyer: Women in Law Face Bias*, ATLANTA J. & ATLANTA CONST., July 30, 1983, at 11A; Tracy Thompson, *Private Law Firms Liable for Bias*, ATLANTA CONST., May 23, 1984, at 1A. For discussion of Hishon's age and her memorial service held at Sacred Heart Church, see *Hishon*, ATLANTA J.-CONST., Jan. 10, 1999, at F11.
133. On Edenfield's career, see Duane Riner, *That 12-Lb. Bass Worries Edenfield*, ATLANTA CONST., June 16, 1967, at 35.
134. *Hishon*, 24 Fair Empl. Prac. Cas. (BNA) at 1305.
135. *See Hishon*, 678 F.2d at 1024.

136. *See* Hishon v. King & Spalding, 467 U.S. 69, 71–73 (1984).

137. *See Hishon*, 24 Fair Empl. Prac. Cas. (BNA) at 1306.

138. *See* Greg McDonald, *Law Firm Argues It's Exempt from Rule in Bias Case*, ATLANTA CONST., Nov. 1, 1983, at 10A.

139. Stewart, *supra* note 127, at 1 (internal quotation marks omitted).

140. Tony Mauro, *Yes, Law Firms Do Discriminate*, USA TODAY, Nov. 1, 1983, at 10A.

141. For confirmation of Powell as the speaker, see *id.*; *Lawyers Ask High Court to Exempt Them from Civil Rights Regulations*, ALEXANDRIA DAILY TOWN TALK, Nov. 1, 1983, at A1. For the quotations, see Transcript of Oral Argument at 24, Hishon v. King & Spalding, 467 U.S. 69 (1984) (No. 82-940).

142. *See* Kathleen Sylvester, *Minorities in Firms: Women Gaining, Blacks Fall Back*, NAT'L L.J., May 21, 1984, at 1.

143. *See* Jeffrey Gordon, *Nixon Nominee Firm Charged with Race Bias*, ROCKY MOUNTAIN NEWS, Oct. 23, 1971, at 5.

144. *See id.*; JOHN C. JEFFRIES, JR., JUSTICE LEWIS F. POWELL, JR. 234, 503 (1994); *Powell Denies Hiring Bias Against Blacks*, L.A. TIMES, Oct. 24, 1971, at B4.

145. *See* 113 J. EXEC. PROC. SENATE U.S.A. 534 (1972).

146. Gordon, *supra* note 143, at 5 (quoting Jeroyd W. Greene) (internal quotation marks omitted).

147. For Powell's response to the *Rocky Mountain News* story, see *Powell Denies Hiring Bias Against Blacks*, *supra* note 144, at B4. For the membership policies of the Country Club of Virginia and the Commonwealth Club, see Gordon, *supra* note 143, at 5.

148. *See* DESTINY PEERY, NAT'L ASS'N OF WOMEN LAWS., 2020 SURVEY REPORT ON THE PROMOTION AND RETENTION OF WOMEN IN LAW FIRMS 8, 40 (2020).

149. *See* Hishon v. King & Spalding, 467 U.S. 69, 72–73, 78–79 (1984).

150. *See, e.g.*, ELLEN BERREY ET AL., RIGHTS ON TRIAL: HOW WORKPLACE DISCRIMINATION LAW PERPETUATES INEQUALITY 54–73 (2017); Kevin M. Clermont & Stewart J. Schwab, *Employment Discrimination Plaintiffs in Federal Court: From Bad to Worse?*, 3 HARV. L. & POL'Y REV. 103, 103–32 (2009).

151. *Hishon*, 467 U.S. at 81 (Powell, J., concurring).

152. *See* Furman v. Georgia, 408 U.S. 238, 450 (1972) (Powell, J., dissenting).

153. *Hishon*, 467 U.S. at 78–79.

154. James B. Stewart, *Sex Bias Suit that Led to Partnership Ruling Is Settled by Law Firm*, WALL ST. J., June 15, 1984, at 13 (quoting "source close to the negotiations") (internal quotation marks omitted).

155. 582 U.S. 47 (2017).

156. *See Morales-Santana*, 582 U.S. at 51.

157. *See* Nationality Act of 1940, Pub. L. No. 76-853, § 205, 54 Stat. 1137, 1139–40.

158. *See Morales-Santana*, 582 U.S. at 51–54.

159. *See id.* at 51, 54–55.

160. *See id.* at 51–54. For the governing statutory provision, see Immigration and Nationality Act, Pub. L. No. 82-414, § 309(c), 66 Stat. 163, 238–39 (1952).

161. *See Morales-Santana*, 582 U.S. at 54–55.

162. *See id.* at 52–55. For the governing statutory provisions, see Immigration and Nationality Act §§ 301(a)(7), 309(a).

163. *See Morales-Santana*, 582 U.S. at 51, 54.

164. *See id.* at 76.

165. *Id.* at 62.

166. *Id.; see also id.* at 67.

167. *Id.* at 62–64 (citation, alteration marks, and internal quotation marks omitted).

168. *Id.* at 57.

169. *See* Immigration and Nationality Act Amendments of 1986, Pub. L. No. 99-653, § 12, 100 Stat. 3655, 3657. Congress later clarified that section 12 of the 1986 statute applies "to persons born on or after November 14, 1986." Immigration Technical Corrections Act of 1988, Pub. L. No. 100-525, § 8(r), 102 Stat. 2609, 2619.

170. Immigration and Nationality Act Amendments of 1986 § 13. For clarification on when section 13's requirements went into effect, see Immigration Technical Corrections Act of 1988 § 8(r).

171. *See Morales-Santana,* 582 U.S. at 72–73.

172. *See id.* at 73–77.

173. *See id.* at 65–66.

174. *See* 533 U.S. 53, 58–59 (2001).

175. *See id.* at 59–62.

176. For the initial requirement, see Nationality Act of 1940, Pub. L. No. 76-853, § 205, 54 Stat. 1137, 1139–40.

177. Franklin D. Roosevelt, Revision and Codification of the Nationality Laws of the United States, Exec. Order No. 6115 (Apr. 25, 1933).

178. 1 H. COMM. ON IMMIGR. & NATURALIZATION, 76TH CONG., NATIONALITY LAWS OF THE UNITED STATES: MESSAGE FROM THE PRESIDENT OF THE UNITED STATES TRANSMITTING A REPORT PROPOSING A REVISION AND CODIFICATION OF THE NATIONALITY LAWS OF THE UNITED STATES, PREPARED AT THE REQUEST OF THE PRESIDENT OF THE UNITED STATES, BY THE SECRETARY OF STATE, THE ATTORNEY GENERAL, AND THE SECRETARY OF LABOR 18 (Comm. Print 1939) (citation and internal quotation marks omitted).

179. *See Nguyen,* 533 U.S. at 57.

180. For an interview where Boulais shared that information, see Steve Lash, *An Issue of Sexism,* HOUS. CHRON., Sept. 10, 2000, at 1A.

181. For discussion of intimate deception in this context, see JILL ELAINE HASDAY, INTIMATE LIES AND THE LAW 160–61 (2019).

182. LeBrun v. Thornburgh, 777 F. Supp. 1204, 1206 (D.N.J. 1991).

183. Sessions v. Morales-Santana, 582 U.S. 47, 62, 64 (2017).

184. *Nguyen,* 533 U.S. at 65.

185. *Id.* at 70.

186. *Morales-Santana,* 582 U.S. at 66 (citation and internal quotation marks omitted).

187. *See id.* at 51.

188. *See* Ruth Bader Ginsburg & Barbara Flagg, *Some Reflections on the Feminist Legal Thought of the 1970s,* 1989 U. CHI. LEGAL F. 9, 10–11, 14–17.

189. *See Nguyen,* 533 U.S. at 74, 76, 86–92, 94 (O'Connor, J., dissenting).

190. For the Justices joining Ginsburg's majority opinion, see *Morales-Santana,* 582 U.S. at 50.

191. For Kennedy's authorship, see *Nguyen,* 533 U.S. at 56.

192. For Rehnquist's vote, see *id.* On Roberts clerking for Rehnquist, see Charles Lane, *Former Clerks Salute 'Chief,'* WASH. POST, June 19, 2005, at A1.

193. *See* ARIANE HEGEWISCH, INST. FOR WOMEN'S POL'Y RSCH., PUB. NO. C473, THE GENDER WAGE GAP: 2017, at 3 tbl.2 (2018).

194. *See supra* Chapters 1 & 3.

195. Kahn v. Kahn, 78 So. 2d 367, 368–69 (Fla. 1955).

196. Phillips v. Phillips, 150 N.Y.S.2d 646, 649–50 (App. Div.) (citation and internal quotation marks omitted), *aff'd mem.*, 138 N.E.2d 738 (N.Y. 1956).

197. McCarthy v. McCarthy, 276 N.E.2d 891, 895 (Ind. App. 1971); Stern v. Stern, 332 A.2d 78, 81 n.3 (Conn. 1973); *see also* Waskiewicz v. Waskiewicz, 303 A.2d 28, 28–29 (Conn. Super. Ct. 1972); *In re* Marriage of Beeh, 214 N.W.2d 170, 173 (Iowa 1974).

198. On Hayes chairing the Assembly's Judiciary Committee, see CAL. LEG., 1969 REG. SESS., ASSEMBLY FINAL HISTORY 13. On Hayes as coauthor, see CAL. LEG., 1969 REG. SESS., SENATE FINAL HISTORY 75 [hereinafter SENATE FINAL HISTORY]. For Hayes's own account of his work on the legislation, see Carlos Vásquez, Oral History Interview with James A. Hayes 117–25 (1990) (copy on file with author; California State Archives, State Government Oral History Program). For more on no-fault divorce, see JILL ELAINE HASDAY, FAMILY LAW REIMAGINED 116–17, 123–24, 128–30 (2014).

199. Act of Sept. 4, 1969, ch. 1608, § 8, 1969 Cal. Stat. 3312, 3333.

200. *See* SENATE FINAL HISTORY, *supra* note 198, at 75.

201. Letter from James A. Hayes, Chairman, Assembly Comm. on Judiciary, to Bob Monagan, Speaker, and Members of the Assembly (Aug. 8, 1969), *in* CAL. LEG., 1969 REG. SESS., ASSEMBLY DAILY JOURNAL 8053, 8053 [hereinafter ASSEMBLY DAILY JOURNAL].

202. Cal. Assemb. Comm. on Judiciary, Report of 1969 Divorce Reform Legislation, *in* ASSEMBLY DAILY JOURNAL, *supra* note 201, at 8054, 8062.

203. *See Judge Considering Hayes' Request to Halt Alimony*, VAN NUYS NEWS & GREEN SHEET, Feb. 18, 1973, at 3B.

204. *See* Property Settlement Agreement at 5 (Sept. 27, 1966), *admitted in evidence in* Hayes v. Hayes, No. D 700518 (Cal. Super. Ct. June 27, 1969).

205. The alimony obligation appeared in the interlocutory judgment of divorce, as amended. *See* Hayes v. Hayes, No. D 700518, slip op. at 2 (Cal. Super. Ct. June 27, 1969); Hayes v. Hayes, No. D 700518 (Cal. Super. Ct. Aug. 4, 1969).

206. For the final judgment of divorce, see Hayes v. Hayes, No. D 700518 (Cal. Super. Ct. Nov. 6, 1969). For the effective date of the Family Law Act, see Act of Sept. 4, 1969, ch. 1608, § 37, 1969 Cal. Stat. 3312, 3351.

207. James A. Hayes, *California Divorce Reform: Parting Is Sweeter Sorrow*, 56 A.B.A.J. 660, 663 (1970) (emphasis omitted).

208. *See Hayes Appointed L.A. Supervisor*, L.A. TIMES, Aug. 29, 1972 (pt. I), at 1.

209. *See* Bill Boyarsky, *Busch Reelected; Ward Ousts Dorn; Hayes Easy Victor*, L.A. TIMES, Nov. 8, 1972 (pt. I), at 1.

210. For James's salary, see Respondent's Financial Declaration at 1, Hayes v. Hayes, No. D 700 518 (Cal. Super. Ct. Dec. 13, 1972).

211. On James's remarriage, see Respondent's Order to Show Cause (Marriage) at 6, Hayes v. Hayes, No. D 700 518 (Cal. Super. Ct. Dec. 13, 1972).

212. *See id.* at 4.

213. Respondent's Opening Points and Authorities and Declaration of George E. Wise at 8–9, Hayes v. Hayes, No. D 700 518 (Cal. Super. Ct. Feb. 21, 1973) (citation and internal quotation marks omitted). For James's pursuit of alimony termination, see *id.* at 12–13.

214. *See* Points and Authorities of Petitioner Janne M. Hayes in Opposition to Opening Points & Authorities of Respondent at 11–13, Hayes v. Hayes, No. D 700 518 (Cal. Super. Ct. Mar. 2, 1973).

215. *Id.* at 11.

216. *Id.* at 13.

217. *See* Hayes v. Hayes, No. D 700 518, slip op. at 1–2 (Cal. Super. Ct. Mar. 23, 1973).

218. *See* Respondent's Financial Declaration at 1, Hayes v. Hayes, No. D 700 518 (Cal. Super. Ct. June 18, 1974).

219. *See* Respondent's Order to Show Cause (Marriage) at 4, Hayes v. Hayes, No. D 700518 (Cal. Super. Ct. June 18, 1974).

220. *See* Hayes v. Hayes, No. D 700518, slip op. at 3 (Cal. Super. Ct. June 2, 1975).

221. *See Hayes' Ex-Wife Seeks Welfare, Food Stamps*, L.A. TIMES, June 6, 1975 (pt. I), at 29; *Hayes' Former Wife Asks for Food Stamps*, PRESS-TELEGRAM (Long Beach), June 6, 1975, at A8.

222. *Hayes 'Not Embarrassed' in Flap*, PRESS-TELEGRAM (Long Beach), June 9, 1975, at A10 (quoting James Hayes) (internal quotation marks omitted). For a similar account, see *Not Upset by Former Wife, Hayes Says*, L.A. TIMES, June 10, 1975 (pt. I), at 25.

223. *See* Hayes v. Hayes, 2d Civil No. 45168, slip op. at 6–16 (Cal. Ct. App. Oct. 30, 1975).

224. *See, e.g.,* Hayes v. Hayes, No. D 700518 (Cal. Super. Ct. July 5, 1977).

225. *See* Petitioner's Notice of Motion (Marriage) at 4, Hayes v. Hayes, No. D 700 518 (Cal. Super. Ct. June 17, 1977).

226. *See* EMILY A. SHRIDER ET AL., U.S. DEP'T OF COM., INCOME AND POVERTY IN THE UNITED STATES: 2020, at 47 tbl.A-7 (2021) (1979 statistics).

227. *See* EMP. & TRAINING ADMIN., U.S. DEP'T OF LAB., EMPLOYMENT AND TRAINING REPORT OF THE PRESIDENT 189 tbl.B-7 (1981).

228. Grinold v. Grinold, 348 A.2d 32, 33 (Conn. Super. Ct. 1975); *see also* Turner v. Turner, 385 A.2d 1280, 1281 (N.J. Super. Ct. Ch. Div. 1978); Kover v. Kover, 278 N.E.2d 886, 888 (N.Y. 1972); Christ v. Christ, 75 Pa. D. & C.2d 499, 500–01 (Ct. Com. Pl. Northumberland County 1976).

229. Spotts v. Spotts, 355 So. 2d 228, 230 (Fla. Dist. Ct. App. 1978); *see also* Thigpen v. Thigpen, 277 So. 2d 583, 585 (Fla. Dist. Ct. App. 1973); Beard v. Beard, 262 So. 2d 269, 272 (Fla. Dist. Ct. App. 1972) (per curiam).

230. 279 N.E.2d 486, 487–89 (Ill. App. Ct. 1972).

231. *See id.* at 487.

232. *See id.* at 487–88.

233. Transcript of Proceedings at 13, Tan v. Tan, No. 63 S 49 (Ill. Cir. Ct. Aug. 3, 1970) (testimony of Margaret Sullivan, formerly Margaret Tan).

234. *Id.* at 16 (testimony of Margaret Sullivan, formerly Margaret Tan).

235. *Id.* at 18 (testimony of Margaret Sullivan, formerly Margaret Tan); *see also id.* at 14–17 (testimony of Margaret Sullivan, formerly Margaret Tan).

236. *Tan*, 279 N.E.2d at 488.

237. *Id.*

238. Parniawski v. Parniawski, 359 A.2d 719, 721 (Conn. Super. Ct. 1976); *see also* Scherer v. Scherer, 292 S.E.2d 662, 665–66 (Ga. 1982); Volid v. Volid, 286 N.E.2d 42, 46–47 (Ill. App. Ct. 1972); Edwardson v. Edwardson, 798 S.W.2d 941, 944–45 (Ky. 1990); Lebeck v. Lebeck, 881 P.2d 727, 733 (N.M. Ct. App. 1994).

239. 581 A.2d 162 (Pa. 1990).

240. *See id.* at 163.

241. *See* Simeone v. Simeone, No. 1847, slip op. at 7 (Pa. Ct. Com. Pl. Philadelphia County Mar. 17, 1988), *aff'd*, 551 A.2d 219 (Pa. Super. Ct. 1988), *aff'd*, 581 A.2d 162 (Pa. 1990).

242. *See Simeone*, 581 A.2d at 167.

243. *See id.* at 164.

244. *See id.* at 163, 167; *Simeone*, slip op. at 4.

245. *See Simeone*, 581 A.2d at 163.

246. For the child's birthdate, see *Simeone*, slip op. at 2 n.1.

247. *See Simeone*, 581 A.2d at 164.

248. *See* Report of Hearing of January 28, 1985 and Recommendation at 4, 6, Simeone v. Simeone, No. 84-00852 (Pa. Ct. Com. Pl. Philadelphia County Apr. 1, 1985).

249. *See* Terry V. Boyce, *Time and Two Seats, Distilled: The Simeone Foundation Experience*, Auto. Q., Third Quarter 2008, at 74, 76, 81, 83.

250. *Simeone*, 581 A.2d at 166–68.

251. *Id.* at 165.

252. A concurring opinion observed that the majority's declarations that "all vestiges of inequality between the sexes have been erased and women are now treated equally under the law" were "inconsistent with reality." *Id.* at 168 (Papadakos, J., concurring).

253. *See* Jill Elaine Hasday, *Contest and Consent: A Legal History of Marital Rape*, 88 Calif. L. Rev. 1373, 1392–406 (2000).

254. *See id.* at 1413–27.

255. Letter from Elizabeth Cady Stanton to Gerrit Smith (Dec. 21, 1855), *reprinted in* 1 History of Woman Suffrage 839, 840 (Elizabeth Cady Stanton et al. eds., New York, Fowler & Wells 1881).

256. Letter from Lucy Stone to Antoinette Brown Blackwell (July 11, 1855), *in* Friends and Sisters: Letters Between Lucy Stone and Antoinette Brown Blackwell, 1846–93, at 143, 144 (Carol Lasser & Marlene Deahl Merrill eds., 1987).

257. I have found no nineteenth-century efforts to prosecute a husband for personally raping his wife and only one case from the early twentieth century, where an appellate court reversed a husband's conviction for assault with attempt to rape. *See* Frazier v. State, 86 S.W. 754, 754–55 (Tex. Crim. App. 1905).

258. Apostle v. Pappas, 277 N.Y.S. 400, 404 (Sup. Ct. 1935).

259. *See* Alaska Stat. § 11.41.432 (2023); Ariz. Rev. Stat. Ann. § 13-1407(D) (2020); Cal. Penal Code § 261(a)(1) (West 2024); Iowa Code Ann. § 709.4 (West Supp. 2023); Ky. Rev. Stat. Ann. § 510.035 (LexisNexis 2014); Mich. Comp. Laws Ann. § 750.520*l* (West Supp. 2024); Nev. Rev. Stat. Ann. § 200.373 (LexisNexis 2021); N.H. Rev. Stat. Ann. § 632-A:2(III) (LexisNexis Supp. 2023); S.C. Code Ann. § 16-3-658 (2015); S.D. Codified Laws § 22-22-7.4 (Supp. 2024); Va. Code Ann. §§ 18.2-61, 18.2-67.1, 18.2-67.2 (2021); Wyo. Stat. Ann. § 6-2-307(a) (2023).

260. *See* statutes cited *supra* note 259.

261. *See* Hasday, *supra* note 253, at 1494–98.

262. 315 S.E.2d 847 (Va. 1984).

263. *See id.* at 847–48.

264. *See id.* at 848.

265. *See id.* at 848–49.

266. *See id.* at 847.

267. *See id.* at 848. On the jury determining the sentence, see Commonwealth v. Weishaupt, No. 38553 (Va. Cir. Ct. Dec. 23, 1982), *reprinted in* Appendix at 150–51, Weishaupt v. Commonwealth, 315 S.E.2d 847 (Va. 1984) (No. 830616).

268. *See Weishaupt,* 315 S.E.2d at 847–48.

269. *See id.* at 847–50. For the statutory language, see *id.* at 850 n.3.

270. *Id.* at 849.

271. *Id.* at 855.

272. *Id.* at 852.

273. *Id.* at 853.

274. *Id.* at 854.

275. *Id.*

276. *Id.* at 853 (missing space between words added).

277. *See id.* at 856 (Compton, J., concurring in the result). For a list of the seven Virginia Justices who decided *Weishaupt,* see 227 Va. iii (1984).

278. *Weishaupt,* 315 S.E.2d at 856 (Compton, J., concurring in the result).

279. *See* Kizer v. Commonwealth, 321 S.E.2d 291, 292 (Va. 1984).

280. *Id.* at 294.

281. *See* VA. CODE ANN. § 18.2-61 (2021).

282. 597 U.S. 215, 231–32, 240, 256, 292, 300–01 (2022).

283. For the statute, see Gestational Age Act, ch. 393, § 4(b), 2018 Miss. Laws 606, 609.

284. For the overruling of those decisions, see *Dobbs,* 597 U.S. at 231, 292, 302.

285. *See id.* at 233–34.

286. *See id.* at 222.

287. *See* Memorandum from Samuel A. Alito to the Solic. Gen. 8–9, 17 (May 30, 1985) (copy on file with author; National Archives and Records Administration, Record Group 60, Department of Justice files of Deputy Assistant Attorney General Charles Cooper, 1981–85, Accession 060-89-216, box 20, Thornburgh v. American College of Obstetricians & Gynecologists folder).

288. *Dobbs,* 597 U.S. at 224, 268.

289. *See id.* at 236–37.

290. *Id.* at 288–89; *see also id.* at 259, 282–83, 292.

291. *See* Brief for Petitioners at 4–5, 29–30, 34–35, Dobbs v. Jackson Women's Health Org., 597 U.S. 215 (2022) (No. 19-1392); Brief of 240 Women Scholars and Professionals, and Prolife Feminist Organizations in Support of Petitioners at 1–4, 13–17, 29–35, Dobbs v. Jackson Women's Health Org., 597 U.S. 215 (2022) (No. 19-1392).

292. *Dobbs,* 597 U.S. at 258 (footnotes omitted).

293. *See* DONNA L. HOYERT, NAT'L CTR. FOR HEALTH STAT., MATERNAL MORTALITY RATES IN THE UNITED STATES, 2022, at 1 (2024); Katherine Kortsmit et al., *Abortion Surveillance— United States, 2021,* MORBIDITY & MORTALITY WKLY. REP., Nov. 24, 2023, at 1, 28 tbl.15.

294. *See, e.g.,* CARLY MCCANN & DONALD TOMASKOVIC-DEVEY, CTR. FOR EMP. EQUITY, UNIV. OF MASS. AMHERST, PREGNANCY DISCRIMINATION AT WORK: AN ANALYSIS OF PREGNANCY DISCRIMINATION CHARGES FILED WITH THE U.S. EQUAL EMPLOYMENT OPPORTUNITY COMMISSION 2–4, 8–9 (2021); Patrick Ishizuka, *The Motherhood Penalty in Context:*

Assessing Discrimination in a Polarized Labor Market, 58 DEMOGRAPHY 1275, 1275–77, 1294–96 (2021).

295. On insurance, see SARAH SUGAR ET AL., U.S. DEP'T OF HEALTH & HUM. SERVS., ISSUE BRIEF NO. HP-2022-09, HEALTH COVERAGE FOR WOMEN UNDER THE AFFORDABLE CARE ACT 3 (2022). On paid family leave, see SARAH A. DONOVAN, CONG. RSCH. SERV., PAID FAMILY AND MEDICAL LEAVE IN THE UNITED STATES 5 tbl.1 (2023).

296. MISS. CODE ANN. § 37-13-171 (Supp. 2023).

297. *See id.* § 97-29-1 (2020).

298. *See* Michelle J.K. Osterman et al., *Births: Final Data for 2022*, NAT'L VITAL STAT. REPS., Apr. 4, 2024, at 1, 27 tbl.8.

299. *See* MISS. STATE DEP'T OF HEALTH, MISSISSIPPI MATERNAL MORTALITY REPORT, 2016–2020, at 14–15 (2023).

300. For a prohibition on sex discrimination in state employment, see MISS. CODE ANN. § 25-9-149 (2018).

301. Anna Wolfe, *Abortion Bill Clears House*, CLARION LEDGER (Jackson), Feb. 3, 2018, at 1A (quoting Rep. Sonya Williams-Barnes) (internal quotation marks omitted); *see also* Jeff Amy, *State Pushes Abortion Ban at 15 Weeks*, GREENWOOD COMMONWEALTH, Feb. 4, 2018, at 4A; Bracey Harris & Geoff Pender, *Abortion Ban Awaits Bryant's Signature*, CLARION LEDGER (Jackson), Mar. 9, 2018, at 1A.

302. *See* MISS. CODE ANN. § 43-17-5 (2021).

303. *See* OFF. OF FAM. ASSISTANCE, U.S. DEP'T OF HEALTH & HUM. SERVS., TANF: AVERAGE NUMBER OF APPLICATIONS RECEIVED, CALENDAR YEAR 2022, at 1 (2023); OFF. OF FAM. ASSISTANCE, U.S. DEP'T OF HEALTH & HUM. SERVS., TANF: AVERAGE NUMBER OF APPLICATIONS APPROVED, CALENDAR YEAR 2022, at 1 (2023); OFF. OF FAM. ASSISTANCE, U.S. DEP'T OF HEALTH & HUM. SERVS., TANF: AVERAGE NUMBER OF APPLICATIONS DENIED, CALENDAR YEAR 2022, at 1 (2023).

304. For the decision, see Nat'l Fed'n of Indep. Bus. v. Sebelius, 567 U.S. 519, 585 (2012) (opinion of Roberts, C.J.).

305. *See* SUGAR ET AL., *supra* note 295, at 7 fig.5, app. at 9 tbl.A.

306. *See* Brief for Women Legislators and the Susan B. Anthony List as *Amici Curiae* Supporting Petitioners at 1–22, Dobbs v. Jackson Women's Health Org., 597 U.S. 215 (2022) (No. 19-1392).

307. *Dobbs*, 597 U.S. at 289.

308. *Id.* at 261.

309. *See supra* Chapters 1 & 3.

310. *See* MISS. CONST. art. 12, §§ 241, 249A.

311. *See* CHRISTOPHER UGGEN ET AL., SENT'G PROJECT, LOCKED OUT 2020: ESTIMATES OF PEOPLE DENIED VOTING RIGHTS DUE TO A FELONY CONVICTION 16 tbl.3, 17 tbl.4 (2020).

312. *See* Hopkins v. Watson, 108 F.4th 371, 375 (5th Cir. 2024) (en banc).

313. *See* ELEC. COOPS. OF MISS., MISSISSIPPI 2018 LEGISLATIVE ROSTER 11, 23 (2018).

314. On Governor Phil Bryant's advocacy, see *15-Week Abortion Ban Moves Closer to Law*, ENTER.-J. (McComb), Mar. 7, 2018, at A4. On Bryant's signing ceremony, see Jeff Amy & Sarah Mearhoff, *15-Week Abortion Ban Faces Lawsuit*, CLARION LEDGER (Jackson), Mar. 20, 2018, at 1A. On Bryant's predecessors, see THE GOVERNOR'S MANSION: A PICTORIAL HISTORY 60–64 (1975); MICHAEL WATSON, MISS. SEC'Y OF STATE, MISSISSIPPI OFFICIAL & STATISTICAL REGISTER: BLUE BOOK, 2020–2024, at 541–49 (2021).

Chapter 6

1. Fred Perry Powers, *Feminism and Socialism*, 3 UNPOPULAR REV. 118, 118 (1915).
2. L.P. BROCKETT, WOMAN: HER RIGHTS, WRONGS, PRIVILEGES AND RESPONSIBILITIES 332 (Cincinnati, Howe's Subscription Book Concern 1869).
3. 2 DEBATES AND PROCEEDINGS OF THE CONSTITUTIONAL CONVENTION OF THE STATE OF CALIFORNIA 1006 (Sacramento, State Office 1881) (statement of James Caples); *see also* Editorial, DAILY INDEP. (Santa Barbara), Jan. 2, 1895, at 2; Mrs. G.H. Shaw, *Reasons Against Woman Suffrage*, REMONSTRANCE, Jan. 1908, at 1, 2; *Why Women Should Not Vote*, RUTLAND DAILY HERALD, Feb. 23, 1911, at 7.
4. *See, e.g.*, Midge Decter, *The Liberated Woman*, COMMENTARY, Oct. 1970, at 33, 43.
5. *See* H.R.J. Res. 75, 68th Cong. (1923); S.J. Res. 21, 68th Cong. (1923).
6. For committee hearings before August 1970, see *Equal Rights Amendment to the Constitution: Hearing on H.R.J. Res. 75 Before the H. Comm. on the Judiciary*, 68th Cong. (1925); *Equal Rights Amendment: Hearing on S.J. Res. 64 Before a Subcomm. of the S. Comm. on the Judiciary*, 70th Cong. (1929); *Equal Rights: Hearing on S.J. Res. 52 Before a Subcomm. of the S. Comm. on the Judiciary*, 71st Cong. (1931); *Equal Rights Amendment to the Constitution: Hearing on H.R.J. Res. 197 Before the H. Comm. on the Judiciary*, 72d Cong. (1932); *Equal Rights for Men and Women: Hearing on S.J. Res. 1 Before a Subcomm. of the S. Comm. on the Judiciary*, 73d Cong. (1933); *A Bill to Provide for Equal Rights: Hearing on H.R.J. Res. 1 Before a Subcomm. of the H. Comm. on the Judiciary*, 75th Cong. (1937); *Equal Rights for Men and Women: Hearings on S.J. Res. 65 Before a Subcomm. of the S. Comm. on the Judiciary*, 75th Cong. (1938); *Amend the Constitution Relative to Equal Rights for Men and Women: Statements on H.R.J. Res. 49 Presented to Subcomm. No. 2 of the H. Comm. on the Judiciary*, 79th Cong. (1945); *Equal Rights Amendment: Hearing on S.J. Res. 61 Before a Subcomm. of the S. Comm. on the Judiciary*, 79th Cong. (1945); *Equal Rights Amendment to the Constitution and Commission on the Legal Status of Women: Hearings Before Subcomm. No. 1 of the H. Comm. on the Judiciary*, 80th Cong. (1948); *Hearings on S.J. Res. 67 Before the Subcomm. of the S. Comm. on the Judiciary*, 80th Cong. (1948); *Equal Rights: Hearings on S.J. Res. 39 Before a Subcomm. of the S. Comm. on the Judiciary*, 84th Cong. (1956); *The "Equal Rights" Amendment: Hearings on S.J. Res. 61 Before the Subcomm. on Const. Amends. of the S. Comm. on the Judiciary*, 91st Cong. (1970) [hereinafter The "*Equal Rights" Amendment*].
7. For committee reports before August 1970, see S. REP. NO. 75-1641 (1938); S. REP. NO. 78-267 (1943); H.R. REP. NO. 79-907 (1945); S. REP. NO. 79-1013 (1946); S. REP. NO. 80-1208 (1948); H.R. REP. NO. 80-2196 (1948); S. REP. NO. 81-137 (1949); S. REP. NO. 82-356 (1951); S. REP. NO. 83-221 (1953); S. REP. NO. 88-1558 (1964); S. REP. NO. 89-458 (1965).
8. For the House committee, see H.R. REP. NO. 79-907, at 1. For the Senate committee, see S. REP. NO. 79-1013, at 1. For the Senate debate, see 92 CONG. REC. 9219, 9223–29, 9293–97, 9302–35, 9397–405 (1946). For the Senate vote, see *id.* at 9405. For constitutional amendment requirements, see U.S. CONST. art. V.
9. In 1950 and 1953, the Senate passed a modified version of the ERA that included a rider stating: "The provisions of this article shall not be construed to impair any rights, benefits, or exemptions now or hereafter conferred by law upon persons of the female sex." 96 CONG. REC. 870, 872–73 (1950); 99 CONG. REC. 8973–74 (1953).

10. *See* Maurice Carroll, *Emanuel Celler, Former Brooklyn Congressman, Dies at 92*, N.Y. TIMES, Jan. 16, 1981, at D16.

11. *See* Eileen Shanahan, *House Vote Expected Tomorrow on Amendment for Equal Rights for Women*, N.Y. TIMES, Aug. 9, 1970, at 29.

12. *See* 89 CONG. REC. A1771–72 (1943) (statement of Rep. Emanuel Celler).

13. Frances Lewine, *Still Burning Issue? Equal Rights Bill Divides Women's Groups, Congressmen*, L.A. TIMES, July 23, 1957 (pt. II), at 5 (quoting Emanuel Celler) (internal quotation marks omitted).

14. *See* Richard L. Madden, *Mrs. Chisholm Defeats Farmer, Is First Negro Woman in House*, N.Y. TIMES, Nov. 6, 1968, at 1.

15. 115 CONG. REC. 13,380 (1969) (statement of Rep. Shirley Chisholm).

16. *See The "Equal Rights" Amendment, supra* note 6, at 331 (statement of Gloria Steinem); Ms., Spring 1972, at 4 (masthead).

17. *The "Equal Rights" Amendment, supra* note 6, at 333 (statement of Gloria Steinem) (typographical error in original corrected, scare to scarce).

18. For Griffiths and Title VII, see *supra* Chapter 1. For the discharge vote and onset of floor debate, see 116 CONG. REC. 28,004 (1970).

19. For the House vote, see 116 CONG. REC. 28,036–37 (1970). On the ERA dying in the Senate, see *Equal Rights for Women Amendment Dropped in Senate*, 26 CONG. Q. ALMANAC 706, 706 (1970).

20. For the Senate vote, see 118 CONG. REC. 9598 (1972). For the House vote, see 117 CONG. REC. 35,815 (1971).

21. H.R.J. Res. 208, 92d Cong., 86 Stat. 1523 (1972).

22. For constitutional amendment requirements, see U.S. CONST. art. V.

23. For the book, see PHYLLIS SCHLAFLY, A CHOICE NOT AN ECHO (1964). For discussion of the book's publication and circulation, see STEPHEN SHADEGG, WHAT HAPPENED TO GOLDWATER? THE INSIDE STORY OF THE 1964 REPUBLICAN CAMPAIGN 124, 262, 266 (1965); *'Choice' Book on GOP Rule Best Seller*, DEMOCRAT & CHRON. (Rochester), July 14, 1964, at 2A; Donald Janson, *Extremist Book Sales Soar Despite Criticism in G.O.P.*, N.Y. TIMES, Oct. 4, 1964, at 76; Russell Kirk, *Holding LBJ Up by the Ears*, S.F. EXAM'R, Oct. 11, 1964 (Book Week), at 5; Lewis Nichols, *In and Out of Books*, N.Y. TIMES, Oct. 4, 1964 (§ 7), at 8.

24. On the election, see David S. Broder, *GOP Elects Mrs. O'Donnell*, WASH. POST, May 7, 1967, at A1; Thomas J. Foley, *Mrs. O'Donnell Elected to Head GOP Federation*, L.A. TIMES, May 7, 1967, at A1; *The Making of a President*, TIME, May 12, 1967, at 21. On her rival's support for the ERA, see *Equal Rights 1970: Hearings on S.J. Res. 61 and S.J. Res. 231 Before the S. Comm. on the Judiciary*, 91st Cong. 344–49 (1970) (statement of Gladys O'Donnell, President, National Federation of Republican Women).

25. For the allegations, see *NFRW Club Action*, PHYLLIS SCHLAFLY REP., Aug. 1967, at 3. Schlafly solicited donations to the Eagle Trust Fund on the same page.

26. *See* Warren Weaver Jr., *Defeated Leader Sets Up a Rival Group for Republican Women*, N.Y. TIMES, Aug. 9, 1967, at 21.

27. *What's Wrong with "Equal Rights" for Women?*, PHYLLIS SCHLAFLY REP., Feb. 1972, at 1.

28. *See The Growing Momentum Against Busing*, PHYLLIS SCHLAFLY REP., Mar. 1972, at 1.

29. *The Fraud Called the Equal Rights Amendment*, PHYLLIS SCHLAFLY REP., May 1972, at 3.

30. This chapter will discuss many of those newsletters. For examples of public appearances, see *A Heated Debate on the ERA*, WASH. POST, Mar. 17, 1977, at D17; Louise Solomon, *Schlafly, MacKinnon Debate Women's Rights*, STAN. DAILY, Jan. 27, 1982, at 1. For the manifesto, see PHYLLIS SCHLAFLY, THE POWER OF THE POSITIVE WOMAN (1977).

31. On the founding of Stop ERA in 1972 and Eagle Forum in 1975, see *A Short History of E.R.A.*, PHYLLIS SCHLAFLY REP., Sept. 1986, at 1. On Schlafly's centrality, see sources cited *infra* notes 114–115.

32. *See* Reed v. Reed, 404 U.S. 71 (1971).

33. *See* EMILY A. SHRIDER ET AL., U.S. DEP'T OF COM., INCOME AND POVERTY IN THE UNITED STATES: 2020, at 47 tbl.A-7 (2021).

34. *What's Wrong with "Equal Rights" for Women?, supra* note 27, at 2.

35. *Id.* at 1.

36. *Id.* at 3.

37. *Id.* at 4.

38. SCHLAFLY, *supra* note 30, at 35.

39. *Id.* at 138.

40. *Id.* at 29.

41. *See id.* at 34–35, 69–70, 118–19; *The Right to Be a Woman*, PHYLLIS SCHLAFLY REP., Nov. 1972, at 3; *ERA Won't Help Women in Education*, PHYLLIS SCHLAFLY REP., Sept. 1973, at 1; *HEW Regulations About "Sexism" in the Schools*, PHYLLIS SCHLAFLY REP., Aug. 1974, at 1; *E.R.A.'s Assist to Abortion*, PHYLLIS SCHLAFLY REP., Dec. 1974, at 2; *How E.R.A. Will Hurt Men*, PHYLLIS SCHLAFLY REP., May 1975, at 2; *Big Money and Tough Tactics to Ratify E.R.A.*, PHYLLIS SCHLAFLY REP., June 1975, at 1; *The Hypocrisy of ERA Proponents*, PHYLLIS SCHLAFLY REP., July 1975, at 2; *Women's Magazines Promote ERA -- but Deny Equal Rights*, PHYLLIS SCHLAFLY REP., Dec. 1979, at 3; *A Short History of E.R.A., supra* note 31, at 2.

42. *The Right to Be a Woman, supra* note 41, at 3 (internal quotation marks omitted).

43. *A Short History of E.R.A., supra* note 31, at 2.

44. *ERA Won't Help Women in Education, supra* note 41, at 1.

45. On women's mobilization for the sex discrimination prohibition in Title VII of the 1964 Civil Rights Act, see *supra* Chapter 1.

46. For Goldwater's 1972 vote, see 118 CONG. REC. 4948 (1972). For Goldwater's 1964 vote, see 110 CONG. REC. 14,511 (1964). For Goldwater explaining his 1964 vote, see *id.* at 14,318–19.

47. On the April 27, 1976, rally, see *ERA Opponents Rally in Rotunda of Capitol*, DECATUR HERALD, Apr. 28, 1976, at 27.

48. *See id.*

49. For publication of this photograph, see *Magnifying Her Voice Against ERA*, CHI. TRIB., Apr. 28, 1976 (§ 1), at 5. For the image, see Getty Images (editorial no. 933169356; copy on file with author).

50. *See, e.g.*, FREMONT P. WIRTH, UNITED STATES HISTORY 689–90 (1949); *supra* Chapter 4.

51. *See A Handshake—Then a Clash*, U.S. NEWS & WORLD REP., Aug. 3, 1959, at 71, 71; *The Two Worlds: A Day-Long Debate*, N.Y. TIMES, July 25, 1959, at 1.

52. *Encounter*, NEWSWEEK, Aug. 3, 1959, at 15, 16 (quoting Richard Nixon) (internal quotation marks omitted).

53. *What's Wrong with "Equal Rights" for Women?*, *supra* note 27, at 2; *see also* SCHLAFLY, *supra* note 30, at 30–31; Vicki Rutledge, *You've Come a Long Way Baby, but Who Gave You a Lift?*, PHYLLIS SCHLAFLY REP., Jan. 1974, at 4.

54. *See* RUTH SCHWARTZ COWAN, MORE WORK FOR MOTHER: THE IRONIES OF HOUSEHOLD TECHNOLOGY FROM THE OPEN HEARTH TO THE MICROWAVE 199–201, 210–16 (1983).

55. For a notorious example from "The Ford International Weekly," see *The International Jew: The World's Problem*, DEARBORN INDEP., May 22, 1920, at 1. Ford was so antisemitic that Adolf Hitler admired him. *Mein Kampf*, Hitler's 1925 manifesto, praised Ford as a "great man." ADOLF HITLER, MEIN KAMPF 639 (Ralph Manheim trans., Houghton Mifflin 1962) (1925). American newspapers reported in the 1920s that Hitler had a large photograph of Ford on a wall in his office and was circulating Ford's anti-Jewish propaganda in Germany. *See Berlin Hears Ford Is Backing Hitler*, N.Y. TIMES, Dec. 20, 1922, at 2; Raymond Fendrick, *"Heinrich" Ford Idol of Bavaria Fascisti Chief*, CHI. DAILY TRIB., Mar. 8, 1923, at 2. In 1938, Hitler awarded Ford "the Grand Cross of the German Eagle," and Ford accepted the award from one of Hitler's representatives during his seventy-fifth birthday celebration in Detroit. *Hitler Honors Four Americans*, PHILA. INQUIRER, Sept. 10, 1938, at 3.

56. SCHLAFLY, *supra* note 30, at 32.

57. *The Fraud Called the Equal Rights Amendment*, *supra* note 29, at 4; *see also* SCHLAFLY, *supra* note 30, at 33.

58. *What's Wrong with "Equal Rights" for Women?*, *supra* note 27, at 3.

59. *The Right to Be a Woman*, *supra* note 41, at 4; *see also* SCHLAFLY, *supra* note 30, at 70–79; *The Precious Rights ERA Will Take Away from Wives*, PHYLLIS SCHLAFLY REP., Aug. 1973, at 1–4; *Effect of ERA on Family Property Rights*, PHYLLIS SCHLAFLY REP., Jan. 1974, at 1; *Why Virginia Rejected ERA*, PHYLLIS SCHLAFLY REP., June 1974, at 1–2; *The Legislative History of ERA*, PHYLLIS SCHLAFLY REP., Nov. 1976, at 2.

60. SCHLAFLY, *supra* note 30, at 138.

61. *See id.* at 166. For more denigration, see *id.* at 12, 25, 89–93, 95, 140–42, 164; *How E.R.A. Will Hurt Men*, *supra* note 41, at 2.

62. *See* SCHLAFLY, *supra* note 30, at 89–92; *ERA and Homosexual "Marriages,"* PHYLLIS SCHLAFLY REP., Sept. 1974, at 1; *E.R.A.'s Assist to Abortion*, *supra* note 41, at 2; *The Hypocrisy of ERA Proponents*, *supra* note 41, at 3; *Who Will Profit from ERA?*, PHYLLIS SCHLAFLY REP., July 1975, at 4; *A Short History of E.R.A.*, *supra* note 31, at 2.

63. SCHLAFLY, *supra* note 30, at 50; *see also id.* at 93.

64. *Id.* at 50; *see also id.* at 54–55; *How E.R.A. Will Hurt Men*, *supra* note 41, at 2–3.

65. SCHLAFLY, *supra* note 30, at 165; *see also id.* at 23–24, 94; *Unemployment -- Causes and Solutions*, PHYLLIS SCHLAFLY REP., Nov. 1975, at 1–2.

66. SCHLAFLY, *supra* note 30, at 38; *see also id.* at 37.

67. SCHLAFLY, *supra* note 30, at 38.

68. *Id.* at 39.

69. On Schlafly's 1952 campaigning, see O.T. Banton, *State GOP Pledges Change in Truck Fee Law, Names 10 Taft Delegates*, DECATUR HERALD, June 24, 1952, at 1; *Mrs. Phyllis Schlafly Drives for District Seat in Congress*, ALTON EVENING TEL., Feb. 27, 1952, at 2; *Mrs. Schlafly Glad McGlynn Opposes Her*, BELLEVILLE DAILY ADVOC., Mar. 27, 1952, at 1. On Schlafly's 1952 loss, see *Price Is Winner 112,889 to 61,866*, ALTON EVENING TEL., Nov. 5, 1952, at 1. On Schlafly's 1970 campaigning, see *Barbecue for Phyllis Schlafly Attended*

by Many Saturday, ALTAMONT NEWS, Oct. 15, 1970, at 1; Adam Clymer, *Illinois Race's Key Is Locality*, SUN (Baltimore), Sept. 14, 1970, at A8; *Schlafly: Must Defeats Dems*, DIXON EVENING TEL., Oct. 13, 1970, at 2. On Schlafly's 1970 loss, see source cited *infra* note 77.

70. For Schlafly offering explanations for her 1970 loss, see G. Robert Hillman, *Mrs. Schlafly Shatters Mold*, INDIANAPOLIS NEWS, Jan. 4, 1978, at 20.

71. *Woman Wins Nomination for Congress*, DIXON EVENING TEL., Apr. 10, 1952, at 13.

72. Mary Kimbrough, *Housewife Who's Running for Congress*, ST. LOUIS POST-DISPATCH, Mar. 3, 1952, at 2D.

73. *She's Cooking Up Campaign*, STATE J. (Lansing), Apr. 10, 1952, at 12.

74. Clymer, *supra* note 69, at A8.

75. Taylor Pensoneau, *Shipley-Schlafly Race: Battle of Sexes*, ST. LOUIS POST-DISPATCH, Oct. 25, 1970, at 3C (quoting Phyllis Schlafly) (internal quotation marks omitted).

76. Richard H. Icen, *Ideology an Issue in Congressional Race*, DECATUR SUNDAY HERALD & REV., Oct. 25, 1970 (§ 4), at 1 (quoting Phyllis Schlafly) (internal quotation marks omitted).

77. *See Shipley Decisively Defeats Mrs. Schlafly*, DECATUR HERALD, Nov. 5, 1970, at 29.

78. Jon Margolis, *A Turn to Right?*, CHI. TRIB., Nov. 9, 1980 (§ 2), at 1 (quoting Phyllis Schlafly) (internal quotation marks omitted).

79. *See* John Hanchette, *ERA Opponent Suggests She May Get Reagan Post*, RENO EVENING GAZETTE, Nov. 19, 1980, at 9; Susan Page, *Her Smile Casts a Long Shadow*, NEWSDAY (Long Island), July 10, 1980 (pt. II), at 3; Carol Stocker, *Friedan: 'It Doesn't Look Good...'... as Schlafly Looks Beyond ERA*, BOS. GLOBE, Nov. 29, 1980, at 9.

80. *See* Joan Beck, *1980 Had Its Share of Good, Bad Nonevents*, CHI. TRIB., Dec. 29, 1980 (§ 6), at 2; Vera Glaser, *Women Anchor Only 10 of 110 Transition Slots*, MIA. HERALD, Nov. 20, 1980, at 16A.

81. *See* Glaser, *supra* note 80, at 16A; Owen Ullmann, *Women, Minorities Absent from Cabinet*, OAKLAND TRIB., Dec. 17, 1980, at E1.

82. On Thomson's acquisition of the position, see June Simpson, *Forum Seeks to Save Traditional Values*, SUNDAY PANTAGRAPH (Bloomington-Normal), Nov. 2, 1975, at D1.

83. ROSEMARY THOMSON, THE PRICE OF *LIBERTY* 47 (1978) (internal quotation marks omitted). For confirmation that Thomson was still the Eagle Forum's Illinois director in 1978, see *Eagle Forum Attacks ERA Extension OK*, DAILY PANTAGRAPH (Bloomington-Normal), Oct. 7, 1978, at A3.

84. THOMSON, *supra* note 83, at 61, 50 (internal quotation marks omitted); *see also id.* at 64; Rosemary Thomson, *What's Behind the Equal Rights Amendment?*, MOODY MONTHLY, Feb. 1974, at 48.

85. *See* Katie Brown, *Equal Rights Law Not What It Appears, Opponents Claim*, FORT WORTH STAR-TELEGRAM, Sept. 2, 1974, at 1B; Marsha Comstock, *Women's Group Fighting Legal Equality of Sexes*, ABILENE REP.-NEWS, July 24, 1974, at 12A.

86. On the leaflet's circulation, see Robert C. Chandler, Letter to the Editor, MIA. NEWS, Apr. 21, 1975, at 10A (Florida); Maria Gallagher, *Attention Focuses on Women's Rights Amendment*, GRAND PRAIRIE DAILY NEWS, Nov. 27, 1974, at 1 (Texas); *Hansen Blasts Repeal Move*, LAS CRUCES SUN-NEWS, Feb. 9, 1975, at 3 (New Mexico); Douglas E. Kneeland, *The Equal Rights Amendment: Missouri Is the Target Now*, N.Y. TIMES, Feb. 7, 1975, at 37 (Missouri); *Ladies! Have You Heard?*, CARROLL DAILY TIMES HERALD, Oct. 6, 1976, at 7 (advertisement) (Iowa); J.C. Martin, *Who's Afraid of ERA?*, ARIZ. DAILY STAR, Apr. 30,

1976, at C1 (Arizona); Jenta Winternitz, *Conversion to the ERA*, HONOLULU ADVERTISER, Sept. 2, 1976, at A18 (Hawaii). For use of the "pink sheet" nickname, see Debbie Byrd, *Not All Women Support Equal Rights*, AUSTIN AM.-STATESMAN, Jan. 12, 1975, at B1; Mary Jo Carr, *ERA Foes Query, 'Do You Want Your Husband to Sleep in Barracks with Women?*,' ARGUS (Fremont-Newark), Aug. 27, 1975, at 14; Brenda French, *From Pedestal to Protest*, MARSHALL NEWS MESSENGER, Dec. 1, 1974, at 1D; Gallagher, *supra*, at 1.

87. Ladies Ladies Ladies Ladies Ladies Have You Heard? 1–2 (copy on file with author; Emory University, Stuart A. Rose Manuscript, Archives, and Rare Book Library, Kathryn Fink Dunaway Papers, box 3, folder 9) (capitalization and emphasis omitted).

88. *Id.* at 1 (capitalization omitted).

89. *Id.* at 2 (internal quotation marks omitted).

90. *Id.* at 1.

91. BEVERLY LaHAYE, WHO BUT A WOMAN? 25 (1984).

92. BEVERLY LaHAYE, I AM A WOMAN BY GOD'S DESIGN 132 (1980).

93. TIM LaHAYE & BEVERLY LaHAYE, THE ACT OF MARRIAGE: THE BEAUTY OF SEXUAL LOVE 21 (1976). For discussion of Beverly LaHaye's career and marriage, see Tim LaHaye, *Introduction* to *id.* at 7, 7; *The LaHayes Returning for Family Life Seminar*, DAILY SENTINEL (Grand Junction), Nov. 3, 1979 (Search), at 3. For the book's sales, see Julia Duin, *20-Year-Old CWA Struggles to Find, Retain New Leader*, WASH. TIMES, Sept. 12, 1999, at C1; Gayle White, *Evangelical Power Couple*, ATLANTA J.-CONST., July 7, 2001, at B1.

94. LaHAYE, *supra* note 92, at 134–35.

95. *Id.* at 132.

96. *See Conservative Protestant Leaders*, CONSERVATIVE DIG., Aug. 1979, at 16, 16; Steve Hill, *Falwell Seeking 'Moral Majority*,' TAMPA TRIB., Aug. 25, 1979 (Logos), at 6; Charles Slack, *Liberty Campus: Not for Ambivalent*, RICHMOND TIMES-DISPATCH, May 10, 1987, at A1.

97. For the *Brown* decision, see 347 U.S. 483 (1954).

98. Jerry Falwell, *Segregation or Integration: Which?*, WORD OF LIFE, Oct. 1958, at 1, 1 (copy on file with author; University of North Carolina, Wilson Special Collections Library, Frye Gaillard Papers, folder 5).

99. *Id.* at 4.

100. *See* Roy Reed, *Freedom March Begins at Selma; Troops on Guard*, N.Y. TIMES, Mar. 22, 1965, at 1.

101. *See* JERRY FALWELL, MINISTERS AND MARCHES, at title page (1965).

102. *Id.* at 2.

103. *Id.* at 17.

104. On Falwell, see Hill, *supra* note 96, at 6. On Tim LaHaye, see Louis R. Carlozo, *In World of 'Left Behind,' End Is Weird*, CHI. TRIB., Dec. 6, 2005 (§ 5), at 3; White, *supra* note 93, at B1.

105. *Local Persons Attend 'I Love America' Rally*, J. GAZETTE (Mattoon), May 12, 1980, at 6 (internal quotation marks omitted).

106. *Id.* (quoting Jerry Falwell) (internal quotation marks omitted). For more on the rally, see Bob Springer, *'I Love America' Rally Attacks ERA*, DECATUR HERALD, May 7, 1980, at A19.

107. JERRY FALWELL, LISTEN, AMERICA! 19 (1980).

108. *Id.* at 151 (quoting *Ephesians* 5:23).

109. *Id.* at 152–53.

110. *See* U.S. CONST. art. V.

111. *See* H.R.J. Res. 208, 92d Cong., 86 Stat. 1523 (1972).

112. *See* H.R.J. Res. 638, 95th Cong., 92 Stat. 3799 (1978).

113. *See A Short History of E.R.A., supra* note 31, at 1; Julia Malone, *Phyllis Schlafly: Wife, Politician Who 'Does It All Without the ERA,'* CHRISTIAN SCI. MONITOR, June 25, 1982, at 22; Megan Rosenfeld, *Hits from the Mrs.,* WASH. POST, Mar. 23, 1979, at C1.

114. *See, e.g.,* SUSAN J. DOUGLAS, WHERE THE GIRLS ARE: GROWING UP FEMALE WITH THE MASS MEDIA 232 (1994); CAROL FELSENTHAL, THE SWEETHEART OF THE SILENT MAJORITY: THE BIOGRAPHY OF PHYLLIS SCHLAFLY 258 (1981).

115. *See* JANE J. MANSBRIDGE, WHY WE LOST THE ERA 110 (1986); Donald T. Critchlow & Cynthia L. Stachecki, *The Equal Rights Amendment Reconsidered: Politics, Policy, and Social Mobilization in a Democracy,* 20 J. POL'Y HIST. 157, 165 (2008); *ERA Debate Marred,* CHICO ENTER.-REC., Nov. 18, 1982, at 2B; Joseph Lelyveld, *Should Women Be Nicer Than Men?,* N.Y. TIMES, Apr. 17, 1977 (§ 6), at 126; Alan Wolfe, *Mrs. America,* NEW REPUBLIC, Oct. 3, 2005, at 32, 32 (book review).

116. *See, e.g.,* SUZANNE VENKER & PHYLLIS SCHLAFLY, THE FLIPSIDE OF FEMINISM: WHAT CONSERVATIVE WOMEN KNOW—AND MEN CAN'T SAY 38–43 (2011); Ginia Bellafante, *A Feminine Mystique All Her Own,* N.Y. TIMES, Mar. 30, 2006, at F1; J.T. Leonard, *Schlafly Cranks Up Agitation at Bates,* SUN J. (Lewiston), Mar. 29, 2007, at A1.

117. ROBERT H. BORK, SLOUCHING TOWARDS GOMORRAH: MODERN LIBERALISM AND AMERICAN DECLINE (1996).

118. For Bork's posthumously published memoir about this phase of his career, see ROBERT H. BORK, SAVING JUSTICE: WATERGATE, THE SATURDAY NIGHT MASSACRE, AND OTHER ADVENTURES OF A SOLICITOR GENERAL 14–19, 69–113 (2013).

119. For the nomination, see 123 J. EXEC. PROC. SENATE U.S.A. 1207 (1982). For the confirmation, see 128 CONG. REC. 1005 (1982).

120. For the nomination, see 129 J. EXEC. PROC. SENATE U.S.A. 493 (1988).

121. For the testimony, see *Nomination of Robert H. Bork to Be Associate Justice of the Supreme Court of the United States: Hearings Before the S. Comm. on the Judiciary (pt. 3),* 100th Cong. 3537–38 (1989) (statement of Beverly LaHaye). For the committee's membership, see *id.* at II.

122. *See* 133 CONG. REC. 29,121–22 (1987).

123. Letter from Robert H. Bork to Ronald Reagan, 1 PUB. PAPERS 40, 40 (Jan. 7, 1988).

124. BORK, *supra* note 117, at 2–3. On the book's sales, see *Best Sellers,* N.Y. TIMES, Feb. 2, 1997 (§ 7), at 26 (reporting eighteen weeks on bestseller list).

125. BORK, *supra* note 117, at 3.

126. *Id.* at 194.

127. *Id.* at 195 (emphasis added).

128. *Id.*

129. *Id.* at 228.

130. *See Group Preferences and the Law: Hearings Before the Subcomm. on the Const. of the H. Comm. on the Judiciary,* 104th Cong. 153 (1996) [hereinafter *Group Preferences*] (statement of Laura A. Ingraham).

131. *See* Students for Fair Admissions, Inc. v. President & Fellows of Harvard Coll., 600 U.S. 181, 230 (2023).

132. *See Group Preferences, supra* note 130, at 153 (statement of Laura A. Ingraham).

133. On the origins of the Independent Women's Forum, see Paul M. Barrett, *A New Wave of Counterfeminists Is Providing Conservatism with a Sophisticated Female Face*, WALL ST. J., Oct. 13, 1995, at A16 (internal quotation marks omitted). For Hill's testimony, see *Nomination of Judge Clarence Thomas to Be Associate Justice of the Supreme Court of the United States: Hearings Before the S. Comm. on the Judiciary (pt. 4)*, 102d Cong. 36–40 (1993) (statement of Professor Anita F. Hill). For Thomas's confirmation, see 137 CONG. REC. 26,354 (1991).

134. Martin Fletcher, *'There Is No Male Conspiracy,'* TIMES (London), Dec. 29, 1995, at 13 (quoting Barbara Ledeen, misspelled LeDeen) (internal quotation marks omitted).

135. For Ingraham's clerkship, see *Group Preferences, supra* note 130, at 143 (statement of Rep. Charles Canady). For Ingraham's membership on the advisory board, see Laura A. Ingraham, *Enter, Women*, N.Y. TIMES, Apr. 19, 1995, at A23. For media attention, see, e.g., James Atlas, *The Counter Counterculture*, N.Y. TIMES, Feb. 12, 1995 (§ 6), at 32.

136. Megan Rosenfeld, *Feminist Fatales*, WASH. POST, Nov. 30, 1995, at D1 (quoting Barbara Ledeen) (internal quotation marks omitted).

137. *Group Preferences, supra* note 130, at 154 (statement of Laura A. Ingraham).

138. *Id.* at 156 (statement of Laura A. Ingraham).

139. Ingraham, *supra* note 135, at A23; *see also* Laura A. Ingraham, *Perspectives on Affirmative Action: Is It an Institutional Crutch or Essential to Women's Progress?*, L.A. TIMES, Apr. 19, 1995, at B7.

140. For more examples, see Jennifer Gonnerman, *Angry White Women: A Right-Wing Women's Group Sets Out to Crush Feminism*, VILL. VOICE, July 11, 1995, at 17; Ellen Ladowsky, *That's No White Male . . .*, WALL. ST. J., Mar. 27, 1995, at A20.

141. *See* Anita K. Blair, *Paperwork Won't Stop Violence Against Women*, AUSTIN AM.-STATESMAN, Aug. 15, 1995, at A9.

142. For Blair as the counsel of record, see Brief of *Amici Curiae* Independent Women's Forum et al. at 15, United States v. Virginia, 518 U.S. 515 (1996) (Nos. 94-1941 & 94-2107).

143. *See id.* at 2–8.

144. *Id.* at 14 (emphasis omitted).

145. *Id.* at 15.

146. *See* United States v. Virginia, 518 U.S. 515, 519 (1996).

147. *See VMI Will Admit Women*, DAILY PRESS (Newport News-Hampton), Sept. 22, 1996, at A1.

148. K.C. Swanson, *She's No Feminist, and She's Proud of It*, NAT'L J., Jan. 4, 1997, at 34, 34 (quoting Anita K. Blair) (internal quotation marks omitted).

149. Stephen Goode, *Armed with Common Sense, Anita Blair Attacks Feminism*, INSIGHT, Nov. 24, 1997, at 31, 33 (quoting interview with Anita Blair).

150. *Id.* at 31 (quoting Anita Blair) (emphasis and internal quotation marks omitted).

151. *Id.* at 33 (quoting interview with Anita Blair).

152. *Id.* (quoting interview with Anita Blair) (internal quotation marks omitted).

153. *See* OFF. OF THE FED. REG., NAT'L ARCHIVES & RECS. ADMIN., THE UNITED STATES GOVERNMENT MANUAL 2002/2003, at 182 (2002).

154. For the article, see F. Carolyn Graglia, *We're All Tramps Now*, WOMEN'S Q., Autumn 1997, at 9.

155. F. Carolyn Graglia, Domestic Tranquility: A Brief Against Feminism 120 (1998); *see also id.* at 9, 114–15, 249. On affirmative action, see *id.* at 2, 12, 17–19, 114, 135–36. On the ERA, see *id.* at 27, 105, 137–38, 189.

156. *Id.* at 111–12; *see also id.* at 19–23, 33, 356.

157. *See id.* at 112.

158. *See id.* at 1–2, 9, 17–19, 113.

159. *Id.* at 27; *see also id.* at 28, 133–35.

160. *Id.* at 113 (emphasis added).

161. Lisa Schiffren, *Family First*, Wall. St. J., Mar. 19, 1998, at A16 (book review).

162. Janet Wilson, *Lawyer Made Her Case for Being Home with Kids*, Austin Am.-Statesman, Nov. 5, 1998, at E1.

163. *See* Rosenfeld, *supra* note 136, at D1.

164. For Sommers's article adapted from her speech, see Christina Hoff Sommers, *The 'Fragile American Girl' Myth*, Am. Enter., May/June 1997, at 73, 73. On Bork at the American Enterprise Institute, see James Warren, *Bork Blames Yale for Decline of Western Civilization*, Chi. Trib., Dec. 8, 1996 (§ 2), at 2.

165. Sommers, *supra* note 164, at 73.

166. For the introduction to the *Guide*, see Bryanna T. Hocking & Dawn Scheirer, *Letter from the Editors, in* The Women's Guild, The Guide: A Little Beige Book for Today's Miss G 2, 2 (Bryanna T. Hocking & Dawn Scheirer eds., 1997) (copy on file with author; Georgetown University Archives, Student Handbooks, box 9) [hereinafter Guide]. For acknowledgment that the "IWF provided advice, assistance and support for the publication of this Guide," see *Special Thanks to, in* Guide, *supra*, at 2, 2 (emphasis omitted). For reports on how much the IWF spent, see Aaron Davis, *A 'Little Beige Book,' a Lot of Controversy*, Hoya, Oct. 10, 1997, at 1 ("estimated between $4,000 and $5,000"); Julia Duin, *Students at GU Upset by Pamphlet for Freshman Girls*, Wash. Times, Oct. 28, 1997, at A2 ("$5,000").

167. *See* Davis, *supra* note 166, at 1; Hocking & Scheirer, *supra* note 166, at 2.

168. *See* Sarah Blustain, *Ladies of the Right*, Lingua Franca, Oct. 1999, at 8, 8; Davis, *supra* note 166, at 1.

169. Hocking & Scheirer, *supra* note 166, at 2.

170. Dawn Scheirer, *A Lie a Day Keeps the Truth Away, in* Guide, *supra* note 166, at 9, 12.

171. Bryanna T. Hocking, *I Am Woman, Hear Me Purr, in* Guide, *supra* note 166, at 18, 19.

172. Suzanne Fields, *I Am Woman, Hear Me Purr*, Wash. Times, Oct. 9, 1997, at A19.

173. *Special Thanks to*, Portia, Fall 1998, at 2, 2 (copy on file with author; Yale University, Sterling Memorial Library, Manuscripts and Archives).

174. D.L.S., *Letter from the Editor*, Portia, Fall 1998, at 2, 2 (emphasis and internal quotation marks omitted).

175. Deborah Schmuhl, *Are We Liberated Yet?*, Portia, Fall 1998, at 6, 7.

176. Nancy M. Pfotenhauer, *Bush Had Message for Women*, Kan. City Star, Jan. 30, 2003, at B7 (emphasis added).

177. For Palin's memoir recounting the experience, see Sarah Palin, Going Rogue: An American Life 209–339 (2009).

178. *Sarah Palin 2008 Acceptance Speech* (C-SPAN television broadcast Sept. 3, 2008).

179. *CBS News* (CBS television broadcast Sept. 30, 2008) (transcript copy on file with author).

180. *See* Ledbetter v. Goodyear Tire & Rubber Co., 550 U.S. 618, 628–29 (2007).

181. *See* Lilly Ledbetter Fair Pay Act of 2009, Pub. L. No. 111-2, § 3, 123 Stat. 5, 5–6. For more on Lilly Ledbetter, see *infra* Chapter 7.

182. *See* Julia Edwards, *Cleta Mitchell*, Nat'l J., July 14, 2012, at 31, 31; Jane Mayer, *The Big Money Behind the Big Lie*, New Yorker, Aug. 9, 2021, at 30, 33–34; Michael S. Schmidt & Kenneth P. Vogel, *Top Lawyer's Cover Is Blown by Trump Tape*, N.Y. Times, Jan. 5, 2021, at A14; Elizabeth Williamson, *Riding Shotgun on Campaign Trail*, Wall. St. J., Oct. 30, 2010, at A6.

183. Cleta Mitchell, *No Room for Dissent in 'Feminist Club,'* N.Y. Times, Apr. 2, 2017, at F3. For an interview with Mitchell along similar lines, see Susan Chira, *Since When Is Being a Woman a Liberal Cause?*, N.Y. Times, Feb. 12, 2017, at SR9.

184. *See* Stuart A. Thompson et al., *Election Fraud? Deniers Quiet as Trump's Win Became Clear.*, N.Y. Times, Nov. 8, 2024, at B5; Alexandra Berzon, *Republicans Flag False Threat to Election: Immigrant Voting*, N.Y. Times, Sept. 7, 2024, at A1; Alexandra Berzon & Nick Corasaniti, *Trump Allies Quietly Push to Reduce Key Voter Rolls*, N.Y. Times, Mar. 4, 2024, at A15; Alexandra Berzon & Ken Bensinger, *A Group Fueled by Falsehoods Stands Ready to Challenge Votes*, N.Y. Times, Nov. 8, 2022, at A1; Alexandra Berzon, *Election Denier Musters 'Army' to Watch Vote*, N.Y. Times, May 31, 2022, at A1; Mayer, *supra* note 182, at 33–34; Schmidt & Vogel, *supra* note 182, at A14.

185. *See* Elizabeth Larson, *Question: Is It Time to End Affirmative Action for Women? Yes: Women Don't Need Extra Help*, Insight, Apr. 24, 1995, at 18, 18.

186. *Id.* at 20–21 (emphasis added).

187. *Id.* at 21.

188. *See* Diana Furchtgott-Roth, *Q: Should Women Be Worried About the Glass Ceiling in the Workplace? No: The So-Called Glass Ceiling Is a Myth, but We're All Paying Plenty to Tear It Down*, Insight, Feb. 10, 1997, at 25, 25 [hereinafter Furchtgott-Roth, *Myth*]. For confirmation that the book "is a publication of the Independent Women's Forum," see Diana Furchtgott-Roth & Christine Stolba, Women's Figures: The Economic Progress of Women in America, at copyright page (1996).

189. Furchtgott-Roth, *Myth*, *supra* note 188, at 27.

190. *Id.* at 25.

191. *Id.* at 27.

192. *See* Emma Hinchliffe, *The Share of Fortune 500 Companies Run by Women CEOs Stays Flat at 10.4% as Pace of Change Stalls*, Fortune, June 4, 2024.

193. On Sidak's role as Chief of Staff to Reagan's Secretary of Transportation, see Off. of the Fed. Reg., Nat'l Archives & Recs. Admin., The United States Government Manual 1988/89, at 435 (1988).

194. For some of the overwhelming evidence Sidak denied, see Off. on Smoking & Health, U.S. Dep't of Health & Hum. Servs., The Health Consequences of Involuntary Smoking: A Report of the Surgeon General (1986); Pub. Health Serv., U.S. Dep't of Health, Educ., & Welfare, Pub. No. 1103, Smoking and Health: Report of the Advisory Committee to the Surgeon General of the Public Health Service (1964).

195. Leonard Buder, *Council to Consider Ban on Cigarette Machines*, N.Y. Times, May 4, 1990, at B3 (quoting Melinda Sidak) (internal quotation marks omitted).

196. *See id.*; Dan Koeppel, *An Ethical Plan for Tobacco Marketers*, Adweek's Mktg. Wk., May 28, 1990, at 18, 18.

197. *See* N.Y.C., N.Y., Local Law 67 (Nov. 27, 1990).

198. *Affirmative Action in Employment: Hearings Before the Subcomm. on Employer-Employee Rels. of the H. Comm. on Econ. & Educ. Opportunities*, 104th Cong. 284 (1995) (statement of Melinda Ledden Sidak).

199. For Chavez's recounting of her work in the Reagan administration, see LINDA CHAVEZ, AN UNLIKELY CONSERVATIVE: THE TRANSFORMATION OF AN EX-LIBERAL [OR, HOW I BECAME THE MOST HATED HISPANIC IN AMERICA] 169–86 (2002).

200. Linda Chavez, *Many Women Don't Want to Break Glass Ceiling*, TENNESSEAN, Mar. 23, 1995, at 15A. For the statistic in the report Chavez was dismissing, see Robert B. Reich, *Message from the Chairman, in* FED. GLASS CEILING COMM'N, GOOD FOR BUSINESS: MAKING FULL USE OF THE NATION'S HUMAN CAPITAL, at iii, iv (1995).

201. *See* CARRIE L. LUKAS, THE POLITICALLY INCORRECT GUIDE TO WOMEN, SEX, AND FEMINISM, at back cover (2006).

202. *Id.* at xiv (citation and internal quotation marks omitted).

203. *Id.* at 18.

204. Sabrina L. Schaeffer, *Principle Is More Important than Gender When It Comes to Public Office*, TELEGRAPH (Macon), Oct. 16, 2015, at 7A (internal quotation marks omitted).

205. *See* Sam Roberts, *Kate O'Beirne, National Review Editor, 67*, N.Y. TIMES, Apr. 25, 2017, at B12.

206. KATE O'BEIRNE, WOMEN WHO MAKE THE WORLD WORSE: AND HOW THEIR RADICAL FEMINIST ASSAULT IS RUINING OUR FAMILIES, MILITARY, SCHOOLS, AND SPORTS (2006).

207. *Id.* at xviii.

208. *See id.* at 23–46.

209. *Id.* at 23.

210. *See Caring for America's Children—A Congressional Symposium on Child Care and Parenting: Hearing Before the Subcomm. on Child. & Fams. of the S. Comm. on Lab. & Hum. Res.*, 105th Cong. 65 (1998) [hereinafter *Caring for America's Children*] (statement of Sen. Daniel Coats); Joyce Price, *No 'Angry Agenda,' No Feminists at New Women's Quarterly*, WASH. TIMES, Sept. 13, 1995, at A2.

211. *Caring for America's Children, supra* note 210, at 67 (statement of Danielle Crittenden). For an article adapted from her testimony, see Danielle Crittenden, *The Mother of All Problems*, WOMEN'S Q., Spring 1998, at 2.

212. DANIELLE CRITTENDEN, WHAT OUR MOTHERS DIDN'T TELL US: WHY HAPPINESS ELUDES THE MODERN WOMAN 177 (1999); *see also id.* at 173–74.

213. *Caring for America's Children, supra* note 210, at 69 (statement of Danielle Crittenden).

214. *Id.* at 68 (statement of Danielle Crittenden).

215. *See, e.g.*, H.R. Res. 432, 103d Cong. (1994); Marla Dickerson, *ERA Activists Try to Start Again: 'No Time Limit on Justice,'* DETROIT NEWS & FREE PRESS, Mar. 27, 1994, at 1B; Allie Corbin Hixson, *Equal Rights Amendment*, COURIER-J. (Louisville), June 1, 1992, at A6; Eileen Stilwell, *Women's Groups Hoping to Revive Fight for ERA*, COURIER-POST (New Jersey), Mar. 22, 1994, at 3A.

216. *See, e.g.*, H.R.J. Res. Constitutional Amendment 5, 90th Gen. Assemb., 1997 Sess. (Ill. 1997); H.R.J. Res. 41, 89th Gen. Assemb., 2d Reg. Sess. (Mo. 1998).

217. *See ERA Foes Attack Vote*, SUNDAY STATE J. (Lansing), Oct. 8, 1978, at B4; Diane Haithman, *Elaine Donnelly: Still a Woman with a Cause*, DETROIT FREE PRESS, May 17, 1984, at 1B; John Hanchette, *ERA Now 'Dead as a Doornail,'* LANSING STATE J., Nov. 23, 1980, at

D1; Ron Russell, *ERA R.I.P.: The Winner*, Detroit News, June 27, 1982, at 1C; Willah Weddon, *'Stop ERA' Leader No Little Old Lady*, State J. (Lansing), July 12, 1974, at D4.

218. Dickerson, *supra* note 215, at 1B (quoting Elaine Donnelly) (internal quotation marks omitted). For more on Donnelly's opposition to women in combat, see The Presidential Comm'n on the Assignment of Women in the Armed Forces, Report to the President 42–79 (1992) (alternative views).

219. Stephanie Simon, *Activists Seek to Bring ERA Back to Life*, L.A. Times, Mar. 9, 2000, at A5 (quoting Vicky Hartzler) (internal quotation marks omitted).

220. George F. Will, *The Return of that '70s Thing*, Wash. Post, Apr. 1, 2007, at B7.

221. David Crary, *Equal Rights Fight*, Phila. Inquirer, Aug. 11, 2014, at A5 (quoting Phyllis Schlafly) (internal quotation marks omitted).

222. Journal of the Senate of the State of Nevada, Seventy-Ninth Session 170 (2017) (statement of Sen. Michael Roberson). For Roberson's vote against ratification, see *id.* at 172. For more examples, see Cathi Herrod, *The Irony of the Equal Rights Amendment*, Ariz. Republic, Feb. 27, 2019, at 19A; Ed Vogel, *Panel Revives Equal Rights Amendment Effort*, Las Vegas Rev.-J., Feb. 25, 2005, at 6B.

223. Rebecca Catalanello, *Equal Rights Amendment Sinks in Legislative Tide*, St. Petersburg Times, May 2, 2007, at 6B (quoting Ronda Storms) (internal quotation marks omitted).

224. Nicole Gaudiano, *Fight for ERA Draws New Interest*, Burlington Free Press, Sept. 12, 2014, at 11A (quoting Margaret Ransone) (internal quotation marks omitted).

225. Victoria Cobb, *Modern Feminism Commands Respect—Without the ERA*, Richmond Times-Dispatch, Mar. 5, 2018, at A11.

226. *See* S.J. Res. 2, 2017 Nev. Stat. 4551.

227. *See* S.J. Res. Constitutional Amendment 4, 2018 Ill. Laws 8987.

228. *See* S.J. Res. 1, 2020 Va. Acts 4627; H.D.J. Res. 1, 2020 Va. Acts 4283.

229. For the archivist's responsibility, see 1 U.S.C. § 106b.

230. For the opinion, see Ratification of the Equal Rights Amendment, 44 Op. O.L.C., slip op. at 1–3, 24–25, 37 (Jan. 6, 2020). For discussion of the opinion's public release on the first day of Virginia's 2020 legislative session, see Patricia Sullivan, *Too Late to Ratify ERA, Justice Dept. Says in Opinion*, Wash. Post, Jan. 9, 2020, at B3.

231. *See* Ratification of the Equal Rights Amendment, *supra* note 230, at 36–37. For legislation purporting to rescind prior ratifications, see Legislative Res. 9, 1973 Neb. Laws 1547; S.J. Res. 29, 1974 Tenn. Pub. Acts 1921; H.R. Con. Res. 10, 1977 Idaho Sess. Laws 950; S.J. Res. 2, 1979 S.D. Sess. Laws ch. 2, at 28; S. Con. Res. 4010, ch. 539, 2021 N.D. Laws 2219. In 1978, Kentucky's acting governor, Lieutenant Governor Thelma Stovall, vetoed the state legislature's attempt to rescind. *See* 124 Cong. Rec. 37,923 (1978) (statement of Sen. Birch Bayh) (reprinting Stovall's veto message).

232. Press Release, Nat'l Archives & Recs. Admin., NARA Press Statement on the Equal Rights Amendment (Jan. 8, 2020) (copy on file with author).

233. *See* Joseph R. Biden, Jr., Statement on the Equal Rights Amendment (Jan. 27, 2022) (copy on file with author).

234. For a letter urging that action, see Letter from Carolyn B. Maloney, U.S. Rep., to Joseph R. Biden, Jr., U.S. President, and Kamala Harris, U.S. Vice President (Jan. 22, 2021) (copy on file with author).

235. Effect of 2020 OLC Opinion on Possible Congressional Action Regarding Ratification of the Equal Rights Amendment, 46 Op. O.L.C., slip op. at 2 (Jan. 26, 2022).

236. *See* Illinois v. Ferriero, 60 F.4th 704, 709–10 (D.C. Cir. 2023); Equal Means Equal v. Ferriero, 3 F.4th 24, 26–27 (1st Cir. 2021).

237. For recent bills, see H.R.J. Res. 82, 118th Cong. (2023); H.R.J. Res. 25, 118th Cong. (2023); S.J. Res. 39, 118th Cong. (2023); S.J. Res. 4, 118th Cong. (2023); H.R. Res. 891, 117th Cong. (2022); H.R.J. Res. 17, 117th Cong. (as passed by House, Mar. 17, 2021); S.J. Res. 1, 117th Cong. (2021); H.R.J. Res. 79, 116th Cong. (as passed by House, Feb. 13, 2020); H.R.J. Res. 38, 116th Cong. (2019); S.J. Res. 6, 116th Cong. (2019).

238. 167 Cong. Rec. H1421 (daily ed. Mar. 17, 2021) (statement of Rep. Debbie Lesko); *see also* 166 Cong. Rec. H1130 (daily ed. Feb. 13, 2020) (statement of Rep. Debbie Lesko); *id.* at H1026 (daily ed. Feb. 11, 2020) (statement of Rep. Debbie Lesko).

239. *See* Dobbs v. Jackson Women's Health Org., 597 U.S. 215, 231 (2022). For more on *Dobbs*, see *supra* Chapter 5.

240. H.R. Rep. No. 116-378, at 19 (2020) (dissenting views by Rep. Doug Collins); *see also id.* at 22 (dissenting views by Rep. Doug Collins); 166 Cong. Rec. H1139–40 (daily ed. Feb. 13, 2020) (statement of Rep. Doug Collins).

241. 166 Cong. Rec. H1132 (daily ed. Feb. 13, 2020) (statement of Rep. Jackie Walorski).

242. *Id.* at H1135 (daily ed. Feb. 13, 2020) (statement of Rep. Virginia Foxx).

243. *Id.* at H1134 (daily ed. Feb. 13, 2020) (statement of Rep. Kay Granger). For other congressional opponents in 2020, see *id.* at H1135 (daily ed. Feb. 13, 2020) (statement of Rep. Carol Miller); *id.* at H1141–42 (daily ed. Feb. 13, 2020) (statement of Rep. Christopher Smith); *id.* at H1027 (daily ed. Feb. 11, 2020) (statement of Rep. Ann Wagner).

244. 167 Cong. Rec. H1421 (daily ed. Mar. 17, 2021) (statement of Rep. Debbie Lesko); *see also* 166 Cong. Rec. H1130 (daily ed. Feb. 13, 2020) (statement of Rep. Debbie Lesko); *id.* at H1026 (daily ed. Feb. 11, 2020) (statement of Rep. Debbie Lesko).

245. 167 Cong. Rec. H1423 (daily ed. Mar. 17, 2021) (statement of Rep. Vicky Hartzler); *see also* 166 Cong. Rec. H1132 (daily ed. Feb. 13, 2020) (statement of Rep. Vicky Hartzler).

246. 167 Cong. Rec. H1422 (daily ed. Mar. 17, 2021) (statement of Rep. Marjorie Taylor Greene). For other congressional opponents in 2021, see *id.* at H1424 (daily ed. Mar. 17, 2021) (statement of Rep. Tom McClintock); *id.* at H1425 (daily ed. Mar. 17, 2021) (statement of Rep. Michelle Fischbach); *The Equal Rights Amendment: Achieving Constitutional Equality for All: Hearing Before the H. Comm. on Oversight & Reform*, 117th Cong. 40 (2021) [hereinafter *Achieving Constitutional Equality*] (statement of Rep. Andrew Clyde); *id.* at 45 (statement of Rep. Yvette Herrell).

247. *The Equal Rights Amendment: How Congress Can Recognize Ratification and Enshrine Equality in Our Constitution: Hearing on S.J. Res. 4 Before the S. Comm. on the Judiciary*, 118th Cong. (2023) (transcript at 4; copy on file with author) [hereinafter *Congress Can Recognize*] (statement of Sen. Cindy Hyde-Smith).

248. *Id.* at 13–14 (statement of Sen. Lindsey Graham).

249. 167 Cong. Rec. H1420 (daily ed. Mar. 17, 2021) (statement of Rep. Michelle Fischbach); *see also id.* at H1425 (daily ed. Mar. 17, 2021) (statement of Rep. Michelle Fischbach).

250. *Achieving Constitutional Equality, supra* note 246, at 5 (statement of Rep. James Comer); *see also id.* at 52 (statement of Rep. James Comer).

251. *Id.* at 35 (statement of Rep. Fred Keller).

252. *Id.* at 39 (statement of Rep. Andrew Clyde).

253. 167 Cong. Rec. H1423 (daily ed. Mar. 17, 2021) (statement of Rep. Vicky Hartzler); *see also* 166 Cong. Rec. H1131 (daily ed. Feb. 13, 2020) (statement of Rep. Vicky Hartzler);

Congress Can Recognize, supra note 247, at 4 (statement of Sen. Cindy Hyde-Smith); *id.* at 13 (statement of Sen. Lindsey Graham).

Chapter 7

1. *See, e.g.,* Act of Mar. 20, 2024, Act No. 2024-34, 2024 Ala. Laws; Act of May 3, 2021, 2021 Ark. Acts 5652; Act of June 8, 2021, ch. 163, 2021 Iowa Acts 415; Act of May 15, 2023, ch. 2023-82, 2023 Fla. Laws 1015; Act of Apr. 22, 2022, ch. 2022-72, 2022 Fla. Laws 534; Act of Mar. 28, 2022, ch. 2022-22, 2022 Fla. Laws 248; Act of June 25, 2021, ch. 91, 2021 N.H. Legis. Serv. 107; Act of May 7, 2021, ch. 426, 2021 Okla. Sess. Laws 1642; Act of Mar. 21, 2022, ch. 39, 2022 S.D. Sess. Laws 67; Act of Apr. 8, 2022, ch. 818, 2022 Tenn. Pub. Acts 859; Act of May 25, 2021, ch. 493, 2021 Tenn. Pub. Acts 1546; Act of Sept. 17, 2021, ch. 9, 2021 Tex. Gen. Laws 3928; *see also* Va. Exec. Order No. 1 (Jan. 15, 2022).
2. *See supra* Chapters 1 & 4.
3. *See supra* Chapter 4.
4. *See* 6 THE HISTORY OF WOMAN SUFFRAGE 131–33, 341 (Ida Husted Harper ed., 1922); *"Go to the Polls and Vote," Urges Suffrage Leader,* ATLANTA CONST., Nov. 1, 1920, at 1; *Mississippi Women Are Not in a Hurry,* JACKSON DAILY NEWS, Sept. 18, 1920, at 3.
5. *See* S. Res. 304, 1970 Ga. Laws 951.
6. *See* H.R. Con. Res. 30, ch. 537, 1984 Miss. Laws. 802.
7. *See supra* Chapters 1 & 3.
8. *See supra* Chapters 1 & 5.
9. For more on *Muller,* see *supra* Chapter 1. For examples using the term "protective labor legislation," see Cal. Fed. Sav. & Loan Ass'n v. Guerra, 479 U.S. 272, 290 (1987); ELIZABETH FAULKNER BAKER, PROTECTIVE LABOR LEGISLATION (1925); SUSAN LEHRER, ORIGINS OF PROTECTIVE LABOR LEGISLATION FOR WOMEN, 1905–1925 (1987); WOMEN'S BUREAU, U.S. DEP'T OF LAB., INTERNATIONAL REPORT NO. 5, WOMEN IN THE WORLD TODAY: PROTECTIVE LABOR LEGISLATION FOR WOMEN IN 91 COUNTRIES (1963).
10. For an article exploring this theme across multiple contexts, see Jill Elaine Hasday, *Protecting Them from Themselves: The Persistence of Mutual Benefits Arguments for Sex and Race Inequality,* 84 N.Y.U. L. REV. 1464 (2009).
11. *See supra* Chapter 1.
12. *See supra* Chapter 3.
13. *See* Fair Labor Standards Act of 1938, ch. 676, § 8(c), 52 Stat. 1060, 1064.
14. For contemporary discussion of excluded occupations, see Women's Bureau, U.S. Dep't of Lab., *The Federal Wage-Hour Law and Women Workers,* WOMAN WORKER, July 1938, at 3, 3.
15. For the overtime provision, see Fair Labor Standards Act § 7.
16. *See id.* § 2.
17. *See supra* Introductory Chapter.
18. 208 U.S. 412, 416–23 (1908).
19. 302 U.S. 277, 279–84 (1937).
20. 335 U.S. 464, 465–67 (1948).
21. 368 U.S. 57, 58–69 (1961).
22. 597 U.S. 215, 231 (2022).
23. *See supra* Chapter 1.

24. 163 U.S. 537, 543 (1896); *see also id.* at 544–45; Civil Rights Cases, 109 U.S. 3, 25 (1883); Shelby County v. Holder, 570 U.S. 529, 547–57 (2013).

25. *See supra* Chapter 1.

26. *See supra* Chapter 2.

27. *See, e.g.,* Julia Halperin, *Smithsonian Women's History Museum Names Director,* N.Y. TIMES, Mar. 13, 2024, at C5.

28. On anti-feminism, see *supra* Chapters 2 & 6.

29. For conservative criticism along these lines, see May Mailman, *Women's Museum Needs a Course Correction,* WACO TRIB.-HERALD, Apr. 8, 2023, at A6.

30. *See supra* Chapter 2.

31. For more on the ERA, see *supra* Chapter 6. For more on voting, see *supra* Chapters 1, 3 & 5. For more on reproductive autonomy, see *supra* Chapters 1–6.

32. *See* Fritz Hahn, *Museum Celebrates Journey to Women's Suffrage,* WASH. POST, Aug. 14, 2020 (Weekend), at 6.

33. On suffragists jailed at Occoquan, see INEZ HAYNES IRWIN, THE STORY OF THE WOMAN'S PARTY 261–91 (1921); DORIS STEVENS, JAILED FOR FREEDOM 192–209 (1920).

34. *See* STEVENS, *supra* note 33, at 356.

35. *See, e.g.,* Lucy Burns Museum, Taking It to D.C.'s Streets; The Activist Alternative; Under Arrest: Imprisoned at the Occoquan Workhouse; Life in the Cells; Summer of Protest; Political Prisoners; Suffragists Behind Bars; From Prison to the Vote (museum display panels; copies on file with author). For a panel that extends past the Nineteenth Amendment's ratification, see Lucy Burns Museum, The African American Fight for Suffrage (museum display panel; copy on file with author).

36. Lucy Burns Museum, Night of Terror (museum display panel; copy on file with author).

37. *See A Week of the Women's Revolution,* SUFFRAGIST, Nov. 24, 1917, at 4, 4–5.

38. Lucy Burns Museum, *supra* note 36 (internal quotation marks omitted). For publication of this note, see *A Week of the Women's Revolution, supra* note 37, at 5.

39. *See* MONUMENT LAB: CREATIVE SPECULATIONS FOR PHILADELPHIA 97 (Paul M. Farber & Ken Lum eds., 2020); Ken Lum, *Memorializing Philadelphia as a Place of Crisis and Boundless Hope, in id.* at 16, 17–18; Jodi Throckmorton, *The Meaning of Absence: Sharon Hayes's* If They Should Ask, *in* MONUMENT LAB, *supra,* at 98, 98; Stephan Salisbury, *Who Deserves a Monument?,* PHILA. INQUIRER, Sept. 14, 2017, at A1.

40. *See* MONUMENT LAB, *supra* note 39, at 97; Lum, *supra* note 39, at 18.

41. *See* Throckmorton, *supra* note 39, at 98–99.

42. *Id.* at 99 (internal quotation marks omitted).

43. For the number of names, see Natalie Pompilio, *Philly Project Evaluates Meaning of Monuments,* REPUBLICAN HERALD (Pottsville), Sept. 5, 2017, at 14.

44. *See* MONUMENT LAB, *supra* note 39, at 97; Throckmorton, *supra* note 39, at 99; Salisbury, *supra* note 39, at A1.

45. *See* RUTH SERGEL, SEE YOU IN THE STREETS: ART, ACTION, AND REMEMBERING THE TRIANGLE SHIRTWAIST FACTORY FIRE 5, 21–22 (2016); Clyde Haberman, *Choosing Not to Forget What Is Painful to Recall,* N.Y. TIMES, Mar. 26, 2010, at A19; Michael Molyneux, *Memorials in Chalk,* N.Y. TIMES, Apr. 3, 2005 (§ 14), at 12.

46. For discussion of the complete list of victims, see Joseph Berger, *A Century Later, the Roll of the Dead in a Factory Fire Now Has All 146 Names,* N.Y. TIMES, Feb. 21, 2011, at A13.

47. On the absence of safety measures, see DAVID VON DREHLE, TRIANGLE: THE FIRE THAT CHANGED AMERICA 161–64 (2003). On cotton's flammability, see *id.* at 118–19, 236.

48. *See id.* at 4, 62–63, 86.

49. *See id.* at 123, 127–28, 164, 219–20, 254–55, 265.

50. *See id.* at 185, 206–18, 267.

51. *See* SERGEL, *supra* note 45, at 21–22.

52. *See id.* at 21–23.

53. *See id.* at 22–23.

54. *See* Pompilio, *supra* note 43, at 14.

55. *See supra* Chapter 2.

56. *See* RETURN OF THE WHOLE NUMBER OF PERSONS WITHIN THE SEVERAL DISTRICTS OF THE UNITED STATES 4 (London, J. Phillips 1793).

57. For discussion of early voting restrictions on white men, see Donald Ratcliffe, *The Right to Vote and the Rise of Democracy, 1787–1828*, 33 J. EARLY REPUBLIC 219 (2013). For an appendix listing "Property Qualifications in First State Constitutions and Election Laws," see WILLI PAUL ADAMS, THE FIRST AMERICAN CONSTITUTIONS: REPUBLICAN IDEOLOGY AND THE MAKING OF THE STATE CONSTITUTIONS IN THE REVOLUTIONARY ERA 315–27 (Rita Kimber & Robert Kimber trans., expanded ed. 2001). New Jersey's 1776 Constitution entitled "all Inhabitants" to vote if they met age, property, and length of residency requirements. N.J. CONST. of 1776, art. IV. In 1807, however, the New Jersey Legislature specified that every voter had to "be a *free, white, male citizen,*" disenfranchising women, people of color, and aliens. Act of Nov. 16, 1807, ch. 2, § 1, 1807 N.J. Laws 14, 14.

58. RETURN OF THE WHOLE NUMBER OF PERSONS WITHIN THE SEVERAL DISTRICTS OF THE UNITED STATES, *supra* note 56, at 4.

59. Dianna M. Náñez, *Do You Vote for Harriet Tubman on the $20 Bill?*, ARIZ. REPUBLIC, May 16, 2015, at 16A (internal quotation marks omitted).

60. For more on this history, see *supra* Chapter 1.

61. For the establishment of June 9 as "Fannie Lou Hamer Day" in Winona, see Proclamation from the Mayor and Board of Aldermen of the City of Winona, Mississippi, Fannie Lou Hamer (Apr. 19, 2022) (copy on file with author) (capitalization omitted). For the unveiling of the historical marker, see Tish Butts, *Bridging the Gap: Hamer Celebrated*, WINONA TIMES, June 16, 2022, at 1.

62. For a published photograph of the marker, see Butts, *supra* note 61, at 1.

63. *See* Trial Transcript at 1, United States v. Patridge, No. WCR6343 (N.D. Miss. 1963) (copy on file with author; Florida State University Libraries, Special Collections & Archives, Davis Houck Papers) [hereinafter Trial Transcript]; *Jury Frees Officers*, STUDENT VOICE (Atlanta), Dec. 9, 1963, at 1.

64. For the length of jury deliberations on December 6, 1963, see Trial Transcript, *supra* note 63, at 1134–37. For references to the jury being all-male, see *id.* at 505, 1073, 1090. For a news report that the jurors were all white men, see *5 Officers in Mississippi Cleared of Mistreatment*, N.Y. TIMES, Dec. 7, 1963, at 31.

65. *See* Trial Transcript, *supra* note 63, at 90–95 (testimony of Annell Ponder); *id.* at 147–49 (testimony of Fannie Lou Hamer); *id.* at 234–35 (testimony of James Harold West); *id.* at 399–406 (testimony of Lawrence Guyot); *id.* at 444–46 (testimony of Euvester Simpson); *id.* at 468–71 (testimony of Rosemary Freeman); *id.* at 506–15 (testimony of June Elizabeth Johnson).

66. *See supra* Chapter 1.

67. *See supra* Chapter 1.

68. *See* Photograph on Madison Place, N.W., Washington, D.C. (copy on file with author).

69. *See supra* Chapters 1–2.

70. *See Militants to Lose Cameron Mansion*, WASH. POST, July 10, 1917, at 1; *Woman's Party Ousted*, N.Y. TIMES, July 11, 1917, at 7.

71. For reporting on the new headquarters, see *Washington House for Woman's Party*, YONKERS HERALD, July 22, 1929, at 6.

72. For designation as a national historic site, see Act of Oct. 26, 1974, Pub. L. No. 93-486, § 202, 88 Stat. 1461, 1463. For designation as a national monument, see Barack Obama, Proclamation No. 9423, 3 C.F.R. 69 (2016). For discussion of battles against threatened demolition, see *Party Alarmed over Idea of Losing Capitol Hill Site*, WASH. POST, Jan. 25, 1931, at 1; L. Lamar Matthews, *A Woman's Lobby*, MONTGOMERY ADVERTISER, July 28, 1935, at 6; *National Woman's Party Fights Eviction*, SUNDAY STAR (D.C.), Mar. 18, 1956, at D5.

73. *See* ARIANE HEGEWISCH ET AL., INST. FOR WOMEN'S POL'Y RSCH., PUB. NO. C527, GENDER AND RACIAL WAGE GAPS WORSENED IN 2023 AND PAY EQUITY STILL DECADES AWAY 1 (2024).

74. For a photograph of the current National Debt Clock, see Matt Phillips, *Debt Hawks' Red Line? We Passed It Back in June*, N.Y. TIMES, Aug. 24, 2020, at B1. For discussion of an earlier version of the National Debt Clock, see Ben Upham, *Debt Clock, Calculating Since '89, Is Retiring Before the Debt Does*, N.Y. TIMES, May 14, 2000 (§ 14), at 6. On the Climate Clock, see Colin Moynihan, *Union Square's Climate Clock Is Ticking with Good News*, N.Y. TIMES, Apr. 20, 2021, at C6. The Doomsday Clock is displayed at the University of Chicago. *See* Photograph of Doomsday Clock (copy on file with author).

75. For discussion of 1997's "Pay Equity Awareness Day," see Gracie Bonds Staples, *Women, Should You Ask for a Raise Tomorrow?*, FORT WORTH STAR-TELEGRAM, Apr. 10, 1997, at F1.

76. *See* Joseph R. Biden, Jr., Proclamation No. 10,710, 89 Fed. Reg. 18,529, 18,529–30 (Mar. 11, 2024).

77. *See id.*; *Honoring "Equal Pay Day": Examining the Long-Term Economic Impacts of Gender Inequality: Hearing Before the H. Comm. on Oversight & Reform*, 117th Cong. 1 (2021) (statement of Rep. Carolyn Maloney); Sami Edge, *Plaza Rally Targets Gender Inequality*, SANTE FE NEW MEXICAN, Apr. 5, 2017, at A7; *Rally Promotes Women's Equal Pay*, DETROIT FREE PRESS, May 12, 2000, at 2B.

78. Alice Paul, *Women Will Be Real Equals in 2023*, WASH. TIMES, Dec. 28, 1922, at 24.

79. *See* CTR. FOR AM. WOMEN & POL., RUTGERS UNIV., WOMEN IN THE U.S. CONGRESS 2024 (2024); CTR. FOR AM. WOMEN & POL., RUTGERS UNIV., WOMEN IN STATE LEGISLATURES 2024 (2024).

80. For 1924, see *National Woman's Party Issues Call for Parley Aug. 15*, WASH. POST, Aug. 3, 1924, at 6; *Women-for-Congress Drive to Be Opened at Westport*, CHRISTIAN SCI. MONITOR, Aug. 13, 1924, at 1. For 1926, see *Campaigners Stop Here on 10,000 Mile Trip to Put More Women in Congress*, INDIANAPOLIS TIMES, Mar. 4, 1926, at 1; *Women Have Not Been Given Fair Chance in Congressional Races, National Party Leader Here Contends*, DAYTON DAILY NEWS, Mar. 3, 1926, at 9.

81. *See* OFF. OF THE HISTORIAN, U.S. HOUSE OF REPRESENTATIVES, WOMEN IN CONGRESS, 1917–1990, at 135–36, 183–84 (1991).

82. *See id.* at 119–20, 219–20.

83. *See id.* at 207–08; *Interest Centers on Woman Member*, EVENING STAR (D.C.), Nov. 11, 1916 (pt. I), at 2.

84. *Woman Against War*, NEWSWEEK, Feb. 14, 1966, at 12, 12 (quoting Jeannette Rankin) (internal quotation marks omitted).

85. *See* OFF. OF THE HISTORIAN, *supra* note 81, at 21–22, 57–58, 85–86, 89–90, 93–94, 99–100, 127–28, 163–64, 171–72, 177–78, 213–14, 237–39, 249–50, 253–54.

86. *See, e.g., 'The Year of the Woman,'* NEWSWEEK, Nov. 4, 1974, at 20 (internal quotation marks omitted); James Hohmann, *#Metoo May Lead to a New Holder of Year of the Woman Title*, WASH. POST, Nov. 23, 2017, at A24; sources cited *infra* notes 93, 95.

87. *See, e.g.,* Melinda Beck et al., *The Feminization of Politics*, NEWSWEEK, July 23, 1984, at 29; Thomas B. Edsall, *2000 Brings 'Feminization of Politics,'* IOWA CITY PRESS-CITIZEN, Mar. 12, 1999, at 11A (internal quotation marks omitted).

88. *See, e.g.,* Sheryl Gay Stolberg, *'Pink Wave' May Complicate Race for Speaker*, N.Y. TIMES, Nov. 16, 2018, at A14 (internal quotation marks omitted); Charlotte Alter, *A Pink Wave Crashes on the Capitol*, TIME, Nov. 19, 2018, at 36.

89. For Thomas's confirmation, see 137 CONG. REC. 26,354 (1991).

90. *See* Eleanor Clift, *Congress: The Ultimate Men's Club*, NEWSWEEK, Oct. 21, 1991, at 32, 32.

91. *See Nomination of Judge Clarence Thomas to Be Associate Justice of the Supreme Court of the United States: Hearings Before the S. Comm. on the Judiciary (pt. 4)*, 102d Cong. (1993).

92. *See, e.g.,* Jill Abramson, *Reversal of Fortune: Image of Anita Hill, Brighter in Hindsight, Galvanizes Campaigns*, WALL ST. J., Oct. 5, 1992, at A1; Bill Steigerwald, *Anita Hill Fight Echoes in Pennsylvania Senate Race*, L.A. TIMES, Aug. 6, 1992, at A5. For more on Biden's role, see Douglas Frantz & Sam Fulwood III, *Senators' Private Deal Kept '2nd Woman' off TV*, L.A. TIMES, Oct. 17, 1991, at A22.

93. *See, e.g.,* R.W. Apple Jr., *Primary Victories Bring Year of the Woman Closer*, N.Y. TIMES, June 9, 1992, at A24; Laurent Belsie, *Primaries Suggest 1992 May Be 'Year of the Woman,'* CHRISTIAN SCI. MONITOR, Apr. 30, 1992, at 1.

94. *See The Changing Face of Congress*, CHI. TRIB., Jan. 3, 1993 (§ 1), at 6.

95. For examples of such declarations, see *From Anita Hill to Capitol Hill: A Flurry of Fresh Female Faces Vindicates "The Year of the Woman,"* TIME, Nov. 16, 1992, at 21; Guy Gugliotta, *'Year of the Woman' Becomes Reality as Record Number Win Seats*, WASH. POST, Nov. 4, 1992, at A30; *'Year of the Woman,' as Predicted*, N.Y. TIMES, Nov. 4, 1992, at A1.

96. *See supra* Chapter 6.

97. THIS WOMAN'S PLACE IS IN THE HOUSE: THE HOUSE OF REPRESENTATIVES (1970) (copy on file with author; Columbia University, Rare Book & Manuscript Library, Bella Abzug Papers, box 64).

98. *See* Grace Lichtenstein, *Farbstein Faces a Strong Challenge by Bella Abzug*, N.Y. TIMES, June 9, 1970, at 30; Richard L. Madden, *Badillo Wins House Race; Rooney, Scheuer Victors*, N.Y. TIMES, June 24, 1970, at 1.

99. *See, e.g., A Woman Whose Place Is in the House (of Representatives): Mary McCain Taylor*, DELTA DEMOCRAT-TIMES (Greenville), Aug. 1, 1971, at 14 (advertisement); Nancy Kruh, *Like "Alice in Liberated Land" All the Big Names Were There*, MANHATTAN MERCURY, Feb.

18, 1973, at D1; *A Woman's Place Is in the House of Representatives*, YORK DISPATCH, Nov. 5, 1988, at 4 (advertisement); *Week in Review*, MISSOULA INDEP., Feb. 7, 2008, at 6; Georgiana Vines, *2 Dems Have Backgrounds in Health Care*, NEWS SENTINEL (Knoxville), May 19, 2012, at 4A.

100. Taylor Pensoneau, *Shipley-Schlafly Race: Battle of Sexes*, ST. LOUIS POST-DISPATCH, Oct. 25, 1970, at 3C (quoting Phyllis Schlafly) (internal quotation marks omitted).

101. The Ripoff of the Taxpayers Known as: *The Commission on International Women's Year or, Bella Abzug's Boondoggle*, PHYLLIS SCHLAFLY REP., Jan. 1976, at 1 [hereinafter Ripoff].

102. *See Abzug, Schlafly Debate ERA, the Constitution*, KY. ADVOC., Apr. 22, 1979, at 1; *Abzug, Schlafly Debate Potential Effects of ERA at Danville*, COURIER-J. (Louisville), Apr. 22, 1979, at B10.

103. James Crutchfield, *It's Man vs. Woman and UAW vs. AFL-CIO*, DETROIT FREE PRESS, Aug. 7, 1978, at 10B (quoting Daisy Elliott's bumper sticker) (capitalization and internal quotation marks omitted). For other early variations on this theme, see David Wilkening, *Conservative, Insists Mrs. Hansel*, SENTINEL STAR (Orlando), Aug. 29, 1976, at 27A; Brenda Ingersoll, *Plymouth Woman Believes Her Place Is Nelson's Seat*, MINNEAPOLIS STAR, Oct. 19, 1976, at 6D. For a version phrased as the opinion of the potential candidate's husband, see Andy Bowen, *To Run or Not to Run—Paula Hawkins*, TAMPA TRIB., Apr. 13, 1974, at 5B.

104. Linda Stasi, *Hillary Has You Covered*, DAILY NEWS (New York), May 27, 2015, at 19 (capitalization and internal quotation marks omitted); Maureen Dowd, *Donald the Dove, Hillary the Hawk*, N.Y. TIMES, May 1, 2016 (Sunday Review), at 1 (capitalization and internal quotation marks omitted).

105. On Chisholm, see *Mrs. Chisholm Bids for Sarasota Votes*, TAMPA TRIB., Feb. 9, 1972, at B3. On Ferraro, see Nancy J. Schwerzler, *Ferraro Fever Captures Convention: She Applauds Symbolism*, SUN (Baltimore), July 20, 1984, at 1A; Bill Peterson, *House Welcomes Ferraro Home*, WASH. POST, July 25, 1984, at A4; Becky Richards, *Ferraro's Birthday Observed*, TAMPA TRIB., Aug. 27, 1984, at 3B; *Dems Highlight Detroit Labor Rally*, LANSING STATE J., Sept. 4, 1984, at 1B; Laura Mecoy, *Crowd Pleaser*, SACRAMENTO BEE, Oct. 28, 1984, at A10.

106. *See* OFF. OF THE HISTORIAN, *supra* note 81.

107. Dave Smith, *Hats off to Bella Abzug*, L.A. TIMES, Oct. 15, 1975 (pt. IV), at 1 (quoting Bella Abzug) (internal quotation marks omitted); *see also* Pam Carlson, *Caucus Success Rated High*, GLOBE-GAZETTE (Mason City), Sept. 23, 1974, at 8; Martin Tolchin & Susan Tolchin, *These Days It's a Political Plus If You're a Woman Candidate*, N.Y. TIMES, Oct. 18, 1974, at 49; *Women Demand Equal Rights and Pay—NOW!*, MINNEAPOLIS TRIB., Oct. 25, 1975, at 3A; Eleanor Randolph, *Bella Without the Brawling*, CHI. TRIB., Nov. 30, 1975 (§ 9), at 28; Maurice Carroll, *Democrats Hear 5 in Senate Race*, N.Y. TIMES, Mar. 15, 1976, at 1; Woodie Fitchette, *Bella Enjoys Contest*, ITHACA J., Aug. 10, 1976, at 7.

108. 597 U.S. 215, 261 (2022). On the absence of an affirmative constitutional right to vote, see *supra* Chapter 3.

109. *See supra* Chapters 1 & 5.

110. *See supra* Chapter 5.

111. BLUEPRINT POLLING, MISSISSIPPI ACLU SURVEY, JUNE 28–JULY 6, 2022, at 1 (2022).

112. *See* ELEC. COOPS. OF MISS., MISSISSIPPI 2018 LEGISLATIVE ROSTER 11, 23 (2018); *supra* Chapter 5.

113. *See supra* Chapter 5.

114. *See* S. 1, 118th Cong. § 1011 (2023).

115. *See id.* § 1031.

116. *See id.* §§ 1201, 1301–05.

117. *See id.* §§ 5001–08. For the House bill, see H.R. 11, 118th Cong. (2023).

118. *See* H.R. 14, 118th Cong. (2023); H.R. 4, 117th Cong. (as passed by House, Aug. 24, 2021). For the Supreme Court decision, see Shelby County v. Holder, 570 U.S. 529, 556–57 (2013).

119. For more on *Dobbs*, see *supra* Chapter 5.

120. *See* Udi Sommer et al., *The Political Ramifications of Judicial Institutions: Establishing a Link Between* Dobbs *and Gender Disparities in the 2022 Midterms*, 9 Socius 1, 1–2, 5–6, 10, 12–13 (2023).

121. For a caption on another photograph from the same day that identifies the protestor as Soraya Bata, see John Fritze, *Roe v. Wade No More*, Ariz. Republic, June 25, 2022, at 1A. The woman in the blue shirt is Carrie McDonald. *See id.*

122. For the image by Brandon Bell, see Getty Images (editorial no. 1404877823; copy on file with author).

123. Fannie Lou Hamer, Testimony Before the Credentials Committee at the Democratic National Convention, Atlantic City, New Jersey, August 22, 1964, *in* The Speeches of Fannie Lou Hamer: To Tell It Like It Is 42, 44–45 (Maegan Parker Brooks & Davis W. Houck eds., 2011); *see also supra* Chapter 1.

124. For examples of anti-abortion bills, see S. 4840, 117th Cong. (2022); H.R. 8814, 117th Cong. (2022). For examples of pro-choice bills, see S. 701, 118th Cong. (2023); H.R. 12, 118th Cong. (2023).

125. For examples of rights-protecting legislation, see Act of Jan. 13, 2023, Pub. Act No. 102-1117, 2023 Ill. Laws 8896; Act of Apr. 5, 2023, Act No. 11, 2023 Mich. Pub. Acts; Act of Apr. 27, 2023, ch. 31, 2023 Minn. Laws 294; Act of Jan. 31, 2023, ch. 4, 2023 Minn. Laws 23. For examples of rights-restricting legislation, see Act of Apr. 13, 2023, ch. 2023-21, 2023 Fla. Laws 487; Act of Apr. 5, 2023, ch. 310, 2023 Idaho Sess. Laws 947; Act of July 14, 2023, ch. 1, 2023 Iowa Acts 1519; Act of May 25, 2023, Act No. 70, 2023 S.C. Acts 383; Act of Mar. 15, 2023, ch. 301, 2023 Utah Laws 2501.

126. *See* Kate Zernike, *Abortion Rights Ballot Measures Succeed in 7 States, but Break Win Streak*, N.Y. Times, Nov. 7, 2024, at A14.

127. Dobbs v. Jackson Women's Health Org., 597 U.S. 215, 258 (2022).

128. Michael J. McMonagle, *Elect a Pa. Governor Who'll Abolish Abortion*, Phila. Inquirer, May 8, 2022, at E4.

129. House Courts and Criminal Code Committee, Indiana General Assembly, Archived Video for 2022 Special Session (Aug. 2, 2022) (statement of Marek Kizer) (copy on file with author).

130. Glenda Gray, Letter to the Editor, St. Louis Post-Dispatch, Feb. 13, 2022, at A14.

131. Bob Alley, Letter to the Editor, Tennessean, June 4, 2022, at 19A; *see also* LeRoy Schlangen, Letter to the Editor, St. Cloud Times, June 12, 2022, at 11A; William A. Wittik, Letter to the Editor, Valley News (West Lebanon), Dec. 4, 2022, at C3.

132. Crisitello v. St. Theresa Sch., 299 A.3d 781, 786 (N.J. 2023).

133. *See id.* at 786–87.

134. *Id.* at 796 (quoting Deacon John J. McKenna) (capitalization and internal quotation marks omitted). For the school's litigation victory, see *id.* at 786.

135. *See* Complaint at 2–3, Syring v. Archdiocese of Louisville, No. 21-CI-003391 (Ky. Cir. Ct. June 11, 2021).

136. *See id.* at 3–7.

137. Answer at 3, Syring v. Roman Cath. Bishop of Louisville, No. 21-CI-003391 (Ky. Cir. Ct. Aug. 1, 2021).

138. *See* Reich v. Diocese of Harrisburg, No. CV-2019-260, slip op. at 1–2 (Pa. Ct. Com. Pl. Northumberland County May 10, 2019).

139. For the approximate date of termination, see *id.* at 2. For the letter, see Letter from Sister Mary Anne Bednar, Principal, Our Lady of Lourdes Reg'l Sch., to Naiad Reich 1 (undated), *reprinted in* Complaint at 14, Reich v. Diocese of Harrisburg, No. CV-2019-260 (Pa. Ct. Com. Pl. Northumberland County Feb. 1, 2019) (exhibit 2).

140. Defendants' Answer, New Matter, and Affirmative Defenses to Plaintiff's First Amended Complaint at 10, Reich v. Diocese of Harrisburg, No. CV-2019-260 (Pa. Ct. Com. Pl. Northumberland County Mar. 4, 2020); Response to Plaintiff's Motion for Preliminary Injunction at 9, Reich v. Diocese of Harrisburg, No. CV-2019-260 (Pa. Ct. Com. Pl. Northumberland County Mar. 6, 2019).

141. *See* statutes cited *supra* Chapter 5.

142. *See* Jill Elaine Hasday, *Contest and Consent: A Legal History of Marital Rape*, 88 CALIF. L. REV. 1373, 1494–98 (2000).

143. Pers. Adm'r v. Feeney, 442 U.S. 256, 279 (1979) (internal quotation marks omitted); *see also supra* Chapter 4.

144. *See* HEGEWISCH ET AL., *supra* note 73, at 7 tbl.3.

145. *See id.* at 8 tbl.3.

146. *See, e.g.*, ELISE GOULD ET AL., ECON. POL'Y INST., WHAT IS THE GENDER PAY GAP AND IS IT REAL? THE COMPLETE GUIDE TO HOW WOMEN ARE PAID LESS THAN MEN AND WHY IT CAN'T BE EXPLAINED AWAY 6–7 (2016); Francine D. Blau & Lawrence M. Kahn, *The Gender Wage Gap: Extent, Trends, and Explanations*, 55 J. ECON. LITERATURE 789, 797–807 (2017); Katie Meara et al., *The Gender Pay Gap in the USA: A Matching Study*, 33 J. POPULATION ECON. 271, 301 (2020).

147. *See supra* Chapter 6.

148. *See* Corinne A. Moss-Racusin et al., *Science Faculty's Subtle Gender Biases Favor Male Students*, 109 PROC. NAT'L ACAD. SCIS. U.S. 16,474, 16,475 (2012).

149. *See id.* at 16,477.

150. *See id.* at 16,475.

151. *See* Rhea E. Steinpreis et al., *The Impact of Gender on the Review of the Curricula Vitae of Job Applicants and Tenure Candidates: A National Empirical Study*, 41 SEX ROLES 509, 513–15 (1999).

152. *See id.* at 522.

153. *See, e.g.*, Alan Benson et al., "Potential" and the Gender Promotion Gap 1–6 (Mar. 4, 2024) (unpublished paper) (copy on file with author); Emilio J. Castilla & Stephen Benard, *The Paradox of Meritocracy in Organizations*, 55 ADMIN. SCI. Q. 543, 543 (2010); Mark Egan et al., *When Harry Fired Sally: The Double Standard in Punishing Misconduct*, 130 J. POL. ECON. 1184, 1188 (2022).

154. Claudia Goldin & Cecilia Rouse, *Orchestrating Impartiality: The Impact of "Blind" Auditions on Female Musicians*, 90 Am. Econ. Rev. 715, 737–38 (2000).

155. *See* Emilio J. Castilla, *Gender, Race, and Meritocracy in Organizational Careers*, 113 Am. J. Socio. 1479, 1506–07 (2008).

156. *See* Shelley J. Correll et al., *Getting a Job: Is There a Motherhood Penalty?*, 112 Am. J. Socio. 1297, 1328 (2007).

157. *See id.* at 1331 tbl.6.

158. For evidence on the prevalence of pay history questions, see Robert E. Hall & Alan B. Krueger, *Evidence on the Incidence of Wage Posting, Wage Bargaining, and on-the-Job Search*, 4 Am. Econ. J.: Macroeconomics 56, 56–57, 66–67 (2012).

159. *See* Equal Pay Act of 1963, Pub. L. No. 88-38, 77 Stat. 56.

160. *See* Lauderdale v. Ill. Dep't of Hum. Servs., 876 F.3d 904, 908 (7th Cir. 2017); Wernsing v. Dep't of Hum. Servs., 427 F.3d 466, 467–70 (7th Cir. 2005); Taylor v. White, 321 F.3d 710, 719 (8th Cir. 2003).

161. *See* Nat'l Women's L. Ctr., Progress in the States for Equal Pay 6 (2023).

162. For the legislation, see Act of May 19, 2023, ch. 52, art. 19, § 56, 2023 Minn. Laws 810, 1154–55.

163. *See* Benjamin Hansen & Drew McNichols, *Information and the Persistence of the Gender Wage Gap: Early Evidence from California's Salary History Ban* 16–17 (Nat'l Bureau of Econ. Rsch., Working Paper No. 27054, 2020); Sourav Sinha, US Salary History Bans: Strategic Disclosure by Job Applicants and the Gender Pay Gap 3 (Feb. 9, 2022) (unpublished paper) (copy on file with author); Jason Sockin & Michael Sockin, A Pay Scale of Their Own: Gender Differences in Variable Pay 4, 24–25 (Jan. 2023) (unpublished paper) (copy on file with author).

164. *See* James Bessen et al., *Perpetuating Inequality: What Salary History Bans Reveal About Wages* 16 (B.U. Sch. of L., Pub. L. & Legal Theory Paper No. 20-19, 2020).

165. *See id.* at 29.

166. *See* H.R. Rep. No. 117-13, at 8–15 (2021). For some recent attempts, see H.R. 1600, 118th Cong. (2023); H.R. 17, 118th Cong. (2023); H.R. 7, 117th Cong. (as passed by House, Apr. 15, 2021); H.R. 7, 116th Cong. (as passed by House, Mar. 27, 2019).

167. *See* Advancing Pay Equity in Governmentwide Pay Systems, 89 Fed. Reg. 5737, 5737 (Jan. 30, 2024) (to be codified at 5 C.F.R. pts. 531, 532, 534, 930).

168. *See* Pay Equity and Transparency in Federal Contracting, 89 Fed. Reg. 5843, 5843 (proposed Jan. 30, 2024) (to be codified at 48 C.F.R. pts. 1, 2, 12, 22, 52).

169. *See* Shengwei Sun et al., Inst. for Women's Pol'y Rsch., Pub. No. C494, On the Books, off the Record: Examining the Effectiveness of Pay Secrecy Laws in the U.S. 2, 4, 9 (2021).

170. *See* Ledbetter v. Goodyear Tire & Rubber Co., 550 U.S. 618, 643 (2007) (Ginsburg, J., dissenting).

171. *See* Brief for the Petitioner at 7 & n.5, Ledbetter v. Goodyear Tire & Rubber Co., 550 U.S. 618 (2007) (No. 05-1074).

172. *See Ledbetter*, 550 U.S. at 643 (Ginsburg, J., dissenting).

173. *See id.* at 650; Brief for the Petitioner, *supra* note 171, at 26; Joint Appendix at 56–57, 89, Ledbetter v. Goodyear Tire & Rubber Co., 550 U.S. 618 (2007) (No. 05-1074).

174. *Justice Denied? The Implications of the Supreme Court's Ledbetter v. Goodyear Employment Discrimination Decision: Hearing Before the H. Comm. on Educ. & Lab.*, 110th Cong.

10 (2007) (statement of Lilly Ledbetter). For the month she received the note, see LILLY LEDBETTER WITH LANIER SCOTT ISOM, GRACE AND GRIT: MY FIGHT FOR EQUAL PAY AND FAIRNESS AT GOODYEAR AND BEYOND 145–46 (2012).

175. *See Ledbetter*, 550 U.S. at 643–44 (Ginsburg, J., dissenting).

176. *See id.* at 628–29 (majority opinion).

177. *See* Lilly Ledbetter Fair Pay Act of 2009, Pub. L. No. 111-2, § 3, 123 Stat. 5, 5–6.

178. *See* NAT'L WOMEN'S L. CTR., *supra* note 161, at 8.

179. *See* Marlene Kim, *Pay Secrecy and the Gender Wage Gap in the United States*, 54 INDUS. RELS. 648, 653–54, 664 (2015); Sockin & Sockin, *supra* note 163, at 4, 24–25.

180. *See* Barack Obama, Non-Retaliation for Disclosure of Compensation Information, Exec. Order No. 13,665 § 2, 3 C.F.R. 240, 241 (2014).

181. *See* Cintas Corp. v. NLRB, 482 F.3d 463, 464–66 (D.C. Cir. 2007); NLRB v. Main St. Terrace Care Ctr., 218 F.3d 531, 537–38 (6th Cir. 2000); Wilson Trophy Co. v. NLRB, 989 F.2d 1502, 1510–11 (8th Cir. 1993); NLRB v. Brookshire Grocery Co., 919 F.2d 359, 362 (5th Cir. 1990); Jeannette Corp. v. NLRB, 532 F.2d 916, 918–19 (3d Cir. 1976).

182. *See* 29 U.S.C. § 152(3).

183. *See* BE&K Constr. Co. v. NLRB, 536 U.S. 516, 529 (2002).

184. *See* H.R. REP. NO. 117-13, at 8–15 (2021). For some recent attempts, see H.R. 17, 118th Cong. (2023); H.R. 7, 117th Cong. (as passed by House, Apr. 15, 2021); H.R. 7, 116th Cong. (as passed by House, Mar. 27, 2019).

185. *See, e.g.,* H.R. 1599, 118th Cong. (2023).

186. *See* NAT'L WOMEN'S L. CTR., *supra* note 161, at 3–5.

187. *See* Act of May 17, 2024, ch. 110, art. 7, § 42, 2024 Minn. Laws.

188. *See* Pay Equity and Transparency in Federal Contracting, *supra* note 168, at 5843.

189. *See* Michael Baker et al., *Pay Transparency and the Gender Gap*, 15 AM. ECON. J.: APPLIED ECON. 157, 157–59 (2023).

190. For some recent bills, see S. 1714, 118th Cong. (2023); H.R. 3481, 118th Cong. (2023). For international comparisons, see SARAH A. DONOVAN, CONG. RSCH. SERV., PAID FAMILY AND MEDICAL LEAVE IN THE UNITED STATES 16–18 (2023).

191. *See* DONOVAN, *supra* note 190, at 5 tbl.1.

192. *See* Family and Medical Leave Act of 1993, Pub. L. No. 103–3, §§ 101–02, 107 Stat. 6, 7–11.

193. *See* SCOTT BROWN ET AL., ABT ASSOCS., EMPLOYEE AND WORKSITE PERSPECTIVES OF THE FAMILY AND MEDICAL LEAVE ACT: RESULTS FROM THE 2018 SURVEYS, at ii, 6 (2020).

194. *See* U.S. DEP'T OF THE TREASURY, THE ECONOMICS OF CHILD CARE SUPPLY IN THE UNITED STATES 6 (2021).

195. *See* ALLISON H. FRIEDMAN-KRAUSS ET AL., NAT'L INST. FOR EARLY EDUC. RSCH., THE STATE OF PRESCHOOL 2020: STATE PRESCHOOL YEARBOOK, at 6–7, 30 tbl.4 (2021).

196. *See* NINA CHIEN, U.S. DEP'T OF HEALTH & HUM. SERVS., DATA POINT: ESTIMATES OF CHILD CARE ELIGIBILITY & RECEIPT FOR FISCAL YEAR 2020, at 1 (2024).

197. *See* LIANA CHRISTIN LANDIVAR ET AL., U.S. DEP'T OF LAB., CHILDCARE PRICES IN LOCAL AREAS: INITIAL FINDINGS FROM THE NATIONAL DATABASE OF CHILDCARE PRICES 1 (2023).

198. *See id.* at 1–2, 7.

199. *See* CHILD CARE AWARE OF AM., PRICE OF CARE: 2023, at 22–23 tbl.XI (2024).

200. *See id.* at 26–27 tbl.XIII.

201. *See* Liana Christin Landivar et al., *Are States Created Equal? Moving to a State with More Expensive Childcare Reduces Mothers' Odds of Employment*, 58 Demography 451, 466 (2021); Leah Ruppanner et al., *Expensive Childcare and Short School Days = Lower Maternal Employment and More Time in Childcare? Evidence from the American Time Use Survey*, 5 Socius 1, 9–10 (2019).
202. *See* Jonah B. Gelbach, *Public Schooling for Young Children and Maternal Labor Supply*, 92 Am. Econ. Rev. 307, 308, 320–21 (2002); Taryn W. Morrissey, *Child Care and Parent Labor Force Participation: A Review of the Research Literature*, 15 Rev. Econ. Household 1, 1, 19 (2017).
203. For the policy change, see Memorandum from Ash Carter, Sec'y of Def., to the Sec'ys of the Mil. Dep'ts et al. 1 (Dec. 3, 2015) (copy on file with author).
204. Nat'l Coal. for Men v. Selective Serv. Sys., 141 S. Ct. 1815, 1816 (2021) (statement of Sotomayor, J.). For more on *Rostker*, see *supra* Chapter 5.
205. National Defense Authorization Act for Fiscal Year 2017, Pub. L. No. 114-328, §§ 551(a), 555(c)(2)(A), 130 Stat. 2000, 2130, 2135 (2016).
206. *See National Commission on Military, National, and Public Service Forum, Day 2, Part 2* (C-SPAN television broadcast Apr. 25, 2019). For the research my testimony drew on, see Jill Elaine Hasday, *Fighting Women: The Military, Sex, and Extrajudicial Constitutional Change*, 93 Minn. L. Rev. 96 (2008).
207. *See* Inspired to Serve: The Final Report of the National Commission on Military, National, and Public Service 8, 111–23 (2020).
208. *See Recommendations of the National Commission on Military, National, and Public Service: Hearing Before the H. Comm. on Armed Servs.*, 117th Cong. (2021); *To Receive Testimony on the Final Recommendations and Report of the National Commission on Military, National, and Public Service: Hearing Before the S. Comm. on Armed Servs.*, 117th Cong. (2021).
209. *See* Immigration and Nationality Act Amendments of 1986, Pub. L. No. 99-653, § 13, 100 Stat. 3655, 3657; *supra* Chapter 5.
210. *See* Nguyen v. INS, 533 U.S. 53, 58–62 (2001); *supra* Chapter 5.
211. H.R.J. Res. 208, 92d Cong., 86 Stat. 1523 (1972).
212. For the 1972 joint resolution, see *id.* For recent bills, see H.R.J. Res. 82, 118th Cong. (2023); H.R.J. Res. 25, 118th Cong. (2023); S.J. Res. 39, 118th Cong. (2023); S.J. Res. 4, 118th Cong. (2023); H.R. Res. 891, 117th Cong. (2022); H.R.J. Res. 17, 117th Cong. (as passed by House, Mar. 17, 2021); S.J. Res. 1, 117th Cong. (2021); H.R.J. Res. 79, 116th Cong. (as passed by House, Feb. 13, 2020); H.R.J. Res. 38, 116th Cong. (2019); S.J. Res. 6, 116th Cong. (2019).
213. 307 U.S. 433, 435–37 (1939).
214. *Id.* at 456; *see also id.* at 450, 454.
215. *The Originalist*, Cal. Law., Jan. 2011, at 33, 33 (quoting interview with Antonin Scalia).
216. U.S. Const. amend. XIV, § 1.
217. For examples of those descriptions, see *supra* Chapter 5.
218. *See supra* Chapter 5.
219. *See* Doe v. State, No. 62-CV-19-3868, slip op. at 4 (Minn. Dist. Ct. July 11, 2022); Weems v. State, 529 P.3d 798, 812–13 (Mont. 2023); Wrigley v. Romanick, 988 N.W.2d 231, 245 (N.D. 2023); Access Indep. Health Servs., Inc. v. Wrigley, No. 08-2022-CV-01608, slip op.

at 4–5 (N.D. Dist. Ct. Sept. 12, 2024); Okla. Call for Reprod. Just. v. Drummond, 526 P.3d 1123, 1132 (Okla. 2023) (per curiam); Planned Parenthood S. Atl. v. State, 882 S.E.2d 770, 774 (S.C. 2023).

220. *See* Frederic A. Birmingham, *Jill Ruckelshaus: Lady of Liberty*, SATURDAY EVENING POST, Mar.–Apr. 1973, at 50, 51; Mary Anne Butters, *Jill to Lead Women at GOP Convention*, INDIANAPOLIS STAR, Aug. 20, 1972 (§ 5), at 1; James F. Clarity, *Jill Ruckelshaus Is No Follower*, N.Y. TIMES, Aug. 3, 1973, at 15; Clare Crawford, *Couples: From Watergate to Womankind, Bill and Jill Ruckelshaus Fight for Their Ideas*, PEOPLE, Apr. 12, 1976, at 41, 42, 44; Lois Romano, *Jill Ruckelshaus, Back in the Fishbowl*, WASH. POST, May 18, 1983, at B1.

221. PHYLLIS SCHLAFLY, THE POWER OF THE POSITIVE WOMAN 135 (1977) (internal quotation marks omitted); Ripoff, *supra* note 101, at 1 (internal quotation marks omitted); *Big Money and Tough Tactics to Ratify E.R.A.*, PHYLLIS SCHLAFLY REP., June 1975, at 1 (internal quotation marks omitted).

222. On the convention and Ruckelshaus as co-founder of the National Women's Political Caucus, see *ERA Passage Top Priority of Women's Political Caucus*, RENO EVENING GAZETTE, Sept. 28, 1977, at 6; John Stanton, *Carter, Court, Congress Rapped on Abortion Issue*, PALO ALTO TIMES, Sept. 10, 1977, at 1.

223. Jill Ruckelshaus, Speech at the National Women's Political Caucus Convention California (1977), *reprinted in* N.O.W. NEWS: BAY AREA CHAPTER, Oct. 1984, at 2, 2 (indentation omitted and final period added).

Index